Latin America Online:
Cases, Successes and Pitfalls

Mila Gascó-Hernández
International Institute on Governance of Catalonia, Spain

T0321980

IRM Press
Publisher of innovative scholarly and professional
information technology titles in the cyberage

Hershey • London • Melbourne • Singapore

Acquisition Editor:	Kristin Klinger
Senior Managing Editor:	Jennifer Neidig
Managing Editor:	Sara Reed
Assistant Managing Editor:	Sharon Berger
Development Editor:	Kristin Roth
Copy Editor:	Shanelle Ramelb
Typesetter:	Michael Brehm
Cover Design:	Lisa Tosheff
Printed at:	Yurchak Printing Inc.

Published in the United States of America by
    IRM Press (an imprint of Idea Group Inc.)
    701 E. Chocolate Avenue, Suite 200
    Hershey PA 17033-1240
    Tel: 717-533-8845
    Fax: 717-533-8661
    E-mail: cust@idea-group.com
    Web site: http://www.irm-press.com

and in the United Kingdom by
    IRM Press (an imprint of Idea Group Inc.)
    3 Henrietta Street
    Covent Garden
    London WC2E 8LU
    Tel: 44 20 7240 0856
    Fax: 44 20 7379 0609
    Web site: http://www.eurospanonline.com

Product or company names used in this book are for identification purposes only. Inclusion of the names of the products or companies does not indicate a claim of ownership by IGI of the trademark or registered trademark.

Library of Congress Cataloging-in-Publication Data

Latin America online : cases, successes, and pitfalls / [edited] by Mila Gascó-Hernández.
   p. cm.
 Includes bibliographical references and index.
 ISBN 978-1-59904-057-8 (hardcover) -- ISBN 978-1-59904-059-2 (ebook)
 1. Internet in public administration--Latin America--Case studies. I. Gascó Hernández, Mila.
 JL959.5.A8L38 2007
 352.3'802854678--dc22
                2006033753

British Cataloguing in Publication Data
A Cataloguing in Publication record for this book is available from the British Library.

All work contributed to this book is new, previously-unpublished material. The views expressed in this book are those of the authors, but not necessarily of the publisher.

Latin America Online:
Cases, Successes and Pitfalls

Table of Contents

Section III: Local Studies

Foreword[1]

It has basically been during the last decade that countries in the Latin American and the Caribbean (LAC) regions have repeatedly expressed their political will to use information and communication technologies (ICT) as a means to achieve their development objectives, and as a way to improve the efficiency, transparency, and competitiveness in LAC public administration. It is then when the countries began to realize the economic and social impact of ICT, and the benefits of participating and promoting national and international events in the areas of electronic government and the information society.

These efforts have been identified in a large number of events, producing declarations and recognizing the need to promote information technology in the context of economic and social development for countries of the region. For instance, the Declaration of Florianopolis recognizes information and communication technologies as the central focus of a knowledge-based economy and the foundation for new forms of organization and production worldwide. Additional international events were the Declaration of the Presidents of South America, the Summit of the Americas, and the European Union-Latin America and Caribbean Summit, in which heads of state and government of the region declared their desire to accelerate government efforts, with the participation of the private sector and civil society, to take advantage of the new opportunities offered by electronic government, the information society, and the knowledge-based economy.

The governments, concerned with the issues surrounding globalization and the digital divide, have initiated electronic-government strategies and action plans that will help create a knowledge-based society and stimulate economic and social growth for efficient, equitable, and sustainable development. The level of success or failure of these initiatives will depend on major political, technical, and administrative efforts and understanding. Due to this fact, we describe electronic government as a complex and multidisciplinary phenomenon for which, despite the risks involved, there are a great number of benefits, including lower costs, greater efficiency and quality of service, more effective communication between citizens and government, enhanced management efficiency and transparency, as well as greater citizen participation and commitment.

It is also important to realize that the government plays an essential role in the process of change. It provides the leadership in making proper use of information and communication technology and serves as a catalyst for development and innovation in the use of ICT. Nowadays, the countries of Latin America and the Caribbean launch programs to reform their public administrations and to enhance their capacity, processes, and techniques of electronic government. However, this does not mean that governments should rush blindly ahead in creating electronic government without first understanding the essential requirements and procedures for implementation. Before any program is undertaken, all the social, technological, political, economic, and environmental risks must be thoroughly considered. It is also important to understand the capacity and resources of the country or municipality where these programs will be implemented.

Working at the Inter-American Development Bank in the areas of electronic government and institutional strengthening in ICT, I have learned the importance of a good design project and that sometimes, good e-government projects go through difficult times during the implementation phase due to the lack of planning, articulation, or coordination. So, there are times when the governments, pressured by political issues and tied agendas, tend to jump into the implementation phase without the proper articulation, vision, or road map. Although it may initially take longer, it is strongly advisable that governments should start to develop their e-government strategies and methodologies on the basis of previous e-readiness studies to establish a baseline and build the road map. It is also important that governments consider giving stronger support to private investment, making joint investments, deregulating monopolies, and reinforcing the private market in the communications sector. Training is always needed to keep up with the new demands and become more competitive. Consideration should be given to allocate the budget for knowledge management and for the provision of training to senior managers in the public and private sectors so that they can establish joint strategies and policies for economic development and restructuring. Achieving progress with economic transformation will require a joint effort from all players (government, private business, and civil society). Finally, it is important that governments assess their own needs and take into account other electronic-government experiences instead of just adopting recipes, which in turn could become a recipe for disaster.

Another important benefit of electronic government is the provision of online services to help governments and citizens interact with each other while reducing the cost of services and making them available to everyone. E-government has the potential to integrate, into a single efficient community, a whole range of social groups—citizens, providers of goods and services, contractors, other government institutions, and international agencies. When we speak about the integration into a single efficient and collaborative community, we must not think just about the capability of sending and receiving e-mail. Electronic government goes beyond that. It is also about improving managerial, administrative, and control systems and processes; it is about skills and building knowledge management and it is also about the regulatory framework and political will. The more interrelated these ingredients are, the greater the level of integration in e-government will be. In the new economy, e-government allows systems at government institutions to interact with other systems from public and private organizations and to establish effective communication and coordination. Some examples of these ICT projects that I have supported throughout the years are (a) the modernization of state programs (the Modernization of the Comptroller's General Office Programs in Chile and Colombia, the Modernization of Justice Reform Programs in Honduras and Paraguay), (b) social programs (the Citizen Security Programs in Honduras, Nicaragua, Guatemala, and Panama; the Primary Education Programs in Argentina, El Salvador, and Jamaica), (c) trade programs in Bolivia, Argentina, and Chile, (d) a customs program for Mesoamerica, and (e) electronic-government programs in Guatemala, Honduras, Jamaica, Panama, and Peru. Also, many of these programs support the decentralization of functions, by distributing the load of work to the regional and municipal levels, as part of the process of reforming the government administration. This decentralization process will depend on integrated communications and platforms that will allow decentralized sectors to communicate and exchange information with each other. The IADB has been successful in promoting and supporting e-government projects in the Latin American and the Caribbean regions by modernizing the public administrations in the countries with the use of ICT, expanding the institutional and human capacity, and improving and creating new processes, policies, systems, and techniques for the benefit of the public administration and the citizens.

The above issues are widely discussed in *Latin America Online: Cases, Successes and Pitfalls*. This book is indeed one of the products that best describes the state of the art in electronic government in the Latin American region. The studies presented in this book are an important part of the ongoing debate and search for methodologies for the establishment of e-government. It introduces the organizational, technical, and financial activities currently developed, and it puts into perspective the modernization and decentralization efforts carried out by the public administration to become more effective and transparent by increasing investment in information and communication technologies as a means to achieve greater interoperability, integrity, and applicability of ICT systems at the central and municipal levels.

Enjoy the reading!

Eduardo Rodal
Washington, DC, USA
December 2006

Endnote

[1]   The ideas and opinions expressed in this foreword are those of the author and do not necessarily represent the official position of the Inter-American Development Bank (IADB).

Eduardo Rodal holds a master of science in telecommunications and a bachelor of science in electrical engineering from the University of Maryland in the United States. He is an operations specialist of the Information Technology for Development Division of the Sustainable Development Department at the IADB in Washington, DC. Since 1994, Mr. Rodal has been working in different positions of the bank in the field of information technology. His responsibilities include project preparation in the areas of ICT institutional strengthening and electronic government. Mr. Rodal has been managing and providing strategic, technical advice and backstopping in almost every country in Latin America and the Caribbean. Before joining the IADB, he worked for the Biomedical Engineering Department at the National Institute of Health in Bethesda, Maryland. Mr. Rodal has participated at several workshops, seminars, and conferences, and has written several papers and reports.

Preface

Although the conceptual roots of what has been called the information society go back to several decades, it was during the '90s that they became popular as a consequence of several factors such as the liberalization of the telecommunications sector all over the world; the spread of a technological change that brought about the informatics, microelectronics, and communications revolutions; and the acceleration of the globalization process that has motivated important social and economical transformations associated with the new technologies.

There is no doubt that this new situation requires the implementation of effective actions by the different actors of the new society and economy. Access to the Internet and knowledge about the use of computers have become expectations and obligations for economic, social, political, and civic participation. That is why not only private-sector efforts are welcome, but public initiatives (among them the electronic-government ones) are also critical.

Broadly defined, e-government has to do with the use of all information and communication technologies to support the actions of public administrations as well as political processes. Thus, electronic-government initiatives include changing the inside of public-sector organizations (what has been called back-office adjustments), improving service delivery, and promoting participation and democracy (often referred to as e-governance or e-democracy). These different types of initiatives are aimed at promoting more efficient and effective governments, facilitating more accessible government services, allowing greater public access to information and participation, and making governments more accountable to citizens. In sum, e-government projects pursue citizens' satisfaction and therefore are about transforming governments to be more citizen centered. That is why they have to be understood as part of the public administration and state reform processes that have been changing public-sector organizations in order to improve their performance.

Although several projects have been carried out all over the globe, the truth is that the development of electronic-government initiatives is unequal depending on the region of the world (what is more, on the country) where they take place. Thus, while countries such as the United States, Great Britain, Sweden, Singapore, Australia, or Canada are the leaders when it comes to implementing electronic-government programs, the same cannot be said about most Latin American nations.

It is therefore the intention of this book to understand how several Latin American governments and public administrations have chosen to pursue their e-government initiatives.

Benchmarking E-Government

For the past 5 years, several e-government global, regional, and local benchmarks have been carried out. Although not all of them have included Latin America in their analysis, the ones that have coincide in their perceptions about the implementation of e-government in this region. Generally speaking, Latin America usually ranks below both North America and Europe and only a little above the world average. In *Benchmarking E-Government*, Ronaghan (2002) classified the region as one with medium e-government capacity and interactive presence.[1] Despite the fact that Latin America performed better than East Asia and Africa, it was still far from the most developed nations such as the United States, New Zealand, or the United Kingdom.

The United Nations' *World Public Sector Report 2003*, on the other hand, also placed Latin America in a better position than South and Southeast Asia, Oceania, and Africa, but still worse than North America and Europe. As a matter of fact, its E-Government Readiness Index score of 0.4420 was only a little higher than the world average (0.4020).[2]

One year later, in the United Nations *Global E-Government Readiness Report 2004*, Latin America's score had only increased by an insignificant 0.0138.[3] Although the region was still ahead of Africa, Oceania, and South and Central Asia, for the first time, it was behind Southeast Asia. Also, the breach between Latin America, and North America and Europe expanded. Finally, in the most recent United Nations report (2005) available,[4] not only did the

Table 1. E-Government Readiness Index 2003-2005: A comparative approach

Region	Index 2003	Index 2004	Index 2005
North America	0.8670	0.8751	0.8744
Europe	0.5580	0.5866	0.6012
Southeast Asia	0.4370	0.4603	0.4922
South and Central America	0.4420	0.4558	0.4643
West Asia	0.4100	0.4093	0.4384
The Caribbean	0.4010	0.4106	0.4282
South and Central Asia	0.2920	0.3213	0.3448
Oceania	0.3510	0.3006	0.2888
Africa	0.2460	0.2528	0.2642
World average	0.4020	0.4130	0.4267

distance between Latin America and the most developed countries widen, but the gap between the region's score and the world average decreased. The following table summarizes the described trends.

The previous data prove the existence in Latin America of what can be called an "e-government divide," that is, a digital gap that occurs between those public administrations and governments that are effectively, appropriately, and successfully implementing and delivering online services to citizens and those that are not (Gascó, 2005). In particular, the figures show a global, cross-country, or international e-government divide: a divergence of implemented e-government actions between developed and developing countries.[5]

Although as earlier showed, generally speaking, Latin America has tended to lose out in the set of world comparative rankings, recently the region has designed and implemented several projects aimed at introducing the new information and communication technologies in the public sector. Therefore, I believe that some of the poor results displayed are not due to government inactivity. Instead, there are other variables that play an essential role in Latin American e-government success or failure.

Several authors have already reported that a limited human and technological infrastructure has a decisive impact on how a country performs in terms of e-government. Latin America is not an exception. But this cause-effect view is, from my perspective, too narrow. As a consequence, this book makes evident the existence of other more structural factors that also influence e-government accomplishment. Therefore, the different chapters that it contains focus on other variables, besides ICT penetration level (digital divide) and illiteracy, that have to be considered to understand why the region is not always being successful in its efforts. In particular, the initiatives presented highlight the importance of both Latin American formal (such as public-administration modernization and state reform processes) and informal institutions (for example, patronage and clientele practices).

Institutions (Also) Matter

As I have already stated (see, for example, Gascó, 2005), the ICT penetration level as well as the availability of trained human resources and financial means condition the development of digital-government initiatives. Certainly, on one hand, if access and connectivity are insufficient or limited, only a few will be able to benefit from ICT use and, therefore, from the advantages to which e-government may give rise. The data that can be found at the *Internet World Stats* Web page (http://www.internetworldstats.com/stats.htm) makes this evident. Thus, back in March 2006, only 14.4% of the Latin American population had access to the Internet, a very low percentage if it is compared to the European 36.1% and the North American 68.6%, but still above the ratio of less developed regions, such as Africa (2.6%) or Asia (9.9%). What is more, if technology adoption is poor and slow, governments and public administrations will experience their own technical and managerial difficulties when implementing digital projects aimed at provisioning online services.

On the other hand, technology and also recruiting and training IT professionals are expensive, and money is often in short supply in the public sector. Resource scarcity or abundance is strongly influenced by a country's economic and social composition, which is usually numerically represented by the Human Development Index that is developed on an annual basis by the United Nations Development Program (see http://hdr.undp.org/).

In short, as Ronaghan (2002, p. 2) well summarizes, digital-government initiatives depend on key factors such as the state of a country's telecommunications infrastructure, the strength of its human capital, the political will and commitment of the national leadership and shifting policy and administrative priorities… Each of these factors influences how decision makers, policy planners and public sector managers elect to approach, develop, and implement e-government programs.

Nonetheless, to stop the analysis here would not be wise since I believe that there is another important factor that explains the e-government disparities between countries: the stage of evolution of public-administration changes. Gascó (2005, p. 692) says,

According to this variable, those regions that have designed and implemented successful e-government programs have already gone through an important state reform process that has produced an institutional change and therefore new public rules and ways of operating. They have indeed left behind the bureaucratic administration model to adopt the new public management one, or even, I add now, the governance paradigm.

In the case of Latin America, and despite the fact that modernization processes have been designed and implemented in several countries, only a few have gone through a real institutional transformation (Oszlack, 2001). This is so because, although these experiences have inexorably given rise to organizational changes,[6] it is not clear that they have also motivated institutional changes, that is, both formal and informal institutional reform processes or, as the economist Douglass North (1990) said, game-rules reforms or, strictly speaking, constrains that men impose on the economic, political, or social interaction (Gascó, 2003). As a result, the different initiatives, and the e-government ones among them, have not been able to solve the underlying conflict between the technical rationality and the cultural and political conditions (or, better said, institutions) of the context within the projects where implemented.

In order to understand why organizational change does not necessarily give rise to an institutional transformation, the following two statements have to be taken into consideration (Gascó, 2003):

1. On one hand, institutional change occurs whenever an alteration of relative prices is perceived by one of the parties taking part in a transaction as a win-win situation for that party or for all the participants involved. Therefore, institutional change depends on the actors' perceptions with respect to the gains (the payoffs, indeed) to be obtained.

2. On the other, institutions determine the payoffs.[7]

As a consequence, any reform strategy is strongly influenced by the current institutions of government because the parties involved determine the choices they make depending on the incentives systems within those structural arrangements. E-government initiatives are therefore also designed and implemented according to the preferences of government actors that, in turn, have been shaped bearing in mind the formal and informal rules and constraints as well as the enforcement characteristics of both, that is, considering the type of institution they are inserted into.

In particular, Latin American public administrations are still considered bureaucratic organizations that are usually more resilient to change due to its preference for stability, uniformity, and continuity. What is more, some authors such as Ramió (2001) declare that the region's public sector is still characterized by odd, pre-bureaucratic structures that have given rise to patronage practices and patters that condition the performance of any modernization program (Gascó, 2005).

About This Book

Latin America Online: Cases, Successes and Pitfalls is a book aimed at enlightening the above concepts and therefore at analyzing the role of ICT penetration level, but also that of the state reform processes, the informal institutions, and the human and financial resources available in the performance of Latin American electronic-government initiatives. In particular, its overall objectives are the following:

1. To describe how e-government initiatives are taking place in several Latin American countries, both at the national and the local level
2. To provide insightful analysis about those factors that are critical in an e-government design and implementation process
3. To discuss how contextual factors affect e-government projects' success or failure
4. To explore the existence of a Latin American e-government model
5. To propose strategies to move forward and to address future challenges

The book presents insights gained by leading professionals from the practice, research, academic, and consulting side of the electronic-government field in Latin America. This is why it should be useful to a variety of constituencies including the following:

1. Politicians and public-sector officials (civil servants) who need a convenient source of information on what other governments are doing in terms of their e-government initiatives

2. Latin American practitioners who are looking for solutions to e-government initiatives implemented by their administrations

3. E-government professionals and practitioners who want to further explore the potential of ICT in the Latin American public sector; this target includes headquarters and field-office staff of large development organizations (such as the World Bank or the United Nations Program for Development), nongovernmental-organization staff and volunteers, or staff of bilateral development agencies (such as United States Agency for International Development (USAID), Angecia Española de Cooperación Internacional (AECI), or Canadian International Development Agency (CIDA)).

4. Private-company executives, leaders, and consultants who frequently liaise with government agencies to supply products or services or to carry out e-government projects

5. Academicians, researchers, and students interested in the e-government field

The book is presented in three sections. The first one, "National Case Studies," reviews four electronic-government initiatives implemented at the national level and one executed at the province level. As a result, it introduces a wide range of issues such as the difference between back-office and front-office projects, the benefits of electronic-government initiatives, and the role of e-government in state reform processes.

In particular, Chapter I looks at the experience of the Argentine IT Professionals Forum, a cross-agency network that involves all the IT professionals of the Argentine public administration. This back-office initiative is especially interesting because it is an example of a new management model known as "community of practice," a core organizational tool that facilitates the implementation of innovation processes.

Chapter II presents another back-office initiative that has been implemented in Brazil. Specifically, it is aimed at analyzing the results obtained by the Brazilian government strategy in the use of a specially developed e-government procurement system, Compras.Net, which has been recognized worldwide and praised due to the high level of innovation that it entails.

Chapter III portrays the adoption of e-government in Chile within the framework of the state reform and modernization process. In particular, the text presents both the technological and the institutional contexts that gave rise to the Chilean e-government strategy and describes some of its most successful experiences.

Chapter IV examines e-government in Brazil as a tool for increased civic participation and effectiveness. Particularly, a front-office initiative, the income e-tax system, is described and analyzed in the framework of the promotion of the Brazilian process of state restructuring and the challenges imposed by the digital divide.

Finally, Chapter V preliminarily evaluates the quality and functionality of four state-government portals in Mexico. It also analyzes their evolution from 2002 to 2005 and uncovers some general trends. In short, the research finds out that Mexican state-government portals seem to be mainly information catalogs with some transactional capabilities, although the observed portals also show a pattern of changing toward a more user-centered design, the integration of more electronic services, and an increasing concern for transparency and citizens' participation.

Section II, "Regional Comparative Studies," presents two regional studies that allow the reader to obtain some comparative knowledge about how the different Latin American countries are performing in relation to e-government.

Therefore, Chapter VI provides a comparative analysis of e-government in Latin America (both intra- and interregional comparisons) with the main objective of elevating e-government literature to a more quantitatively rigorous and sophisticated level. In order to do so, the authors introduce the United National Global E-Government Readiness Reports with particular focus on the Latin American region.

Chapter VII analyzes the existing disparity regarding the achievements of electronic-government development in the Latin America Southern Cone area (and specifically in Argentina, Chile, and Uruguay), underlining the important role of each country's own institutional framework.

Section III, "Local Studies" approaches several e-government issues at the local level. In particular, the final part of the book presents two chapters that compare the state of e-government and e-democracy in Latin American municipalities, one individual case study in one of Latin America's largest cities, and one project conducted at the local level that shows a cooperation strategy between Europe and Latin America.

As such, Chapter VIII examines e-government practices in 15 Latin American cities. It does so taking into account five significant variables: privacy and security, usability, content, services, and citizen participation. Although the chapter does not take into consideration all e-government local practices in Latin America, it does provide benchmark cases for cities in the Latin American region.

Chapter IX aims at defining and measuring the level of development of electronic democracy in the following 17 Latin American local governments: Asunción, Bogotá, Brasilia, Buenos Aires, Caracas, Guatemala, La Paz, Lima, Managua, Mexico Distrito Federal (DF), Montevideo, Panama, Quito, San José, San Salvador, Santiago, and Tegucigalpa. In doing so, the author pays particular attention to the impact of ICTs on local political processes from an institutional point of view.

Chapter X introduces a conceptual framework and a case study (the genesis of the communes in Buenos Aires, Argentina) to make evident the relationship between the information and knowledge society, development, and democracy. It emphasizes the contribution of ICTs to the consolidation of a public space where multiactor, open, well-informed, and transparent participatory processes can take place.

Finally, Chapter XI presents a European Union Alliance of the Information Society (@LIS) project, Electronic Government Innovation and Access (eGOIA), with the goal of provisioning demonstrators that show future-oriented public-administration services to a broad public in Latin America. The text focuses on the description of this European Union and Latin American cooperation initiative in São Paulo (Brazil) and some Peruvian municipalities.

References

Gascó, M. (2003). New technologies and institutional change in public administration. *Social Science Computer Review, 21*(1), 6-14.

Gascó, M. (2005). Exploring the e-government gap in South America. *International Journal of Public Administration, 28*(7 & 8), 683-701.

North, D. (1990). *Institutions, institutional change and economic performance.* Cambridge, United Kingdom: Cambridge University Press.

North, D. (1994). Institutional change: A framework of analysis. *Working papers in economics.* Retrieved May 2, 2006, from http://129.3.20.41/eps/eh/papers/9412/9412001.pdf

Oszlak, O. (2001). *El servicio civil en América Latina y el Caribe: Situación y retos futuros.* Washington, DC: Inter-American Development Bank.

Ramió, C. (2001). Los problemas de la implantación de la nueva gestión pública en las administraciones públicas latinas: Modelo de estado y cultura institucional. *Reforma y Democracia, 21.* Retrieved May 2, 2006, from http://www.clad.org.ve/rev21/ramio.pdf

Ronaghan, S. (2002). *Benchmarking e-government: A global perspective.* New York: United Nations Division for Public Economics and Public Administration & American Society for Public Administration.

Thomas, J. M., & Bennis, W. G. (Eds.). (1972). *The management of change and conflict.* Baltimore: Penguin.

United Nations. (2003). *World public sector report 2003: E-government at the crossroads.* New York: Author.

United Nations. (2004). *Global e-government readiness report 2004: Towards access for opportunity.* New York: United Nations Department of Economic and Social Affairs & United Nations Division for Public Administration and Development Management.

United Nations. (2005). *Global e-government readiness report 2005: From e-government to e-inclusion.* New York: United Nations Department of Economic and Social Affairs & United Nations Division for Public Administration and Development Management.

Endnotes

[1]   The study by Ronaghan presents the E-Government Index, a measure
of a country's e-government environment that incorporates a country's
official online presence, evaluates its telecommunications infrastructure,
and assesses its human development capacity. The index classifies the
different countries as follows: (a) high e-government capacity countries
that index above 2.00, (b) medium e-government capacity countries that
are placed between 1.60 and 1.99, (c) minimal e-government capacity
countries that score between 1.00 and 1.59, and (d) deficient e-government capacity countries, which score below 1.00. Also, it considers the
existence of the following five stages when implementing e-government
initiatives: emerging (an official government online presence is established), enhanced (government sites increase and information becomes
more dynamic), interactive (users can download forms, e-mail officials,
and interact through the Web), transactional (users can actually pay for
services and other transactions online), and seamless (full integration
of e-services across administrative boundaries is accomplished).

[2]   The report presented the E-Government Readiness Index, a composite
index comprised of a Web measure index, a telecommunications infrastructure index, and a human capital index, aimed at measuring online
generic availability of information and services in quantitative terms.
The index ranked between 0 and 1.

[3]   The index used in this report is the E-Government Index already used
to measure worldwide e-government progress and development in the
United Nations' *World Public Sector Report 2003*. More information
about the composition and evolution of this index can be obtained from
"A Comparative Analysis of E-Government in Latin America: Applied
Findings from United Nations E-Government Readiness Reports," a
chapter in this book by Gregory Curtin and Christopher Walker.

[4]   See Endnote 3.

[5]   However, it is also interesting to note that if data had been further disag-
gregated, two other e-government divides could have also been observed.
On one hand, there is the regional e-government divide or the digital
gap that refers to e-government actions between the different countries
of Latin America. On the other, there is the domestic e-government divide, which explains the difference between the advanced online public
administrations and the more backward ones in the framework of one
Latin American specific country.

6   According to Thomas and Bennis (1972), an organizational change refers to the design and implementation, in a deliberate way, of a structure innovation, a policy, a new goal, or an operational transformation.

7   North (1994, p. 1, 4) is very illustrative about this assertion:

Institutions are the structure that humans impose on human interaction and therefore define the incentives that together with the other constraints (budget, technology, etc.) determine the choices that individuals make that shape the performance of societies and economies over time...[For example,] if the highest rates of return in a society are to be made from piracy, the organizations will invest in knowledge and skills that will make them better pirates; if organizations realize the highest payoffs by increasing productivity then they will invest in skills and knowledge to achieve that objective.

Acknowledgments

The editor would like to acknowledge the help of all involved in the collation and review process of the book, without whose support the project could not have been satisfactorily completed.

Once more, deep appreciation and gratitude is due to Kristin Roth, my development editor and a dear friend. She is a great professional and a better person. Her editorial support, her encouragement, and her good advice during the last 2 years have turned this project into a worthwhile book. Special thanks also go to all the staff at Idea Group Inc., whose contributions throughout the whole process from inception of the initial idea to final publication have been invaluable. In particular, thanks go to Mehdi Khosrow-Pour, whose enthusiasm motivated me to initially accept his invitation to take on this project, and to Jan Travers, who kindly granted me a deadline extension when she found out about my personal situation.

I also want to sincerely thank all those who offered constructive and comprehensive input for the different chapters. And, above all, I wish to thank all the authors for their insights and excellent contributions to this book, and to most of them for making an effort to translate their texts into English. Thank you to all of you for helping me to disseminate your expertise and knowledge about Latin American electronic government initiatives.

Last, but not least, I would like to thank my beloved husband Fran for his continuous support. As has been the case in the past, this new book would not have come out without his encouragement and understanding throughout the years.

This book is dedicated to Marcos and Hawa, my children, the sunshine of my life.

Mila Gascó, PhD
Barcelona, Spain
December 2006

Section I

National Case Studies

This section reviews several electronic-government initiatives implemented at the national and state or province level. A wide range of issues are introduced in this first part of the book such as the difference between back-office and front-office projects, the benefits of electronic-government initiatives, and the role of e-government in state reform process.

Chapter I

The Argentine IT Professionals Forum:
Building the Basis for the Back Office Through Communities of Practice[1]

Ester Kaufman,

Facultad Latinoamericana de Ciencias Sociales (FLACSO), Argentina

Abstract

This chapter introduces the experience of the Argentine IT Professionals Forum (ITPF) that enriches the definition of processes involving the tasks of e-government. The ITPF has become a cross-agency network that involves all the IT professionals of the public administration. It was created in 2002 as a response to the institutional crisis in Argentina in order to solve problems associated with the IT areas. The most important contribution of the ITPF is the basis for the back office as an interesting management model, theoretically known as "communities of practice" (CoPs) and networks, which have become core organizational tools as far as carrying out difficult innovation processes, such as the development of free software, cross-agency applications, and interoperability. However, traditional government structures have found it hard to deal with this kind of processes. Among the specific tasks involved, it is worthwhile mentioning the development of suitable software, the creation of cross-agency consensus, the generation of institutional networks, and so forth.

Introduction

The experience of the Argentine IT Professionals Forum (ITPF[2]) enriches the definition of processes involving the tasks of e-government. The ITPF has become a cross-agency network that involves all the IT professionals of the public administration (in Argentina it is called Foro de Responsables Informáticos[3]). It was created in 2002 as a response to the institutional crisis in Argentina in order to solve problems associated with the IT areas. The most important contribution of the ITPF is the basis for the back office as an interesting management model. The components of this model are theoretically known as "communities of practice" (CoPs) and "networks," which have become core organizational tools as far as carrying out difficult innovation processes, such as the development of free software, cross-agency applications, and interoperability. However, traditional government structures have found it hard to deal with this kind of processes, such as the setup of the back office. Among the specific tasks involved, it is worthwhile mentioning the development of suitable software, the creation of cross-agency consensus, the generation of institutional networks, and so forth. The new institutional forms are based on knowledge management (KM) related to ongoing learning and innovation within organizational environments. These new models were incorporated into e-government plans in order to solve the problems of the integration of technological, institutional, and cultural systems. Nowadays, such models are at the core of knowledge theories and are being used in real e-government experiences.

To consider the ITPF experience and the usefulness of the CoPs in the development of e-government (including back-office plans), I will deal with the following items: the background, including definitions and theoretical approaches; the context in which the ITPF took place; and the technological models at the time and the current problems they have been generating. Then I will describe the different periods of the ITDF and other experiences (future and emerging trends), and finally I will lay out the conclusion of those experiences.

Background

Much research to date has focused on the front office—on the use and take-up of electronic public services by citizens and businesses. However, no systematic research has dealt with the way public agencies are using ICT to reorganize in order to change the relationship between the front and back offices. Bearing this in mind, I would like to discuss, in detail, a striking experience of the ITPF within the Argentine central government. Its most important contributions are the following:

1. The creation of the basis for the back office, consisting of cross-integration among IT areas at the national government level, as the first step toward further development.
2. The implementation of a management model that guarantees this back office. This model is based on KM techniques that take up institutional forms such as networks and CoPs.
3. The design of new perspectives, differentiated from those in force in the '90s (new public management [NPM] and the technological model).
4. The awareness of the huge task involved in solving the basic problems generated by the approaches of the past decade.

In the following sections I will develop these contributions, taking into account the models and underlying views.

The Basis for the E-Government Back Office

The tasks involved in this basis take place prior to the development of back offices for specific services to citizens and businesses, such as driving licenses, passports, and payment of taxes. These tasks consist of organizing the information systems in such a way that they enable the government to share the data. They include, for example, the following:

1. How to use standards for feeding people's names to the systems
2. How to recognize state employees
3. How to locate files

4.   How to agree on shared software developed by specific IT public areas (in case the proprietary software is not available, is unsuitable, or is too expensive)

In its final report (Danish Technological Institute, 2004), the European Commission takes these tasks for granted in defining the back office. According to them:

the "back office" is a term relative to the front office which in this context is a user interface to an online service. The back office receives and processes the information which the user of a service enters in order to produce and deliver the desired service. This may be done completely manually, fully automatically or by any combination of both. In some cases such a service is produced by one unit or back-office, in other cases several back-offices of the same service supplier agency or of different agencies, at the same government level or at different levels may be involved. (p. 16)

In developing countries, such as Argentina, the above-mentioned previous tasks do not take place due to the institutional weakness of the governments as well as their lack of technical rationality (Weber, 1992). Therefore, lines of action should be set up for the development of the back office. For that reason, I would like to describe a successful experience that would be useful as far as showing the lines of action to be taken.

New Management Models Underlying the ITPF Experience: Networks and CoPs

In order to understand the management model developed by the ITPF, it is essential to define and differentiate networks and CoPs, considering that this forum is a mixture of both forms. A community of practice is a group of peers with a common sense of purpose who agree to work together to share information, share a common repertoire of resources, build knowledge, develop expertise, and solve problems. CoPs are characterized by the willing participation of members and their ongoing interaction in developing a chosen area of practice and competencies. Identity and autonomy are essential to enhance CoPs.

On the other hand, networks allow a mutually negotiated specialization: They are made of heterogeneous agents whose cognitive activity is to exchange knowledge. They interact together through informal and formal meetings, and the recruitment rule is mutual trust" (Cohendet, Creplet, & Dupouët, 2001, p. 6).

The CoPs describe groups of people who share a concern or a passion for something they do and who interact regularly to learn how to do it better[4] (Lave & Wenger, 1991). On entering these types of communities, every new member learns from the veteran members participating in certain activities related to the practice performed by the community. Thus, their participation progresses from the periphery until it reaches a full integration (Falivene, Silva, & Gurmendi, 2003).

The fact that the ITPF has functioned alongside traditional structures is also an enriching experience. It gives strength to new institutional models empowering e-government plans through the ICT networks tissue, which constitutes an essential feature of the information society.

Contexts and Models in the Last Decade: New Outlooks

Globalization has meant for many countries the inability to function in an autonomous way. This effect has been even more startling in developing countries such as Argentina. In the last decade, the government model responsible for this lack of autonomy was a limited version of NPM.[5]

NPM in Argentina was applied only to privatizations and downsizing in public agencies. Less attention was given to the training and recruitment of professionals by public agencies. Instead, recruitment was organized mainly around political cronyism. Because of this, the government did not count on specialized professionals to carry out its policies. Neither did it develop sound methods for enhancing the quality of its human resources, a key strategy to implement the e-government agenda. In Argentina, bureaucracies usually lack any behaviour toward Weberian "technical rationalities." The state is trapped by political interests and sluggish routines.

With regard to state personnel, every administration appoints its own public officials. The result of this chronic practice is that once a new administration takes power—bringing along a new set of appointees—the former members usually keep their jobs but are highly mistrusted. This is a recurring cycle in public administrations.

Every new administration announces its own e-government project that is seldom fulfilled.

The above-mentioned scenario makes it difficult to develop a sustainable e-government plan because deep restructuring is called for in order to achieve a step-by-step integration of the public sector. Ironically, this limited NPM seemed to be working by the mid-'90s, fed by an overabundance of foreign funding (by multilateral organizations) and political oversight with regard to the public debt that was being accrued. Parts of those funds were allotted to the purchase of ICT for government use.

It was in this context that a technological model of e-government was set up as a supposed emulation of American politics. This model was supported on the still-current belief that the incorporation of ICT was mainly an IT issue rather than a public-policies issue. The reliance of the government on a technological model meant profits for some businesses as well as for some public officials who allowed the random purchase of technology at high costs. This only improved the efficiency of a few isolated areas of the public administration such as tax collection. The government has not yet grasped the potential of ICT to offer better performance in order to help develop the information society.

Up to the present, the Argentine administrations have only applied general formulas suggested by international organizations that have been repeated automatically by government officials and consulting agencies. These formulas present a straightforward and mechanical view of development in four consecutive and cumulative stages:

1. Informative stage
2. Interactive stage
3. Transactional stage
4. Integrational stage

However, no logic can guarantee this lineal development. Considering the self-centeredness that characterizes many third-world administrations, the above process is unthinkable except for tax collection and e-procurement. Otherwise, many third-world administrations have no interest in sharing information or interchanging different points of view with fellow citizens or users. That is to say, Stages 2 through 4 never take place, which goes to show that e-government policies are not carried out seriously. Had they been taken seriously, a reengineering of structures and processes together with cultural changes would have been taken into account.[6] In contrast with first-world governments, the Argentine administrations did not understand these complex processes. E-government policies were limited to the purchase and installation of technology and the setting up of sloppy informational Web sites. These isolated courses of action brought about a negative connotation concerning the potential of e-government. Argentine citizens were under the impression that such policies had been motivated by shady businesses, which meant a profit for government officials. In some cases, these suspicions were proved true (Herzog, 2002).

Even if no corruption was involved, officials used e-government as a purely technological model. Considered as such, some basic concepts associated with this model are as follows:

1. The assumption that technology acquisition automatically implies positive effects

2. The fact that it is a self-centered model, which generates incomplete institutional information without any degree of participation from non-governmental actors

3. E-government is considered a matter that belongs to IT professionals, not an issue concerning the generation of public policies.

4. The implementation of e-government consists of building portals featuring some official information (informative model), a little technology, and some governmental internal electronic procedures, all overlapping the existing bureaucratic structure.

The Awareness of the Basic Problems of the Technological Model

Bruce Rocheleau (1997) points out the failures of a related model applied to the reinvention policies launched by Al Gore in the United States. This author emphasizes that sharing information is made difficult in an organization in spite of advances in the ability to share. Politicians have resorted to the Internet as a way of providing easy access to information. This ability of technology to solve problems has raised a false optimism in the political spectrum given that there is more hope than empirical proof.

Rocheleau (1997) suggests the need to examine information-system failures more closely in order to draw lessons on how to improve their performance. These difficulties could be traced to what I call "the basis of the back office."

Rocheleau (1997) identified some basic problems of this model and their possible causes. Among them, he mentioned inadequate training, caused by lack of investment, low priority, and poor quality of training; poor quality of data caused by inadequate oversight, lack of technical controls, and organizational resistance; and obstacles to sharing data caused by interoperability problems, database incompatibilities, and organizational obstacles.

Since its inception in 2002, the ITPF has tried to solve some of the kinds of problems mentioned by Rocheleau. The following list of proposals was devised in one of its first meetings:

1.   Availability of IT application systems such as keeping track of files, human-resource management, income and expenditure control, patrimony, and training

2.   Use of standards to classify goods and services

3.   Design of basic outlines to develop government Web sites

4.   Development of techniques to improve interoperability, and the definition of standard and metadata schemes

5.   Improvement and optimization of agencies' connectivity and the use of the Internet through safety tools

6.   Compilation of strategic issues to generate specific training

The ITPF: Functioning, Strengths, and Challenges

Functioning of the ITPF

In order to set up the present ITPF, created at the beginning of 2002, representatives of over 100 national public agencies were invited to participate. Ninety organizations and 200 technicians are now involved in different processes within the forum. This methodology was developed in Argentina by the Latin American School of Social Sciences (FLACSO).The KM applied consists of articulating several work meetings where the accomplished tasks are agreed upon and new actors incorporated. The meetings may be plenary, thematic, or group meetings. They are mainly face-to-face gatherings.

The global structure of the activities depends on a core group open to all members of the ITPF led by the ITPF coordinator. Their purpose is to develop a strategic viewpoint of ITPF, and plan the meetings according to the topics already agreed upon by the whole group in previous meetings.

Participants of the plenary meetings are professionals in the IT areas within the national government, although over time professionals from other local governments as well as from the academic sector have joined in. The average turnout was 100 people with monthly meetings throughout 2002 and 2003. Lately, the meetings have been less frequent due to the widespread growth of the virtual forum.

The plenary meetings are divided into three stages:

1. Presentation and consensus of the tasks accomplished by the core group and by the work groups and new lines of action

2. Work performed in workshops, where new ideas and proposals are discussed openly

3. Conclusion with a shared presentation of the subjects addressed in the workshops and action plans. At this point, new work groups are set up, and the existing ones may be modified. Should a relevant topic require discussing in depth, external specialists are called in to present experiences and existing papers at a special plenary meeting.

Goals are established in each meeting in order to connect one meeting with the next. These goals are written up in a record of proceedings. Taken together, these documents allow the members to trace the steady quality of the interchange, the building of a balance of information among the different actors, a prospective analysis, as well as the history of the process. Likewise, the collective conceptualizations enable the upgrading of the level of understanding and the monitoring of tasks, advances, or setbacks.

The work groups are fully dedicated to the development of leading issues for the back office of an electronic government, including, for example, the following:

1. **Free Software Group:** It performs discussion and legislative support activities on draft laws dealing with that subject. It relays the existing developments in the state as an input for its own work on software development.

2. **Cross-Agencies Applications Group:** It focuses on the need to incorporate IT processes into the ordinary administrative ones in different areas within the state, such as human resources, files, hospital administration, and financial administration. Its line of action is to identify best practices, coordinating their transfer, and to generate upgraded applications.

3. **Interoperability Group:** The aim of this group is to create a framework of technological standards and data structure that enable the users to interchange information. Interoperability is the ability of a system or a product to work with other systems or products without special effort on the part of the user.

ITPF Strengths and Challenges

These strengths are to be found in the following:

1. In the steady attendance of its members, considering that the initiatives are generated by the permanent or quasi-permanent staff

2. In the certainty that the work that has been produced will be implemented given that the practitioners who present the innovations coincide with the ones who implement them

3. In the legitimacy of its productions due to the general consensus regarding their suitability

4. In its transparency and responsibility as a result of periodic and steady collective control of the initiatives, processes, and products

The challenges the ITPF has to confront are as follows:

1. Its continuity beyond changes in government

2. The need for greater resources considering the extraordinary growth of its activities, especially for the development of free software

3.   The channeling of foreign funding destined to information technologies for their use and control via the forum

4.   The use of the virtual ITPF as its own efficient means

The Importance of the ITPF

The ITPF has become a key actor in the development of the first stages of e-government initiatives by putting into operation the basic platform that could solve such problems as interoperability, cross-agency applications, and the development of suitable software, among others.[7]

The work performed by the ITPF suggests solutions to problems regarding the basic conditions that would ensure the enforcement of an elementary e-government and that would enable upgrading in order to make up networks of different levels (local, state, national, international) and origins (public or private), that is to say, the creation of "back networks."[8, 9]

By elementary e-government, I mean one that starts the creation of the missing basic platform of the back office in order to interconnect several government agencies. These agencies offer a front office where services will be integrated cohesively according to the customers' needs. This process will eventually lead to a "one-stop shop" enabling access to services that will be grouped together and classified by subject. The development of the back office must lead up to reorganization as well as a redefinition of processes and structures. Further, it must also contemplate changing organizational cultures. This basic platform of the back office should also be the basis for a progressive technological development that could establish sensible criteria for purchasing hardware and software. Likewise, this technological development could pave the way for the creation of suitable software to ensure better services and to protect confidential government data.

For the time being, this concept of the basic platform of the back office is carried out only by the ITPF. The forum has provided prompt responses in contrast to the lack of action on the part of the authorities responsible for e-government politics. After President Menem's second term in office, the relationship between ICT and the government went on a discouraging downward path. The miracle recipes of the '90s never materialized, unjustly discrediting the potential of ICT and hence putting at risk the placement of our country with respect to the new economy. E-government policies suffered likewise.

This loss of credibility mirrored the descent of the IT National Office[10] (ITNO) in government hierarchies. Having been an undersecretariat (during Menem's administration), it became a lower ranking office (Dirección Nacional) deprived of power to regulate ICT activities within the state.

This is the context in which the ITPF developed.

Development of the ITPF

I deal with the ITPF experience separating it in two steps. The first started with the creation of the ITPF (during the 2002 crisis) and finished when President Kirchner took office in May 2003. The second step deals with overcoming the crisis, and the relationship between ITPF and the new authorities and teams. I also deal with other similar international experiences. Finally, I arrive at the conclusions centered on the liaison between the traditional and emerging institutions.

In order to describe the above-mentioned sequences, I go back to the ITPF's inception.

Step One: The Crisis. Setting up the ITPF[11]

The ITPF came about in response to the institutional crisis that started in Argentina in December 2001. The forum designed within the public-management undersecretariat as an interinstitutional network, cutting across bureaucratic management tiers linked to the ITNO to solve problems associated with these fields.

In the past, experts from international organizations, such as the World Bank, the Inter-American Development Bank, and consulting companies, were sought after for the design and implementation of technological policies. However, these experiences failed due to the lack of contact between these agencies and the local staff who would have developed the knowledge gained by these experiences. When the crisis set in, the default was declared by the authorities, generating isolation from the international framework. Therefore, the government was left without economic resources to keep up expenditures related to outsourced consultants. As a result, the local IT staff started to assemble the ITPF invited by the ITNO.

Other forums were created as a result of the above-mentioned crisis. Indeed, during the crisis, government policies were focused on overcoming bureaucratic limitations. One of the most important government directives was informality. Different public sectors were called to create CoPs and networks. This gave rise to forums through which organizational knowledge could be accessed to generate competencies and in this way overcome the crisis. Thus, cross-agency forums were created with reference to the following activities: human resources, file management, documentation centers, IT areas, budget management, statistics, international cooperation units, and so forth.

Finally, technology enabled the government to overcome the communication problem through the use of e-mail, thus solving inconveniences such as the lack of paper or ink for printers (crucial at the time). ICT provided a solution for these shortages in an informal way, ensuring an adequate number of functioning computers, something that could not be taken for granted at the time.[12] This issue is related to the IT area, as well as the supply of software programs. However, considering that it is next to impossible to afford proprietary software licenses, IT experts have continually faced the challenge of creating new applications.

The above-mentioned situations involve almost all the information pertaining to the state. With this in mind, the ITPF tackles these tasks in a highly motivated way, thus enhancing its members' self-esteem. The result has been that this forum is already providing effective answers to core IT questions that politicians had not been able to confront.

As already mentioned, the ITPF has outperformed other forums in the sense that it has acquired a quasi-autonomous profile due to the ability of its members to face constant innovation.[13]

I should mention that these forums were originally created having in mind training objectives at zero cost. This goal was perfectly accomplished by the ITPF using the KM model, which relies on the challenge of learning by doing and sharing experiences, thus transforming them into a common asset. This practice, never before applied in the booming '90s, turned out to be vital in the absence of other training resources. The only available source of expertise at the time was the knowledge developed throughout decades by the ITPF members.

Step Two: Overcoming the Crisis

As of 2003, the different groups have widened the scope of their tasks. This came about because the ITPF members became familiar with the KM tools. Another reason for this positive result was the stability that the Kirchner administration has achieved. Thus, the groups have been able to envision long-term core activities.[14]

Up to the present, an important activity has been the creation of the Web Space Group that deals with the ITPF Web site, where the interaction between the members is enhanced through virtual support.

Besides this, it is worthwhile noticing the development of the Free Software Group. It created three subgroups:

1. **Training Group:** It organizes training based on an inter-sectorial co-operative-practices model. A training scheme was developed in LINUX for three learning levels on which different organizations have been contributing complementary resources (tutors, classrooms, and computers).[15]

2. **Software Licenses Group:** It works on two items: the incorporation of free software developed outside the state, and state developments and internal transferences among public organizations.[16]

3. **Interstate Knowledge Network:** It is constantly being upgraded on the ITPF Web site, where successful public free-software experiences can be accessed. A support desk is under way thanks to the voluntary and anonymous help of the ITPF members.[17]

The other work groups continue improving their lines of action.[18]

The development of the ITPF can be seen as contrasting with bureaucratic structures that so far have failed to provide an integration proposal for a back office.

I will try go over the following issues in the light of the strained relationship between the network and stiff bureaucratic structures.

With regard to the network's range of action in the face of political institutional power that continues to manage institutions in the traditional hierarchical way, it can be declared that the relationship between traditional hierarchical institutions and the ITPF was the main concern in the first period of the process.

The beginning of this process signaled the change from a negative view toward informal working relationships. The resulting benefits started to be seen inasmuch as these informal relationships decreased bureaucratic drawbacks, such as the following:

1. Lack of shared effort and a tendency toward fragmentation
2. Reduced capacity to integrate innovation
3. Censorship related to such innovation
4. Self-centeredness

The forums brought "fresh air" into bureaucratic behaviours

The ITPF's range of action was wide from the very beginning. The national authorities overlooked IT areas (ITNO), thus leaving this field open for the ITPF to operate in. It can then be concluded that the government did not delegate to the ITPF the responsibility of handling IT policies in a legal fashion. The ensuing problem was that the available tools managed by the ITPF were applied in a random way. If the back office tasks are understood as standard practices that implement an interoperable system, the lack of general rules brings about a difficult problem to solve. However, little by little, this situation has been changing as the institutions gain stability and the crisis diminishes. During 2003, President Kirchner achieved a general consensus that enabled an increasing inflow of economic resources. The growth of tax revenue generated some resources for the public sector. This brought about many difficulties in the relationship between the ITPF and the political authorities due to the well-known mistrust between the newly appointed personnel and the already-operating staff. The first measure taken by the new director of the ITNO was to appoint a reliable team. The environment generated by the new team produced a distance between the ITPF and these authorities, who perceived the ITPF to be a powerful as well as an amorphous group of manage.

The new administration soon noticed that the ITPF had a power of its own. This was owing to the fact that it had reached a strong identity among its members, obtained through the sharing of common goals.

On the other hand, many of its participants held significant positions whether in the IT arena or in their own organizations. It is worthwhile bearing in mind that due to the cross-agency nature of the ITPF, many IT representatives from different agencies attended the forum. Some of these agencies have, even nowadays, a higher rank than the ITNO in terms of political and economic relevance. The ITPF continued growing and generating projects and innovations.[19]

In time, certain politicians became aware of the ITPF's importance as a problem-solving resource. In this respect, the present ITNO director and chief officer of the e-government plan claims that in view of the weak state of the ITNO as opposed to the powerful position that the ITPF has achieved, it is necessary to balance both organizations by means of human resources, infrastructure, and suitable policies developed by the ITNO itself. According to the director, only a strong ITNO could standardize the innovation taking place in the ITPF.[20]

However, the ITPF is likely to be included in further plans in charge of certain tasks.

On the other hand, as time goes by, the usual turn of events, as far as management occurs, mainly, the new officials get to know the old ones and a bond of trust is established between them.[21,22] Besides, ITNO has fount it hard to consolidate due to the following factors:

1.   ICTs are not relevant in the public agenda, despite the efforts made by certain ITNO directors.

2.   The ITNO was left in a weakened position (such as in the state in general) as a consequence of applying new public management.

Therefore, the expected balance between the ITNO and the ITPF has not yet been achieved.

The authorities lack a strong support to implement the projects they announce. As a consquence of this, the ITPF keeps generating IT solutions and recommendations that the government does not apply immediately. Nevertheless, they are stored and may become available for the political authorities to be used when they encounter difficulties in carrying out plans that need sound results. The suitability of many of these solutions could bring forth closer bonds between the government and the ITPF as long as a technical rationality is enforced as regards political decisions.[23]

A second issue is the political authorities' indifference toward the networks.

Actually, regarding underlying networks, CoPs, and political authorities, there are different logical ways of thinking as well as different foci of interest.

As far as networks and CoPs are concerned, their goal is to solve daily issues associated with their needs or professional practices. In the case of networks, they solve these by means of complementary actions. In the case of CoPs, issues are solved by means of KM and innovation (Cohendet et al., 2001).

The networks and CoPs within the state are driven by a technical rationality aimed at solving difficulties in management. In contrast, for most political authorities, their main interest lies in their party relationships, political commitments, and state agenda. Many issues are not included in this agenda. In view of the present crisis Argentina is going through, with its resulting poverty, hunger, and unemployment, it would seem politically incorrect to develop technological policies in order to improve the state's performance. This is the case with the E-Government National Plan because it would mean an expense in hardware and software, which is not a priority. The ITNO falls under this context, making it hard to fulfill its goals.

With respect to the informal structure of networks and CoPs, governmental control is limited, causing certain uneasiness in political authorities. This situation could be reverted if the government became familiar with their functioning.

In other countries, there are also misunderstandings. Snyder and Souza Briggs (2003, p. 51) state that:

there are several ways to address these concerns: by seeing the emergence of CoPs as an evolutionary process, not a cataclysmic revolution; by distinguishing the knowledge-building and knowledge-sharing functions of these communities with the primarily transactional focus of product- and service-delivery units; and by understanding that collaborative, boundary-crossing networks need not mark the loss of government's public-service identity and influence, but rather serve as an expansion of both.

Another interesting topic has to do with the possibilities to develop free software in a context of scarcity of resources.

Indeed, it is a hard task to develop software without the necessary resources.

However, it should be remembered that the ITPF is made up of several organizations that may be working on software developments with their own resources (for example, the AFIP, the Argentinean tax agency; ANSES, the pension funds administrator, and the Central Bank). This software is usually made available in order to test its applicability in other sectors.

It goes without saying that every agency where the software is applied will need its own resources so that the software can be implemented and the necessary training supplied. In some cases, directives from the ITNO are required.

I have mentioned earlier some ways in which it has been possible to generate a network for the creation of LINUX training courses. I should add that the group of tutors is made up of IT experts who share their knowledge. Their tutoring is almost free. Moreover, they have designed courses for public officials. It should be noticed that it would have been hard to find enough LINUX teachers for this task, and the few available ones would have charged very high fees. If this had been the case, the courses would not have started.

The fourth challenge I would like to refer to is how the ITPF can broaden the professional competencies of IT experts.

The ITPF has come a long way. At its inception, the members were against interacting with other systems, actors, or forums. Nowadays, they are starting to change this attitude of isolation, interacting with legislators, scholars, lawyers, human-resources directors, and front-desk chiefs.

The evolution of the ITPF is also reflected in the language its members have been adopting. Rather than just using IT jargon, they have integrated IT terms into an interlinguistic field. This attitude helps to include the addressees' needs by letting them have a say in their decisions. Broadly speaking, IT experts are responsible for showing the way in which technology can be used to improve decision-making processes. Thus, they should be familiar with public-administration rules and the specific needs of public officials. The ITPF has contributed to collective knowledge about the culture of organizations in connection with information and technology, the rules of the game, as well as the implicit hierarchies and their informal structure.

Through their own experience at the ITPF, its members have also learned to work in networks to perceive the environment, communicate skills, and so forth. They confront the challenge of bridging the gaps with non-IT areas, taking into account that the latter are constantly producing data. This data needs to be standardized in order to be included in IT systems and to feed new developments. This compatibility should be the priority of the back office. Yet, it proves difficult to achieve given that IT and non-IT experts are used to working based on different disciplinary logics. Therefore, the job of IT experts is to match these differences.[24]

It is also interesting to know the processes that have led to interdisciplinary relationships with non-IT expert customers. These interchanges took place due to the following:

1.   The gradual awareness by IT experts of the customers' needs
2.   The gradual incorporation of basic IT logics by non-IT experts

The massive use of ICT together with its inadvertently growing daily use led customers to become more participative. Moreover, users have started to demand solutions tailored to their needs as they rely increasingly on ICT tools. These practices are being developed through daily routines that are giving way to a certain familiarity. Needless to say, the ITPF is involved in these processes. Although at first the forum rejected any kind of interchange with other actors, little by little it abandoned such reluctance. [25]

As regards the incoporation of basic IT logic by non IT experts, and viceversa, we should remember that interaction among CoPs may take the shape of border meetings where some of the members of two or more CoPs get together in order to foster an interchange of practices and to trigger thinking processes into the community itself or in the border practices. For example, the ITPF needed to acquire competencies developed by librarians in order to be able to classify the developments spotted by the Free Software Group. The Forum of Documents Center, in turn, needed to incorporate competencies from the former in order to work with digital documents and to be able to deal with them. It was necessary to learn, among other issues, how to keep these documents from disappearing from the Internet.

This phenomenon also takes place with non-IT actors in general as they try to become familiar with the use of ICT (Falivene & Kaufman, 2005).

Finally, a last question remains: Why are IT public officials more likely to work in networks, incorporating IT, therefore becoming the main support of the e-government back office?

The ITPF experience, as well as other empirical cases, shows a trend of many IT experts to develop systems that enable a horizontal flow of information. This behaviour is a strong core identity mechanism in their CoPs.[26] Needless to say, it forms part of the development of an IT professional. It is as obvious as mentioning the physician's predisposition to heal. The fact is that such behaviour concerning the horizontal flow of information is not neutral as regards public-administration practices. That is to say, it generates a conflict when confronted with political and bureaucratic points of view. Usually, the hierarchies in these CoPs are synonymous with professional pride and know-how. So, these different perspectives constitute dissociated worlds sharing common environments.

On the other hand, many IT experts do not conceive institutional or personal power as isolated compartments. This fragmented view of power has always existed within the Argentine government, preventing the consolidation of a strong and efficient state.

Nevertheless, ICTs are in a way becoming a dangerous-enough weapon to injure the Achilles heel of fragmentation. Many IT experts understand the crucial importance of these tools and are willing to generate positive changes. To make this happen, they are building other institutional architectures (usually informal ones) that enable the inflow of information to legitimate addressees.

IT experts may not be the champions of transparent processes or of participation through ICT. They may just be good professionals.

Other Experiences

Some current government policies encourage CoPs as strategic lines of action, such as in Canada,[27] the United States, Australia,[28] and other countries. These lines of action are oriented toward reinforcing federal policies as well as supporting government

structures in complex processes. This is the case of e-government plans when a government wants to change and integrate the institutional, cultural, and technological systems.

The developments implemented by the above-mentioned administrations have key government authorities as their sponsors. Such was the case with Al Gore in the United States when he was the vice president of that country ("Reinventing Government," 1998). Conversely in Argentina, as far as IT areas, this initiative stems from the public-management undersecretariat and the ITNO (which depends on the former). In view of this categorization, it is difficult to undertake a political strategy as strong as those from the previously mentioned countries.

This emerging complementary relationship between CoPs and the bureaucratic structures is an interesting strategy given that CoPs constitute an effective way of solving unusual problems, sharing knowledge beyond traditional structural borders through the coexistence of informal integration models and bureaucratic models. Within these interrelationships, formal structures can be fed by the production generated in turn by CoP members. The different CoPs intertwine in a blurred way and cut across the organizational arena (Tuomi, 1999). These CoPs also contribute the improvement of teams that are set up for specific government projects (such as e-government), recognizing that formally managed projects work best when the following are true:

1.   Problems can be clearly defined.
2.   Reliable, quantifiable measurements are established.
3.   An authority structure is in place to ensure that project results get implemented.

Additionally, communities are most effective when they follow certain criteria, as follows:

1.   Problems are complex and dynamic or very situation specific.
2.   Measures require stories to link cause and effect.
3.   Authority is decentralized and depends more on professionals' intrinsic commitment to getting results (vs. extrinsic appraisals and incentives).

In the United States, the IBM Center for the Business of Government has performed case studies, led by Snyder and Souza Briggs (2003), that reveal the strategic relevance the U.S. federal government has placed on the development of CoPs to support a variety of state-related issues, such as children's health, highway controls, antiterrorism, e-government, and so forth. Specifically, the federal e-government encourage the development of CoPs to generate a cross-agency pilot community because it addressed a strategic concern that aligned with a new government-wide legislative mandate, the Government Paperwork Elimination Act, which required agencies to streamline processes and reduce paperwork by October 2003 (Snyder & Wenger, 2003).

The Australian government has also included CoPs in its experience of e-government. The Australian Government Information Management Office (AGIMO) states:

CoPs are practical vehicles for sharing and building knowledge and promoting better practice... In this spirit, AGIMO's role is that of a catalyst and facilitator, providing initial structure, while encouraging ownership and engagement by community of practice members. Facilitation of the CoPs is shared with other government agencies.[29]

As mentioned before,[30] the Australian CIO Forum is an alternative version of the ITPF.[31]

On the Web page of the AGIMO, it is possible to find the following excerpt:

The CIO Forum has been established to provide a mechanism for CIOs across the Australian Government to share information and enhance linkages to the Chief Information Officer Committee (CIOC) and the Information Management Strategy Committee (IMSC). The objectives of the CIO Forum are to:

1. *Share information about better practice approaches and key strategic issues being faced by agencies in their use of ICT to facilitate better government.*

2. *Provide a mechanism for CIOs across government to hear about Chief Information Officer Committee (CIOC) and Information Management Strategy Committee (IMSC) activities.*

3. *Explore opportunities to contribute to CIOC activities and provide CIOC with non CIOC perspectives.*

4. *Explore and pursue collaborative and cooperative opportunities.*

Conclusion

Some Thoughts about International Experiences

Since the creation of the ITPF, I have been researching the process of building the back office. I always thought I was witnessing a new practice and my belief was confirmed by all the practitioners who attended the events where I put forward this experience.

At the same time, I was devoted to relaying a bibliography on the following subjects: CoPs, epistemic communities, and networks, and their relationship with KM. In this respect, I found mainly theoretical approaches with some practical references to private environments.

At first, the subjects bore no relationship in my mind. But little by little, they began to fit a certain pattern. I could integrate CoPs and e-government. Therefore, I changed my theoretical outlook toward the ITPF experience.

I considered this approach a very innovative one. On finishing my first draft of this chapter, some workmates[32] discovered that in several countries, this model of relationships was put into practice as a political strategy for e-government programs. CoPs were becoming an essential tool. This realization became a shared joy for the ITPF and the ITNO authorities since they felt less lonely in their initiative.

However, I found no detailed descriptions of how these relationships (formal-informal) operated within the framework of the back office. Therefore, I consider it useful to state the specific experience of the ITPF, giving more accurate information and detailed reflections.

Final Thoughts

Historically, the traditional structures of government have failed to provide integral answers to e-government plans, above all in third-world countries such as Argentina (Kaufman, 2005). This seems also to be the case in first-world countries, as seen from the examples of Canada, the United States, and Australia, even though they have support policies regarding CoPs. Traditional structures have very sharp internal boundaries marking isolated compartments. Therefore, it is hard for them to incorporate functions and actors to interact within different contexts, even when a strong political environment encourages this. Informal institutions, such as CoPs, should support such goals as the production of information and services within a network tissue model with the understanding that e-government has a main function to perform in the information society.

Manuel Castells (1997) has defined the information society as a society where the central processes of knowledge generation, economic productivity, political and military power, and media have been deeply transformed by an informational paradigm. This paradigm has been shaped by the new technological medium that follows the logic of interconnection among systems (networks morphology). The development of a society bearing these characteristics depends on the capacity of its agents to generate processes and efficiently apply information based on knowledge and to organize itself on a global scale.

It can be said that the function of e-government consists of being a trigger for the integration of networks, permitting their articulation through information and services that e-government produces (alone or with other partners within networks). This should also facilitate the articulation of private actors on a global scale in order to permit adequate insertion in the new economy.[33]

This scenario is light years away from e-government conceived by Latin American politicians, although the region needs the economic development that would be made possible by efficient articulation. This region needs all its available resources to strengthen its states: the maximum effort (public and private) at a minimum cost. There is a big difference between this region and the first world, which can encourage these developments with a lot of funding. Latin America has only been receiving foreign money to pay consultancies that work in a superficial, nonsystematic and nonintegrative way. Most government, university, nonprofit, and business actors should integrate resources to support key policies leading to a way out of economic stagnation. For this reason, the tasks of integration into networks and CoPs (public and private) are fundamental. An important part of these tasks is carried out in the back office of a type of e-government that I call associative, in which the back office has already become back networks.

With reference to associative e-governments, it is worth mentioning that technology enables society and government to interact. Furthermore, it can transform the players or stakeholders into partners together with the government. If this is the case, on entering the e-government portal, users are at the same time entering the digital city where they can find all the services, whether public or private, that each society or government chooses. In an associative model, many segments of society can participate in the decision making about the kind of services that the government and each social and economic segment have to provide through the Internet. Also, each particular segment, stakeholder, or partner decides on the implementation and evaluation of such services and can monitor them. Each and every part is essential to build up the back networks where users can find unions, small and medium enterprises, civil and cultural organizations, universities, ICT enterprises, and so on. Some of the Net workers could work interconnected with others. For instance, the enterprises could work with schools, universities, and unions in order to develop the kind of workers and professionals that the market needs. In this kind of relationship, the government is not self-centered. It works as a strong coordinator, although it is not the only one (Kaufman, 2003a).

Most Latin American governments are not in a position to carry out the necessary tasks of integration of the back networks, nor are they interested in them (Kaufman, 2003b). The ambitions of those in power within the state have weakened the state itself in a swamp of corruption and spurious special interests. This weakness of the state might be corrected through networks and CoPs, allowing the weaving of a fabric that had never been finished. Such new interventions may also function as controls. Furthermore, networking in itself makes it possible to demand participation in political decision making.

It is my belief that these networks promote the common good because, together with an increasing use of ICT, they can sharpen a watchful gaze on matters that until recently were kept in the dark. The ICT put into effect mechanisms that impede total control over information.[34]

The profound transformations brought about by the information society often occur in a disorganized and chaotic fashion. They can never be entirely taken into account by public policies precisely because many are the fruit of forms of self-organization that exceed the responsibility of the state.

However, some specific courses of action may help or hinder these transformations, such as the ones developed by the ITPF. It is essential to achieve a cross-technological alignment of the different public agencies so that they become interoperable in order to build a networks system (or back networks) in accordance with the morphological model of the information society. The courses of action adopted by the ITPF present a different perspective to the fixed e-government models that satisfy mainly technology suppliers and associated consultants. CoPs, such as the ITPF, are key structures to counteract special interests and poor models of e-government. These should allow accessing more ambitious projects that address the common good, such as the associative e-government. In Argentina, no other mechanisms have as yet paved the way for these processes.[37]

Yet these mechanisms are not enough. Needless to say, specific e-government and information-society policies, as well as a strong political will, are missing. Some decisions should be made within the framework of a strategic e-government plan. They should address issues such as the following:

1.   Who does the plan target?
2.   Who are its stakeholders?
3.   What are the available resources?
4.   What methodology is to be used?
5.   What are the priorities?
6.   What are the expected results?

The belief that CoPs and networks may make the above decisions would mean continuing with the assumption of the "magic" role of IT professionals, though they may have contributed their knowledge as in the case of the ITPF.

References

Castells, M. (1997). *La era de la información: Economía, sociedad y cultura* (Vol. 1). Madrid, Spain: Alianza Editorial.

Cohendet, P., Creplet, F., & Dupouët, O. (2001). *CoPs and epistemic communities: A renewed approach of organisational learning within the firm.* Retrieved November 22, 2004, from http://www.marsouin.org/IMG/pdf/dupouet.pdf

Community Intelligence. (2003). *Innovation and CoPs: The "great symphony" paradox. The innovation potential of bridging structural holes.* Retrieved April 2, 2004, from http://www.communityintelligence.com/pdf/Communities_&_Innovation.pdf

Danish Technological Institute. (2004). *Reorganisation of government back offices for better electronic public services: European good practices (Back-office reorganisation). Final report to the European Commission.* Retrieved March 3, 2004, from http://www.cio.gv.at/news/files/Back_office.pdf & http://hw.oeaw.ac.at/0xc1aa500d_0x0010b255

Falivene, G., & Kaufman, E. (2005). The potential of CoPs in Argentina to articulate public organizations and training through knowledge management approach. In E. Coakes & S. Clarke (Eds.), *Encyclopedia of communities of practice in information and knowledge management.* Hershey, PA: Idea Group Reference.

Falivene, G., Silva, G., & Gurmendi, L. (2003). *El e-learning como mecanismo articulador de procesos de gestión del conocimiento y formación continua en las organizaciones públicas: El caso del Sistema de Información Universitaria.* Retrieved September 19, 2004, from http://www.clad.org.ve/fulltext/0048201.pdf

Gascó, M., & Equiza, F. (2002). Formulación de políticas públicas de transición a la sociedad del conocimiento: El caso argentino. *Desarrollo Humano e Institucional en América Latina (DHIAL), 36.* Retrieved December 20, 2002, from http://www.iigov.org/dhial/?p=36_04_

Gualtieri, R. (1998). *Impact of the emerging information society on the policy development process and democratic quality.* Paris OECD Public Management Service. Retrieved November 14, 1998, from http://www.alfa-redi.com//apc-aa-alfaredi/img_upload/a63473ef6aa82c7a2b2cc688d7e635dd/12E81094.doc

Herzog, R. (2002). Internet und politik in Lateinamerika: Argentinien. In R. Herzog, B. Hoffman, & M. Schulz (Eds.), *Internet und politik in Lateinamerika: Regulierung und nutzung der neuen informationsund kommunikationstechnologien im kontext der politischen und wirtschaftlichen transformationen* (pp. 100-112). Frankfurt, Germany: Vervuert Verlag. Retrieved September 12, 2002, from http://www1.uni-hamburg.de/IIK/nikt/Argentinien.pdf

Kaufman, E. (2003a). *Associative model for e-gov including digital cities.* Retrieved December 5, 2003, from http://www.cities-lyon.org/es/articles/203

Kaufman, E. (2003b, November). *Panorama latinoamericano de gobiernos electrónicos: Modelos existentes.* Paper presented at the Second Argentinean Conference on Public Administration, Córdoba, Argentina. Retrieved March 1, 2004, from http://www.aaeap.org.ar/ponencias/congreso2/Kaufman_Ester.pdf

Kaufman, E. (2004). E-gobierno en Argentina: Crisis, burocracia y redes. In R. Araya & M. Porrúa (Eds.), *América Latina puntogob* (pp. 151-187). Santiago, Chile: FLACSO Chile & Organization of American States.

Kaufman, E. (2005). E-government and e-democracy in Latin America: Stages of development. In S. Marshall, W. Taylor, & X. Yu (Eds.), *The encyclopedia of developing regional communities with information and communication technology.* Hershey, PA: Idea Group Reference.

Klijn, E., & Coppenhan, J. (2000). Public management and policy networks: Foundations of a network approach to governance. *Public Management, an International Journal of Research and Theory, 2*(2), 135-158. Retrieved February 3, 2001, from http://www.inlogov.bham.ac.uk/pdfs/readinglists/Klijn%20and%20Koppenjan%20on%20policy%20network%20theory.pdf

Lave, J., & Wenger, E. (1991). *Situated learning: Legitimate peripheral participation.* New York: Cambridge University Press.

Nonaka, I., & Takeuchi, H. (1995). *The knowledge-creating company: How the Japanese companies create the dynamic of innovation.* New York: Oxford University Press.

Rocheleau, B. (1997). Governmental information system problems and failures: A preliminary review. *Public Administration and Management: An Interactive Journal, 2*(3). Retrieved May 25, 1999, from http://www.pamij.com/roche.html

Snyder, W. M., & Souza Briggs, X. (2003). Communities of practice: A new tool for government managers. *Collaboration series of the IBM Center for the business of government.* Retrieved December 22, 2004, from http://www.businessofgovernment.org/pdfs/Snyder_report.pdf

Snyder, W. M., & Wenger, E. (2003). *Communities of practice in government: The case for sponsorship.* Retrieved December 30, 2004, from http://www.ewenger.com/pub/pubusfedcioreport.doc

Tuomi, I. (1999). *Corporate knowledge: Theory and practice of intelligent organizations.* Helsinki, Finland: Metaxis.

Weber, M. (1992). *Economía y sociedad.* Mexico: Fondo de Cultura Económica.

Wenger, E. (1998). *Communities of practice: Learning, meaning and identity.* New York: Cambridge University Press.

Wenger, E. (2000). Communities of practice and social learning systems. *Organization, 7*(2), 225-246.

Endnotes

[1]   A debt of gratitude goes to the IT Directors Forum coordinator, José Carllinni, for his help in developing this chapter. I also wish to acknowledge the help of Julie Taylor (Department of Anthropology, Rice University, Texas, USA) and Diana Stalman, who assisted me in translating and editing this chapter.

[2]   In some English-speaking countries, this kind of forum is referred to as a CIO (chief information officer) forum. I have chosen to use ITPF because CIO indicates the participation mainly of upper level IT areas. By contrast, ITPF also includes its broader membership.

[3]   See http://www.sgp.gov.ar/sitio/foros/foro_rrii.html.

[4]   See http://www.ewenger.com.

[5]   In its complete version, NPM consists of (a) privatizations of public enterprises, (b) a downsizing of government agencies, (c) a trend toward an increase of middle-management skills through the requirement of professionals, (d) the setting of performance standards, (e) an emphasis on outcomes, (f) the decentralizing of areas of competence in government agencies, (g) the advancement of competences and rivalry among participants, and (h) more control in the use of resources.

[6]   According to Gascó and Equiza (2002), digitalizing the government is not synonymous with having a few computers installed. Nor does it mean to design a Web site offering information. Rather, it aims at transforming the fundamental relationship between the government and the citizens.

[7]   See the ITPF methodology in the previous section.

[8]   This term was coined by José Luis Tesoro.

[9]   These improvements obviously depend on public politics. In this respect, the ITPF can only help by widening its CoPs and networks since it faces some limitations, such as (a) the voluntary nature of its members, (b) its limited scope, since it functions mainly within the national government, and (c) its independence from public-policy agendas (an issue associated with politician authorities).

[10]   The IT National Office (Oficina Nacional de Tecnología Informática, ONTI) has as its main objective to assist the public-management undersecretary to design politics and implement the process of development and IT innovation for the transformation and modernization of the state. It is the state regulating office in charge of furthering the integration of new technologies and their compatibility and interoperability, as well as promoting technological standardization. Among its projects are digital signatures, IT security, a government portal, as well as the e-government program. Each project is managed by a special team. Every IT area of the national government falls under the coordination of this regulating office, which sets norms and functioning standards related to IT. Its relationship with the ITPF and the state's bureaucratic structure may be seen in the annex at the end of this chapter. For more information, see http://www.sgp.gov.ar/sitio/institucional/oficinas/onti.html.

[11]   The first year of this experience has been analyzed by Kaufman (2004).

[12]   These kinds of difficulties are still present throughout the state.

[13]   The ITPF coordinator has his office at the ITNO. Meetings are held in public-management undersecretariat offices. The support team as well as the ITPF coordinator is within the government payroll in order to run the ITPF. This shows that this forum is not a totally self-organized CoP, but it was set up by the government, which provides it with resources. Regarding the ITPF activities, they are mainly self-organized.

[14]   The work groups are organized in the plenary meetings by the consensus of all the attendees. See more details in the previous section.

[15]   These courses have a very low cost ($0.30 per student). A further project proposes a team of LINUX coaches and tutors.

[16]   This subgroup is made up of lawyers from different public organizations together with software chambers, universities, and IT experts.

17   Anonymity was the chosen course of action in this task in the face of the offers made by private firms to ITPF members, siphoning them away from the public sphere.

18   See Endnote 2.

19   At this stage, the ITPF widened its variety of members to include IT experts with no specific hierarchy within the government, for instance, young programmers who worked in the free-software area.

20   The present director is Carlos Achiary, and his opinion has especially been recorded for this research.

21   Concurring this particular point, Mr. Achiary explained that he decided not to include the ITPF as a relevant actor in the E-Government National Plan because this degree of institutionalization would take away the ITPF's innovation force, caused by its informal style of bringing different participants together. The ITPF was meant to be an informal source of solutions for the e-government plan.

22   Notice that Mr. Achiary has been actively participating in the lastest plenary meeting ("Criteria for Recommendations for the Implementation of Free Software"an "Interoperability") as a member.

23   Up to the present, the collaboration between the ITPF and ITNO has increased. Some ITPF solutions have been carried out by the ITNO. This is the case of Web services and also the one-stop-shop file system follow-up.

24   This issue is neglected by the political authorities. In Argentinean public agencies, acquired technologies could have triggered an upgrading of the processes. Nevertheless, this upgrading never took place due to the existing gap between technology data administration, workflows, and management.

25   If these interchanges were regarded from a CoP approach, a border area could be identified since belonging to a community establishes a difference between the outside and the inside. It also reminds us of a bridge. The CoPs are connected to other collective subjects, their shared undertakings are linked, their members are in turn members of other communities, and their artifacts and tools are usually available to several groups. These bridges have a high potential. They offer the communities the possibility of confronting difference, experimenting with a cognitive dissonance between their own practice and others; of counteracting the risk of group thinking trapped at the community boundaries, incorporating

new resources, themes, languages, and behaviours; and of meeting the challenge of building a language to accomplish meaningful interchanges among the communities (Falivene & Kaufman, 2005).

[26]   This tendency is stressed by some youngsters who have made an ideological issue out of free software; their culture is a culture of gift giving and reputation.

[27]   http://www.communities-collectivites.gc.ca

[28]   http://www.agimo.gov.au

[29]   See http://www.agimo.gov.au/resources/cop.

[30]   See Endnote 2.

[31]   See http://www.agimo.gov.au/government/cio_forum.

[32]   They were José Carllinni (the ITPF coordinator) and Graciela Silva (an expert in CoPs).

[33]   To make all this possible, the government must also generate orchestrated policies for digital access that guarantee skillful and informed use of ICT. These functions must be applied for the successful integration into the information society.

[34]   In fact, this may lead to a trivialization of politics (suffice it to watch the superficial level of the media and political speeches). To read further on this matter, see Gualtieri (1998).

Appendix

Figure 1. The Argentine national authorities, the ITNO, the ITPF, network, CoPs and other public organisations

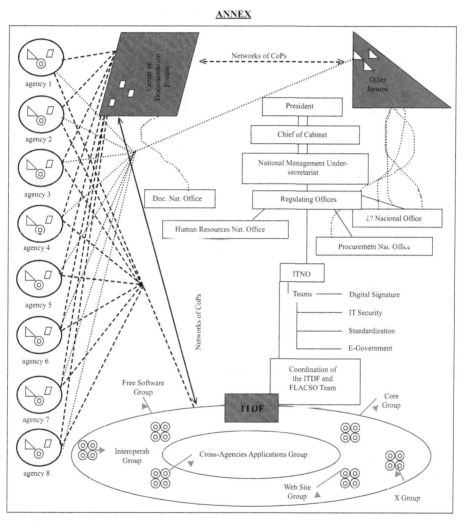

ANNEX

◎   CIO and IT expert from different public agencies

▱   Documental Directors from different public agencies

◺   Directors from other agencies (in charge of: human resources, budgetary, procurement, etc.)

Chapter II

E-Government Strategy in Brazil:
Increasing Transparency and Efficiency Through E-Government Procurement

Marcos Ozorio de Almeida,
Ministerio De Planejamento, Oramento e Gestao, Brazil

Abstract

The role of SIASG/Comprasnet in promoting efficiency and transparency in government procurement (GP) in Brazil has generated great interest in the international scenario of e-commerce and in the transformation of public administration, related to the e-government initiative. Several international organizations and some national governments have elected this experience as a best practice in e-government in the government-to-business (G2B) classification. Some of the innovations implemented by the system are the use of the e-reverse auction (e-RA) and the publishing of information of all the phases of the tendering process. This chapter has the aim of analyzing the results obtained by the Brazilian government strategy in the use of a specifically developed e-government procurement (e-GP) system (http://www.comprasnet. gov.br). It is composed of a structuring system, operated internally by the *government, coupled with a Web interface for suppliers and the general public that covers the whole GP cycle (including post-award contract administration) of commodities (sundries and standard quality goods and services). The analyzed e-GP application accounts for expenditures of around $8.5 billion. This amount is equivalent to 15% of the budget (1.5% of GDP).*

Introduction

Studies conducted by international non-government organizations, such as Transparency International, hint that public-sector inefficiencies, including corruption practices, may account for a waste of 3% to 10% of GDP (gross domestic product), thus reducing national growth by up to 2%. The public sees the procurement of goods, services, and civil works, especially with the lack of transparency and the subjectivity permitted by closed-door traditional tendering methods, as the main area for inefficiency in public spending. The implementation of e-government procurement (e-GP) has been considered one of the most promising and feasible paths to be followed by public administration in rendering transparency and efficiency in the acquisition of goods and services for the public sector.

This chapter has the aim of analyzing the results obtained by the Brazilian government strategy in the use of a specifically developed e-GP system named SIASG/Comprasnet (Sistema Integrado de Serviços Gerais, Integrated General Services System; http://www.comprasnet.gov.br). This system is composed of a structuring system, that is, a robust back-office application, running on legacy-based technology, which is operated internally by the government, coupled with a Web interface with suppliers and the general public that enables one to process the whole procurement cycle (including post-award contract administration) of commodities (sundries and standard quality goods and services), as well as the critical phase of the tendering cycle. The system is responsible for the processing of around $5 billion to $6 billion worth of supplies for the federal public sector, which is equivalent to about 10% of the net federal budget, that is, 1% of the GDP. If one aggregates the transparency rendered to the execution of civil works through the coupling of the SIASG/Comprasnet with the SIASG/Obrasnet (responsible for guiding and informing the execution of civil-works contracts), the e-GP applications implemented by the government account for up to $8.5 billion. This amount is equivalent to 15% of the budget (1.5% of GDP).

The role of SIASG/Comprasnet in promoting efficiency and transparency in the GP of the Brazilian government has rendered great interest in the international dissemination of e-commerce and in the transformation of public administration in the context of the e-government initiative. Several international organizations and some national and local governments[1] have elected this experience in their concept of best practices in e-government in the government-to-business (G2B) classification.[2] Some of the innovations implemented by the government in using the system are the use of the e-reverse auction (e-RA) and the publishing of information about most of the phases of the tendering process. These characteristics have gained widespread acceptance in other levels of government, and already over 15 of the 27 Brazilian state governments, the main capital cities, and some big municipalities are using and/or implementing e-GP.

The federal government has three main objectives in promoting the use of SIASG/Comprasnet:

1.   **Efficiency:** By the promotion of more streamlined acquisition processes and better planning in public spending

2.   **Control:** By making management information available to the government authorities and operational personnel

3.   **Transparency:** By rendering online real-time information for stakeholders outside government (suppliers and civil society)

As an added asset to the use of SIASG/Comprasnet, the government has also discovered that it enhances supplier participation in each bidding process by having over 30% more suppliers participating on average than before the use of the system. Besides this, the number of SMEs (small and medium-sized enterprises) available for government contracts tripled over the last decade and at present account for at least 60% of the suppliers on the registry. Therefore, even taking into consideration the liability of having to cope with the digital divide in Brazil, especially for SMEs, in paradox it has fomented suppliers' participation in contracting. (They are now responsible for around 10% of the monetary value of goods and services procured.)

Evolution of the Legal Framework for Procurement

In the late 1960s, the federal government of Brazil undertook a significant policy reform in the area of public management. A 1967 decree consolidated administrative reform and regulated the general legal framework that public entities would adopt in order to interact with the private sector (Decree-Law 200/67). The 19 articles of this decree lay down the basic policy features of GP with the establishment of principles and procurement methods, but all particulars of bidding and contract documents (i.e., qualification requirements and types of contract) were dealt with in each invitation to bid. In 1986, in response to public demand for more democratic institutions and clamors for transparency in public procurement and contracts, the government issued a new procurement law that had a better structure and was based on sound legal doctrines (Decree-Law 2.300/86). In 1993, the emergence of the issue of corruption as a dominant public concern caused the government to pass new legislation regulating procurement (Law 8.666/93). Reflecting that concern, the procedural requirements of the procurement process, as established by the 1993 law, were elaborate and difficult to modify through administrative action due to their statutory basis. The legislation, which is currently effective, is very detailed, as indicated by its many (125) articles on procurement, reflecting the legalistic traditions of the Brazilian public administration.

However, after almost 12 years, experience has shown that this sophisticated process does not necessarily lead to the best choice of bids. The 1993 law gives more weight to formal rather than to substantive aspects. This specific course of action often causes protracted disputes, which are quite often taken to court. As a consequence, the federal government recognizes that on average, 60% or more of federal public procurement is carried out through noncompetitive methods, mainly in order to avoid the time-consuming bidding process. To exemplify the plight of public organizations when using competitive bidding to acquire simple articles, such as office supplies, the whole process may take between 3 to 6 months, that is, if it is not challenged by some unsatisfied participant taking the matters to justice. In the latter case, the conclusion of the process becomes uncontrollable. In these cases, the procuring agency or entity will have little choice but to apply the several uncompetitive methods provided by the law. Strikingly, Article 24 of Law 8,666/93 allows for many departures (27 reasons) from truly competitive procedures. It is important to note, however, that the excessive use of direct contracting in Brazil, as exemplified above, is not necessarily linked to corrupt or fraudulent practices.

Notwithstanding the constraining environment imposed by the 1993 law, the federal government has experimented with potentially significant technological innovations whose institutionalization and expansion have been occurring slowly but steadily. In this regard and in response to those challenges, the government is moving toward e-government and e-GP. The new method, used in the purchase of off-the-shelf goods and noncomplex services, is a reverse auction or pregão (Portuguese denomination). In the RA (established by Law 10.520, dated July 17, 2002[3]), following the appropriate advertisement of the bidding opportunity, bidders submit an initial price proposal in a sealed envelope. During a public session that is fully recorded, bidders are encouraged to offer discounts until the lowest possible price is reached. In this method, qualification requirements[4] are assessed on an ex post basis. The government also developed an Internet-based system to implement the electronic version of the reverse auction (e-RA), which can be accessed through Comprasnet (http://www.comprasnet.gov.br), which is the Web platform for e-GP of the federal government. Since its inception in 2001, the use of the reverse auction has reduced the number of contracts awarded through noncompetitive methods by more than 20%.

The use of e-GP, in which the e-RA is a central instrument to promote efficient and transparent procurement methods, is part of the overall Brazilian e-government strategy of enabling social inclusion through digital inclusion, and with that permits the citizen his or her rights in the form of social control. Therefore, it is important to emphasize that e-GP is part of the e-government strategy also related to e-democracy in Brazil. Other examples of this are the recent creation of the public-transparency Web site with the control of public spending (http://www.portaltransparencia.gov.br), access to the most critical services of the general ombudsman of the federal government (http://www.presidencia.gov.br/cgu), as well as the well-known online tax system called Receitanet (http://www.receita.fazenda.gov.br). Additionally, the government has also invested heavily in providing online social services, such as social security and medical assistance by portals such as http://www.mpas.gov.br and http://www.comprasnet.gov.br/PortalMed/principal/default.asp. To enable a one-stop window to all services rendered by the government and a comprehensive overview of the strategy, the administration centralized all links to the government network portal and the e-government Web site, respectively accessible through http://www.e.gov.br and http://www.governoeletronico.e.gov.br/governoeletronico/index.html.

It has been unanimously agreed on that the successful implementation of this new procurement method may be credited to the following basic factors: (a) It gives more weight to ensuring transparency, economy, and efficiency, but it does not disregard formal requirements, which are kept to the minimum necessary; (b) it opts for the postqualification of bidders, which leaves little room for frivolous complaints since the price is known before a decision on the respective qualification is made; and (c) the pregoeiros (the only public servants able to conduct the reverse-auction sessions) are selected from professionals who have been accredited after having received specific intensive training.

The government has also been putting a lot of effort into increasing transparency and improving the supervision of government procurement by making use of e-GP mechanisms, such as Comprasnet and Obrasnet, both of which are ICT systems that generate managerial information. The latter includes a database of costs, progress reports of works, photography, and material regarding civil works implemented by the federal government, based on information available from the National Court of Accounts (TCU) and the Government Housing Development Bank (CAIXA). Remarkably enough, as far as e-GP is concerned, Brazil has played a leading role in its implementation in the region and supported the exchange of information, visits, and agreements that have been made possible with countries such as Bolivia, Nicaragua, Guatemala, Colombia, and Peru to promote familiarity with e-GP in the region.

About Reverse Auctions

Background

The RA was introduced into the Brazilian framework first by means of the General Telecommunications Law (Law 9.472/97, dated July 16, 1997), which granted the possibility of the regulatory agency of the telecommunications sector (Agência Nacional de Telecomunicações, ANATEL) the right to use the modality if it is more advantageous to the administration. During the next 3 years, ANATEL was the sole public entity of the Brazilian federal government allowed to use the RA.

In 2000, the federal government was in the midst of drawing up the PPA[5] (plano plurianual) for the 2001 to 2003 period. One of the management-improvement programs set up in the government investment plan was to "reduce costs in the acquisition of goods, services and civil works" (hppt:// www/abrasil.gov/br/anexos/download/relatorio.pdf). Amongst the lines of action adopted was the study of the impacts of ANATEL's experience with reverse auction, as well as the designing of an implementation plan to extend it to the rest of the public administration (including states and municipalities besides the federal administration).

The initial benefits derived from using the RA were quite clear, that is, price reductions in the procurement of goods and services. Even though ANATEL had the right to use the modality, not many reverse auctions had been conducted by the agency. The reasons for the low usage rate may be enumerated as the following:

1.   Lack of a guide to enactment and the need to train the procurement staff in the use of a new procurement tool

2.   Resistance on the part of the administration in using something so far apart from the traditional method

3.   Nonbinding use of the RA, which is just another modality available for procurement

4.   Lack of definition of the goods and services that could be procured under the RA

From the studies conducted, the proposal for creating the RA was consolidated into the proposal of the Medida Provisória (Provisional Measure) 2.182, dated August 23, 2001.[6]

Even though at first the objective of the government was not to go directly into e-RA, the government decided to do so in one of the reeditions of the provisional measure, placing the target of having a functional information-technology system tested and operating by the end of the year 2000.[7] Another important point to make is that the Brazilian legislator, in following the tradition of the administrative law practice, as well as the model adopted by Law 8.666/93, brought a substantive amount of the procedures into the law itself and linked these with those stated in the general procurement law

(Law 8.666/93). The regulation of the RA was limited therefore to Decrees 3.555 and 3.693,[8] which established amongst other matters, an annex with the goods and services eligible for procurement through RAs.

Definition

An RA is a tendering procedure for the procurement of goods and services in which tenderers are provided with information on the other tenders, and can amend their own tenders on an ongoing basis to beat other tenders. In an e-RA, tenderers then post tenders electronically through an electronic auction site. They can view in electronic form the progress of the tenders as the auction proceeds and amend their own accordingly. The auction may take place over a set time period, or may operate until a specified time period has elapsed without a new tender.

Auctions offer the potential for better value if used in an appropriate manner.[9] This is because of, inter alia, increased pressure on suppliers to offer their best possible price, more transparency in the markets (especially important in the short and medium term), and the incentive toward more careful procurement practices, such as more precise specifications of non-price award criteria and the greater aggregation of requirements. They can also be more transparent than other procurement methods. In particular, to the extent that information on other tenders is available and the outcome of the procedure is visible to the participants, there is reduced scope for favoring suppliers by violating the confidentiality of the tenders or abusing discretion in tender evaluation. Auctions can also speed up the tendering process and reduce transaction costs. Electronic technologies have facilitated the use of the reverse auction by greatly reducing the transaction costs. However, there are also potential problems, such as encouraging an excessive focus on price, and encouraging suppliers to submit unrealistic prices.

When analyzing the impact of the transition costs, one faces very little research conducted in this field. One of the most comprehensive studies conducted in Brazil was done in 2004 by Florência Ferrer,[10] in which empirically she added all the inputs involved in the traditional process, that is, the number of people working on the specific tender, the electricity consumed, postage, the amount of paper consumed, and so forth, and compared them with those in the electronic process. The study does not consider the fixed asset cost, initial investments, or maintenance costs of the e-GP system, nor does it consider the depreciation of the equipment. Even with such drawbacks, the said study demonstrated that the transaction cost of the e-RA was around only 8% to 15% of the traditional method according to the item being tendered.

RAs are commonly used for standardized products and services for which price is the only or at least a key award criterion since it is generally price alone that is featured in the auction phase or is evaluated in the auction process. However, other criteria can be used; these can be built in to the auction phase or evaluated in a separate phase in the overall procedure.

It is useful to distinguish, for regulatory purposes, three models, all of which to some extent are practiced by agencies and bodies subject to procurement laws:

1.   Assessment limited to aspects tendered through the auction: Under this model, all aspects of tenders that are to be compared in selecting the winning supplier are submitted through the auction itself. Lowest price is the sole award criterion in competitions conducted entirely through an auction. Under this model, suppliers can see during the auction how they stand in relation to other tenderers, and when the auction finishes know from this information whether or not they have won the contract.

2.   Procedure with prior assessment of aspects submitted outside the auction phase: A contract could also be awarded on the basis of both criteria that are subject to competition in the auction phase, and other criteria (such as product quality) assessed prior to the auction. Before the auction phase, the aspects of the tender that are not to be submitted in the auction phase are evaluated and converted into a price equivalent. During the auction phase, suppliers are provided with information on their position that takes into account all aspects of other tenders, including those assessed prior to the auction.

3.   Procedure without prior assessment of aspects submitted outside the auction phase: Auctions are also sometimes used in a procedure that considers both criteria subject to competition in the auction phase, and other criteria, but without suppliers receiving any information on how the nonauction criteria affect the result of the auction. During the auction phase, suppliers have information only on how they compare with their competitors in respect to those criteria that are subject to the auction process (usually just the price). Thus, when the auction closes, the suppliers do not know whose is the best tender; this is established once the nonauction aspects of the tender have been factored in. From

a value-for-money perspective, the absence of full information means that the auction phase does not generate the same pressure to improve tenders during the auction.

e-RAs, especially of the first two models, are increasingly being used by public organizations. For example, they have been used in the United Kingdom, by a wide variety of purchasers, in the United States,[11] and by some entities in Singapore. The federal government, states, and municipalities, as mentioned above, have also used them in Brazil.

The decision on which model is best suited to the needs of the procurement system and the agency (or agencies) involved with the process should consider the complexities of the goods and services to be procured. As stated before, the third model should be avoided due to the introduction of nonobjective evaluation criteria that subverts the main purpose of the e-RA, which is transparency and cost efficiency. Because the government decided not to run risks in the beginning that could discredit the use of e-RA in Brazil, the Brazilian system is based on the first model.

Breaking the Resistance in Reverse Auction

In the more than 4 years that Brazil has been using the RA (including the electronic version), the modality, even though not mandatory, has grown from a few processes done in 2000 to over 25% of the total procurement done by the federal government's direct administration, foundations, and agencies last year; it has a projected growth of another 5 percentage points this year. The total amount of goods and services procured by the over 200 organizations involved in the aforementioned universe averages around 13 to 15 billion Brazilian reals (BRL), that is, $6 billion.[12] The RA, including the electronic version, accounts for approximately 3.5 to 4 billion BRL, which is equivalent to $1.6 billion. In the case of the e-RA, the absolute amounts are not so spectacular, but the modality has achieved consistent growth over the live RA. In 2001, there were just a handful of e-reverse auctions. The modality was responsible for 3.2% of the auctions in 2002 and grew to 12% in 2003. Around 30% are to be procured by e-RA this year.

One of the reasons for the slow start of the e-RA is the cultural resistance to change, quite natural in a legalistic environment like the Brazilian public administration. Seeing that the modus operandi of the procurement process not only does not favor innovation but also cracks down on initiatives for innovation, procurement staff was very resistant to departing from well-known and more objective evaluation methods. In their view, subjectivity was created by the introduction of the auction phase. The first step in the strategy to overcome resistance was to create the post of the reverse auctioneer.[13] The idea was to capacitate a public servant who had an adequate profile in the areas of negotiation techniques, group work, and leadership so as to be able to conduct the reverse-auction process. An unforeseen resistance group, which voices opposition up to the present, is those that believe that a discretionary power has been given to the reverse auctioneer.[14] It is interesting to note that even though to the general public this could be perceived as an added advantage by reducing the cost of buying goods and services, in the eyes of the public servant, who has to abide to strict conduct rules with little space for initiative and creativity, the discretionary power was thought to subvert the public-service conduct rule. To counter such, the legislation is very detailed and limits the space for discretion in the evaluation procedures. In the first 2 years of the reverse auction, almost 3,000 procurement staff were trained in the art of RA. That accounts for around 10% of the workforce dedicated to procurement in the federal government.

The other step was to create manuals and an online simulator for different users of the RA and e-RA. These are not limited to the internal users in the government, but also include potential suppliers and even the general public. Based on the materials generated by the government, a series of private entities became interested in the reverse auction and created parallel training programs for suppliers and state and municipal governments. To counter the commercialization of the training process for the public sector, ENAP (Escola Nacional de Administração Pública) trained multipliers of the basic course and commissioned the state's public-administration schools to give the courses.

Besides having physically available all the manuals and orientations, as well as the normative framework published in the official journal, all the material is also available on the Comprasnet Web site, which is linked to most federal-government portals and Web pages.

About Electronic Reverse Auctions

Electronic Reverse Auction in Practice: Common and Distinctive Regulatory Features

Before going through the steps of the e-RA, it is important to distinguish that the SIASG/Comprasnet, as will be detailed later on in the chapter, is the environment in which e-RAs are done. Besides being the platform for e-RA, the system also enables the information flow of the traditional procurement methods and even newer pilot-stage methods, such as the electronic quotation.[15] The following are the main features and phases of the e-RA of the SIASG/Comprasnet:

1. **Prequalification requirements:** Registration as a federal-government supplier: First of all, anybody interested in supplying to the federal government has to register on a central suppliers' registry, called the SICAF (Sistema de Cadastramento de Fornecedores, Suppliers' Registry System). SICAF was established by an internal orientation of the Ministry of Federal Administration and State Reform (MARE; superseded by the Ministry of Planning, Budget and Management, MP), which supervises the procurement function across the federal public organizations of the direct administration, foundations, and agencies. The problem is that TCU has ruled that the normalization of the SICAF is inadequate, and the ministry is in the process of changing the mandatory registration to a voluntary one on the SICAF, in which case the services rendered to the supplier would be a differential in relation to those not registered. The draft of a decree to do so has already circulated inside the ministry but has not been edited yet.

    When registering online (the supplier may also come to one of the more than 2,000 procurement offices across the country to register[16]), the supplier will fill a form in which the following information is required: (a) statutory information of the firm or professional (for an individual), (b) financial information, such as statements of the last 3 years, (c) information on obligations to the government (federal, state, and municipal, if included by agreement), that is, taxes, levies, social-security contributions, labor obligations, and so forth, (d) data on the supplier's products and/or services, (e) areas of the country in which the supplier works, and (f) the types of procurement opportunities the supplier is interested in.

Once registered on the SICAF, the supplier will receive automatically generated e-mails with basic information on the procurement opportunities it is interested in. The procurement opportunities generated by the system are not limited to RA or e-RA.

2. **Registering for a specific e-reverse auction:** Once the supplier has decided on participating in an e-RA, the next step is to register on the specific process and prepare the bid. Legislation obligates the bid (in all modalities) to be composed of fiscal qualification documentation (in one envelope), technical specifications when necessary (in a separate envelope), and price (in a third envelope). e-RA dispenses with the need to present the technical specifications, seeing that the goods and services eligible to procurement by this method are so-called commodities.[17] Since the supplier is also registered on the SICAF, the presentation of the qualification documents is waived because the winner will have its checked on the SICAF. This is one of the biggest departures from the other procurement modalities, in which the first step is to check and disqualify any supplier not compliant with the qualification criteria. Therefore, the supplier only has to upload the price for each item of its bid before the stated time to open the RA.

3. **Publication of upcoming e-reverse auctions:** e-RAs, like all procurement opportunities over 8,900 BRL ($3,500), have to be published. Unlike the other modalities, the e-RA may be published only on the Comprasnet Web site.

    One may question if the limiting of the publishing of e-RAs only on the Comprasnet Web site would render transparency. In this case, the answer is simply yes due to the fact that all suppliers eligible to do business with the government has to first register on the SICAF to be able to participate. Therefore, the Web site is the natural point of contact between public contractors and suppliers. Added to this, it reduces the price of doing business not only for suppliers that have to buy and research several journals and newspapers daily to actively maintain their search for public-sector business, but also for the government, which does have to pay for expensive bidding advertisements in national papers.[18]

4. **Time frame for procurement conducted by electronic means:** The publicity period of the other procurement methods varies according to the value thresholds. These range from 30 to 60 days. If taken into

consideration the time span for the preparation of the process, which is usually very bureaucratic, the evaluation period, and possible suspensions in the process due to complaints filed, the process may range up to 6 months. On average, tenders take around 4 months to be adjudicated.

The RA and the e-RA, due to simplicity, have a publicity period of as little as 15 and 8 working days respectively, and most are adjudicated inside 20 working days.

5. **Regulation of the procedure and evaluation criteria:** The regulation of the procedure and the evaluation criteria are established in Law 10.520 and Decree 3.555 that are also subordinated to the General Procurement Law 8.666, with the amendments, in the dispositions that do not conflict. In the case of conflicting interpretation, Law 10.520 dispositions prevail.

6. **International bidding promoted by the publication of relevant documents other than in a local language:** In the case of Brazil, which is a country with a much diversified economy, whose suppliers are capable of providing goods and services in sufficient quantity and quality for the public sector, the volume of international bidding in general is very limited. Even though the general procurement law has provisions for the use of international bidding, in the last 3 years, the amount procured through international competitive bidding fell from around 3% of the total volume to less than 1% in 2003, and this year the trend seems to be the same.

The e-RA, as foreseen by the RA law, also provides for international bidding if more advantageous for the administration. But up to the present, there have not been any e-reverse auctions done with the participation of international suppliers. Brazilian suppliers, including constituted branches of multinational companies, relate the contributing factors for this scenario to the language barrier since the law specifies that the official language is Portuguese. Besides this, goods and services eligible for electronic reverse auction are readily available in sufficient amount and diversity on the local market.

An interesting experiment is being set up between the Brazilian government and the multilateral banks (World Bank and Inter-American Development Bank [IADB]), in which the idea is to extend the use of RA and the e-RA under the SIASG/Comprasnet platform to funding made available under the loans made by these banks. The differences are in the establishment of thresholds and the limitation to only goods.[19]

7.   **Restrictions placed in the system on the type of procurement that can be operated under the procedure and the possibility of amendments:** The restrictions placed on the use of e-RA are the limited number of goods and services eligible for procurement under this modality. Decree 3.555 establishes the list of around 74 goods and services that meet the criteria of goods and services. Being a presidential decree, the list is limited to the procurement conducted by federal entities. States and municipalities may establish their own regulations as to what attends to the classification under the law.

Seeing that the restrictions placed are dealt with under executive order, the possibilities for amendments are easer to be achieved. The federal government is at present considering that the idea of the list has achieved the initial purpose of serving as a guideline to the delimitation as to what goods and services may be classified as commodities. The problem now is that in the modern economy, new commodities are always appearing: The need to periodically change the list may be cumbersome and may not bring the desired flexibility (one example is the incorporation of generic medical supplies for the Unified Health System [SUS]) to the efficiency of the reverse auction and electronic reverse auction. In this sense, the Ministry of Planning, Budget and Management has drafted a new decree to substitute the list for the definition of eligibility on the premise that the concept is well known by now.

8.   **Other restrictions found, such as (but not limited to) the size of the procurement, the level of detail in the relevant specification or other descriptive document that must be provided, and the variables that can be bid:** In principle, there are no restrictions other than those provided by Decree 3.555 and its amendments once the idea is to increase competition under the e-RA by facilitating the participation of potential suppliers. Therefore, under the dispositions of the e-RA, restrictions placed related to terms of delivery and other more subjective criteria are not admissible. If the bidding documents state such criteria, suppliers may file complaints.

However, restrictions are placed on widespread participation if taken into consideration the fact that only the suppliers registered on the SI-CAF can participate, as well as the criteria placed by Law 8.666 on the participants' eligibility. Other restrictions may be placed on the need to attend to commercial and quality specifications.

9. **Suspension procedures:** Suspensions of the e-RAs are permitted when there are communications problems between the procuring entity and bidders. Article 11 of Decree 3.697 established that in the event that there is a systems or communications failure during the competitive phase of the auction, the auctioneer resumes the RA as early as possible without prejudice to the process done before the failure. When the connection is interrupted for more than 10 minutes, the auction session is suspended and only resumes after participants receive communication to that effect. Another case for suspension may be by restraining court order, in which case the reopening of the session depends on a new judicial decision. Temporary suspensions may also be requested by and granted by the reverse auctioneer to give time to bidders to rethink bids or to better their offered bids.

    The suspension is always published on the Comprasnet Web site so as to be transparent on the time span and the related motives.

10. **Publishing of results of an electronic reverse auction and its procedures:** All the proceedings of the e-RA are published on the Comprasnet Web site. These include (a) the name and detailed information on the bidders and the procuring organization, (b) the items of the procurement and the budgeted unit price for each, (c) the initial price proposal of all bids, (d) the initial and closing time of the reverse-auction session and eventual suspensions, (e) all decisions taken by the reverse auctioneer, (f) the communications exchanged between bidders and the reverse auctioneer in chat sessions,[20] (g) the complaints files, if any, and decisions taken on them, (h) clarifications requested and given, and (i) the complete information on the adjudication procedure and any procedure that would be dealt with in the real world, such as the testing of samples and so on. All this information (automatically generated by the system), in the form of a memoir of the proceedings, is electronically signed by the reverse auctioneer and assistants, and is published on the Web site at the end of the session. An extract is also generated and automatically sent to the official journal for publication the next day. The official journal publishes in paper and in the journal's virtual edition. Usually, the procuring organization also publishes extracts of the results on its Web site, too.

The Specifics of RA and e-RA

Operation of the Electronic Reverse Auctions

The e-RA is only operated by means of e-GP systems. In the case of the federal government, all e-RAs are operated by the SIASG/Comprasnet platform.[21] There are presently an estimated 15 platforms in operation by several public entities at state and municipal levels, such as the Electronic Procurement Exchange (Bolsa Electrônica de Compras, BEC) of the Sate of São Paulo, the e-RA systems maintained by the Bank of Brazil and the National Confederation of Municipalities (CNM) made available to interested parties.

Effectiveness of Limiting E-Reverse Auctions to a Standardization of Products or to a Price Cap as a Way to Limit Lowballing

One has to take into consideration that lowballing[22] in GP is not an absolute and simple phenomenon. On the one hand, there is not a clearly defined line between objective and subjective factors in the establishment of the lowest price for which a supplier may make a profit from a procurement opportunity. On the other, no two suppliers with equivalent goods and/or services have the same price structure or cost-benefit relationship. Therefore, lowballing as a whole would be difficult to define in all its amplitude in the legislation.

However, some factors may be established in what is illegal competition on the part of some suppliers that would enable unrealistic prices and curb competition in the long run in public procurement. One of them is not meeting fiscal and labor obligations, in which case the supplier could deduct these costs from its bids. In this case, the legislator has established the need to present evidence of the payment of taxes, social security, and labor levies at the federal and state levels (the municipalities that have agreements with the federal government are also checked).

The other is to establish a set of rules for goods and services that may participate and be objectively evaluated.

Other Issues Related to the Regulation of E-Reverse Auctions

So as to be able to able to reduce subjectivity, the Brazilian e-RA has been regulated to take into account only the price factor. The quality issues (that the United Kingdom model may take into account) are regulated by having set out in the bidding documents a minimum qualification requirement; if met, suppliers are not set aside. Besides this, the quality requirements are already established when cataloguing the goods and services in the materials and services catalogues (CATMET and CATSERVE). Otherwise, other quality issues may be construed as a discriminatory issue when legislation does not render specific provisions for such measure to be supported in bidding documents.

Other Aspects that Impact the Procurement Regime

In the case of confidentiality, the system does not permit the bidders or the reverse auctioneer to view each other during the critical phases of the procedures. Once the initial bids are opened and classified by the reverse auctioneer on the system (according to the bidders eligible to participate in the RA), inside the phase of submitting lower bids, the system only provides an identification number to the bidders so that the reverse auctioneer may control the receiving of bids from the different bidders but not be able to identify them physically. On the other side, the bidders themselves have sufficient information to perceive only which is the lowest bid and if it is theirs. Only after closing the session and generating the memoir of the e-RA will all the information (to enable transparency for the general public and interested parties) be made available. The SIASG/Comprasnet system also generates and keeps logs for the purpose of doing system audit.

On data protection, the records of the different databases (i.e., SICAF, adjudications, RA information, etc.) are kept physically separate. The generation of logs[23] enables a track record of any possible tampering and/or violations. The Comprasnet development team works in a separate environment and does not access the operational environment. Also, by keeping the development restricted to SERPRO (Serviço Federal de Processamento de Dados, Federal IT Company) and the Secretariat of Logistics and Information Technology (SLTI) of the MP, which are not end users of the system, the space for tampering is greatly reduced.

Besides this, the e-RA uses cryptography and authentication resources to ensure security in all phases of the procedure. Attributing an identification key and a personal and nontransferable password to access the electronic system accredits the users. Identification keys and passwords are used in any electronic auction unless the bidder cancels or is excluded from the SICAF. The use of the access password, both in transactions conducted directly or by the bidder's representative, is the bidder's own and exclusive responsibility. Neither the system provider nor the procurement entities are liable for any loss resulting from undue use of the password, even if by third parties.

Nondiscrimination is a more complex issue in the case of the e-RA, seeing that, first of all, the supplier may only participate in the procurement process if registered on the SICAF. Besides this, one may argue that limiting access to bid through the Internet is also discrimination to those that do not have access or knowledge to be able to access the SIASG/Comprasnet. This is more relevant in the case of a country in which the Internet penetration is low and unevenly shared amongst the different income levels. Another possible discriminatory factor is the quality of the connection. It is probable that in the same reverse auction, suppliers with secure and/or high-speed access would, in principal, have advantages over those in areas with poor telecommunications infrastructure and dial-up connections.

These are difficult and external issues to deal with due to the novelty of the use of electronic reverse auctions, but, if not adequately addressed by the legislation and policies to promote the development and compensation of the infrastructure in more backward areas, they may be a real discrimination to the entry of new suppliers in the field of GP. This is especially true for SMEs.

In Brazil, to counter the above-mentioned discriminatory issues, the federal government is implementing policies to bridge the digital divide, to enable public Internet access for SMEs, to capacitate society to be able to manage ICT and work in the area of the information society, and to promote the participation of SMEs in the e-RA.

The procedures for filing appeals, including those by a bidder during the e-RA, are conducted through the Web site in appropriate form, available on the SIASG/Comprasnet system. Given the transparency and the confidence in the equal treatment rendered to the participants of the e-RA, the number of complaints and grievances of suppliers is much lower in the e-RA. This became clear after a study that was conducted by SLIT in 2002 concluded that the number of complaints filed dropped from over 10% in the paper-based procurement methods to less than 2% in the e-RA.

An interesting aspect of the bid review mechanism of the reverse auction is that contrary to the other modalities, the filing of complaints does not suspend the bidding process at the administrative level. To suspend an e-RA at any time, the supplier voicing a grievance would have to get a restraining order from the judiciary.

About Comprasnet as the Framework Where e-RA Takes Place

Comprasnet: An Overview

The SIASG/Comprasnet is the sole information system for the cycle of the procurement process of the direct administration, including foundations and autonomous agencies, as well as the public companies that receive funding from the federal budget or have voluntarily adopted the system. The greater part of the procurement cycle may be divided into the following categories: (a) specification and funding arrangements, (b) tendering- and bidding-document preparation, (c) notice giving and supplier invitations, (d) the submittal of proposals and evaluations, (e) awards and contract management and execution, and (f) post-execution controls and evaluation.

Characteristics of the SIASG/Comprasnet

1. **Application:** This is an e GP system set up by the SLTI/MP. The system is a Web-based online procurement system used by the more than 2,000 federal-government procurement units. It enables online price quoting and RA commodity purchases. It has a client-server architecture, resident on secure 32-bit Pentium III Xeon corporate servers. The operating system is Windows 2000 Advanced Server. Three Unisys Aquanta STD Web application servers support the front end. The solution software used is the Vesta Business Services Suite.[24] Under Brazilian free-software development, property software are now being phased out and SERPRO is implementing open-code solutions to the platform.

2. **Application description:** SIASG/Comprasnet is the system where federal-government organizations register their procurement needs (i.e.,

goods and services they need to buy). The system automatically informs registered suppliers by e-mail and the supplier may download the bidding documents. The procurement officer uses a federal catalogue to specify the description of the good or service required. If the item is classified as a commodity, the whole process may be done through the Internet using the price-quoting system (which is a 2- to 3-day purchase-posting site for noncompetitive small purchases). For the larger procurement of general-purpose goods and services (such as building-maintenance services or office supplies and equipment), an RA procedure is used. In the RA, the bids (prices the suppliers will charge for that item) are submitted on the Web. Each supplier reduces their bid price competitively with others during the auction, and the one offering the lowest price at a previously agreed end time for the auction will be the one awarded the contract. Auctions and prices are open for inspection by the public, and auction results are posted immediately.

3.   **Application purpose:** SIASG/Comprasnet was introduced to automate the procurement process. The aim of automation is to render the procurement process uniform without centralizing the buying process of the federal organizations. It was also intended to reduce procurement costs and give more transparency to the process. Other aims were to increase the number of government suppliers, to reduce participation costs for these suppliers, and to increase competition among suppliers, which should also bring about cost reductions and better quality of goods and services acquired.

4.   **Stakeholders:** Federal-government agencies and organizations as well as the suppliers of goods and services to the federal government (there are over 210,000 registered suppliers) are the main affected parties. Citizens and society are affected in the sense that e-GP is intended to provide an instrument for the social control of public expenditure through its public transparency.

5.   **Modules of the SIASG/Comprasnet:** The IT system is composed of the following modules.

    a.   **SICAF:** The unified system for the fast and nonbureaucratic pre-registration of federal-government suppliers through the Internet (SICAFWeb) that certifies fiscal compliance through online consultation (online checking of taxes, social security, labor levies, etc.)

    b.   **SIDEC (Electronic Contract Publishing Subsystem):** The electronic application for the posting of purchases and contracts, the forwarding of electronic documents for publication in the federal government's official journal, the automatic posting of invitations to bid and tender results on the Internet, as well as the searching for and downloading of invitations to bid

c.   **SISPP (Practiced Prices Information Subsystems):** The integrated price-posting database that registers and stores the prices paid by the federal administration in previous contracts, and provides public managers with a price reference for the assessment of procurement convenience

d.   **SICON (Contract Management Subsystem):** The contract-management system, which allows the registration and financial monitoring of contracts undertaken within the federal administration

e.   **SISME (Draft Awards Subsystem):** The module for the generation of draft awards that does the automatic issuance of award drafts, is linked to the financial execution of the national treasury Integrated Financial Administration System (SIAFI), and ensures that all federal-administration contracting and purchases go through the system

f.   **CATMAT/CATSER:** The supplies and services catalogues to define specifications and quality standards for supplies and services purchased by the government, which adopt the federal supply classification criteria. At present, they are composed of 130,000 supply items organized into 13,000 supply lines and 2,000 service lines.

Figure 1. Diagram of the SIASG/Comprasnet

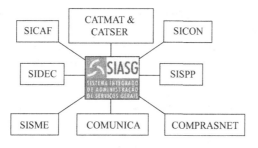

Additionally, they make available a management-information data warehouse that aggregates data on government purchases for the monitoring of indicators and publish the Comprasnet bulletin, which offers monthly statistical information on current expenditures made available to the general public.

g.   Finally, all the normative orientation for procurement officers and doubts brought up by suppliers and other interested parties are made public through the COMUNICA, which is a Subsystem of the SIASG/Comrasnet used to communicate instructions and claifications on the normative functioning of the System.

Issues to be Addressed to Accommodate Electronic Commerce

From the Brazilian experience with e-RA some considerations should be taken into consideration in defining the best approach and strategy to addressing e-RAs. In the first place, even though the e-RA is a form of electronic commerce, the GP aspects of the process, which are more relevant, set it aside from general electronic commerce and need to be treated specifically in a separate legal framework. Second, national legislation on GP usually deals with the traditional aspects of the procurement process and in principal would be the right field to deal with e-RA. However, one has to take into account the environment in which e-RAs are conducted (electronic medium vs. paper-based medium); the main difference is in the reengineering of the process. Therefore, a review of the national legislation would be warranted to take into account the specificities of the process of the RA.

Another important point to make, in the case of the Brazilian model, is that even though the RA and e-RA were established through new legislation, both are, in reality, sets of rules to deal with a phase of the bidding process. The administrative processes before and after the RA and e-RA phase remains substantially the same.

Resistance to the implementation of e-RA may only be countered by the availability of precise information on the advantages and disadvantages of its use, procedures to be followed in using the modality, as well as a comprehensive and extensive capacity-building program, not only for public servants but also for suppliers. In this case, the guide to the enactment of the national legislation is an important and powerful instrument to disseminating the best practices in the field of e-RAs.

Finally, e-RAs should not be treated as a panacea to the solving of the other matters and problems that appear in the field of GP and should be kept simple and restricted in the number of cases in which they may be used to be effective, preventing them from becoming a means to enhance lowballing in the government acquisition of goods and services.

Challenges of Implementing e-GP in Developing Countries

An important issue that needs to be addressed in economies with low communications and/or Internet penetration is the digital divide, especially in relation to potential suppliers so as to not limit competition. The main issues to be taken into account when formulating an e-GP strategy (as has been demonstrated in the case of Brazil) are as follows:

- Concentration of telecommunications infrastructure only in large urban areas, thus limiting possibilities for interested suppliers in small towns and in the countryside

- High local-connection, ISP (Internet service provision), and long-distance tariff costs

- Low quality of connectivity

- Digital illiteracy, lack of familiarity with procurement processes, and lack of trust in the equality of the treatment in the virtual environment (which is the paradox of any new technology)

Coupled with the above, the investments necessary to enable the migration, with transparency and efficiency, of part of the procurement needs of the government to the virtual world have to be lead by the public sector (or by direct investment, financial backing and incentives, generating and enabling a framework for private-sector investment, or even a combination of all of the aforementioned). Authorities perceive this as being less of a priority than other public policies, such as health, education, poverty reduction, and others.

In the case of Brazil, the issues enunciated above were tackled in the following manner. The telecommunications infrastructure, which was state owned and did not meet universalizing criteria, had a broad framework rearrangement and was privatized. Granting licenses to shadow telecom companies instated the competition environment. A flat rate for ISP is under study by the government (to deal with long-distance tariffs). To facilitate the participation of small and medium enterprises in public procurement as well as creating incentives for e-commerce, the Ministry of Development, Industry and International Trade has installed specific SME-oriented public telecenters. There are presently 156 cities attended by the Information and Business Telecenter, and the goal is to attend to the more than 5,600 municipalities until 2007.

On the other hand, as research undertaken in Brazil and abroad has demonstrated, e-GP as part of the overall G2B strategy is a powerful instrument to fomenting e-commerce in a broader sense. As well as this macro-objective, if coupled with active policies for the promotion of SMEs, e-GP may be the first steps toward the building of the bridge to cement the path of digital inclusion, that is, by creating a marketplace for developing e-commerce.

It is important to state that the objectives of the reforms stated above are of broader scope than to have a healthy GP environment. However, on the bottom line, they have contributed immensely to the implementation of e-GP.

Conclusions on Impacts of the RA and e-RA

Role of the Reverse Auction in Promoting Transparency

As an e-government system, the SIASG/Comprasnet has been designed to meet three main objectives:

- To broaden participation in GP
- To speed up the procurement process and make it more efficient by expanding supply and demand
- To provide transparency to GP by reviewing established procedures and public information, and by developing an easy auditing system

The system is coordinated by the SLTI/MP, which delegates operation, maintenance, and development to the federal information-technology company SERPRO.[25] SIASG/Comprasnet aims at benefiting three main stakeholders of GP. First, there is the public at large, which demands easy access to reliable information on public procurement. Second are the government purchasers that need a more efficient, faster, and less bureaucratic procurement process. Besides that, the government has been keen on the use of the system to restore public trust on the part of government spending going to the acquisition of goods and services. And last but not least, the private sector—meaning suppliers, contractors, and consultants—need more transparent, easier, cheaper, and fairer procurement processes.

The SIASG/Comprasnet is linked to other structuring systems[26] of the Brazilian government. This way, the system enables public-procurement officers to check on a series of information that enables the government to set aside suppliers that do not follow the fiscal, labor, social-security, and related fields of legislation, not permitting them to participate in GP opportunities. In other words, the local companies[27] that do not pay their taxes or the employees' social security are not eligible for tendering with the government; this is easily checked by crossing information on the different structuring databases. The system also renders parameters and automated thresholds on practiced prices for the items of the materials and services catalogues, thus avoiding scope for over- and underpricing. Therefore, the scope for under- or overbilling and under- or overpayment of commissions is greatly reduced.

Another innovation introduced is the linking of the SIASG to the SIAFI during the awards phase. In the past, it was common for public administrators at the end of the year to rush a series of tenders for goods and services without the corresponding budget allocation, which generated the need for supplementing the budget. Thus, there was a negative impact on the public deficit of the next year.

Role of SIASG/Comprasnet in Reducing Human Interference and Subjectivity in the Procurement Process

Besides creating strict rules and regulations to try and curb human interference in the GP process as well as subjectivity in specifications and evaluation criteria, which is the role of the legislation framework, a good e-GP system has the capability of rendering the space for malpractices and corruption less attractive to those interested in perpetrating such practices. This is achieved by several means, of which the following may be considered the major ones:

- Generation of information that enables more stakeholders to participate in the decision process
- Better tools for control and auditing, and the possibility of more productivity in the auditing process itself (by means of online real-time data)
- Transparency rendering social control due to the low cost and high availability of information for the whole of society
- Benchmark data inputs for the establishment of technical and procedure inputs in the tendering process

The public perception is that the corruption in Brazil is ingrained in the public sector.[28] In the eyes of the independent observer, Brazil has made little progress in fighting corruption. In fact, Brazil has made important steps to systematically combat corruption. In order to combat corruption more effectively, the government created the Controladoria-Geral da União (CGU) under the presidency of the republic with the mission to provide due diligence to the complaints on corruption in the federal government. Subsequently, the Federal Secretariat of Internal Control (SFC)[29] was moved to CGU for further independence from the ministries. In July 2002, Brazil ratified the Inter-American Convention to Fight Corruption of Caracas.

The evidence in public records shows that CGU received more than 6,000 complaints of irregularities since its creation, resolved 2,680, is investigating 2,233, and is seeking additional information regarding 1,087. CGU has performed actively in the cases that received ample coverage in the media (National Department for Road Administration (DNER), North East Regional Development Superintedency (SUDENE), Northern Region Development Superintendency (SUDAM), Labor Support Fund (FAT), and Land Administration Agency of the Capital (TERRACAP)). These appear to be big numbers; however, there are more than 800,000 federal government employees in Brazil out of which more than 30,000 carry out government procurement functions.

With respect to the internal and external auditors, according to the World Bank evaluation, both SFC and TCU[30] appear to function adequately as professional audit institutions. The SIASG/Comprasnet managerial and technical information modules support most of the auditing activities. There are several cases in which the audited institutions were required to reimburse the project's account for small expenditures considered by SFC to be wrongly procured, that is, less than three quotations in shopping or direct purchases.

The World Bank also stated that, in addition to the comprehensive report of the president, an annual report prepared by each of the federal entities contains an audit opinion from SFC. These annual reports are not published widely, but can be obtained under Brazil's Freedom of Information Legislation if desired. The reports are forwarded to TCU for their financial statements to be judged. The reports comprise, inter alia, a report on activities prepared by management of the organization and a certification by SFC on financial statements, legal compliance, and efficiency.

In sum, the government has set up working internal and external auditing and anticorruption mechanisms that are greatly based on information rendered by the SIASG/Comprasnet, enabling the different levels of public prosecutors to exchange information and technology, and follow up and monitor the prosecution by the relevant judiciary authorities.

Evaluation of e-RA and Online Procurement: Impacts, Benefits, and Difficulties

Impacts of the SIASG/Comprasnet

As mentioned before, the SIASG/Comprasnet processes all the contracting of the federal administration at a total value of around 14 billion BRL, which is around $4.83 billion, for more than 2,000 decentralized procurement units, based on the SICAF registry of government suppliers and contractors of 210,000 firms and individuals. More than 30,000 federal-government employees carry out procurement activities based on the system on a regular basis.

A great part of the procuring methods are still undertaken under the guidance of Law 8.666/93, entailing highly bureaucratic morose and inefficient tendering processes. In order to modify that profile, SLTI/MP undertook a modernization process including the use of RAs and other new procurement procedures designed to speed up and simplify the processing. In the last 4 years, progress was achieved and trends characterize the federal government procurement as follows. The total procurement of goods and services equals around $6 billion per year (2001/2004). The total procurement of

Table 1. SIASG/Comprasnet development and maintence cost

Funding/Year	1995	1996	1997	1998	1999	2000	2001	2002	2003	Total
Budget Funding										
BRL	1,500,0	2,300,0	3,500,0	4,000,0	11,000,0	6,300,0	8,000,0	6,000,0	7,800,0	50,400,0
USD	1,744,2	2,421,1	3,181,8	3,333,3	7,051,3	3,315,8	2,797,2	1,714,3	2,600,0	28,159,0
Private Investment										
BRL	—	—	—	—	—	—	20,000,0	16,000,0	—	36,000,0
USD	—	—	—	—	—	—	6,993,0	4,571,4	—	11,564,4
Total Funding										
BRL	1,500,0	2,300,0	3,500,0	4,000,0	11,000,0	6,300,0	28,000,0	22,000,0	7,800,0	86,400,0
USD	1,744,2	2,421,1	3,181,8	3,333,3	7,051,3	3,315,8	9,790,2	6,285,7	2,600,0	39,723,4

sundry items for administrative function ranges around $4 billion per year. In 2004, procurement through RA represented about 20% of the government procurement at $1.2 billion. Reportedly, the use of RA has rendered savings estimated at 22% of the cost, that is, $264 million. Until December 2004, over 4,200 (accumulated in the period) RAs had been carried out. It is projected that pregão will be used in 40% of the government procurement purchased through competitive procedures, representing $2.4 billion a year by 2005.

The federal government started a state-reform program in 1995 following two guiding principles. These principles are de-bureaucratization and simplification. In order to achieve these objectives, the reform included actions aiming at making use of information technology in the public administration. SLTI/MP is responsible for coordination in the use of information technology.

Impact in Costs and Benefits

During SIASG/Comprasnet's existence, the federal government spent about $40 million on system development and maintenance, as demonstrated by Table 1.

During the first 3 years of online reverse-auction use, the federal government is estimated to have saved up to $315 million. Besides this positive return on investment, the system enables better and more transparent procurement, as well as reducing the red tape in the process. For example, a normal procurement process takes more than 2 months. The online reverse auction may be completed in less than 15 working days.

The use of online procurement has also increased the participation of small businesses in government supplies. This might sound like a paradox, more overly to the fact that SMEs are in general less connected to the Internet. This is especially true in developing nations and Brazil is no exception. Because of that, the government has been investing heavily on bridging the digital divide by reducing the cost of buying equipment (through tax rebates and long-term subsidized public financing). The market has also helped in making accessible communications and interfacing technology that enables households and small businesses with Internet connections at a very competitive cost. On the other hand, SMEs have had the need to connect themselves with clients and suppliers in the private-sector supply chain to enable e-commerce and electronic data interchange. Therefore, the mining of government contracts by SMEs is a value-added by-product of their connectivity.

Under the traditional procurement methods, the cost of participation in government tenders is relatively high due to the time and effort to be implemented by suppliers participating in the tender. Besides not having a very transparent process, in which the supplier could be ascertained that it is receiving fair and equal treatment relative to other participants, the supplier is not assured that it will be able to recuperate the investment spent on participating in the tender. Even more, seeing that governments are not especially renown for on-time payments for goods and services acquired, this becomes an added risk to the supplier. All these factors add up as incentives for small and medium enterprises not to participate in GP. On the other hand, e-GP not only brings down the participation cost of the supplier, but it gives more transparent, and therefore fairer, treatment to all parties involved. And last but even more important, in the case of the SIASG/Comprasnet, it guarantees timely payments for the goods and services acquired through the portal by linking the financial-management system (SIAFI) with the e-GP system. This assures that the agency or entity not only has available budget resources, but all financial availability.

Besides this, as seen in Table 1, the total investment in the SIASG/Comprasnet system to date has been around $40 million, and during the same time span, the federal government has saved around $310 million, which gives us a 7.75 ratio on the investment. If taken into consideration other factors of the cost-benefit ratio (using adapted methodologies, developed for measuring the unit cost reduction in Internet banking) and the marginal cost of acquisition for the traditional paper-based process and the e-GP process, this gives the government a very positive outlook, especially dealing with the tendering

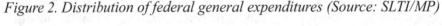

Figure 2. Distribution of federal general expenditures (Source: SLTI/MP)

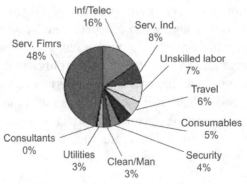

Figure 3. Spending on goods and services by the federal government in 2003

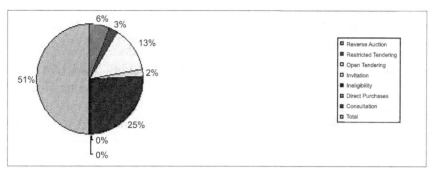

of high-frequency, small-valued purchases (that have a low aggregated cost, such as office supplies and services). According to studies developed by the government of the state of São Paulo coupled with simulations conducted by the author on a sample of the registered tenders posted on the SIASG/Comprasnet, the reduction in transaction cost is over 10:1 in favor of the SIASG/Comprasnet over the traditional procurement processes.

Transparency and Efficiency

The transparency and effectiveness of public procurement can be much enhanced through an increased use of the Internet to publicize business opportunities, to download tender documents, to publicize and adjudicate contracts, and to deliver proposals. The scope of the work carried out by SLTI/MP and SERPRO, in particular on the use of the Internet as a tool in the conduct of procurement, compares favorably with the best international experiences. This has generated great interest in technical cooperation and capacity-building activities with international organizations such as the World Trade Organization (WTO), the World Bank, the IADB, the Organization of American States (OAS), and the United Nations Commission on International Trade Law (UNCITRAL), as well as with neighboring countries, particularly Bolivia, Guatemala, Colombia, Nicaragua and Peru. In the case of multilateral organization, the Brazilian government has been invited to share experiences and expertise with other developing nations, as well as to take part in the capacity building of these organizations' staffs to implement reforms in government procurement in countries where they implement public-sector reform programs. Brazil has also organized some technical visits for neighboring countries and even entered into a technical cooperation agreement with the Bolivian government to help implement the Comprasnet in Bolivia.

The SIASG/Comprasnet in this sense has been considered by several organizations as a cornerstone of e-procurement. The World Bank carried out an assessment with detailed background information and characteristics in which it considered Comprasnet to be a cutting-edge system providing transparency, economy, and efficiency to government procurement. The bank together with the IADB, as part of their efforts to harmonize procurement regulations and adopt efficient and transparent national systems, is doing a pilot project this year based on the SIASG/Comprasnet. According to this pilot, parts of the system will be used as a vehicle of bank lending. It is expected that within a few years and after certain improvements suggested, the use of the SIASG/Comprasnet in the bank's operations will increase.

Evaluation: Failure or Success?

Notwithstanding the constraining environment that is imposed by Law 8,666/93, SLTI/MP has experimented with potentially significant technological innovations whose institutionalization has solidified through Law 10.520/02 (RA) and whose expansion is occurring gradually. In this regard and in response to those challenges, the federal government is moving rapidly toward e-government and e-GP. Moving further toward modern practices, the government also developed the e-RA. In the period of 2001 to 2003, the use of RA and e-RA reduced the number of contracts awarded through noncompetitive methods by around 20%. But still, less than 50% of the government procurement follows real competitive procedures. Figure 3 shows the profile of government procurement.

The success in implementing this new procurement method may be credited to some factors such as (a) more weight on economy and efficiency, not dispensing formal requirements, which are kept to a minimum, (b) the post-qualification of bidders, leaving little room for frivolous complaints, and (c) intensive capacity-building training for those directly involved, that is, the pregoeiros.

The government has also been putting a lot of effort into increasing transparency and improving the supervision of the government's procurement by making use of e-GP mechanisms. The two main systems as stated before are the SIASG/Comprasnet and SIASG/Obrasnet.[31] The measure of the success of the Brazilian government has been the number of frauds in traditional procurement methods since it began to cross-check the data available on the systems.

There are many criticisms that may be levied against a radical swing of the GP practice to e-GP, especially in developing nations. Those related to the digital divide have been dealt with above, as well as the steps the Brazilian government is taking to deal with them. Other problems related to e-GP are information security, for which it is important to mention encryption, the identification of participants, the enforcement of actions and violation, and the capture and/or modification of information in transit through the Net, amongst others. On the legal side, issues such as the authentication of digital documents, and legislation on criminal and civil actions perpetuated by participants or third parties must be taken into consideration by the legislators, law enforcement agencies, and courts in setting up the necessary framework for doing public procurement through the Internet. Also, as mentioned before, specific regulations as to what is appropriate to procure by electronic means must be clearly set up so as to not generate market distortions or bankrupt local businesses in unfair competition with large companies, or even, reduce competition, which is one of the main objectives of adopting e-GP.

As mentioned before, the Brazilian government at the appropriate stages of the development of the SIASG/Comprasnet considered all these issues, although in the Brazilian case many of the now existing criminal (hacking and cracking) practices were still in infancy and security measures were taken care of in an ad hoc fashion. Presently, these issues should necessarily be taken into account already in the design phase of the public entity deciding to adopt the e-GP approach.

Meeting the Balance on Electronic Public Procurement and the Government Procurement Market

A lot has been said over the last 2 years after the implementation of the RA and e-RA about the economic advantages of the use of information technology in the acquisition of goods and services by the public sector. With such a success in the final cost of buying common-use goods and services (commodities), besides the federal government, an increasing number of states and municipalities, as mentioned before, have begun adopting this modality. Even

Table 2. Total yearly inverse auctions in the federal government

Year	Number of Electronic Processes	Volumes (BRL 1,00)
2000	1	67.200.00
2001	63	8.687.300.00
2002	181	17.864.500,00
2003	1,107	154.785.000,00
2004	2,848	374.400.000,00

though there is not yet a consolidated statistic on the number of units in the federation, the 7,866 odd inverse auctions done up to November of last year by the federal government attest to the full acceptance of the modality.

The e-RA has the tendency of following the same path of the RA, growing at triple the pace of the traditional tenders each year in the federal public administration. Especially after the conversion of the provisional measure into Law 10520/2002, which extended this modality to the states and municipalities, the e-RA consolidated itself as an interesting option to all levels of government. Seeing that legislation enables the public administrator to decide on the adoption of the e-RA, besides the use of the application of the SIASG/Comprasnet and the BEC (Electronic Buyer's Market) of the São Paulo government, a series of new electronic procurement systems have appeared with great profusion. The Bank of Brazil and the CAIXA have already launched their e-GP systems, and states such as Mato Grosso, Minas Gerais, and Paraná have also developed their own e-GP solutions to do RAs. Besides this, companies are marketing e-RA applications to municipal administrations.

To disseminate the use of the e-RA, legislation does not limit the possibility of the choice of architecture, systems, applications, and/or technological solutions. This strategy is to avoid the generation of a market reserve for a determined company or group of enterprises that would have the ability of imposing conditions on supplying the IT system. E-RA is a success and promotes expressive disbursement economies by promoting competition among suppliers. Bid by bid, the winner is announced at the lowest price.

At this point, it is important to consider the experience observed in other sectors that have incorporated the concept of virtual transactions through the Internet. Not only in the case of electronic commerce, but also banking transactions, home banking, and tax payments, the only known formula to reach financial-economic feasibility is in the incorporation of economies of scale. In this way, the Achilles heel is the proliferation of e-RA systems in the states and their potentially small volume generation in the future, making for uneconomical operation in the view of the development and permanent updating needs to maintain such systems up to the technological state of the art.

Using available data, one may observe in the case of the federal government, which is one of the experiences with longest operation, the following volumes.

The equilibrium equation to be sought for the annual investment on maintenance and technological innovations is expressed by the following:

$$CIDM \leq PEP,$$

where:

CIDM is the opportunity cost of investing in development and maintenance and

PEP is the percentage of process economy.

It is possible to calculate the PEP by the following formula:

$$PEP = CPV/CPF,$$

where:

CPF is the physical process cost and

CPV is the virtual process cost.

To calculate the CPV, the formula to be applied is:

$$CPV = (CPF \times (EP + EF)) \times PLV,$$

where:

EP is the percentage of process economy,

EF is the percentage economy on final price, and

PLV is the percentage of virtual processes in the universe of goods and services acquired.

The economy on the final price has been historically at around 20% to 25% on average for the live and e-RAs done by the federal government. Because a way of calculating the process economy has not yet been made public in Brazil or the rest of the world (at least not to the knowledge of the author), as a formula to input costs in the public-administration process, we suggest the application of the following simplified equation:

$$CPF = (R \times N \times USAGs) + (PGT \times (T + E + P + S + I) \times DUT) \times UASGs,$$

where:

R is the daily servant's salary (including benefits),

N is the number of servants involved in the live traditional tender process,

USAGs is the total number of general-services units in the federal government,

PGT is the percentage of the total expenditures of the organization (excluding expenditures with labor force),

T is the monthly communications costs of the tendering organization (telephone, fax, Internet, and postal services),

E is the monthly energy bill of the tendering body,

P is the monthly paper consumption of the tendering body,

S is the cost of outsourced maintenance and support services of the tendering body,

I is the indirect costs (taxes, levies, contributions, etc.) of the tendering body, and

DUT is the number of working days of the servants involved in the procurement process.

Therefore, applying the formula to the global amount of commodity-type goods and services acquired by the federal government, which is at present around 14 billion BRL annually, as well as the present mapped universe of virtual acquisitions, which is around 2% of the total volumes above mentioned, we may conclude that one needs to invest around 0.1% in maintenance and development of the electronic inverse auction system (e-GP) and 0.1% of the total volume of transactions to make it economically feasible.

As the volumes acquired by electronic means grow, the cost-benefit relationship becomes inversely proportional and directly favorable in such a way that at the attainment of a volume of 20% of virtual acquisitions, one will reach a relation of 0.00001% of investment for each $1 acquired.

Due to the observation of the aforementioned, the thesis of the need to increase volumes of contracting goods and services through e-RA and/or other electronic means, such as permanent quotation (done through the Internet) and the corporative credit card, is reinforced. Based on such a premise, it is important to concentrate investments on the development of only a few systems to make feasible the investments needed to increase continually the efficiency of the public sector, with the participation of the several units of the federation in each of the systems.

We should therefore progress on the concepts of this area in which Brazil already appears as a global paradigm, such as on the issue of transparency in public expenditures. In the future, we understand that the maintenance of the position conquered will not only be through the end economies and process economies achieved in contracting, but also in the investments of public and private funding in the development and maintenance of ever more sophisticated systems geared toward the creation of a complete virtual market for government procurement.

Challenges Faced by an Evolutionary Environment

E-GP is the latest wave to hit the governments of Latin America. Though it has the potential to take care of most of the ills that have afflicted GP, its implementation has become debatable. Many good features of e-GP are not being used on account of the nonaggregation of demands by the several agencies and departments of the governments as they develop separate systems.

The e-GP system enables a large number of tenders at one location, bringing greater participation of suppliers and quicker finalization. Why should this feature not be used to get better transaction costs and best possible price, apart from standardization of the procurement process? Up to now, governments have allowed the procurement of goods and services in a decentralized manner. However, the scenario changed after e-GP started to become a reality. It not only has allowed governments to aggregate the demand of their various agencies and entities, but also helped them by producing much needed information for expenditure analysis, which in turn would permit them to cut down on unnecessary expenditures.

After the long track record of success reached by the Brazilian government, the time has come to try to develop the model to be able to fit the specificities of countries with diverse cultural and institutional backgrounds from Brazil. The experience of Brazil is relevant because it started as a centralized e-GP system for all federal-government entities in 1997 with 61,113 registered vendors. At the end of 2004, about 200,000 suppliers were registered with the system and around 2,000 new registrations are being aggregated every month. Besides the number of suppliers, the volume of transactions on the e-GP system is quite substantial, ranging in the tens of thousands a year. Even though as stated before the law enables other systems to independently coexist, the issue of volume continues to be fundamental if the best cost-benefit ratio is to be sought. Therefore, for several years the federal government has been seeking to sign agreements with states and municipalities to foster the use of the SIASG/Comprasnet at other levels of government so as to bring down the total transaction cost of the e-GP system.

In contrast to this scenario, many Latin American governments, at national and sub-national levels, under their e-government strategies have put in their priorities the development or acquisition of e-GP systems to become what they envision as a fix to their traditional procurement methods. Even though this may be justifiable on the transparency stance, individual governments and/or agencies and entities with 200 to 1,000 tenders a year are going for e-GP on their own. Naturally, the transaction costs are higher, and the ultimate beneficiaries will be the suppliers of e-GP systems who sell more systems or get a higher transaction fee even though they use the common resources for all such governments and their agencies and entities.

The multilateral development banks are now developing E-GP guidelines. These posit a valid framework for the public sector of each country to develop their e-GP strategies under sound premises based on the internationally recognized best practices. If most of the governments of the region follow the same general guidelines and principals, then why should there be any dissimilarity in the procurement process? Of course, the local language interface will have to be provided to ensure its acceptability. After all, the several experiences worldwide have shown huge savings of resources by the adoption of the e-GP system. By analogy, seeing that governments are taking the steps to integrate their online tax systems with common features and be part of the network to share information on taxpayers and their doings inside and out of each country, there should not be any problem in adopting a limited number of e-GP systems in the region.

Conclusion: Government Procurement in Brazil is Efficient and Transparent

Success in Promoting Efficiency

Particularly in comparison with its neighbors, government procurement in Brazil is well structured and is functional. Moreover, in the last few years, it has introduced notably interesting features and methods for government e-procurement that are worldwide references. There is insufficient data from a broad-enough range of stakeholders to describe the system as a total success, but it can certainly be described as largely successful, bringing an estimated average 22% reduction of final price for goods and services acquired through reverse auction and price quoting. Suppliers also see it as successful due to it being linked to the financial payment system, guaranteeing timely payments on supplies sold to the government. The immediate benefits of the modernization of public services and functions include more transparency, increased business opportunities, and lower prices. These benefits appear to be in place through the actions in the new model of government procurement, which kicked off in 1999 with SIASG/Comprasnet. Two new procedures for buying goods and services for the government units are in place: pregão and cotação eletrônica (electronic purchases).

Success in Promoting Transparency

On the bottom line, the SIASG/Comprasnet has served to promote quantitative and qualitative transparency in government procurement by facilitating the implementation of centralized control while enabling decentralized execution of funding for government supplies. Besides this, the public and main local stakeholder and those abroad involved in the procurement process have perceived the change in environment with the implementation of e-GP. One of the statistics to corroborate the generation of fair practices on the part of the procuring entities is that the number of complaints filed on average in the electronic inverse auction vis-à-vis the traditional methods have plummeted from around 6% to less than 1%. This is mainly due to the transparency and efficiency of the online process.

Enablers and Critical Success Factors

In the arena of political will inside the government, one may mention the following:

- External pressures, particularly from citizens and citizens' groups, for greater transparency and efficiency in government spending
- Acceptance by suppliers of the benefits derived from transparency in the procurement process

Related to the constraints and challenges, we may highlight the following.

- Technological factors that give rise to the temporary unavailability of the system at times
- Legislative delays caused by the need for new legislation and rules to allow for new forms of procurement

The recommendations are as follows.

- **Get the technology right:** This system needs a robust platform, scalability, and a basis in open systems, with heavy investment in back-office sustainability.
- **Provide intense training:** This is needed to cover users on both government and supplier sides.

- **Adopt a phased approach:** This project worked well by having modules, the first of which could provide a demonstration effect for the system that would develop usage and interest.

References

Almeida, M. O. (2001). O que é governo eletrônico. *Tema Magazine, 153*, 30-42.

Almeida, M. O. (2002). E-procurement by Brazil's federal government. *eGovernment for Development: Success/Failure Case Study, 12*. Retrieved January 31, 2006, from http://www.egov4dev.org/brazeproc.htm

Almeida, M. O. (2004). *Case study on electronic government procurement in Brazil: Use of information and communications technologies to increase transparency and efficiency and reduce corruption in the relationship between the government and suppliers.* Paper presented at CUTS-CITEE, Geneva, Switzerland.

Almeida, M. O., Maza, J. C., & Nisis, E. H. (2004). *Retos en la modernización de las prácticas de compras y contrataciones del estado como un instrumento para el comercio y desarrollo: Realidades y desafíos de los sistemas de compras del estado en la región.* Paper presented at the Organization of American States Fourth International Seminar on Government Procurement, São Paulo, Brazil.

Arrowsmith, S. (2004). Public procurement: An appraisal of the UNCITRAL model law as a global standard. *International and Comparative Law Quarterly, 5*, 17-46.

Brazil's Ministry of Federal Administration and State Reform, Ministry of Planning, Budget and Management. (1995). *Portaria MARE 5.* Retrieved 2005, from http://www.presidencia.gov.br/legislacao/.

Brazil's Presidency of the Republic. (2004). "*Informações sobre o Brasil, Brasil em temas, estrutura da união*" and "*ações do governo federal*". Retrieved December 21, 2005, from http://www.brasil.gov.br/

Brazil's Presidency of the Republic/Civil Cabinet, Ministry of Planning, Budget and Management. (1993). *Law 8.666/93 and modifications.* Retrieved 2005, from http.//www.presidencia.gov.br/legislacao/

Brazil's Presidency of the Republic/Civil Cabinet, Ministry of Planning, Budget and Management. (1994). *Decree 1.094/94.*Retrievêd 2005, from http.//www.presidencia.gov.br/legislacao/

Brazil's Presidency of the Republic/Civil Cabinet, Ministry of Planning, Budget and Management. (2000a). *Decree 3.555/00.*Retrieved 2005, from http.//www.presidencia.gov.br/legislacao/

Brazil's Presidency of the Republic/Civil Cabinet, Ministry of Planning, Budget and Management. (2000b). *Decree 3.693/00.*Retrieved 2005, from http.//www.presidencia.gov.br/legislacao/

Brazil's Presidency of the Republic/Civil Cabinet, Ministry of Planning, Budget and Management. (2000c). *Plano plurianual: Avança Brasil.* Retrieved 2005, from http.//www.presidencia.gov.br/legislacao/

Brazil's Presidency of the Republic/Civil Cabinet, Ministry of Planning, Budget and Management. (2001). *Decree 3.784/01.*Retrieved 2005, from http.//www.presidencia.gov.br/legislacao/

Brazil's Presidency of the Republic/Civil Cabinet, Ministry of Planning, Budget and Management. (2002a). *2 anos de governo eletrônico: Balanço de realizações e desafios futuros.* Retrieved December 21, 2005, from http://www.governoeletronico.e.gov.br

Brazil's Presidency of the Republic/Civil Cabinet, Ministry of Planning, Budget and Management. (2002b). *Law 10.520.*Retrieved 2005, from http.//http.//www.presidencia.gov.br/legislacao/

Brazil's Presidency of the Republic/Secretariat of Federal Administration, Ministry of Planning, Budget and Management. (1992). *Portaria SAF/ PR 2.050.* Retrieved 2005, from http.//www.presidencia.gov.br/legislacao/

Campanário, M., & Da Silva, M. (2002, November). *Modelagem de impacto de sistema eletrônico de compras públicas: Estudo de caso da BEC/SP.* Paper presented at the 22nd Simpósio de Gestão da Inovação Tecnológica, Salvador, Bahia, Brazil.

Fernandes, C. (2004). Impactos dos sistemas de compras eletrônicas na administração pública: O caso do SIASG/Comprasnet. In A. Chahin, M. Cunha, P. Knight, & L. Pinto (Eds.), *E-gov.br: A próxima revolução brasileira,* (pp. 234-244). London: Prentice Hall/Financial Times.

Ferrer, F. (2002). *Bolsa eletrônica do estado de São Paulo.* Retrieved October 15, 2005, from http://www.cqgp.sp.gov.br/downloads/FERRER.BEC. RESUMO.pdf

Ferrer, F. (2004). *E-government: O governo eletrônico no Brasil.* Brasília, Brazil: Editora Saraiva.

Joia, L. A., & Zannot, F. (2002). Internet-based reverse auction by the Brazilian government. *The Electronic Journal on Information Systems in Developing Countries, 9*(6), 1-12. Retrieved December 24, 2005, from http://www.is.cityu.edu.hk/research/ejisdc/vol9/v9r6.pdf

United Nations Commission on International Trade Law (UNCITRAL). (1993). *UNCITRAL model law on procurement of goods and construction.* Retrieved February 14, 2006, from http://www.uncitral.org/uncitral/en/uncitral_texts/procurement_infrastructure/1993Model.html

World Bank. (2003). *Brazil: Country procurement assessment report.* Retrieved 2005, from http://www-wds.worldbank.org/external/default/main?pagePK=64193027&piPK=64187937&theSitePK=523679&menuPK=64187510&searchMenuPK=64187283&theSitePK=523679&entityID=000012009_20040521094555&searchMenuPK=64187283&theSitePK=523679

Yukins, C. R. (2003). *Reform of the UNCITRAL model procurement law: A report on experience in the U.S. procurement system.*Washington, DC: Public Contract Law Journal.

Yukins, C. R., & Schooner, S. L. (2003). Model behaviour? Anecdotal evidence of tension between evolving commercial public procurement practices and trade policy. *International Trade Law & Regulation, 4.*

Endnotes

[1] International organizations, such as WTO, the United Nations, the World Bank, and some Latin American and African national and local governments

[2] Also see the author's proposal on the matrix of relationships for electronic-government models, *Tema Magazine*, 2001.

[3] The full text in Portuguese is available at https://www.planalto.gov.br/ and http://www.comprasnet.gov.br/legislacao/leis/lei8666.pdf.

[4] The qualification requirements are related to the compliance of the winning bidder to the payment of taxes and levies of the federal and state governments, and the legal, economic, and financial information

of the company. The bidders are waived from presenting the compliance documents in paper that are available in the unified registry system (Sistema de Cadastramento Unificado de Fornecedores) and similar systems maintained by the states and the federal district or municipalities.

[5]   The PPA is the multiannual investment budget (governing public investment priorities for 4 years, starting on the second year of the administration and ending the first year of the next).

[6]   At present, the provisional measure in the Brazilian legislative framework is equivalent to a law, which is enacted by the president of the republic and has to be appreciated and validated by the national congress in up to 120 days; otherwise, it loses its validity. At the time of editing the provisional measure of the RA, such instrument was valid for 30 days, and the executive branch could reedit up to the moment of validation or rejection by the congress. Later, the provisional measure was validated as Law 10520/2002, which enabled the states, the federal district, and the municipalities, as well as the public organizations they maintained. The full text in Portuguese is available at https://www.presidencia.gov.br/.

[7]   The Ministry of Planning, Budget and Management on December 29, 2000, did the first e-RA for the acquisition of four automobiles for the ministry's transport services.

[8]   Decrees 3.555 and 3.693, respectively dated August 8 and December 20, 2000, established the list of goods and services eligible for procurement through RA. They later included information-technology desktop equipment as part of the standardized goods. Decree 3.697, dated December 21, 2000, established the possibility of using information technology in the RA process, thus creating the e-RA.

[9]   The tendency experienced by governments in Brazil and other countries that have implemented the auction formula is to try to stretch its use to incorporate non-commodities in which other procurement methods are more adequate. If such practices are not curbed on the outset, governments may drive away or even bankrupt potential good suppliers, thus reducing competition, which is the main goal of the auction.

[10]   For more details on the study, see Florencia Ferrer, *Bolsa Eletrônica de Compras do Estado de São Paulo: FAPESP*, at http://www.cqgp. sp.gov.br/downloads/FERRER.BEC.RESUMO.pdf.

[11] Some examples are found in the OGC publication *eProcurement: Cutting through the Hype* at http://www.ogc.gov.uk/index/asp?id=2314, Annex A. Also see Yukins (2003).

[12] In United States dollar values, the amount has varied substantially due to the exchange rate with the BRL, which was over 3 BRL to $1 during 2002 to 2003, and dropped to around 2.5 BRL to $1 during 2004 to 2005.

[13] Pregoeiro is the Portuguese term for reverse auctioneer.

[14] The power to be able to negotiate price reductions if the outcome of the auction phase still results in prices higher than expected and budgeted

[15] The electronic quotation is a simple method following the general process of the e-RA but without the auction phase, and is suited as a substitute for small-volume direct contracting.

[16] These are called UASGs (Unidades de Serviços Gerais), which are responsible for administering procurement for the federal entities. Depending on the size and decentralization of the organization, an entity may have many UASGs.

[17] Off the shelf, with quality standards established by the market, and in which price is the only differential

[18] The cost of publishing fell from around $500 thousand paid yearly by SLTI for all federal direct administrations procurement announcements to a little under $30 thousand on the first year of enforcement of Decree 3.555.

[19] Under the bank's guidelines on procurement, services fall under the two-envelope (technical and price) criteria.

[20] Not amongst themselves, because there is no communications between bidders. In the experiment with the multilateral banks, one of the issues raised was the possibility of suppliers using the chat function to set up prices. Therefore, they requested SLIT/MP to disable that function on e-RAs conducted with their funding.

[21] Besides the executive branch of the federal government, the legislative and judiciary branches also use the Comprasnet, and SLIT/MP has signed over 200 agreements with other levels of government for the use of the platform by states and municipalities.

[22] Term created to designate abnormally low bids in the tendering process

23   To attend to recommendations made by the World Bank in 2002. It was also an IADB requirement to be able to undertake the pilot to test the possible use in the bank's financed projects.

24   Developed during the phase of the public and private partnership established between SERPRO (a federal IT company) and the Unisys and Vesta private IT companies, selected by a national bidding contest. Since then, the contract was terminated in 2003 and all the development and operation has been reassumed by SERPRO.

25   SLTI/MP plays the functions and develops rules for public procurement. Within the SLTI, staffed with 50 government officials in the area of procurement, the Logistics and General Services Department (DLSG) plays an important role in developing procurement systems and regulations. The secretariat is the second layer of the government hierarchy; the department is in the third layer. SERPRO is the federal IT company that renders information technology and communications services and development to the Ministry of Finance and Ministry of Planning.

26   Structuring systems are information systems developed by the government to support horizontal common issues of administrative and organizational structures. For example, there is a central human-resources organization in the MP to set out planning guidelines, norms, and standards for public servants' salaries, training, contracting, and so forth. In each ministry, there is a sector organization to operate and oversee specific career aspects, for example, teachers in the Ministry of Education. In the indirect administration, there are likewise organizations, such as for medical personnel in public hospitals. The Civil Servants Integrated Administration System (SIAPE) (human resources) is the IT administrative system for the management of around 1.2 million active, retired servants and pensions of the federal government. Other structuring systems are Federal Budget System (SIDOR) (for the budget), Multi-annual Planning System (SIGPLAN) (to manage the government planning), and Active Debt System of the National Treasury (ATIVA) (internal auditing).

27   At present, only companies legally constituted under the Brazilian legislation observe the captioned obligations. Due to the signing of government procurement agreements under the umbrella of regional integration and free-trade agreements, such as MERCOSOUTH and MERCOSOUTH-CAN (already signed and needing congressional

approval to be enforceable), the FTAA, EU-MERCOSOUTH, and MERCOSOUTH-SACU, to mention some under present negotiations by Brazil, the same rules will be extended to foreign companies as they gain access to the national GP market. The federal government is now piloting a project to test the concept in two projects funded by the IADB.

[28] Even though there is a natural tendency for distrust of government intentions in Latin American countries, due to the history of successive authoritarian regimes after their independence, in Brazil, the voter tends to believe that politicians (who are elected by mandatory vote) are naturally bent on using public funds for personal benefits. The public outcry against corruption has been increased by the efficiency of investigative reporting by the press, which in the past was censured and now has the liberty of publishing. The interesting facet of the issue is that the increase in investigation of corruption cases and the number of incriminated parties in successful trials increases the perception of the problem, though decreases the practice in the long run.

[29] Created in 1994 under the Ministry of Finance

[30] TCU is the federal accounts courts, that is, the external control and auditing body the government.

[31] SIASG/Obrasnet is the Web interface created to enable social control and community participation in local municipal small-scale civil-works projects (http://www.obrasnet.gov.br).

Appendix: Acronyms and Abbreviations

BEC/SP	Bolsa Electrônica de Compras de São Paulo (São Paulo Electronic Market)
CATMAT/CATSER	Catálogo de Materiais e Serviços (Services and Materials Catalogue, based on the NATO standards)
CGU	Corregedoria Geral da União (Federal Government Complaints Body, responsible for promoting ethics and supervising the authorities actions)
Comprasnet	SIASG interface for goods and services
DOU	Diário Oficial da União (Official Journal do Federal Government)
e-GP	Electronic Government Procurement

continued on following page

ENAP	Escola Nacional de Administração Pública
EU-MERCOSOUTH	Trade negotiations between the European Union and MERCOSOUTH (as defined in the first item) to implement a free trade agreement between the two Integration Communities
FTAA	Free Trade of Americas Agreement (not yet fully negotiated)
GP	Government Procurement
IADB	Inter-American Development Bank
MERCOSOUTH-CAN	Negotiated between MECOSOUTH (as defined above) and CAN – Andean Community of States (Comprises: Bolivia, Colombia, Equador and Peru and observer nations: Chile, Panama andVenezuela)
MERCOSOUTH	Comom Market of the Soth Cone, (Comprises: Argentina, Brasil, Paraguay, Uruguay – as full members, and Bolivia, Chile, Colombia, Equador, Peru and Venezuela – as associate members)
MERCOSOUTH-SACU	Trade negotiations between MERCOSOUTH (as defined in the first item) and the Southern African Customs Union to implement a free trade agreement between the two Blocks.
NATO	North Atlantic Treaty Organization
Obrasnet	SIASG interface for civil works
Pregão	Reverse Auction
Provisional Measure	Medida Provisória (MP, has the status of laws, but is enacted by the executive branch, immediately coming into force, and has to be converted into law or rejected by the congress in 90 days; otherwise, no other matter may be voted)
BRL	Brazilian Real
SERPRO	Serviço Federal de Processamento de Dados (Federal IT Company, specialized in financial management systems' development and operation)
SIASG	Sistema Integrado de Serviços Gerais (Integrated General Services System that centralizes all executive-branch procurement processes and goods, services, and civil-works contracts)
SICAF	Sistema de Cadastramento de Fornecedores (Suppliers' Registry System, part of SIASG)
SLIT/MP	Secretaria de Logística e Tecnologia da Informação do Ministério do Planejamento, Orçamento e Gestão (Logistics and Information Technology Secretariat of the Ministry of Panning, Budget and Management, responsible for operating the SIASG/Comprasnet)
SME	Small and medium enterprises
TCU	Tribunal de Contas da União (Federal Accounts Court, linked to the national congress and exercises the external control of the executive branch)
UASG	Unidade de Serviços Gerais (General Services Units, directly responsible for procurement and contract management in the several government ministries, agencies, and organizations)
UNCITRAL	United Nations Commission on International Trade Law
World Bank	International bank for reconstruction and development

Chapter III

E-Government in Chile:
Summarising the Policy Process

Patricio Gutiérrez, Ministry General Secretary of the Presidency,
State's Reform and Modernisation Project, Chile

Alberto Etchegaray,
Superintendency of Securities and Insurance Chairman, Chile

Abstract

This chapter describes the incorporation of the concept of e-government in the Chilean government upon the context of the State's Reform and Modernisation Project. It starts by explaining the role of the Reform and Modernisation Project in the transformation of the Chilean government to later concentrate on how e-government has been developed as a strategic public policy. The document summarizes the basic initiatives, both at technological and institutional levels, that originated the e-government process. Finally, this chapter reviews some successful e-government experiences in Chile.

Introduction

The fundamental aim underpinning all the Chilean public-action improvement proposals in the last 15 years has been the placement of the state to the service of the citizens. Initially in an implicit manner and then explicitly, the democratic governments have changed the focus of attention to those who are the aim of any public policy, the people, reestablishing regulations, procedures, and instruments to their right proportion in order to achieve such a goal. One of the most significant mechanisms that the public sector has used in the challenge of giving citizens appropriate service is to strategically commit itself to the development of e-government.

This chapter is organised as follows. After this introduction, it provides a historical outline of the State's Reform and Modernisation Process. Then, the general characteristics, appropriateness, and structure of the e-government strategy in the process of modernisation of the state are analysed. Next the chapter reveals the examples of e-government best practices that Chilean public agencies have implemented. Finally, it establishes some of the main conclusions of the e-government strategy development in Chile and makes recommendations on possible implementations for future administrations.

History of a Progressive Modernising Process

The first post-military democratic government (1990-1994) led by Patricio Aylwin had the main institutional challenge of readjusting the administrative organisations for a democratic context, assuming responsibility for rebuilding, institutionalising, and strengthening a government that was minimised and had no hierarchical organisation at the end of the military administration. Due to the clearly transitional character of the first Coalition of Democratic Parties (Concertación) administration, government adaptation efforts toward the new political reality were focused on political, constitutional, and institutional aspects, thus beginning an incipient reform of the State's. Subsequently, President Eduardo Frei's government (1994-2000) set out to explicitly modernise public management, creating for this purpose the Inter-Ministerial Committee for the Modernisation of the State. It went deeply into the extent and relevance of the modernisation processes in the main public agencies, and, for the first time, generated a strategic plan for the modernisation of public management.

President Ricardo Lagos' administration (200-2006) set out to carry on with a set of changes through the implementation of the State's Reform and Modernisation Project, an initiative that depended on the Ministry General Secretary to the Presidency. A second strategic plan to reform the state and improve its management was formulated. Such a plan had a global focus on institutional transformations and management modernisation, including seven main components: (a) the redesign and reorganisation of the state structure, (b) modernisation of public management, (c) reform of the public-sector human-resource system, (d) service quality (simplification of public procedures, users' rights, information for the users), (e) service management (result budgeting, key performance indicators), (f) citizens' participation, public-sector accountability, and probity, and (g) e-government.

By observing the three Concertación coalition governments, it is possible to conclude that the modernisation of the state has been a continuous and increasing process that has acknowledged the relevance of counting on a modern and efficient administration with a shared strategy regarding objectives, policies, and reforms to be implemented for such purposes, but at the same time having different and autonomous emphasis regarding the areas that need reforming. Thus, it is possible to notice that one of the fundamental components of the State's Reform and Modernisation Project implemented by the current administration has been the development of initiatives in connection with e-government. For the purpose of this chapter, we will concentrate particularly on the e-government component and its connection with the management improvement in Chile.

E-Government in Chile

E-government in Chile has been a main element in the initiatives that have intended to improve public administration in terms of quality, efficiency, and management.

The political will to modernise public management has been clearly expressed in the last two administrations of the Concertación governments, and has been an element of great importance to promote the strategy and explain the achievements reached in relation to e-government.

At the end of 1990, various stakeholders in the Chilean society decided to tackle the challenges the country faced to make its entrance into the information society. With this aim, by mid-1998, a commission representing all the relevant sectors of the country (government, parliament, civilians, the academic world, and the armed forces) was established to advise the president of the republic, Eduardo Frei (Alvarez, 2005). This commission convoked more than 100 experts to debate for more than 7 months, after which a report of proposals[1] was released, presented to, and approved by the president of the republic in January 1999. The report defined a general view, diagnosing the readiness of the country to face the challenges, specifying the objectives, and proposing a set of relevant initiatives.

In 2000, the newly sworn-in president, Ricardo Lagos, gave a huge impulse to digital issues. During his address to the nation on May 21, 2000, Mr. Lagos outlined his priorities for his 6-year tenure of government. One of the highlights of his programme was technological reform. In his speech, the president assumed the following commitments:

- To start up a national network of ICT access centres for the community (infocentres)
- To extend the Enlaces Network[2] to 100% of schools in Chile
- To promulgate a law permitting the accreditation and certification of electronic signatures and providing a safe framework for electronic commerce to expand expeditiously
- To begin the process of public procurement on the Internet
- To make available on the Internet most of the services and procedures provided by the public sector

In order to drive these ICT issues, the president ordered the creation of the Committee of Ministers for Information and Communication Technology, which was instated in June 2000. This committee was created for the purpose of facilitating government coordination in the elaboration and carrying out of the follow-up of ICT policies. Its scope focused on five areas: expansion of Internet access, training of ICT human resources, e-government, ICT in the private sector, and an ICT legal framework. The committee set out to achieve the following aims: to constitute the National Network of Infocentres, to design a campaign for promoting digital literacy, to complete the informational phase and start up the transactional phase of e-government, and to develop a suitable legal framework, especially the electronic-signature law.

Subsequently, the development of e-government got promoted by the drawing up of the e-government presidential set of directions addressed to all the public-sector departments, becoming the cornerstone of the public policies implemented in this regard for it raises the ICT incorporation process to the level of government policy. This set of directions established that the monitoring and coordinating functions for the stipulated direction fulfillment had to be under the supervision of the Ministry General Secretary of the Presidency through the State's Reform and Modernisation Project (Chateau, Márquez, Gutiérrez, Varas, Holgado, Ramírez, et al., 2003).

Therefore, the Chilean e-government structure has been developed through project-coordinating inter-institutional committees.

On the other hand, the e-government presidential set of directions defined three areas of action to make progress in these issues: citizen service, good government, and democracy development.

A brief description of each of them follows:

1. **Citizen service:** This area takes into consideration new ways in which government and citizens interact with each other; these new ways allow the government to give its services efficiently, effectively, and ubiquitously.

    Developments in this area include the fact that all public agencies have Web sites providing information, communication channels with the community, and online procedures. In fact, there are more than 440 public proceedings online, among them income and tax declaration, VAT (value-added tax) payment, customs payment, social- and land-tax payment, electronic invoice, ID and passport blocking, and applications for state funding.

2. **Good government:** It seeks the establishment of new internal processes in the public administration that allow the integration of different service systems, resource sharing, and management improvement.

    Currently, the totality of public agencies has e-mail and Internet servers. Most agencies have introduced ICT to support strategic internal processes and there are agencies that perform automatic transactions with other public agencies through their ICT systems.

3. **Democracy development:** It involves the creation of mechanisms based on ICT that allow the citizens to play an active role in the country's decision making, opening new spaces and ways of citizen's participation.

There are several information portals aimed at opening communication spaces with citizens on the Internet. Some of these are the following:

a.   http://www.elecciones.gov.cl, which provides all information related to presidential, parliamentary, and county elections since 1989

b.   http://www.chilecompra.cl, which contains all the information concerning requests for proposals and procurement processes from public agencies participating in this system

c.   http://www.dipres.cl, which makes the information related to public agencies' finances and budget execution available to the citizens

The relationship between technology and management has been considered as an indissoluble factor in the e-government development strategy. In this way, the dilemma of dealing with both components has been avoided, considering the possibility of moving into a new management era where ICT takes a very important place. This is not just about using ICT as a tool for carrying out the same administrative processes, but it is about understanding e-government as an evaluation of a different way to accomplish management. This approach has facilitated the development of e-government using ICT as a strategic tool to make the government better, making easier the changes that the State's Modernisation Pocess requires. When referring to strategy, it relates to the effects and transformations that are made possible through the rational and appropriate use of ICT, empowered by changes in the way management is conducted.

The cooperation between the public and private sectors for the development of such issues has managed to create a strong bond that is currently consolidated through the joint operation of very relevant projects such as the public purchase portal Chilecompra, or the handing over of identity cards and passports, among others. This relationship is not about a simple dialogue between parts, but it has reached effective cooperation in processes that require management choices and complex technical decisions. The outstanding levels of public-private interrelation are a main consequence of the following causes: (a) The government has established clear rules and coherent incentives for the participation of the private sector, (b) the public and private sectors have reached consensus on country strategy regarding ICT cases, and (c) the state has counted on teams of professionals and technicians of great expertise and leadership regarding ICT cases.

Emblematic E-Government Projects in Chile

No doubt the advance in e-government matters in Chile has been progressive, substantial, and extensible to all of the public administration. Nevertheless, it is possible to identify certain emblematic e-government projects that have been implemented by advanced public agencies, which, in spite of being restricted to their sector of competence, have reached undeniable progress, impact, and demonstration. The e-government strategy recognises these projects as a relevant priority for they have become a referent and an example of best practices for the rest of the public sector due to their acknowledged prestige and effectiveness. In other words, they became reform and modernisation initiatives worth imitating and generated positive externalities in the whole society that go beyond the cost-benefit advantages considered originally. Such externalities have resulted in examples that have clearly motivated the development and innovation concerning ICT cases, becoming a paradigmatic case in which the public-sector initiative has proven to cause motivation and incentive for the private sector to get involved.

When considering variables such as usage levels, innovation, and results, it is possible to mention the following cases among the most significant:

1. **Citizen service area:** Tax compliance for income, implemented by the Internal Revenue Service (IRS) and the Citizen's Portal Tramitefacil, implemented by the State's Reform and Modernisation Project
2. **Good government and democracy development areas:** The e-procurement system, Chilecompra, implemented by the Public Procurement and Contracting Bureau

Tax Compliance for Income (http://www.sii.cl)

The system developed for income declaration (operación renta) is worth the attention, because it has become a standard to be compared to by others worldwide. As displayed in Table 1, Chilean people are increasingly making tax declaration through the Internet. In 2005, more than 95% of the taxpayers declared income and taxes online. The introduction of this system began in 1999 with rather basic functions, and it was not free of difficulties, especially because of the accountants and many taxpayers who were reluctant to change from the traditional paper system to the new electronic one. There was even

Table 1. Tax returns by Internet vs. paper

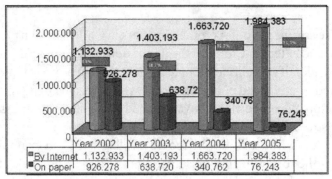

more reluctance when the IRS initially decreed that all private companies in the country were compelled to make an electronic declaration, letting the individual taxpayers choose any of the two systems. However, from the initial complaint, users moved into a general acknowledgement of the system advantages, reaching the usability rate mentioned above.

The introduction of the electronic declaration has generated important reductions in transaction costs, a significant increase in state efficiency, and a reduction of tax-evasion rates. The IRS personnel costs and other resources involved in the process have decreased as well.

Currently, the electronic online income procedure offers a predefined proposal declaration to over 50% of all taxpayers; the user is able to accept, modify, or refuse the given proposal. Moreover, when analysing the income-declaration process for 2005, it was possible to notice that 34.6% of taxpayers accepted the online income-declaration proposal made by IRS systems, 12.1% modified it, and 35.6% used the provided online forms and its incorporated arithmetic tools. The others use authorised software, SMS (short-message service) via mobile-phone network, or partially completed forms provided by the IRS.

The impact for taxpayers has been huge because process time and complexity have been reduced to just clicking to accept the proposal, and people are no longer compelled to hire an accountant for calculating the taxes they will have to pay or how much they will get back. Besides this, there are extra benefits for those who complete these processes through the Internet, such as the extension of deadlines and earlier refunds of tax surplus.

The success in the usage of this system can be explained by the advantages provided by the online tool and by the possibilities of Internet access that are being provided. Regarding this last point, it is worth mentioning that the IRS established a national public-private network of more than 880 centres, adding up to 3,000 connectivity points. Taxpayers were able to do their online income declaration from these centres either free of charge or at a reduced cost. Trained staff helped taxpayers in each of these centres.

The E-Procurement System: Chilecompra (http://www.chilecompra.cl)

The most evident lack that public service has in developing countries is related to the systems of public acquisitions, not only because of transactions accountability problems, but also due to their lack of efficiency in the transaction costs. Therefore, in 1997, a reform of the public purchase and hiring system was proposed by making a Strategic Plan of Public Management Modernisation from 1997 to 2000,[3] creating an electronic Internet acquisition system. In 1999, a pilot model was developed, and in 2000, Chilecompra, the Chilean state procurement portal, was officially launched.

President Lagos' administration decided to give the project a new promotion, turning it from a regular portal into a genuine project directed to ensure public procurement management efficiency. The introduction of this system was not free of difficulty either, mainly because it involved a cultural change of both government employees and private suppliers since both of them were accustomed to dull and uninformed systems. In order to support Chilecompra's full deployment across the public sector, training programmes have been put in place to show the system's value and provide staff with the skills needed to interact with the purchasing system. Since Law N°19.886 (which came into effect May 2003) that regulates the public purchase system came into effect, the requirement of publishing the requests on Chilecompra's portal became compulsory for all of public administration (Gobierno de Chile, 2002). Chilecompra informs about the goods and services that the Chilean state requires, and is designed to distribute and maintain updated information on its requirement operations using the Internet platform. This has led to a standardised institutional behaviour by requiring agencies to make all bidding and awarding procedures and decisions accessible via Chilecompra.

The main objective of this electronic platform is to guarantee high levels of accountability, efficiency, and the use of technology in the government's purchases, benefiting private enterprises, the State, and the public. The num-

Figure 1. Schematic overview of the Chilecompra public procurement system

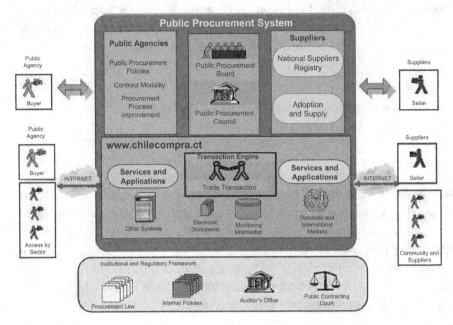

ber of entities that purchase on Chilecompra is over 900, and they belong to public-service organisations of the central government, municipalities, armed forces, and other institutions within the State structure.

The number of suppliers of the Chilean government is about 160,000. This number includes businesses of any size, but most of them are small and medium-sized businesses. More than a third of the active companies in the country were registered as Chilecompra suppliers. The greatest impact is found in medium businesses, where 6 out of 10 are suppliers registered in the system.

As shown in Figure 2, public purchasing through Chilecompra's system has shown a significant growth in the first trimester of 2005, adding up to an operation volume of $432 million, which represents a variation of 104% compared to the same period in 2004.

The total number of business opportunities had a similar expansion, going from nearly 200,000 transactions in 2003 to more than 400,000, a 200% increment. The decrease in the cost of the acquisition process has reached nearly 5%.

Figure 2. Total transactions in Chilecompra (in thousands of dollars)

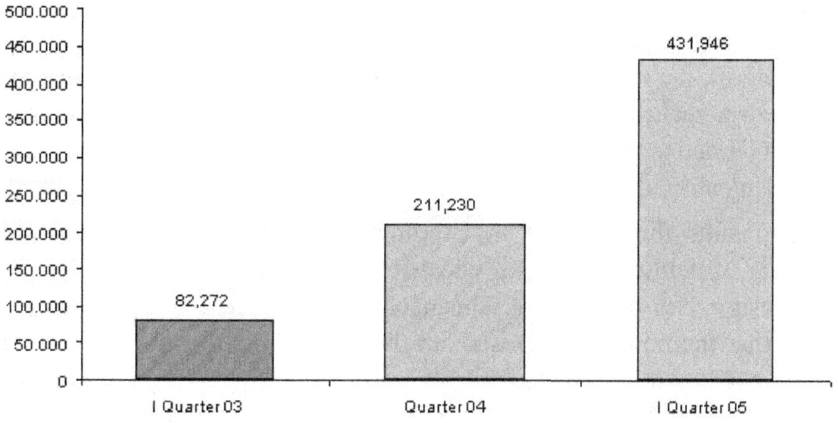

Tramitefacil (http://www.tramitefacil.cl)

It is a portal launched in 2001 as a practical way of putting the government to the citizen's service. It contains information on almost every procedure that citizens must carry out with public agencies.

The goals originally defined for the project were the following:

1. To help and optimize the communication processes between citizens and public agencies, informing about services and products that agencies offer as well as the obligations that people have with each public agency

2. To achieve effective management and a more active and transparent public administration through the utilization of ICT, oriented toward the development and concretion of a State to the service of citizens

3. To promote and extend Internet utilization in the country, making information about the State and its procedures available to everybody in a one-stop shop

4. To increase the number of procedures for the citizens available online

Tramitefacil also allows people to find over 400 high-demand online procedures (including some electronic payments), to download 300 procedures' forms, and to find basic information[4] about 1,500 other procedures.

The site has been built considering a citizen's point of view in order to provide an easy and express navigation. There are several ways of searching for information, the most used being people's logic and needs (i.e., health, jobs, economy, security, environment, sports, education, culture, etc.). This service is intended to help all the people living in the country plus the Chilean citizens living abroad.

Regarding results, this Web site has become a catalyst for simplification and the ordering of public procedures because public agencies have the necessity to redesign their procedures. This necessity originated from the service standards that the new site imposed. At the same time, the site has been a successful channel to approach and solve problems and queries the citizens have with the state. This new role forced the creation of a network of contacts with public agencies to reply to citizens' questions and doubts.

The most popular proceedings in Tramitefacil are certificates from the National Civil and Identification Registry, tax declaration, VAT declaration and payment, and trademark registration.

Conclusion

The state relates to the people in various ways, the most relevant being giving the rights to vote and participate, which legitimise the decisions made by the authority. However, on a daily basis, the state interacts with its people by the legal procedures done. These electronic form fillings have been the centre of the e-government development strategy.

The last three administrations, but particularly the current one of President Lagos, have focused on facilitating the relationship of people with the state, trying to simplify the procedures by which they interact. The information about procedures has clearly improved for both, the ones done personally in public agencies and those done through electronic means mainly through the Internet. During this government, a more integrated focus has been developed, which includes, among other things, the elaboration of a general inventory of procedures that must be done in the administration at all levels (national, regional, and municipal). Also, the Law of Administrative Procedure has been approved and is now in effect. This law includes the concept of "administrative silence" (positive and negative). Finally, great improvement has been attained by incorporating new technologies, which has facilitated the provision of service and the fulfillment of personal or tax obligations by electronic means. For example, the requests for civil certificates and tax declaration, both now available on the Internet, are emblematic cases of a total of over 300 interactive procedures that citizens can do online.

The strategy for the development of e-government in Chile stands out because of the presence of strengths implemented early in the process and consolidated by now. Some of them have been political will when deciding on strategic guidelines, the close relationship between technology and management that the processes have had, the public-private collaboration when taking it into action, and the existence of an organisation-coordinating model that facilitated decentralisation in the development process.

Political will was clearly expressed through the issue of a presidential set of instructions and the designation of a government ICT coordinator.

The close relationship between management and technology was given by guidelines that placed ICT as a strategic resource to make the government better, liaising it together with the State's Modernisation Process.

Public-private partnerships were created through the development of transversal projects. Such projects provided visibility, safety, and confidence in e-government development.

Finally, and in regard to e-government organisational structure, it has been based in the creation of project-coordinating interinstitutional committees (originally the ICT Committee, currently the State's Reform and Modernisation Project and the government ICT coordinator) and the existence of public agencies[4] that have implemented pioneering ICT projects. Such agencies have demonstrated great technological knowledge and leadership in their management and have become models to follow for other public agencies.

References

Alvarez, C. (2005). *As tecnologias de comunicação e informação como parte da estratégia chilena para o desenvolvimento: O presente e os desafios.* Lisboa, Portugal: A Sociedade em Rede e a Economia do Conhecimento: Portugal numa Perspectiva Global.

Chateau, J., Márquez, M. A., Gutiérrez, P., Varas, Holgado, Ramírez, et al. (2003). *Gobierno electrónico en Chile: Estado del arte.* Santiago de Chile, Chile: Gobierno de Chile (Ministerio Secretaría General de la República, Proyecto de Reforma y Modernización del Estado) & Universidad de Chile (Facultad de Ciencias Físicas y Matemáticas).

Gobierno de Chile. (2002). *Public procurement system: Strategic plan 2002-2004.* Santiago de Chile, Chile: Ministerio de Hacienda.

Endnotes

[1]   This document can be accessed at http://www.reuna.cl/central_apunte/docs/chile_hacia_soinfo_1999.pdf.

[2]   Enlaces is part of a national policy to introduce ICT in Chile. It focuses on providing equality access to ICT through the provision and integration of computers and networks in schools along the country.

[3]   This document can be accessed at http://www.modernizacion.cl/1350/article-47999.html.

[4]   Among them, Servicio de Impuestos Internos, la Dirección de Compras y Contrataciones Públicas, el Servicio de Registro Civil e Identificación y el Instituto de Normalización Previsional.

Appendix: Additional Reading

Digital Action Group. (2004). *Digital agenda 2004-2006: Bringing you closer to the future.* Santiago de Chile, Chile: Secretaría Técnica del Grupo de Acción Digital.

Gobierno de Chile. (2006). Gobierno Electrónico en Chile 2000-2005: Estado del Artull. Santiago de Chile, Chile: Gobierno de Chile (Ministerio Secretaría General de la Presidencia, Proyecto de Reforma y Moderización del Estado.

Chapter IV

E-Government in the Context of State Reform in Brazil:
Perspectives and Challenges

Marco Aurélio Ruediger, Brazilian School of Public &
Business Administration of the Getulio Vargas Foundation, Brazil

Abstract

In this chapter, we examine key elements of state reform and the importance of e-government as a tool for increased civic participation and effectiveness. Brazil is taken as an example. We outline the political process behind state reform in Brazil and the importance of e-government in this construction. The successful case of the income-tax system and the problem of the digital divide are briefly discussed. Finally, we conclude considering the possibility of a civic participation strategy in the promotion of a sustainable process of state restructuring.

Introduction

During the 1990s, embedded in a political process of deep state restructuring and following a global governmental reformist tendency, Brazil went through a broad-spectrum public-administration managerial reform (Bresser-Pereira & Spinks, 1998) similar to what occurred in various other countries engaging in modernizing public administration. One of the pillars of state reform in Brazil was the intensive use of information technology to enhance government managerial capacity, decrease general costs, and bring more transparency to public administration as a whole. The implementation of these administrative reforms in Brazil started in the 1990s with the creation of the State Administration and Reform Ministry (MARE). As a key component of this reform, the Brazilian program for the development of Web-based governmental information systems was a central part of a larger political process that brought this reformist agenda and achieved substantial results that had an impact on the restructuring of the state. It also contributed to democratizing a series of key governmental services. The initial e-government experience, therefore, was deeply immersed in a political context related to the effectiveness of the state apparatus and the degree of interpenetration with civil society that this apparatus encourages. It is therefore, as we shall see, an essentially political matter, embedded in a complex political and social process.

In this regard, the e-government implemented by MARE did not result from a standard institutional development process accompanied by the usual bureaucracy. To the contrary, the ministerial program was actually implemented as a result of a political design. For this to occur, macroeconomic stability, the control of inflation, the restructuring of the administrative machine, and privatization, in addition to the redrawing of boundaries for governmental, private, and public operations, were fundamental pillars of the program of the political party in office at that time, namely the Brazilian Social Democratic Party (PSDB, Partido Social Democrata Brasileiro). Not by chance, this occurred in a period when Brazilian society strongly supported general reforms in government, and the new administration team had coupled successfully with the inflationary challenge in the country, achieving a higher level of approval during the 1994 presidential election.

Consequently, the new administration had strong support for reforming the state, including the privatization of state-owned companies and reforming the administration. Although the final results of this political experiment were not fully successful, some important achievements were obtained in relation to increased bureaucratic efficiency and governmental transparency. The e-government experience, although limited in its initial steps, was one of the pillars of these two achievements. This will be the focus of this chapter.

E-Government as a Political Construction

First, we should point out that the perception of a necessary integration and modernization of the state apparatus was paramount among public operators in Brazil as a fundamental complement for the stabilization process in the country during the '80s and '90s. To a certain extent, it represented a window of opportunity to develop e-government, with the support of a modernization project for the Brazilian state. Some of the key concepts of the reform were conceived in academia by a group of intellectuals who were very active in politics. Among them, we can highlight the former president Fernando Henrique Cardoso, well known in the academic world for his theoretical works, such as dependency theory, and Professor Bresser-Pereira, the minister for state reform in charge of MARE. It is clear that the conceptualization of state reform was a socially constructed process integrating large segments of academia, politicians, and state bureaucrats, some performing more than one role at the same time. Also, the use of technology was in general a clear option for these public actors. However, the eagerness to really invest in e-government as a consistent policy was a step conceived once the new government was in office, based on the experience of the United Kingdom, Canada, and some other countries engaged in state reforms.

Therefore, although many of the policies implemented in the administration of MARE had been developed before the intensive deployment of electronic-government systems, those systems became a key instrument to accelerate the reforms proposed by the ministry that supported the development of very successful e-government systems. In these ways, we can say that the electronic-government systems should be considered the symbolic and objective representation of the reforming ethos that ended in 2002 with the election of a new president from an oppositional party, and at that time its design and broadness was a representation of the political will of one politically marked concept of a project for modernizing the structure of the Brazilian state.

Today, after the election of a center-left coalition led by President Lula in the 2002 presidential elections, the efforts to continue government informational integration have been diverted by other questions, such as the use of free software like LINUX. In other words, as we mentioned, it appears that the momentum for managerial reform was lost, at least temporarily, in the intention of using electronic government as an instrument for a deep restructuring of the state. Nonetheless, it also appears that although redesigned in terms of its priorities, the agenda for e-government implementation still continues given its legitimization as an instrument for civil society to access government services, and, in relation to the government itself, for inducing more efficient governmental processing.

Taken together, these questions have a significant impact on the balance of power and special interests in administration, depending more on political resolutions to advance than on sensu stricto technological solutions, which are necessarily built around the generation of collectively agreed agendas (Kingdon, 2003). In this sense, one must ask how efficient this experiment was and what the major obstacles were that academics, as practitioners, faced in implementing it. Also, how successful was this experience in enlarging citizen participation, and in incorporating larger segments of the citizenry in accessing the government agenda and online public resources?

In order to answer these questions, we will discuss some theoretical issues related to e-government and the political adaptation of the Brazilian case, focusing on the results of the governmental income-tax Web system Receitanet, for which an outstanding result was obtained and that is usually used as a proxy of the Brazilian case in general international studies as well as e-procurement systems. In addition to this, we also examine the problem of the digital divide vis-à-vis state reform principles of accountability and transparency. We conclude with considerations on the Brazilian experience and some possible future developments.

E-Tax Collection as an Example of E-Government in Brazil

One of the main objectives of the Brazilian e-government program has been to improve transparency and the speed of service delivery, as well as supporting and meeting targets concerned with dismantling bureaucracy, standardizing models and procedures, digitizing public administration, improving managerial expense controls, increasing competition in tender processes, reducing costs, and increasing state revenues, especially those linked to tax collection.

Figure 1. Federal Services Online: Percentage of Brazilian Federal Government services available on the Internet-2002 (Source: Brazilian Ministry of Planning, Secretary of Logistics and Information Technology)

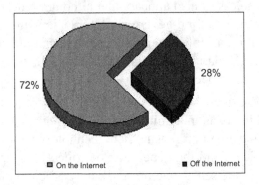

In terms of Internet usage, the program seeks to support initiatives promoting state reform, reduce the government procurement time cycle, improve efficiency, reduce costs, optimize communication channels through procurement portals, improve internal processes, provide a single access point, integrate processes that go beyond the public sector, and finally, promote collaboration between different government bodies and sectors. From a broad perspective, e-government development in Brazil is a successful case, although it still mixes some transactional Web systems with a majority of interactive Web systems. Figure 1 summarizes the status of e-government system development in terms of Brazilian administration (direct administrative areas only; state-owned companies are not included).

Nonetheless, some key Web-based systems such as e-procurement and income-tax returns have not only presented impressive results, but also have an advanced degree of transaction features. More specifically, the income-tax-return Web system called, Receitanet, which we use here as a proxy of these systems evaluated by UN/ASPA (United Nations/American Society for Public Administration), is interrelated with other strategic public-administration systems such as e-procurement systems within the electronic-government development program (Fernandes, 2003). Its proposed themes include the following:

- Providing the public administration with a sophisticated income-tax management system

- Simplifying data processing and transmission of millions of taxpayers
- Reducing the level of error by taxpayers through the use of an interactive and friendly program for processing, checking, and transmitting income-tax data
- Reducing the time schedule for analysis and reporting of income-tax declarations
- Offering taxpayers information about their tax status
- Diminishing the income-tax evasion
- Providing a reliable and secure system with cryptographic certificates
- Promoting transparency in the public-sector treasury

In historical terms, this process of the computerization of the Federal Revenue Service in Brazil began in 1964 with the use of punch cards and mainframe computers without the use of teleprocessing technologies in handling the data. Since then, significant advances have taken place. In 1995, income-tax returns of individuals (IRPF) could be made on a computer disk as well as on the traditional paper form. Since 1997, income-tax returns can also be made over the Internet. Although this service has always been essential for the Federal Revenue Service, this agency has developed a complete e-government solution that provides various services for Brazilian taxpayers.

The impulse for the provision of these services over the Internet, characterizing a more transactional form of e-government, was much more accentuated after 2000, with the numbers of services offered being dramatically increased each year, such as certificates for the absence of debt with the exchequer, as well as the core of the system related to the transmission of income-tax returns, which was not only based on a transmission system but rather on a complete set of facilities including the download of interactive programs for the declaration with a set of accessories including the calculation of tax and the complete checking of the declaration before its final submission.

In addition, we would like to highlight that this recent, more substantial advance was especially due to the increased use of improved digital security-certification protocols. Thus, as a result of the use of state-of-the-art procedures and resources, the integration of the taxpayer with the Federal Revenue Service can incorporate other forms of communication, such as intelligent e-mail systems that seek to answer immediate doubts, to mention just one. The success of these systems that decongest telephones and leave counters empty has encouraged the revenue service to increasingly invest in

Figure 2. Income tax declarations submitted in Brazil, 1991-2004 (Source: Brazilian Federal Revenue Service-Serpro)

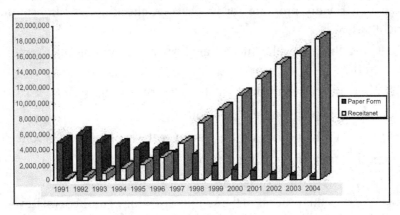

new services, giving a sustained and systematic character to the development process of Brazilian e-government in this area of government. We shall return to the importance of certification later.

Therefore, in summary, the services offered by the income tax return system have a very broad range of functions related to the principles established in state reform, such as tender-process results, transparency, proof of payment, communication via e-mail, online submission, a specialized summary of legislation, and themes of interest to the users. Above all this, the system has links with various critical government systems. In terms of the results achieved, our proxy presented a promising picture given that in 2004, almost 97% of the income-tax declarations using the system were submitted before the deadline, and the total number of declarations submitted by Internet is growing in a sustainable way and passed 18 million in 2004. Figure 2 summarizes these results.

In addition, we would like to conclude this section by observing that currently, following the success of the Internet income tax returns program, the expansion of the use of the digital certification protocol of taxpayers is currently under way based on digital certification. Two recent decisions by the Federal Revenue Service have considerably accelerated the use of digital certificates in the country. The first was the signing of a protocol between the Brazilian Federation of Banks (Federação Brasileira de Bancos, Febraban), the Federal Revenue Service, and the Information Technology Institute (Instituto de Tecnologia da Informação, ITI) for the use of digital certification in the signing of electronic documents and banking transactions, giving preference to the highest level of security, the e-CPF/e-CNPJ (the numbers of individual and company taxpayers in Brazil, respectively) standard, which allows the use of smart cards (cards with chips). The second was the Federal Revenue Service regulation that obliged companies with gross annual revenue above 30 million reals to submit their DCTF (Declaration of Federal Tax Credits and Debits) over the Internet using a digital signature. Initially, this regulation affected 10,000 Brazilian companies.

The impact of these measures should not be underestimated since the extension of e-government services related to the expansion of the provision of interactive services concerned with complex confidential transactions is intrinsically linked to the reliability of the service. In other words, by investing in a sustained form of security and reliability, the Federal Revenue Service can go beyond the provision of services related to the declaration of income, providing a growing number of services and, above all, an increased level of interactivity with citizens and, by extension, the universe of companies established in Brazil, with an obvious impact on the structure of opportunities and the institutional reliability of the productive sector in the set of rules and the transparency of Brazilian governmental institutions. In this way, corroborating what we have stated above, it can be stated that digital government requires a continuous process of technological expansion for its interaction with civil society.

However, although the results are in essence highly auspicious and are very representative of the efforts in Brazil to establish a network of e-government systems, a key question deserves particular attention at this juncture. It concerns the level of accessibility and the problem of a digital divide, which diminishes the scope of possibilities of e-government as a republican structure in which extended popular participation would be possible. We will explore this point next.

Accessibility and the Digital Divide

The problem of physical accessibility to systems of electronic government is, undoubtedly, a complicating factor in the questions discussed above and a necessary element to conceive a true e-government on the demand side.

Although it is significantly more acute in developing countries, like those in Latin America, it is also a problem for developed countries (Norris, 2001). In this way, the result of asymmetric access to new information channels can be felt immediately as it affects services, infrastructure, and quality of life, thereby signaling an increase rather than a decrease in socioeconomic and spatial disparities. At worst, these can have a negative effect on the competitive capacity of a city or even a country and, certainly, of the government in the provision of goods to the citizens and accountability.

In the present analysis, the essential aspect we will focus on is that the specific nature of societies such as Brazil leads us to a triple divide; in other words, we have not only a digital divide and a spatial divide, which is common in developed countries, but also a legacy of social divide. By examining Table 1, we have different perceptions of the same reality. Thus, as we can see more accurately, despite access in absolute terms being highly significant in Brazil, in relative terms, this figure is far below the average for developed countries.

Table 1. Population of selected countries and Internet users (Source: NUA, 2002)

Selected Country	Population (millions)	Internet Users (millions) (Source)	Internet Users per 100 habitants
Argentina	37.4	3.88 (Nielson NetRatings)	10.374
Brazil	174.5	16.84 (Nielson NetRatings)	9.650
Canada	31.6	14.20 (Media Metrix Canada)	44.937
Chile	15.3	3.10 (Int'l Telecom. Union)	20.261
Finland	5.2	2.69 (Taloustukimos Oy)	51.731
France	6.0	16.97 (Mediametrie)	28.283
Japan	126.8	51.34 (NetRatings Japan)	40.489
United Kingdom	59.6	34.00 (Nielson//NetRatings)	57.047
United States	278.0	165.75 (Nielson//NetRatings)	59.622

In the case of Brazil, this translates into less than 5% of the population, while in Canada, for example, the total is approximately 50%. In other words, judging from Table 1, it is clear that the 16.84 million Brazilian Web users represent a sizeable grouping, which places Brazil among the countries with the highest population of Internet users in the world. However, and this is a fundamental point, when we examine these numbers comparatively and not only from the point of view of absolute values, but also in terms of the ratio of Web users and the general population, we see that Brazil has one of the worst ratios in the selected group.

Furthermore, we should remember that the democratization of the virtual state and its policies by information and communication technologies begins out of necessity with the possibility of a multiplicity of interest groups and common citizens having access to these information channels. We can see from Figure 3 that there is not only a very low correlation between users and the population in the Brazilian case, but also a high correlation between higher social-status sectors with the possibility of more intense use of ICT (access to information and communications technologies). This would suggest a higher level of accessibility to information and services precisely among the segments that are already over-privileged in this aspect in Brazilian society. This discussion of the policy question, which seeks to achieve democratization of access to state mechanisms and even to private services via ICT as a standard of the increasing influence of public action should necessarily be added to the public agenda.

For the sake of argument, if we consider that according to the 2000 Brazilian census, 80% of the Brazilian population live in cities, the digital divide becomes a strong additional element of social asymmetry. It clearly has an increasing impact in the extremely dense urban areas, which already have a myriad of problems (Graham & Marvin, 1997), including, amongst others, their own urban development. In this sense, as suggested by Castells (1997), technology and its physical links have created a new social and economic dynamic in a physical space where the spatial flow is superimposed by that of information, being duly influenced by the latter.

We see, therefore, that the distribution of the access to the means through which public information is gathered, increasingly including the state services that are available on the Internet, is more expressive in terms of access to the segments that already have access to the regime, as well as networks of contacts, or even proficiency and ability to use new media. In other words, the latter have higher social status and relationship networks that are closer to

Figure 3. Percentage of households with potential access to the Internet (telephone and computer) per income (units of minimum wage) and region- Brazil 2000 (Source: Brazilian National Census-2000 IBGE)

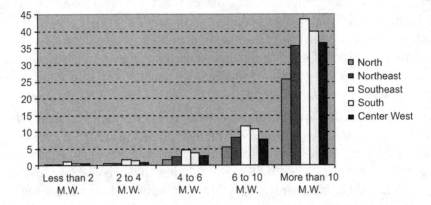

those of the political elite. The Figure 3 and Map 1 seek to survey this situation. In Figure 3, we see a division in regional terms in Brazil with respect to access to the Internet, in terms of region and income, and considering those residences where there is a telephone and a computer simultaneously. We should point out that the north and northeast are the poorest regions and the south and southeast the wealthiest.

The correlation between potential Internet access and income is obvious (Ruediger, 2003). This asymmetric distribution of wealth also occurs at the state and municipal levels. We can better observe this on Map 1, where we used GIS software to study, from a spatial perspective, a particular Brazilian state, Rio de Janeiro, and its capital, the city of Rio de Janeiro, taken here as a proxy. It shows the potential access to the Internet by residences in clusters in differentiated colors, representing percentages of potential access by state region and city neighborhood. Coming down to the local level, as in the detailed map of the city of Rio de Janeiro, we also have a clear divide within the capital. In both cases, the areas represented with darker tones are those with higher potential for access and, in general, associated with a higher social status.

This points to the issue of mechanisms of governance and transparency that are fundamental for the reversal of the problematic scenario both in socio-economic and developmental terms, and which could be greatly assisted by

Map 1. Rio de Janeiro State and City of Rio de Janeiro by potential access to Internet (Source: Brazilian National Census-2000 IBGE)

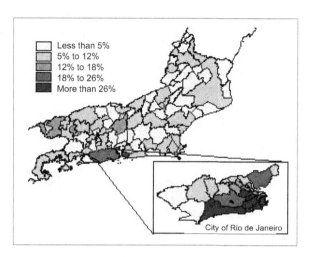

the digital revolution, though obstacles arise due to historic asymmetries in addition to a new asymmetry arising from the digital world itself. The report of the last world meeting of the UN Habitat Agency when discussing local government defined it as: "...the sum of the forms by which individuals and institutions (private and public) plan and manage their common interests. It is an ongoing process which can lead to conflict or mutually beneficial cooperative action" (Habitat, 2001). On those grounds, one can say that developing public policy that can take advantage of digital opportunity is a fundamental element for the development with fairness, but it can also be a vector of efficiency. However, we should also argue about which kind of efficiency can be possible if it is restricted to a certain section of the population, even though this is significant in absolute terms: Will it remain small in a relative perspective? Furthermore, to what extent might this deprivation complicate the construction of social capital and encourage the restructuring and the efficiency of the state? Taking both of these aspects into consideration, might e-government be the field for a republican construction of state? In this case, what are the strategic opportunities for arranging the redefinition of this instrument through political means? We will discuss these aspects in the conclusion.

Conclusion

Throughout this chapter, and from a critical standpoint, we have attempted to examine key elements that we consider to be central to a restructuring of the state in terms of its efficiency linked to the promotion of a republican perception of its relations with civil society. Consequently, backed with modern information technology, we suggested a potential to obtain new levels of efficiency and interactivity with civil society through the use of e-government, making feasible the establishment of a model of public administration capable of confronting the challenges arising in the contemporary complex context, which is increasingly interpenetrated with simultaneously global and local processes. Brazil is taken as an auspicious proxy of the Latin American case, as shown in the example above, related to the income-tax returns Web system in terms of e-government possibilities.

However, we also realize that the e-government experiment faces some key difficulties in the Brazilian case. First, despite the early success of e-government systems, as shown in the examples we presented above, it must be mentioned that we encountered an overall difficulty in galvanizing a deep restructuring of the entire state structure. In other words, although some key systems and areas of government have really developed sophisticated e-government systems and appropriate managerial procedures to support them, others have failed to introduce the same level of sophistication, and, therefore, as a whole, Brazilian e-government is an asymmetric construction, with some very developed areas and others still lacking the necessary commitment to state restructuring and the implementation of transactional mechanisms necessary for a truly digital version of government services.

Second, the lack of continuity concerning e-government as a state policy is disappointing because it is dependent on governmental will and not to be perceived as a state policy to be carried on vigorously despite the political coalition in power. Thus, the development of e-government has been victimized by a stop-and-go process, which has affected the structuring of the opportunity to direct it toward a more comprehensive and deeply integrated transactional model that could integrate more effectively governmental structures and improve state-society relations.

On the other hand, generally speaking, the access presently provided is based on a form of exposition with a subsidiary nature and the specialization of functions, which is still, to a large extent, consolidated and reflected in the supply of ad hoc services. These are restricted or unfettered by intense political concerns in terms of committed citizenship, or are lacking a civic interrelation with access to broad segments of society, which is, in turn, also biased by an asymmetric distribution of the necessary equipment for accessing the Web.

Thus, certain interest groups and governmental agencies as opposed to others are potentially bolstered, while civic pressure is especially reduced for the restructuring and provision of information by the state. To us, this points to an inevitable delay in concretizing the more widespread reform of the state, in which e-government could act as a catalyst for a republican process involving the redesign of the administration. The obstacles are, therefore, both internal and external to the state apparatus and require a complex construction that goes far beyond the simple implementation of systems and routines. In other words, e-government deals with societal interaction as much as organizational change.

Indeed, we have to consider this problem as central to the implementation of reforms from the e-government perspective. By confronting an ad hoc implementation vis-à-vis an integrated and systemic construction of e-government, we find that for information technology to be an efficient tool aimed to promote a more effective state, it must involve bringing together the reform of the state structure, both from a structuralist perspective as well as from the perspective of a political process. From this complementary perspective, we suggest linking the implementation as a strategy based on understanding and modeling processes that cross the organizational structure, but also as an approach toward inducing cultural change. Since e-government promotes a complex interaction between state structure and civil society, these changes must be embedded in an ethos where organizational change, based on cultural transformation, recognizes the interaction of organizational structure with the social structure of civil society, which will demand a more responsive and accountable interaction with the government.

Therefore, the internal barriers of the state could be restructured and eventually mitigated by the pressure of civil society in an interactive process where an increase in demand for services is met by an increase in the supply of information from the state. In this manner, managers could seek incentives to maximize this potential by means of mechanisms geared to the provision of access media, in addition to others linked to the supply of programs and policies related directly to questions of citizenship and the provision of policy feedback. By extension, this feedback can induce a more vigorous impetus toward state reform and e-government advancement.

Obviously, this virtuous circle needs to have a starting point that must be politically constructed. We suggest that this point of departure be mutually agreed on by the main strategic players and representatives of organized civil society and built around a strategic plan for the virtual state. In such a plan, supplementary objectives and strategies would be defined for the restructuring and integration of procedures and functions in addition to the provision of information and access.

The rational incentive for this initiative would be the social awareness of state planners and political society of the incapacity to deal with the present scope of problems using traditional regulatory strategies. This is translated by the state's inability to fully regulate and deal with multiple demands within a globalized context without a better interface with the myriad number of national and international collective players. In this manner, the need for legitimation highlights the rationality for accepting a role with more emphasis on the privileged articulation of networks, thereby mitigating the state's decision-making presence as a major player in terms of the policies outlined. As an example, experiments like Demos[1] (Delphi Mediation Online System), designed to bridge the gap between unilateral mass communication and multilateral discourses among small groups of active experts, seem like promising tools. So, the state remains central, but its centrality is legitimated and empowered by coordination together with civil society (Castells, 1997).

The virtual state needs to be built around a broader consensus precisely in order to deal with these requirements while reinforcing both its supply and demand side. The structuring of this consensus demands the organization and coordination of several political, public, and private players and entrepreneurs. For this to occur, and assuming the risk to sound excessively normative, we believe the consensus between civil society and the bureaucratic structure could be articulated on complementary approaches in which technology is vital.

Therefore, we emphasize the need to establish universal goals and criteria for administration in such a way as to standardize and induce an effective restructuring of the state in terms of processes and routines (Fountain, 2001). More importantly, this would establish the standards for an effective virtual administration in terms of data integration, clusters of services, and transparency of policy designs with seamless agency boundaries and effective mechanisms for virtual accountability and policy feedback. This would have to occur without affecting the specific systems of each agency, articulating both macro and micro levels in an organizational matrix structure.

In addition, the leadership positions in the areas of information technology would be mainly occupied not by technology experts, but by state administrators trained as bureaucrats with emphasis on modern management methods toward the implementation of a managerial state, though keeping some still valid Weberian principles (Evans, 2002). The managers would mould the virtual state respecting the particularities of each unit under the umbrella of the specifications of the strategic plan. This would, at some point, link the different administrative bodies to an agency highly positioned at the executive branch, which would have to act on the two fronts with both the government managers and the strategic planning committee.

In conclusion, based on empirical research and literature on the subject, we would emphasize that, at least technically, the provision of better and more democratic information would be possible by reducing the inefficiency of political choice and increasing the efficiency of state bureaucracy. Above all, the motivating spark of this effort should be, as Mitchell (1999) observed, the belief that emerging civic structures of the digital era can deeply affect economic opportunities, public services, and urban life in general. Therefore, we would add, there is no other alternative for the state than to legitimate itself, paying due heed not only to the monopoly of the use of force or regulation but, principally, to its status as the major repository of data and as the central player in the articulation of civic networks. Of course, in this regard, solving the difficult equation of the digital divide is central to the whole process. For this to occur, and this is the crux of this discussion, we believe there is a need to grant access to other social players to participate in the discussion of electronic government from a political perspective. In essence, we propose that electronic government should be used as the window of opportunity for a civic restructuring of the public administration. In these terms, transparency and interaction between civil society, bureaucracy, and political society could become the basic element in this process, as taken together they are effectively the vertebral axis for the potential restructuring of the state. In this way, its republican and democratic dimension may revert to the political forefront, leading to the organized social construction of the virtual state. However, we must admit that it is still a promise that will need a complex political construction to be fulfilled and, as those involved with government acknowledge, that it can be conceived only as an ongoing process.

Acknowledgments

I would like to express my gratitude to Steven Dutt Ross for the dedication to this project as my assistant and to FGV/EBAPE for providing funds to this research.

References

Bresser-Pereira, L. C., & Spinks, P. (1995). *Reforma do estado e administração pública gerencial.* Rio de Janeiro, Brazil: Editora da Fundação Getúlio Vargas.

Castells, M. (1997). *The rise of the network society* (Vol. 1). Cambridge, MA: Blackwell.

Evans, P. (2002, October). *Hybridity as administrative strategy: Combining bureaucratic capacity with market signals and deliberate democracy.* Paper presented at the CLAD Seventh International Congress on State Reform and Administrative Development, Lisbon, Portugal.

Fernandes, C. (2003). *Sistemas de compras eletrônicas e sua aplicação à administração pública: O caso do SIASG/ComprasNet.* Rio de Janeiro, Brazil: Mimeo-FGV.

Fountain, J. E. (2001). *Building the virtual state.* Washington, DC: Brookings.

Graham, S., & Marvin, S. (1997). *Telecommunications and the city: Electronic spaces, urban places.* New York: Routledge.

Kingdon, J. W. (2003). *Agendas, alternatives, and public policies.* Washington, DC: Longman.

Mitchell, W. J. (1999). *City of bits: Space, place, and the infobahn.* Cambridge, MA: The MIT Press.

Norris, P. (2001). *Digital divide? Civic engagement, information poverty, and the Internet worldwide.* Cambridge, MA: Cambridge University Press.

Ruediger, M. A. (2003, September). *Governança democrática na era da informação.* Paper presented at the 27th Encontro da ANPAD, São Paulo, Brazil.

Endnote

[1]   Demos is a project developed by Professor Rolf Luehrs at the Technical University of Hamburg, Germany.

Chapter V

An Exploratory Study of Electronic Government and State Portals in Mexico

Luis Felipe Luna-Reyes,
Universidad de las Américas-Puebla Business School, Mexico

J. Ramón Gil-Garcia, Center for Technology in Government,
University at Albany, State University of New York, USA

Jennifer S. Rojas-Bandera,
Universidad de las Américas-Puebla Business School, Mexico

Abstract

Many governments have embraced the information revolution by developing information and communication technologies (ICTs) to improve services to citizens. In Mexico, the number of government Web sites has increased from none in 1994 to about 2,800 in 2005. However, there is relatively little research about Mexican government portals. This chapter preliminarily evaluates the quality and functionality of four state government portals in Mexico. It also analyzes their evolution from 2002 to 2005 and uncovers some general trends. In general, Mexican state government portals seem to be mainly information catalogs with some transactional capabilities. However, the observed portals show a pattern of transitioning to a more user-centered design and integrating more electronic services. In addition, Mexican state portals show an increasing concern for transparency and citizen participation.

Introduction

The expansion of information and communication technologies (ICTs) is without a doubt one of the main developments of the last few decades (Thomas & Streib, 2003). ICTs impact on social organization has been compared with that of the steam engine during the industrial revolution.[1] Moreover, the development of ICTs has been considered one of the main catalysts of a new society based upon information and knowledge (Drucker, 1994; Winograd, 2002).

The Internet has probably had the most impact of all ICTs on society. Due to people's acceptance of the Internet, the number of computers connected to it has doubled every year since the early 1980's. In this way, the number of Internet enabled computers around the world has increased from less than 1,000 to more than 73 million in the year 2000 (Commer, 2000). This connectivity has promoted the development of a diversity of applications for information, products and services such as electronic mail, chat rooms, Web blogs, Web pages, electronic commerce, distribution lists, Web feeds, and virtual private networks. This plethora of applications and services has lead to the creation of Web portals, which are developed to facilitate access to information, products or services on the Internet (D. B. Gant, Gant, & Johnson, 2002). Portals can be vertical (when organized around a specific theme) or horizontal (when they cover a diversity of themes) (Eisenmann, 2002).

Governments are also involved in ICTs use and innovation, and many applications have been developed to improve services to citizens. They have joined this trend not only because citizens are looking for the same level of service that they get with private corporations but also because of the increasing governmental tendency of managing for results and citizen satisfaction (Arellano-Gault, 2004; Bardach, 1998; Barzelay, 1992; J. P. Gant & Gant, 2002; Osborne & Gaebler, 1992). In fact, advances in ICTs and the increase in their applications in government are promoting the design of an electronic administration that can lead to better relationships between the state and

Figure 1. Number of Web pages with a gob.mx domain name (1994-2005)
(Source: www.nic.mx)

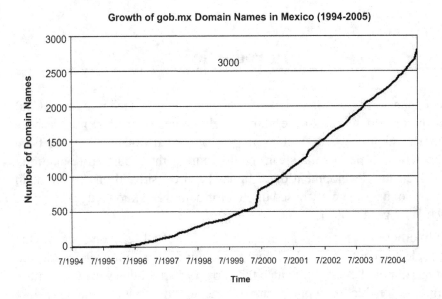

its citizens while creating new opportunities and challenges (Martín, 2001; Sancho Royo, 2003).

Applications of ICTs to improve public administration are known as electronic government, electronic governance or simply e-Gov (Grönlund & Horan, 2004). The Internet plays a critical role in most of these applications. In Mexico, for example, the number of government Web sites has increased from none in 1994 to about 2,800 in 2005 (see Figure 1). Although there are some efforts to assess both the quality and the social impact of such projects in different countries, there is still much to learn about them (Aldrich, Bertot, & McClure, 2002; Basu, 2004; J. P. Gant & Gant, 2002; Ho, 2002; Ke & Wei, 2004; Moon, 2002; West, 2004, 2005). Moreover, there is relatively little research in the context of Latin America and particularly in the context of Mexico (Sandoval & Gil-García, 2005).

This chapter constitutes a preliminary evaluation of the quality and functionality of four state government portals in Mexico. It also analyzes their evolution from 2002 to 2005, uncovering some general trends. Choosing this particular e-Gov application (state government portals) is due to their potential impact in the ways governments do business, as well as the diversity of applications currently included in state Web sites. Most government portals are considered intermediate applications between simple Web pages and complex interorganizational projects involving high levels of collaboration and information integration (Cook et al., 2004; Fountain, 2001).

The chapter is organized into five sections, starting with this introduction. The following section includes a review of relevant literature of electronic government and state portals. The third section describes the research design and methods used to select and analyze the four state portals. The fourth section describes the main findings, and the chapter ends with some preliminary conclusions and suggestions for future research.

Literature Review

ICTs have been impacting government since the 1980s, when personal computers placed processing capabilities on the public manager's desktop. The Internet can be considered "the next step" in the process of transforming government work, changing the previous internal focus on process improvement promoted by early computing technologies to an external focus on interaction with the citizen (Heeks, 1999; Stowers, 1999). In this way, during the last three decades ICTs have promoted organizational changes in terms of internal transformation (efficiency), external transformation (transparency), and relational transformation (relationships to the citizen) (Ndou, 2004). Even those who consider that ICTs have yet had no impact in government activities consider that these technologies can play an important role in the process of transforming public administration (Garson, 2004; Kramer & King, 2003).

This section of the chapter is organized in three subsections. The first one includes some basic concepts of e-government and government portals. The second section describes several approaches to assessing government portals, and the last section consists of data describing the current status of government portals around the world, showing particular interest in the case of Mexico and other Latin American countries.

E-Government and Government Portals

Many different perspectives have emerged and many concepts and terms have been coined with the emergence of electronic government as a field (Grönlund & Horan, 2004). We consider e-Gov to be a very ample concept defined as the:

use of information technologies in government for the provision of public services, the improvement of internal operation management and the promotion of democratic values and mechanisms; as well as the design and implementation of a regulatory framework that facilitates and promotes the development of the information and knowledge society. (Gil-García & Luna-Reyes, 2003, p. 107)

From this perspective, state government portals constitute just an example of electronic government applications, maybe one of the more prominent applications from the citizen's point of view. Portal development in some countries is attributed to public pressure to receive the same kind of service they receive from the private sector (Ndou, 2004). Moreover, portal development also responds to the perception of many potential benefits such as cost reductions, increases in efficiency and quality of service, improvement in transparency and access to public information, better decision-making, and promotion of community development (Gil-García & Martinez-Moyano, 2005; Ndou, 2004). To take advantage of many of these benefits, however, control and audit mechanisms are needed (Martín, 2001).

In broad terms, a government portal is an "integrated gateway into a state government website and provides both external constituents and internal government personnel with a single point of contact for online access to state information and resources" (D. B. Gant et al., 2002, p. 11). Given the versatility of its technical architecture, a government portal has the potential to become a single access point to government information and services, making transparent to the citizen the government office he or she is dealing with (Fletcher, 2002; D. B. Gant et al., 2002; Glassey, 2004; Scavo, 2003).

Approaches to Assessing E-Government Portal Functionality

Although most portals are designed to constitute a 24×7×365 single point of service to citizens, current state government portals show different levels of development and functionality. Studying levels of development in e-Gov applications, Layne and Lee (2001) have classified four stages according to their current functionalities: cataloguing, transaction, vertical integration, and horizontal integration. In their initial stage of development, government portals constitute simply a "catalog" of government office Web sites, most likely just offering basic information about government services offered. In its simplest form, a state portal is just a Web page offering information about public officials and a very basic catalog of offices and services. Portals in the next functionality level contain basic applications allowing citizens to make one or more "transactions" with government agencies. It is also possible that pages integrated or linked from these portals in this second stage of development show some common design elements to facilitate browsing among them. The most developed government portals offer services and transactions "integrating" the same function across different levels of government (vertical integration) or integrating interrelated services offered by two or more government agencies (horizontal integration).

Government portals can be classified with little uncertainty using the stages of development described in the previous paragraph, mainly because stages like the ones proposed by Layne and Lee (2001) have been developed on the basis of empirical exploration of government applications on the Internet.[2] However, some scholars recognize that the characteristics included in these stages are not mutually exclusive and that there is not necessarily a linear progression from one stage to the other (Gil-García & Martinez-Moyano, 2005; Moon, 2002).

Some observers of government portals around the world have concluded that most of them can be placed in the stages of cataloging and transaction (Cullen, O'Connor, & Veritt, 2003; Holden, Norris, & Fletcher, 2003; Reddick, 2004; Sandoval & Gil-García, 2005). Government portals' functionality depends little on technology and it is more a reflection of the level of integration of the underlying processes and services inside and across agencies (J. P. Gant & Gant, 2002). In this way, government information and service providers should maintain commitment to ICT use, but more importantly, they should be committed to collaboration, process integration and resource sharing to allow government transformation (Caffrey, 1998; Dawes & Pardo, 2002). In turn, government transformation will promote better portal development.

Government transformation needs to be guided by clear policies and regulations which encourage and facilitate collaboration across government agencies (Dawes & Pardo, 2002; Fountain, 2001). This transformation process, however, poses an important challenge in Latin America, where the state is perceived as a series of loosely organized agencies with poorly compensated and motivated personnel at the lower levels, and bureaucrats and politicians more interested in their own interests at the upper levels (Gascó, 2004). Institutional arrangements and organizational culture have been found to affect other government reform strategies in Latin American countries and there is no reason to think e-government is different in this respect (Arellano-Gault, 2000, 2004). In addition, there are important inequalities in access to Internet technologies, which may limit the potential of e-government initiatives in these countries (Luna-Reyes & Maxwell, 2003; Mariscal, 2003; Mossberger, Tolbert, & Stansbury, 2003).

To face the challenge of providing useful information and services to citizens through the Internet, researchers and practitioners in the area have considered at least two different approaches. The first of them focuses on the supply side (design of Web portals and Web sites), and the second one focusing on the demand side (understanding citizen needs).

On the demand side, emphasis should be placed in understanding who the main users are and their particular interests and needs. Such knowledge can be obtained by analyzing and understanding their behavior over the Internet, as well as their main uses of government Web sites and services. For instance, Sancho Royo (2003) suggests that creating regulations and promotion strategies for stimulating contact with citizens constitutes an important requirement to provide useful and updated information to them through government portals. Martín (2001) describes the main Web site requirements from the user point of view. These requirements include easy access to information and services, access to services from anywhere at any time, confidentiality, security, privacy, and a personalized and integrated service. Corporate users also demand information useful for market analysis, and a flexible, adaptable, and efficient administration.

Another path to face the challenge is the one suggested by the United Nations (UN) in the second World Public Sector Report on E-Government (UN, 2003). From the UN's point of view, government transformation facilitated by ICTs is a collective endeavor that involves public participation. In a very simplistic way, their proposal consists in questioning ICT applications in terms of the public value they are producing or leveraging. The notion of public value is closely linked to the identification of what citizens really want.

Outcomes of the development process that improve people's quality of life, laws that are necessary and just, services that meet people's needs, fairness, equity, due process, trust and confidence in government that stems from perception of its overall performance are all things that people want and value. (UN, 2003, p. 1)

From the UN point of view, there are three types of e-Gov development: wasteful (uses resources without results), pointless (improves government operations, but in areas of little interest to the public), and meaningful (supports human development, allows participation, and supports values essential for human development). The UN's interest in the development of meaningful e-Gov applications is confirmed in its 2004 report, where they emphasize the need of "real access" for all, considering not only the access to ICTs but a minimum level of literacy and education that allows to use them effectively (UN, 2004).

On the supply side, authors like Winograd (2002), West (2005) and J. P. Gant & Gant (2002) focus mainly on strategy or Web site features and design. Winograd (2002), for example, suggest the use of his Five Star Framework, which includes five key questions to determine the extent to which any government agency enacts design criteria required to succeed in the information era. These five questions focus on five different areas: analysis, alignment, action, accountability and acceptance. The analysis question centers on the organization's use and analysis of current challenges based upon objective information and understanding of external relationships in its preparation to respond to the main challenges. The alignment question focuses on the existence of a vision, mission, values and strategies guiding innovation, learning, individual and organizational growth. At the heart of the action question are program structure and action plans, paying particular attention to their design in terms of incorporating human capital, reviewing and improving business processes, and using technology in a creative manner. The accountability question relates to the establishment of clear and measurable goals, as well as their linkages to budgets and other resources. Finally, the acceptance question refers to the perceived value of any initiative from the point of view of users, employees, and the public. By answering these questions on a regular

Figure 2. A preliminary theoretical framework to evaluate government state portals (Source: Adapted and expanded from J. P. Gant & Gant, 2002)

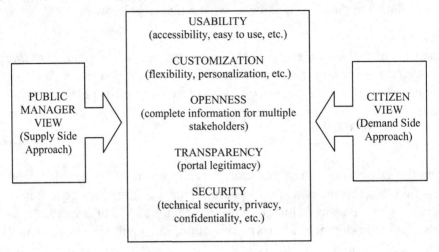

basis, government organizations can self-assess their level of service while promoting a cycle of continuous service improvement.

Using a different approach to assess portal quality, J. P. Gant and Gant (2002) propose assessing portal functionality in terms of four dimensions: usability, customization, openness, and transparency. Transparency refers to the availability of information that allows the user to assess the legitimacy of the portal content, such as the publication date, the content owner and the Webmaster. Openness is related to the extent in which the government portal offers complete information, keeping contact with all relevant stakeholders. Portal design, as well as its degree of compliance to the recommendations of the World Wide Web Consortium (W3C)[3] define portal usability. Finally, customization refers to portal flexibility and the options it offers to the users to adapt the information and the visual displays to its own needs and interests.

J. P. Gant and Gant's (2002) framework includes elements that have been identified as important by both previously mentioned approaches (demand and supply). Figure 2 shows a preliminary theoretical framework to evaluate the functionality of government state portals based on their work. Although privacy and security are included in J.P. Gant and Gant's framework as components of transparency, we have separated them as a fifth dimension.

This distinction responds to the importance of these two issues in any Internet-based government application (Joshi, Ghafoor, Aref, & Spafford, 2002; Tillman, 2003), and the importance of the issue in the 2003 United Nations Report on E-Government (UN, 2003).

Data on E-Government Development

Application of these different frameworks to assess government Web sites around the world yields interesting results mainly describing the state of the art of e-Gov on the Internet. Some of these studies correspond to state government portals and Web sites in the USA (D. B. Gant et al., 2002; Lassman, 2002; West, 2002), and others to national government portals at the international level (UN, 2003, 2004; West, 2004, 2005). In his survey of 198 national level portals, West (2005) found out that only 19% of the sites offered executable online services, and only 6% offered services with some extent of integration. According to this study, the Mexico federal portal is ranked 30th in terms of public access, as well as information and services availability. The ranking is based on a 100-point scale, where Mexico has 29.7 points. Taiwan has the first place with 57.2 points, and the last country in the ranking has 12 points. The range between the 7th and the 102nd countries is about 10 points in the scale (from 35.3 to 25.0 points). The main weaknesses of Mexican portals are the lack of privacy and security policies, and the poor compliance with W3C criteria to warrant access to people with disabilities (West, 2005).

The UN World Public Sector Report "Towards Access for Opportunity" shows that only 20 out of 178 governments with a Web presence around the world have public participation mechanisms through the Internet, and just 38 of them offer electronic transactions such as online forms or payments. There are 13 UN country members without a Web presence (UN, 2004). According to the UN report, Mexico is ranked in 30th place in e-government readiness, and 11th in terms of the Web Measure Index.[4] The only Latin American country that ranks better than Mexico is Chile, which ranks 22nd and 6th, respectively. Argentina and Brazil are the next Latin American countries in terms of ranking, placing 32nd and 35th in e-government readiness, and 22nd and 24th in Web Measure Index. Differences between ranking in e-readiness and Web Measure Index across the four countries are mainly explained by the lack of ICT infrastructure. That is to say, although the four countries are doing important progress in their Internet e-Gov applications, the lack of infrastructure limits access to the services and their potential impact on development.

In terms of electronic participation, which is measured by access to public interest information, electronic consultation and decision making, Chile ranks 11th and Mexico 6th. Argentina and Brazil share the 23rd position. Although the four countries rank similarly in terms of offering public interest information, Chile and Mexico have significantly better developments in terms of consultation and decision making (UN, 2004).

Other surveys show that the progress of e-Gov portals is slowing down over time, given that the increase in Internet maturity was only 5.4% in 2004, compared with a 7.4% and 11.5% increase for 2003 and 2002, respectively ("E-Gov Slowly Gaining Acceptance, but Must Mature," 2004). Some general explanations about the small impact of e-Gov projects consider that government services do not match citizen needs (Winograd, 2002), partly because governments do not have access to information about true citizen demands (Sancho Royo, 2003). There is still a lack of access to technology resources or a digital divide; despite the fact that many governments have a Web presence, only 20% of the world population have access to Internet services (UN, 2003), with only 8.7% of Mexican households having Internet access in 2004 (González Palacios, 2005). As mentioned before, other restraining factors of e-government impact in Latin American are related to the limited coordination of government agencies offering public services. This situation is not unique to Latin America, but it is an important characteristic of the institutional framework in government settings (Dawes & Pardo, 2002; Fountain, 2001).

Most of the information provided in the surveys described in the previous paragraphs corresponds to national government portals, and there is little exploration of developments at the state level in Latin America. Because of this, the current chapter constitutes one of the first systematic attempts to understand Latin American state government portals, describing the specific case of Mexico.

Methods

As described previously, this analysis will focus on state government portals in Mexico. There are two main reasons for the selection of these particular e-government applications. First, government portals are one of the ICT applications that have the potential of transforming government activities and the ways in which they offer information and services to citizens. Second, taking into consideration the current status of national portals and Web sites, state government portals in Mexico are very likely to include a rich variety of information and applications. It is important to mention that there is not a systematic study that ranks all Mexican states in terms of portal functionality.[5] This section describes the research design and methods.

Research Design

The analysis presented in this chapter is qualitative and exploratory in nature. The main purpose is to explore and compare the characteristics and functionalities of state government portals in Mexico. In many senses, the work described in this chapter follows the procedures proposed by the comparative case method (Yin, 1994). This research method has proven useful to answer questions like the ones this chapter is trying to answer: What is the current functionality of Mexican state government portals? How have they evolved over time?

We originally conceived of this research during the summer of 2002 as a cross-sectional analysis of state government portals in Mexico, which would describe their functionality level according to the four dimensions proposed by J. P. Gant and Gant (2002): openness, transparency, usability, and customization. During the summer of 2004, we again visited the state portals under analysis, finding that two of them had made important changes. We initially interpreted this change as a consequence of a gubernatorial election, with a strong link to political leadership and pressures. Thus, we decided to closely observe the other two state portals during the following months, given that they would hold elections during the fall of 2004, changing governors in December 2004 and February 2005 respectively. The main purpose was twofold: to observe if the portals would also change in an important way and to observe the ways in which the transitions would occur. Thus, the current research design is longitudinal in nature. It started with observations of the four selected portals during the summer of 2002, with a second observation during summer 2004, and several observations from December 2004 to August 2005 to see the evolution in the state portals during the transition from one governor to his successor. If political and institutional factors were important determinants of portal functionality, it would be expected to see changes in the content and format of the portals under observation during political transitions.

Selection of the States

Mexico is constituted of 31 states and a Federal District, analogous to the 50 states in the U.S. and Washington, DC. All of the states, as well as the Federal District, have had their own Web portals since at least 2002. Given that the Federal District has had an independently elected government since the late 1990s, it will be considered a 32nd State for the purposes of this analysis.

The state selection is the result of our interest in maximizing learning about state government portals in Mexico (Stake, 1995). Accordingly, we decided to choose four state government portals, taking into consideration their geographic location and their level of economic and social development. Although Mexican states can be subdivided into six or more geographical zones, the geographic regions were reduced to the following three to simplify the selection: North (8 states), Center (18 states), and South (6 states). To assess the state level of development, the income strata created by the National Institute of Geography and Statistics (INEGI) were taken into consideration. Again, the seven strata were grouped into three groups. The two upper strata comprise ten states, the two following strata include another ten states, and the lower level strata consist of twelve states.

Given that the highest concentration of states is in the central part of Mexico, we decided to include one state from the North one from the South, and two from the Central part of the country. There are also slightly more states in the lower income strata; one state was selected from the upper income level, one from the middle income level and two from the lower income level. In this way, the four portals selected were from the states of Nuevo Leon (a prosperous state in the north of Mexico), Queretaro (a state in the middle income level from the central region), Oaxaca (a low income state from the South), and Puebla (a low income state from the central region).

Dimensions of State Portal Functionality

To facilitate the assessment of the level of functionality of the state portals, the four dimensions or evaluation criteria proposed by Gant and Gant (2002) were selected to be used in this study. Although these dimensions were briefly described in the literature review section, the present section will describe them in a more operational way, including the fifth dimension of security and privacy.

- **Openness:** This dimension refers to the extent in which the government portal offers complete information and services with all relevant stakeholders. Openness increases as information, figures, procedures, and links to relevant pages increase. Some indicators of portal openness are information and service diversity, the number of required steps to accomplish a given task, and the extent to which personal information "follows" the user through the Web portal pages.

- **Transparency:** Three of the main problems Internet users face are the difficulty assessing the legitimacy and reliability of the information source, determining the accuracy of the information presented in Web pages, and determining how current information retrieved is. How easy it is for the user to assess content legitimacy and to contact the information providers are the main determinants of the level of transparency of a government portal. In this way, transparency can be assessed by the quantity and quality of the Web elements that identify the author, the person responsible for content management and updating, and the currency of the information produced, posted or updated.

- **Usability:** Portal graphical and conceptual designs determine to a large extent how usable a state portal is. Well-designed portals use a consistent graphical design that facilitates browsing as well as finding information relevant to the user. Unlike e-commerce portals, where the audience can be targeted with some level of specificity, government portals must include a wide audience. This additional requirement poses different technical, content, and design challenges to the portal developer. The main indicators of portal usability are the use of a simple, consistent, and intuitive design and extent to which it complies with W3C recommendations. W3C recommendations are developed to facilitate access to information over the Web to handicapped individuals such as the visually impaired as well as to individuals using different Web browsers or slower computers. To assess portal usability, WebXACT[6] analysis was applied to the four state Government portals selected.

- **Customization:** Customization refers to the flexibility that the portal offers to the user to adapt the feel and look of the portal to his or her own needs. Customization can take place manually or automatically.

Manual customization takes place when users have the ability to choose the information and services to be displayed when they access the portal. Automated customization conducts user behavior analysis to identify relevant patterns of information or service access. These patterns can be used to "push" information that may be relevant users according to their behavior, or the behavior of other users through collaborative filtering. Customization level can be observed when users choose to change the portal display or the portal capabilities to adapt the content dynamically.

- **Security and privacy:** This dimension includes aspects of technical security, privacy and confidentiality assurance. The main indicators for this dimension are the existence of proper encryption methods to conduct transactions with the government, as well as the existence of published policies on security and privacy, which explain to users the ways in which their personal information will be managed and stored (Joshi et al., 2002; Klang, 2001; Kleckner, 2002). Another indicator of concern about privacy consists of rational use of applications such as cookies that, although useful to facilitate customization and conduct transactions, pose threats to privacy (Berghel, 2001). It is important to point out that the original four dimensions included these policies as indicators of transparency of the government portal. We decided to differentiate them as a separate dimension because of its relevance for Internet applications.

Results:
State Government Portals in Mexico

State government portals are still a recent development in Mexico. They are mainly informational in nature, and they offer limited capabilities to make transactions with state governments. It is hard to find across state government Web pages a clear statement of an electronic government policy or strategy, and the ways in which state portals contribute to this strategy. Only one of the portals included in this analysis has a clear policy statement on ICTs and government.

However, it is possible to see some evolution in the portals throughout the last few years. One indicator of their recent development is associated with the presence of governor photos on the home pages of the sites. During the summer of 2002, governors' photographs and biographies were present in three out of the four portals under study (many portals in their early stages of development started with the photographs of CEOs or governors). Although governor activities and profiles are still present in the four state portals as a content category, none of them have governor photos in 2005. Moreover, three of them now have a more stakeholder-centered design, compared with only one portal in 2002. Only half of the observed portals included some online services in 2002, while all four portals are offering services in 2005. The services provided, however, are offered by a single agency (most of them related to state taxes), which is an indicator of the lack of process integration inside and across government offices. Another characteristic of the four government portals is that they intend to be not only a unique entry point to government information and services, but also to the state itself, offering information on history, geography, weather, news, and tourism.

The following sections contain a report of the observations associated with each of our four case studies: Nuevo Leon, Oaxaca, Queretaro, and Puebla. Following the main theoretical constructs presented earlier in this chapter, each section includes a general description of the state government portal in 2002. Then, they highlight some of the most important changes and the evolution of each portal from 2002 to 2005.

Nuevo Leon

The Nuevo Leon portal has been changing over time according to the evolution shown in Figures 3, 4, and 5. Figure 3 presents the portal as it looked during the summer of 2002. As shown in the figure, the portal had an attractive design for the visitor. The basic design components were consistent across other government Web pages, making browsing easy for users through a series of intuitive lists of options. However, there were too many Web elements on a single page. Although including many options on the first page can facilitate access to government information and services, human processing capabilities are limited. In this way, too many components can saturate user processing capabilities, making it more difficult for users to understand the logic of the portal in order to make decisions about where to begin to search for particular information.

In terms of openness, the Nuevo Leon portal was one of the leading state portals in 2002 because it offered a great variety of information and services.

Figure 3. Nuevo Leon state portal captured from the Internet in 2002 (Source: www.nl.gob.mx)

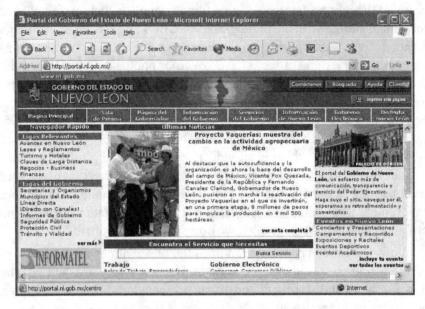

Figure 4. Nuevo Leon state portal captured from the Internet in 2004 (Source: www.nl.gob.mx)

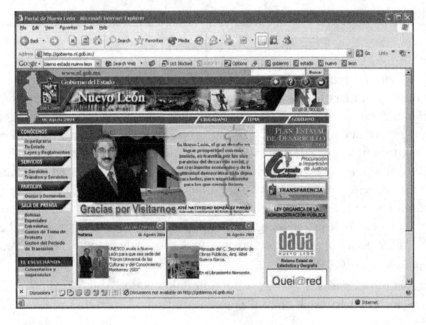

Figure 5. Nuevo Leon state portal captured from the Internet in 2005 (Source: www.nl.gob.mx)

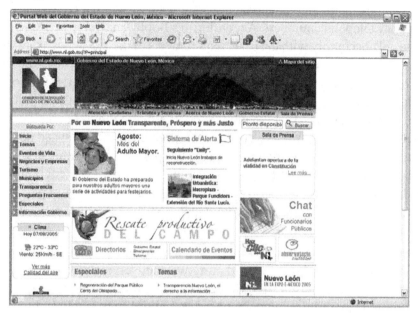

Besides information from the governor's office (government plans, press room, etc.), the portal included information about state laws and regulations, and a complete guide to government procedures from all state offices. Moreover, the portal contained links to Web pages with geographical and visitor information. At that time, the Nuevo Leon portal offered limited capabilities to make transactions. The services offered by the portal were tax-related and a link to the COMPRANET procurement system, which is a federal system made available to state and local governments. It was possible to pay car usage taxes and property taxes through the Nuevo Leon portal. It was possible to contact the governor's office through e-mail, but it was not clear how the questions would be answered.

In terms of transparency, the Nuevo Leon portal offered alternative ways to get in touch with content owners, including telephone numbers or voice mail. Nevertheless, there was no information about the people responsible for the portal, and there was no information about when the information had been posted or updated.

Consistent design contributed to portal usability as well as the existence of additional help such as a site map and a search function. Although there is a link to "online help", the link does not lead to a user manual but to a list of emergency telephone numbers. According to a Bobby analysis (WebXACT), the site did not comply with the basic requirements of the W3C. For example, different "frames" used in the portal did not have a descriptive title, and the images used in Nuevo Leon portal did not have alternative text descriptions, which are necessary for automatic readers used by the visually impaired. There was no language specification, and table usage did not comply with the W3C standards. There were no alternate mechanisms to advanced design components, making it difficult to access the portal from computers with limited capabilities. About half of the computers of the state government would be slow or extremely slow in accessing this portal; 10.5% of personal computers were Intel 80XXX or equivalent, 26% had Pentium processors, and 15% had Pentium II processors in 2001.[7]

The Nuevo Leon portal had no options to customize browsing. There were some "cookies" provided by a third party weather service on the page. Although it is hard to determine if the cookies posed a threat to user privacy, the portal should have advised the user about these third-party cookies. In 2002 the Nuevo Leon portal did not have published security or privacy policies regarding transactions over the site or user data gathered through it. However, the available transactions had a secure connection.

The Nuevo Leon portal is one of the two portals that changed appearance with the accession of a new governor. One change was the inclusion of a large photo of the new governor welcoming people to the state portal (see Figure 4). Portal design changed again in April 2005. This design change seems to respond to an interest to have a more citizen-centered portal. Although we cannot be sure about the reasons for this second change, it seems that there is a general trend from organization-centered to citizen-centered portals in many countries. This may be due to citizens' experience with private sector organizations' Web sites, an attempt to have more citizens using the portal as a result of a more intuitive organization, or simply a way for politicians to present their states as being at the top of portal development and provision of services. We think that these three reasons are important and more research is needed to disentangle the specific impact of each of them.

Certainly, there is an interesting evolution in the design of this portal (impacting portal usability) that can be observed in both Figures 4 and 5. In 2002, the state portal was organized from the government's point of view; information and services were organized in terms of the different government agencies providing them. The first change (see Figure 4) observed in 2004 reflects the intention of changing this organization to a more user-centered view of the content. One indicator of this change in the logic of the portal is the creation of three main options available in the portal date line: citizen (ciudadano), theme (tema), and government (gobierno). Although the government option kept information organized by government agency, the theme option included information grouped by key topics such as starting a business in Nuevo Leon, searching for a scholarship or a job, and others. This interest of organizing information from the user point of view is promoted with the inclusion in 2005 of an option named "Life Events" ("Eventos de Vida" in the left menu of Figure 5). This new option contains information about government services for people planning, for example, to get married or to buy a house. Overall, there is not an important change in the content or services provided by the portal, but in the way they are organized.

A second important change in the Nuevo Leon portal is related to the amount of information (links) provided on the first page. The designs of Figures 4 and 5 seem simpler and easier to understand by the user than the design in 2002. Moreover, the 2004 design (Figure 4) looks much cleaner than the 2005 design (Figure 5), in which more options are included in the vertical and horizontal user menus.

An interesting addition to the portal is the idea of transparency (transparencia) as a topic area. In the Mexican governments, transparency is related to accountability and access to information, and has become an important policy theme. This topic is not important only to government, but also to other stakeholders such as citizens, non-governmental organizations, and private corporations. It appears that this state government is trying to use its portal to improve in this area.

The addition of periodical chats with government representatives reflects the desire to use the Internet as a mechanism of citizen participation. These chats are facilitated by a mediator who selects questions from the online participants to the government representative. About five chat sessions have taken place every month since April 2005, and a transcript of each is available on the portal. In terms of security and privacy, the site no longer has third-party cookies, and contains secure pages for online transactions. The portal has no published security and privacy policies, but each online service page contains a link to a page that briefly explains that the portal complies with security standards.

The Nuevo Leon portal continues to lack information regarding the posting and updating of information as well security and privacy policies. There is no progress in compliance with W3C recommendations according to the WebXACT analysis. However, changes in the conceptual design, as well as the inclusion of clear mechanisms of citizen participation place Nuevo Leon portal in a good position towards becoming a meaningful e-government project.

Oaxaca

Figure 6 shows the Oaxaca portal as observed in 2002. In general, the design was simpler and cleaner when compared to the Nuevo Leon portal in any of its versions. The Oaxaca portal was, and still is, much less open than the Nuevo Leon portal. The Oaxaca portal offered a list of the municipalities in the state, information about the governor, and the state organizational chart. The processes and services of all government agencies were also available in the portal. The portal was linked to other state agency Web sites, but none

Figure 6. Oaxaca state portal captured from the Internet in 2002 (Source: www.oaxaca.gob.mx)

of them offered any online services. Similar to the Nuevo Leon portal, the Oaxaca portal also had a link to the COMPRANET system. There were also links to sites with information for visitors. Some sections of the portal linked to forms that appeared to be interactive forms to send information to the governor or other government officers, but none of them worked as an online form or had directions on how to download or print the form so it could be sent by postal mail or fax.

The Oaxaca portal had a freeware application of a chat room, but there was no particular purpose declared for this application, and it appeared not to have had much activity. An interesting addition to this portal was the existence of job postings, which is a frequently-used application for low-income citizens in other countries (NTIA, 2002). Unfortunately, there were no explicit objectives or rules for participation, and the online form to submit curricula vitae was non-functional. In fact, the form could discourage participation by frustrating users because they only discover it did not work after entering the requested information. In addition, even when it was a relatively simple portal, there were several broken links.

Figure 7. Oaxaca state portal captured from the Internet in 2005 (Source: www.oaxaca.gob.mx)

In terms of transparency, it was impossible to identify which government office was responsible of maintaining sections in the Oaxaca portal. Although it was possible to identify the content owners, there was no information about how current the information was. The Oaxaca portal has no published privacy and security policies.

Integration across agencies is poor, and there was no consistency in the design or the internal logic of the several sites linked through the portal. This promotes a more difficult browsing experience for the user. The Oaxaca portal did not offer any additional help for the user such as a site map, a help section or a search engine. A WebXACT analysis indicated a low level of compliance with the W3C recommendations, with problems very similar to the ones shown in the Nuevo Leon portal. The Oaxaca portal had no mechanism to customize the user browsing experience.

The Oaxaca portal in 2004 had the same look that it had in 2002. However, it was evident the portal had not been maintained between these years, evidenced by the fact there were much more broken links in 2004 than in 2002. The chat room was more active, but the topics discussed there were of no use for improving government services. It was more a place to meet informally with friends and chat about any topic. The transition when the new governor took the office in December 2004 was rather radical. Soon after the transition, the state portal had only one page with an "Under Construction" symbol and the name of the state. In February 2005, the new portal was released (see Figure 7). From informal conversations with citizens from Oaxaca, it seems that the state portal was an important element on the new governor's political strategy, and he wanted the portal to convey the message that there was a new administration with new ideas, programs, and policies for the state.

The Oaxaca portal in its current incarnation contains more information about government offices, addresses and ways to contact them. However, it no longer contains information about government procedures and services. The current portal also includes links to information about state traditions, tourism, and some special interest groups. It appears that the new state government has a special interest to offer information to underrepresented groups such as indigenous Mexicans, women, the elderly, and youth. Information about government programs is organized on the basis of these main themes. Because Oaxaca is one of the Mexican states that "exports" much labor to the U.S., there is a special section oriented to migration (migrantes). Since the portal also aims to attract the business community, it offers information about opportunities, infrastructure and incentives to invest in Oaxaca (invierta). The jobs section now contains a list of job opportunities and a phone number and an address to make further inquiries.

The Web portal also has links oriented exclusively to government personnel, such as access to e-mail through the Web (Webmail). Most of the new content offered by the portal relies on third-party information providers; that is to say, the state government is not creating new information, but relying on other content providers by linking them to the portal. Although the link to the COMPRANET procurement system is no longer a part of the Oaxaca portal, it does offer a couple of online tax-payment applications as well as online forms to be downloaded by the user. The online transactions are not on a secure (encrypted) page, and there are not yet any published policies on security and privacy.

In terms of usability the state portal maintains a very simple and intuitive design despite the addition of more user options. It has added user help options such as a site map and a search function. According to a WebXACT analysis, the portal still does not comply with the W3C recommendations. In terms of transparency, it is possible to identify and have contact with the office in charge of maintaining and updating the portal, as well as the content owners. Finally, there is no significant progress in terms of portal customization. In this way, Oaxaca portal has given important steps in terms of conceptual design and structure, but still does not materialize the effort in terms of meaningful information and services.

Queretaro

Figure 8 shows a picture captured from the Queretaro portal in 2002. The portal had an attractive and relatively "clean" design in terms of the user options, perhaps looking as if it had too little information because of the many photos associated with the last news in the central part of the portal.

In terms of openness, the Queretaro portal offered a similar amount of information and services compared with the Nuevo Leon portal in 2002, with more functionalities than the Oaxaca portal. As additional features, the portal included two interactive components promoting citizen participation in government processes. One of these components consisted of a multiple-choice survey about policy issues that appears to change periodically. Additionally, the portal hosted a survey to get reactions to the long-term state strategic plan, known as Great Vision for Queretaro 2025. Unfortunately, this survey

Figure 8. Queretaro state portal captured from the Internet in 2002 (Source: www.queretaro.gob.mx)

was linked from a section geared toward the business community, potentially limiting participation from the ordinary citizen who is not likely to follow that link (and perhaps also reflecting state government policies and values at that time). In many ways, the selection of the user options in the portal seemed to indicate that the portal's main focus was to attract private investment to the state, which could limit citizens' participation and engagement.

An interesting addition when compared to the state portals previously discussed is a children's section with information about Queretaro and some interactive games. The portal had a section for complaints and a list of job opportunities in the state. Although limited in terms of functionality, this list may be a useful option for the citizen looking for a job.

In terms of transparency, it was clearly stated that the Office of Public Relations was responsible for the Queretaro portal. Unfortunately, it was impossible to identify the agencies that owned the content. The Queretaro portal presented the same privacy concerns associated with third-party cookies observed in the Nuevo Leon portal. The Queretaro portal has incorporated a transparency policy since 2002. Although there were no published privacy and security policies, transactions were placed on secure pages.

In terms of usability, the portal did not have a site map, but offered a search function. Although there was a link that appeared to be linked to online help, this link was actually to the Webmaster's mail address. The design was consistent across Web pages, but the WebXACT analysis shows the same navigation limitations observed in the previous cases. Finally, this portal had no customization options.

The Queretaro portal was the second portal that changed in design at some point during 2003 or early 2004 (see Figure 9). However, a closer look at the choices in the portal makes it apparent that the main changes are not related to content but to general design. In other words, the underlying content and services are about the same, but the way in which they are presented to the user is different.

An important change from one portal to the other is the office responsible for portal maintenance. In the 2004 portal, the office responsible is no longer the office for Public Relations, but the office for Access to the Information.

Figure 9. Queretaro state portal captured from the Internet in 2004 (Source: www.queretaro.gob.mx)

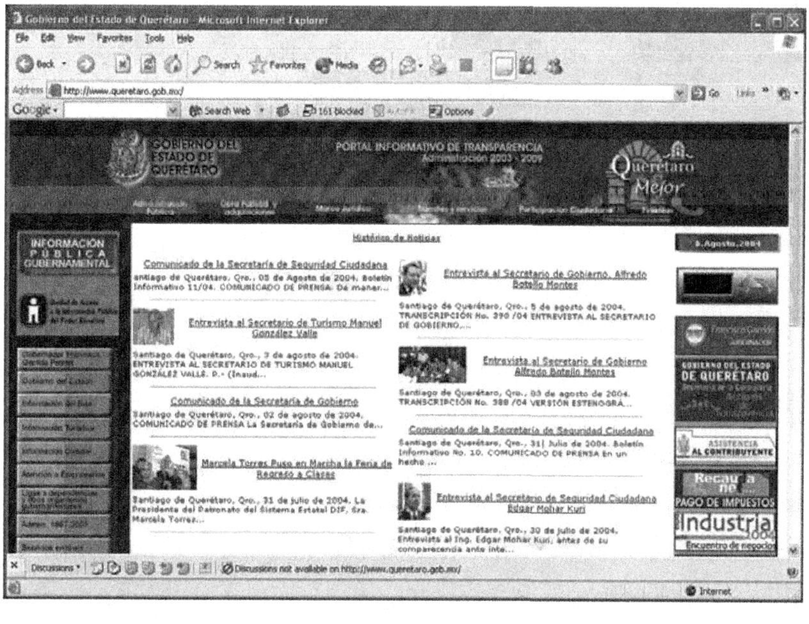

Under the new Webmaster, the emphasis on transparency and citizen participation became more important, and more links to these Web sites were added to the portal. The search function was lost in the change. In general, the Queretaro portal has shown little changes in terms of openness, usability, transparency, and customization. Thus, changes in Queretaro portal have been mainly "cosmetic," showing little progress in terms of pushing the vision of a portal as an effective tool to promote better government.

Puebla

The Puebla portal has displayed interesting Web design and content since 2002 (see Figure 10). In terms of openness, the Puebla portal was similar to the Queretaro and Nuevo Leon portals, including similar amounts of government and state information as well as online services. Similar to Queretaro portal, the Puebla portal had a children's section.

In terms of transparency, the portal contained information about the agency responsible for its maintenance (Department of Finance) as well as informa-

Figure 10. Puebla state portal captured from the Internet in 2002 (Source: www.puebla.gob.mx)

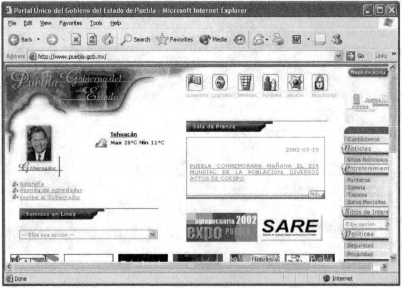

tion about the content owners and update dates. This was, and still is, the only portal with a published statement about security and privacy related to online transactions. All transactions were secure.

Additionally, the Puebla portal had information about a strategic ICT plan, including infrastructure development and online services offered through the Internet. The plan contained short-term and long-term goals as well as success indicators. Information in the Puebla portal also included specific actions to close the digital divide, showing the current situation and access goals for the following years. Including such information not only illustrated government interest in these issues but also concrete actions to solve them.

In terms of usability, the portal had an intuitive and simple design, consistent across Web pages linked to the portal. Moreover, content was not organized in terms of government organizational structure, but in terms of the user need (personal, business, or governmental) or service availability. The Puebla portal had a site map, but did not have a search function or online user help.

Although the portal was not in compliance with W3C recommendations, it subscribed to BetterWeb, which are a series of standards developed by a private party to provide Web designers with a checklist of good practices on design, security, and privacy. Similar to other governance mechanisms on the Internet, BetterWeb is a self-regulated system, implying a commitment to improve access, security, and privacy. It may be that an important limitation of privately developed standards is that they are developed with the private sector in mind. In this way, it is feasible that such standards do not consider the privacy and security levels necessary for democratic processes such as citizen participation in decision making and electronic voting. Similar to the Oaxaca, Queretaro, and Nuevo Leon portals, the Puebla portal did not have customization options.

As expected, the Puebla portal design changed when the new governor took office in March 2005. Although the design changed greatly, the main themes and basic organization are still present, including the transparency topic that emerged as part of the portal since the observation of summer 2004. The transition was managed differently from what was observed in Oaxaca. The only change on the home page was the change of governor photograph. Meanwhile, the whole graphic design was being changed, and a new portal was posted on June 2005 (see Figure 11). Similar to Queretaro, the change is partly explained by a change in the government office responsible for portal maintenance. Puebla portal was maintained by the State Ministry of Finance, and now is maintained by a decentralized public organization in charge of the

Figure 11. Puebla state portal captured from the Internet in 2005 (Source: www.puebla.gob.mx)

State's ICT strategy. At this point, it is difficult to see the ways in which the dimensions will change because there are still many sections under construction, but it looks like the portal will keep its user-centered design, adding important stakeholders like the USA Mexican immigrants from Puebla, and some sections oriented to government personnel.

Discussion:
A Comparison of the Four State Portals

Electronic government is increasingly seen as a tool for governmental administrative reform. Internet technologies in general, and Web portals in particular, have the potential of improving the provision of public services and transforming the relationships between government and citizens. However,

Table 1. State portals in Mexico: Openness

State	Openness Characteristics
Nuevo Leon	▪ Rich information ▪ Links to Web pages with geographic and visitors information ▪ Limited services available ▪ Governor's e-mail available ▪ Interactive chats with government officers
Oaxaca	▪ Limited information ▪ Links to Web pages with information for visitors ▪ Online services were not available in 2002, and limited services in 2005. ▪ Non-functional forms in 2002 change to e-mail links and phone numbers in 2005. ▪ Open-purpose chat room available in 2002, eliminated by 2005 ▪ Job postings
Queretaro	▪ Rich information ▪ Interactive components promoting citizens' participation ▪ Information to visitors ▪ Kids section ▪ Section of complaints and a list of job opportunities ▪ Limited transactions
Puebla	▪ Rich information ▪ Information to visitors ▪ Kids section ▪ Section of complaints and a list of job opportunities in the state ▪ Limited transactions

Table 2. State portals in Mexico: Transparency

State	Transparency Characteristics
Nuevo Leon	▪ Alternative ways to get in touch with content owners, including phone numbers ▪ No information about the person or office responsible of the Web portal ▪ No information about when the information was posted or updated
Oaxaca	▪ It was possible to identify the content owners. ▪ No information about the person or office responsible of the Web portal ▪ No information about when the information was posted or updated
Queretaro	▪ It was possible to identify the content owners. ▪ It was clearly stated that the Office of Public Relations was responsible for the Web portal. ▪ No information about when the information was posted or updated
Puebla	▪ It was possible to identify the content owners. ▪ It was clearly stated that the Department of Finance was responsible for the Web portal. ▪ There was information about updates.

Table 3. State portals in Mexico: Usability

State	Usability Characteristics
Nuevo Leon	• Consistent design, site map, and search function • Online help link leads to emergency telephone numbers. • The site does no comply with the basic requirements of the W3C (according to a WebXACT analysis). • Change to user-centered design
Oaxaca	• No consistency in the design and internal logic of the multiple sites linked to the portal; site map and search added in 2005 • Low level of compliance with the W3C recommendations (according to a WebXACT analysis) • Change to user-centered design
Queretaro	• Consistent design across Web pages; the site does not have a site map, it lost search function in 2003-4. • There is a link to online help, but it leads to the Webmaster e-mail address. • Low level of compliance with the W3C recommendations (according to a WebXACT analysis)
Puebla	• Intuitive and simple design consistent across all Web pages linked to the portal; the portal had a site map, and plans to add a search function (not working yet). • User-centered design since 2002 • Low level of compliance with W3C recommendations • It is subscribed to BetterWeb, a series of standards developed by a private party to provide Web designers with good practices on design, security, and privacy.

there are not enough systematic evaluations of government portals in Latin American countries. This chapter discussed some relevant literature related to electronic government and state portals and described the current status and recent evolution of four state government portals in Mexico. This last section of the chapter discusses some patterns observed in state government portals and suggests some opportunities for future research. It is important to emphasize that the goal of this chapter is not to generalize the results to other realities, but to present some lessons that may be useful to understand similar situations and contexts.

The Mexican state government portals observed seem to be mainly information catalogs with some transactional capabilities. The online services offered by these portals are mainly tax-related. Following models from industrialized countries, scholars have implicitly accepted that more technological sophistication is good in all cases. In fact, most evolutionary models of e-government present the stages as progressive increases in technological

Table 4. State portals in Mexico: Customization

State		Customization Characteristics
Nuevo Leon	▪	No customization available.
Oaxaca	▪	No customization available.
Queretaro	▪	No customization available.
Puebla	▪	No customization available.

Table 5. State portals in Mexico: Security and privacy

State		Security and Privacy Characteristics
Nuevo Leon	▪	Privacy concerns associated with third party cookies in 2002, solved since 2004
	▪	No privacy and security policy, but security statement in each transaction
	▪	Secure transaction enabled
Oaxaca	▪	No published privacy and security policies
	▪	Secure transactions not enabled
Queretaro	▪	Privacy concerns associated with third party cookies in 2002, solved since 2004
	▪	No published privacy and security policies
	▪	Secure transactions enabled
Puebla	▪	Published statement about security and privacy
	▪	Secure transactions enabled

and organizational sophistication (see for example Layne & Lee, 2001). The adequacy of portal development to citizen and other stakeholder needs, however, is not necessarily a straightforwardly appraised. Looking at cases such as Mexico, future research should explore not only the feasibility but also the desirability of different levels of technological and organizational sophistication according to different national contexts, and the creation of public value. It might be the case that for certain contexts lower degrees of sophistication are more effective.

The main limitations and problems observed in the four state portals are consistent with the problems observed at the national level, including the lack of compliance with recommendations to warrant usability (W3C recommendations), and the lack of explicit concerns for privacy and security. Another important area of opportunity for improvement resides in the need for clear policy and strategy for ICT use in government (only Puebla has a published strategy). Future research should explore the motivations and conditions that enable state governments to comply with usability, accessibility, and security standards in Latin American countries. One potential explanation of the lack of compliance is that accessibility advocacy groups in Latin America may not be as strong as in the United States and some European countries, and therefore, governments are not experiencing strong external pressures to require usability and accessibility compliance. Regarding the publication of ICT policies and strategies, several Latin American countries (including Mexico) are promoting e-transparency initiatives. Although 23 Mexican states have openly joined the federal effort for e-transparency by the creation of a transparency comission and a State law regulating access to information, ICT policies are not considered high priority at this point in time. Other information such as budgeting, personnel, and procurement, among other, are more important for institutional contexts in which access to government information has been an issue only in the last few years.

Tables 1 through 5 contain a comparison of the four portals in terms of the five dimensions. In terms of openness, three of the four state portals present rich information, but all of them have very limited online services available. All four portals attempt to be not only a tool to provide government services but also a gateway to the state, presenting geographical, historical, and tourist information. Two of the state portals contain chat rooms, but their strategies were very different. Nuevo Leon has a more active chat room with different government officers. Oaxaca had an open chat room without a clear objective that was eliminated in 2005.

In terms of transparency, it was possible to identify content owners in all four portals, but only Nuevo Leon offers alternative methods of contact. Two of the portals clearly state which government agency was responsible for the state portal. Interestingly, Nuevo Leon does not offer this information. Only the Puebla portal gives information on how often information is updated.

In terms of usability, three of the four state portals have a clear and consistent design (the exception is Oaxaca). However, none of them complies with the requirements of the W3C (according to a WebXACT analysis). Puebla is subscribed to BetterWeb, what can be seen as an attempt to improve its usability, security, and privacy. Three portals have a site map and two have a working search function. Two of the portals included an online help section, but none of them leads to a user manual. Nuevo Leon's online help sections leads to emergency telephone numbers and Queretaro's online help leads to the Webmaster's e-mail address.

None of the state portals offers options to customize the user browsing experience. They have started developing user profiles for students and businesspeople, among others, but there are no ways to customize the display of the information according to user needs and interests. Finally, in terms of security and privacy, only the Puebla portal includes a published statement on security and privacy. However, three of the four portals enable secure transactions (the only exception is Oaxaca), and Nuevo Leon offers a security statement for each transaction.

In general, no pattern showing a relationship between either a state's economy or geographical location and the functionality of the state government portal. It is feasible, however, that portal functionality is related to economic level and size of the state's capital city. In this way, the least developed portal is from the smallest and poorest state (Oaxaca), and the more developed portals are from the two states with the larger capital cities (Nuevo Leon and Puebla). Future research should investigate which factors affect government Web portals and Web site functionality in Latin America. Some of these factors have been identified for industrialized countries such as the U.S. and Canada, but more research is needed for developing countries (see for example Gil-García, 2005). It would be important to understand direct and indirect effects of organizational and institutional factors on the functionality of Latin American e-government initiatives.

Evolution of state portals is at least partially related to changes in elected officials and other trends and external inputs. All portals observed changed their design with the change of governor, but in three out of four cases (the only exception is Oaxaca) the initial change was mainly in terms of graphic design rather than content. However, other trends and external inputs can greatly change the portal organization, such as the case of Nuevo Leon's recent switch to a more citizen-centered organization. Future research should explore how different political factors shape the characteristics of state portals. In fact, Web portals can be used as marketing and communication mechanisms between government officials and citizens. More research that explores these relationships is also needed.

In general, the observed portals show a pattern of changing towards a user-centered design, which tries to organize information and services as they are needed by main stakeholders in the state (i.e. migrants in the cases of Puebla and Oaxaca). Moreover, it is likely that the content will also be organized by life events in the future. This trend is not unique to Mexico, but is also happening in some other countries such as Singapore, whose e-government portal is one of the most advanced. Future research should analyze the impact of these changes in content organization on Web portal usability and overall user satisfaction.

Finally, Mexican state portals also show an important concern for transparency and citizen participation, which is an external input being promoted by the federal government and incorporated in different ways by state governments. In fact, the increase in citizens' participation is an important concern for the international community, and was stated clearly in the last UN report (UN, 2003). Future research should assess the impact of Web portal characteristics on citizens' participation and overall perception of transparency.

Final Remarks

It appears that Web portals will continue to be used by state governments to improve their provision of services, streamline their internal procedures, and promote citizen participation and transparency. Mexican state portals are still at the initial stages and there need additions and improvements. However, this longitudinal study shows a trend to more customer-oriented portals that include not only better content organization but also the provision of more information and services with the necessary security and privacy measures. There might still be some questions about the desirability of the e-government revolution for Latin American countries. However, state governments in Mexico have already embraced Web portals as mechanisms to communicate with and serve their multiple stakeholders. More research will be needed in the coming years. Analyses presented in this chapter suggest some additional ideas for future research. One deals with the systematic evaluation of government portal functionality. Although a cross-sectional design is a useful starting point, a longitudinal analysis has the potential to yield interesting insights about the evolution of state portals. Second, several elements from this initial work suggest that another thread of research should include the analysis of the organizational and institutional factors that either enable or limit the development of government portals. Finally, there is a need for research about the impact of e-government initiatives in both government efficiencies (costs savings, better processes, etc.), and government results (health, education, justice, promotion of a democratic society, etc.).

References

Aldrich, D., Bertot, J. C., & McClure, C. R. (2002). E-government: Initiatives, developments, and issues. *Government Information Quarterly, 19*(4), 349-355.

Arellano-Gault, D. (2000). Challenges for the new public management. Organizational culture and the administrative modernization program in Mexico City (1995-1997). *American Review of Public Administration, 30*(4), 400-413.

Arellano-Gault, D. (2004). *Beyond reinventing government: Fundamentals of new public management and performance-oriented budgets in Latin America.* Mexico City: Miguel Angel Porrua.

Arellano-Gault, D. (2004). *Gestión estratégica para el sector público.* México: Fondo de Cultura Económica.

Bardach, E. (1998). *Getting agencies to work together: The practice and theory of managerial craftmanship.* Washington, DC: Brookings Institution Press.

Barzclay, M. (1992). *Breaking through bureaucracy: A new vision for managing in government.* Berkeley, CA: University of California Press.

Basu, S. (2004). E-government and developing countries: An overview. *International Review of Law, Computers & Technology, 18*(1), 109-132.

Berghel, H. (2001). Caustic cookies. *Communications of the ACM, 44*(5), 19-22.

Caffrey, L. (1998). *Information sharing between & within governments.* London: Commonwealth Secretariat.

Commer, D. (2000). *The Internet book* (3rd ed.). Upper Saddle River, NJ: Prentice Hall.

Cook, M., Dawes, S. S., Juraga, D., Werthmuller, D. R., Pagano, C. M., & Schwartz, B. F. (2004). *Bridging the enterprise: Lessons from the New York state-local Internet gateway prototype.* Albany, NY: Center for Technology in Government, University at Albany, SUNY.

Cullen, R., O'Connor, D., & Veritt, A. (2003). An evaluation of local government Websites in New Zealand. In G. G. Curtin, M. H. Sommer, & V. Vis-Sommer (Eds.), *The world of e-government* (pp. 185-211). New York: The Haworth Press.

Dawes, S. S., & Pardo, T. A. (2002). Building collaborative digital government systems. Systematic constraints and effective practices. In W. J. McIver & A. K. Elmagarmid (Eds.), *Advances in digital government. Technology, human factors, and policy* (pp. 259-273). Norwell, MA: Kluwer Academic Publishers.

Drucker, P. F. (1994). *La sociedad post capitalista*. Bogotá: Grupo Editorial Norma.

E-Gov Slowly Gaining Acceptance, but Must Mature. (2004). *The Information Management Journal, 38*(4), 16.

Eisenmann, T. R. (2002). *Internet Business Models: Text and Cases*. New York: McGraw-Hill Irwin.

Fletcher, P. D. (2002). The Government Paperwork Elimination Act: Operating instructions for an electronic government. *International Journal of Public Administration, 25*(5), 723-736.

Fountain, J. E. (2001). *Building the virtual state. information technology and institutional change*. Washington, DC: Brookings Institution Press.

Gant, D. B., Gant, J. P., & Johnson, C. (2002). *State Web portals: Delivering and financing e-service*. Washington, DC: PriceWaterhouseCoopers (IBM) Endowment for the Business of Government.

Gant, J. P., & Gant, D. B. (2002). *Web portal functionality and state government e-service*. Paper presented at the 35th Hawaii International Conference on System Sciences, Waikoloa, HI (pp. 1627-1636).

Garson, G. D. (2004). The promise of digital government. In A. Pavlichev & G. D. Garson (Eds.), *Digital government: Principles and best practices*. Hershey, PA: Idea Group Publishing.

Gascó, M. (2004). *¿Luces? y sombras de la reforma del Estado en América Latina* (Working Paper). Barcelona, Spain: Institut Internacional de Governabilitat de Catalunya.

Gil-García, J. R. (2005). *Exploring the Success Factors of State Website Functionality: An Empirical Investigation*. Paper presented at the National Conference on Digital Government Research, Atlanta, GA.

Gil-García, J. R., & Luna-Reyes, L. F. (2003). Towards a definition of electronic government: A comparative review. In A. Mendez Vilas, J. A. Mesa-González, V. Guerrero-Bote, & F. Zapico-Alonso (Eds.), *Techno-legal aspects of the information society and new economy: An overview* (Vol. 1, pp. 102-108). Badajoz, Spain: Formatex.

Gil-García, J. R., & Martinez-Moyano, I. J. (2005). *Exploring e-government evolution: The influence of systems of rules on organizational action.* Retrieved May 2005, from http://www.ksg.harvard.edu/digitalcenter/Research/working_papers/gil-garcia_wp05-001.pdf

Glassey, O. (2004). Developing a one-stop government data model. *Government Information Quarterly, 21*(2), 156-169.

González Palacios, M. (2005). *The digital divide.* Retrieved July, 2005, 2005, from http://www.slais.ubc.ca/courses/libr500/04-05-wt2/www/M_Gonzalez/index.htm

Grönlund, A., & Horan, T. (2004). Introducing e-Gov: History, definitions, and issues. *Communications of the AIS, 15,* 713-729.

Heeks, R. (1999). *Reinventing government in the Information Age. International practice in IT-enabled public sector reform.* New York: Routledge.

Hiller, J. S., & Bélanger, F. (2001). Privacy strategies for electronic government. In M. A. Abramson & G. E. Means (Eds.), *E-government 2001* (pp. 162-198). Lanham, MD: Rowman & Littlefield Publishers.

Ho, A. T.-K. (2002). Reinventing local governments and the e-government initiative. *Public Administration Review, 62*(4), 434-444.

Holden, S. H., Norris, D. F., & Fletcher, P. D. (2003). Electronic government at the local level: Progress to date and future issues. *Public Performance and Management Review, 26*(4), 325-344.

Joshi, J. B. D., Ghafoor, A., Aref, W. G., & Spafford, E. H. (2002). Security and privacy challenges of a digital government. In W. J. McIver, Jr. & A. K. Elmagarmid (Eds.), *Advances in digital government. Technology, human factors, and policy* (pp. 121-136). Norwell, MA: Kluwer Academic Publishers.

Ke, W., & Wei, K. K. (2004). Successful e-government in Singapore. *Communications of the ACM, 47*(6), 95-99.

Klang, M. (2001). Who do you trust? Beyond encryption, secure e-business. *Decision Support Systems, 31,* 293-301.

Kleckner, J. E. (2002). E-security 101. *AFP Exchange, 22*(3), 54-56.

Kramer, K. L., & King, J. L. (2003). *Information technology and administrative reform: Will the time after e-government be different?* Unpublished manuscript, Irvine, CA.

Lassman, K. (2002). *The digital state 2001*. Washington, DC: The Progress & Freedom Foundation.

Layne, K., & Lee, J. (2001). Developing fully functional e-government: A four stage model. *Government Information Quarterly, 18*, 122-136.

Luna-Reyes, L. F., & Maxwell, T. (2003). *The digital divide: An integrated approach*. Paper presented at the International Conference of the System Dynamics Society, New York.

Mariscal, J. (2003). *Digital divide in Mexico*. Mexico City: Centro de Investigación y Docencia Económicas.

Martín, T. R. (2001). Proyectos para una administración electrónica en España. *Reforma y Democracia, (20)*, 17.

Moon, M. J. (2002). The evolution of e-government among municipalities: Rhetoric or reality? *Public Administration Review, 62*(4), 424-433.

Mossberger, K., Tolbert, C. J., & Stansbury, M. (2003). *Virtual inequality: Beyond the digital divide*. Washington, DC: Georgetown University Press.

Ndou, V. (2004). E-government for developing countries: Opportunities and challenges. *Electronic Journal on Information Systems in Developing Countries, 18*(1), 1-24.

NTIA. (2002). *A nation online: How Americans are expanding their use of the Internet*. Washington, DC: National Telecommunications & Information Administration.

Osborne, D., & Gaebler, T. (1992). *Reinventing government: How the entrepreneurial spirit is transforming the public sector*. Reading, MA: Addison-Wesley.

Reddick, C. G. (2004). A two-stage model of e-government growth: Theories and empirical evidence for U.S. cities. *Government Information Quarterly, 21*(1), 51-64.

Sancho Royo, D. (2003). Gobierno electrónico y participación. Factores de éxito para su desarrollo. *Reforma y Democracia, (25)*, 11.

Sandoval, R., & Gil-García, J. R. (2005, May 15-18). *Assessing e-government evolution in Mexico: A preliminary analysis of the state portals*. Paper presented at the 2005 Information Resources Management Association International Conference, San Diego, CA.

Sandoval, R., & Gil-García, J. R. (2006). E-government portals in Mexico. In M. Khosrow-Pour (Ed.), *Encyclopedia of e-commerce, e-government and mobile commerce* (pp. 367-372). Hershey, PA: Idea Group Inc.

Scavo, C. (2003). World Wide Web site design and use in public management. In G. D. Garson (Ed.), *Public information technology: Policy and management issues,* (pp. 299-330). Hershey, PA: Idea Group Publishing.

Stake, R. E. (1995). *The art of case study research.* Thousand Oaks, CA: Sage.

Stowers, G. N. L. (1999). Becoming cyberactive: State and local governments on the World Wide Web. *Government Information Quarterly, 16*(2), 111-127.

Thomas, J. C., & Streib, G. (2003). The new face of government: Citizen-initiated contacts in the era of e-government. *Journal of Public Administration Research and Theory, 13*(1), 83-102.

Tillman, B. (2003). More information could mean less privacy. *Information Management Journal, 37*(2), 20-23.

UN. (2003). *World public sector report 2003: E-government at the crossroads.* New York: United Nations Publications.

UN. (2004). *Global e-government readiness report 2004: Towards access for opportunity.* Retrieved May 2005, from http://www.unpan.org/egovernment4.asp

UN & ASPA. (2002). *Benchmarking e-government: A global perspective.* New York: United Nations Division of Public Economics and Public Administration and the American Society for Public Administration.

West, D. M. (2002). *State and federal e-government in the United States, 2002.* Providence, RI: Brown University.

West, D. M. (2004, September, 2004). *Global e-government, 2004.* Retrieved January, 2005, from http://www.insidepolitics.org/egovt04int.pdf

West, D. M. (2005, September, 2005). *Global e-government, 2005.* Retrieved October, 2005, from http://www.insidepolitics.org/egovt05int.pdf

Winograd, M. A. (2002). La gobernanza en la Era de la Información. ¿Qué hacer y cómo hacerlo? *Reforma y Democracia*(22), 17.

Yin, R. K. (1994). *Case study research design and methods* (2nd ed.). Newbury Park, CA: Sage.

Endnotes

[1]   ICTs impact, however, was underestimated in the early stages of computing. Thomas Watson, member of the IBM executive team declared in 1943 that "In the world there is a market for about five computers." Ken Olsen, president and founder of Digital Equipment Corporation, considered in 1977 that there were no reasons for anyone to want a computer at home.

[2]   The e-Gov stages of development proposed by Layne and Lee (2001) is one of the several efforts to describe and classify advances in ICT use in government settings. Although different in some extent, most of them include stages consistent with the ones described in this chapter. Other examples can be found in Hiller and Bélanger (2001), and in documents from the United Nations and the American Society for Public Administration (UN, 2003; UN & ASPA, 2002).

[3]   The World Wide Web Consortium (W3C) is an organization coordinating the development of standards for the Internet. To learn more about the consortium, its mission and activities, visit http://www.w3.org/.

[4]   The e-government readiness index is a composite of three indexes, an index that considers government Web sites (by itself constitutes the Web Measure Index), another that includes the country's telecommunications infrastructure, and a third one considering human capital.

[5]   For a study that evaluates the functionality of all state portals in Mexico, but do not develop an overall ranking see Sandoval and Gil-García (2006).

[6]   WebXACT is a free service provided by Watchfire to assess accessibility as described by W3C. The application was formerly known as Bobby because of the software application initially developed at the Center for Applied Special Technology (CAST). Bobby is now also produced and distributed by Watchfire. Free access to the service to assess individual Web pages is located at http://webxact.watchfire.com/.

[7]   Data about personal computers in Mexican Public Administrations is available at http://www.inegi.gob.mx/est/contenidos/espanol/rutinas/ept. asp?t=tinf003&c=3425

Section II

Regional Comparative Studies

This section presents two regional studies that allow the reader to obtain some comparative knowledge about how the different Latin American countries are performing in relation to e-government.

Chapter VI

A Comparative Analysis of E-Government in Latin America:
Applied Findings from United Nations E-Government Readiness Reports

Gregory Curtin, University of Southern California, USA

Christopher Walker, Harvard University, USA

Abstract

This chapter introduces the United Nations global e-government readiness reports, for which we serve as primary researchers, with particular focus on Latin America. The UN reports provide useful composite scores and rankings on 191 countries worldwide with respect to e-government, e-readiness, and e-participation, as well as highlighting best practices that have been identified throughout the world. In particular, the UN reports provide meaningful insights into the development of e-government in Latin America—facilitating comparative analysis between regions, as well as country comparisons within Latin America.Basing itself on the UN report, the chapter provides a comparative analysis of e-government in Latin America—both intra- and interregional comparisons—with the main objective of elevating e-government literature to a more quantitatively rigorous and sophisticated level. This chapter aims at introducing the UN report, outlining its main findings, and reporting how Latin America compares with the world in e-government readiness and development. It first outlines the background of the UN report, followed by the research methodology. Then it discusses the findings relevant to Latin America, with a brief conclusion on topics for future research and discussion.

Introduction

As researchers for the annual United Nations (UN) global e-government readiness survey, our purpose for this chapter is to expose Latin American public officials, policy makers, and scholars to the valuable resources and knowledge compiled in the annual United Nations global e-government readiness reports (*UN Benchmarking E-Government: A Global Perspective*, 2002; *UN Global E-Government Readiness Report 2004: Toward Access for Opportunity*, 2004; *UN Global E-Government Survey 2003*, 2003).[1]

The UN reports provide useful composite scores and rankings on 191 countries worldwide with respect to e-government, e-readiness, and e-participation, as well as highlighting best practices that have been identified throughout the world. In particular, the UN reports provide meaningful insights into the development of e-government in Latin America—facilitating comparative analysis between regions, as well as country comparisons within Latin America.

While the book as a whole aims at identifying qualitative studies of best practices within Latin America online, this chapter takes a step back to contemplate how Latin America as a region is doing in comparison to the rest of the world, as well as how individual Latin American countries compare with their neighbors and the world. Much of the e-government literature and research have focused on anecdotal case studies (*The 2002 E-Readiness Rankings: A White Paper from the Economist Intelligence Unit*, 2002; Accenture, 2002, 2003; Siew & Leng, 2003), with researchers and policy makers describing practices that have been particularly successful or common pitfalls they have found in implementation, or qualitative comparative surveys (Jupp, 2003; West, 2002, 2003), with researchers scoring Web sites and services based on qualitative impressions of effectiveness and user friendliness. Additionally, a number of researchers and associations have attempted to gather quantitative data through broad, self-reported surveys (International City-County Management Association [ICMA], 2002). However, few, if any, reliable quantitative studies have been undertaken on e-government throughout Latin America or on a global scale.

This chapter introduces the UN report, for which we serve as primary researchers, with particular focus on Latin America. Basing itself on the UN report, the chapter provides a comparative analysis of e-government in Latin America—both intra- and interregional comparisons—with the main objective of elevating e-government literature to a more quantitatively rigorous and sophisticated level. Even given the quantitative approach taken by the researchers on the UN report, the methodology employed, especially the Web-site survey methodology specifically employed to produce the Web Readiness Index, has inherent weaknesses that should be noted. As a good example, simply observing that a national government Web site provides a technically sophisticated and well-implemented online consultation facility does not in and of itself provide any information about the usage of online consultation by citizens, or more important, whether or not the government in question utilizes the online citizen input in policy deliberations and decision making. This and other methodological weaknesses are prime opportunities for follow-up research using the UN report as a foundation.

The chapter establishes a solid foundation for additional chapters on specific e-government initiatives that are taking place in Latin America; it puts these innovations in comparative context and regional perspective. Additionally, some of the unique practices we discovered in Latin American government online are also highlighted as best or emerging practices, which will also be briefly discussed in this chapter.

This chapter aims at introducing the UN report, outlining its main findings, and reporting how Latin America compares with the world in e-government readiness and development. First it outlines the background of the UN report, followed by the research methodology. Then it discusses the findings relevant to Latin America, with a brief conclusion on topics for future research and discussion.

Background

In 2001, the United Nations established the United Nations Information and Communication Technologies Task Force, which aims at boosting global development and competence in information technology (*UNICT*, 2004). UN secretary-general Kofi Annan (2001) outlines the mission of the ICT Task Force:

The new technologies that are changing our world are not a panacea or a magic bullet. But they are, without doubt, enormously powerful tools for development. They create jobs. They are transforming education, health care, commerce, politics and more. They can help in the delivery of humanitarian assistance and even contribute to peace and security. One of the most pressing challenges in the new century is to harness this extraordinary force, spread it throughout the world, and make its benefits accessible and meaningful for all humanity, in particular the poor. The principal mission of this Task Force is to tell us how we might accomplish this ambitious goal.

As part of this initiative, the United Nations began benchmarking e-government with its first report released in 2002, entitled *UN Benchmarking E-Government: A Global Perspective*. This survey's primary purpose was to "objectively present facts and conclusions that define a country's e-government environment and demonstrate its capacity to sustain online development" (p. v). The researchers for the 2002 report (Jafar M. Jafarov of the United Nations Development Programme and several graduate research fellows from Columbia University, New York University, and Rutgers University) limited the survey's scope to a particular form of e-government, broadly defined as "utilizing the internet and the world-wide-web for delivering government information and services to citizens" (p. 1). Analyzing each member country's national Web site, data were collected and analyzed to create an E-Government Readiness Index that could serve as an annual benchmark for policy makers in order to know where their country stands in comparison to the rest of the world and to establish a reference point from which to measure future e-government progress and development.

This initial attempt to measure e-government readiness on a global scale was dramatically improved in 2003 with the *UN Global E-Government Survey 2003*. Others, too, have attempted to benchmark e-government (Graafland-Essers & Ettedgui, 2003), but none have attempted it on such a comprehensive, global basis. The refined and expanded 2003 UN survey once again assessed the 191 UN member countries based on a composite index of e-government readiness, but the index was expanded to cover ministry Web sites in addition to national home pages. Furthermore, the theory behind e-government had developed dramatically in the 1-year time span, and those developments were captured in the quantitative index as well as the theoretical model (pp. 8-17). The overall E-Government Readiness Index was developed comprising three separate, quantitative indices: the Web Readiness Index, the Telecommunications Index, and the Human-Capital Index. With this strengthened tool and approach in hand, the UN research team set forth the following survey objectives:

1. Present a snapshot of the state of comparative e-government readiness of the countries of the world

2. Provide an appraisal of the use of e-government as a tool in the delivery of services to the public in its capacity as consumer of such services

3. Provide a comparative assessment of the willingness and ability of governments to involve the public in e-participation

4. Provide a benchmarking tool for monitoring the progress of countries as they move toward higher levels of digital public-service delivery in the future (*UN Global E-Government Survey 2003*, 2003)

The 2003 UN report encompasses two different surveys—a quantitative survey of e-government readiness and a qualitative study on e-participation. Since most of the data collected involved the quantitative survey, this chapter will focus almost entirely on the E-Government Readiness Index and the UN report's findings on the quantity of information and services provided, not the qualitative analyses. However, the methodology behind the qualitative survey will also be briefly discussed later.

It is important to note that the 2003 UN report, as well as the 2002 and 2004 UN reports, considers e-government to "be the means to an end, the end being the development for all. It is considered to be a tool at the disposal of government" (*UN Global E-Government Survey*, 2003, p. 8) that can be used to effectively enhance the lives of its citizens and improve the functioning of its governance. The survey evaluates only quantitative, not qualitative, evidence of e-government capacity indexed for comparison to all other member countries. Consequently, the results should be placed in context with the country's overall development and capacity. Higher rankings might not necessarily predict better information and services since the survey does not evaluate qualitative issues involved with citizen access and usability. This is admittedly a weakness with the underlying methodology employed in the study; however, it is in line with the stated goals and purpose of the survey. This quantitative survey merely measures information and services provided without making normative or qualitative judgments as to their veracity, accessibility, or usability, or even the level of citizen usage. These are subjects for follow-up research.

The 2003 UN report was the first comprehensive quantitative examination of global e-government readiness and development, aimed at advancing e-government literature from anecdotal success stories and qualitative studies to more empirically proven, quantitative analyses. Since e-government is such a young field of scholarship and public policy, it is imperative that anecdotal and qualitative analyses are combined with quantitative data in order to empirically measure development. Success stories of best practices could be misleading if researchers are not aware of the country's overall e-readiness as compared to its neighbors and other e-government entrepreneurs. Quantitative studies add context and perspective to the traditional case studies and qualitative analysis. To that end, the United Nations embarked on the *UN Global E-Government Readiness Report 2004: Toward Access for Opportunity* (2004), which utilized roughly the same E-Government Readiness Index as the 2003 UN report, but also included a section on access for opportunity. Furthermore, not only does the 2004 UN report allow for intra- and interregional comparisons for the current year, but it also facilitates time-series analyses to measure e-government progress from 2003 to 2004. The UN research team plans to continue this ongoing analysis in 2005 and hopes to make this an ongoing, annual project.

The 2004 UN report aims at improving four e-government objectives by measuring their readiness and development and ranking member countries: "(a) efficient government management of information to the citizen; (b) better service delivery to citizens; (c) improved access and outreach of information; and (d) empowerment of the people through participatory decision making" (*UN Global E-Government Readiness Report*, 2004, p. 4). As with the 2003 UN report, the 2004 UN report aims at measuring five stages of e-government development, as set forth in the Web measure assessment model. The 2004 UN report provides a brief summary of each stage of e-government evolution:

- **Emerging Presence:** Stage I of e-government presents information that is limited and basic. The e-government online presence comprises a Web page and/or an official Web site. Links to ministries or departments of education, health, social welfare, labor, and finance may or may not exist, and links to regional or local government may or may not exist. Some archived information such as the head of states' message or a document such as a constitution may be available online, but most of the information remains static with the fewest options for citizens.

- **Enhanced Presence:** In Stage II, the government provides greater public policy and governance sources of current and archived information, such as policies, laws and regulation, reports, newsletters, and downloadable databases. The user can search for a document and there is a help feature and a site map provided. A larger selection of public-policy documents such as an e-government strategy or policy briefs on specific education and health issues are provided. Though more sophisticated, the interaction is still primarily unidirectional with information flowing essentially from government to citizen.

- **Interactive Presence:** By Stage III, the online services of the government enter the interactive mode with services to enhance the convenience of the consumer such as downloadable forms for tax payment, or applications for license renewal. Audio and video capability is provided for relevant public information. The government officials can be contacted via e-mail, fax, telephone, and post. The site is updated with greater regularity to keep the information current and up to date for the public.

- **Transactional Presence:** Stage IV allows two-way interactions between the citizen and his or her government. It includes options for paying taxes, applying for ID cards, birth certificates and passports, license renewals, and other similar C2G (citizen-to-government) interactions by allowing him or her to submit these online 24/7. The citizens are able to pay for relevant public services, such as motor-vehicle violations, taxes, and fees for postal services through their credit, bank, or debit card. Providers of goods and services are able to bid online for public contracts via secure links.

- **Networked Presence:** Stage V represents the most sophisticated level in online e-government initiatives. It can be characterized by the integration of G2G (government-to-government), G2C (government-to-citizen), and C2G interactions. The government encourages participatory deliberative decision making and is willing and able to involve the society in a two-way open dialogue. Through interactive features such as Web comment forms and innovative online consultation mechanisms, the government actively solicits citizen views on public policy, law making, and democratic participatory decision making. Implicit in this state of the model is the integration of the public-sector agencies with full cooperation and understanding of the concept of collective decision making, participatory democracy, and citizen empowerment as a democratic right (UN Global E-Government Readiness Report, 2004).

The Web measure assessment model serves as the foundation for the research methodology in both the 2003 and 2004 UN reports. As discussed previously, the survey instrument also was crafted to reflect these five stages. This research methodology will be presented in the next part, followed by a discussion of the key findings relevant to Latin America.

Methodology

In total, there were over 50,000 online information features and services evaluated in 178 countries (13 member countries do not have e-government resources) during data collection for the 2004 report (*UN Global E-Government Readiness Report*, 2004). The data collection took place from March to June 2004, with 12 researchers dedicated to country analysis. For each country, the national Web site and five ministry or department Web sites (education, finance, health, labor, and social welfare or their equivalents) were evaluated, utilizing a standard survey instrument with static questions for each country. One research associate fluent in the language used on the national home page was responsible for each country, with a supervising researcher responsible for checking each survey for regional and global consistency.[2]

The data were first entered by hand on paper surveys and then transferred to an online database for composition score calculation and comparison. Scores for each Web site were tabulated and statistically manipulated to generate the Web Measures Index, which created a benchmark for comparing countries and regions and measuring progress over time. The composite index also incorporates two other measures for each country: (a) the Telecommunications Index, which measures the ICT infrastructure capacity, and (b) the Human-Capital Index, which measures the education capacity of the country through literacy rates and primary and secondary school enrollments (*UN Global E-Government Readiness Report*, 2004). Each separate index is weighed equally in the overall composite index—the E-Government Readiness Index.

With respect to the Web measure survey, each question required a quantitative answer (e.g., a dummy variable to determine whether the site offered a particular feature and/or a quantitative variable to measure the number of features offered). In addition to quantitative prompts, one final question asks for a qualitative response: "Rate from 1 to 10 (10 being best) on how useful this site was for you as a national user." Although not incorporated into the Web Measure Index, this question helped normalize the survey responses between researchers and check for inconsistencies in data entry. Ample space for notes and comments was included on the survey instrument as well. Each stage of the Web measure assessment model was evaluated with the following questions asked for each stage.

Stage I: Emerging Presence

Stage I evaluates whether the country has a national Web site with links to regional and ministry sites. Thirteen of the 181 member nations did not have a national Web site, but the other 168 had some level of emerging presence. The questions for this section entailed the following:

1. Is there a national government home page?
2. How many cabinet-level ministry or department Web sites are linked from the national government home page only (can include substantial subsites or subsections at the national site)?
3. Are there links from the national government home page to the following?
    a. Other national, nongovernment sites
    b. Government ministries or departments
    c. Regional- or local-government Web sites
    d. Departments other than executive branches of government (e.g., parliament)

Stage I analysis was not included in the ministry Web-site evaluation since these questions apply specifically to the national government's Web presence.

Stage II: Enhanced Presence

Stage II concerns whether the country Web site provides current and archived information on law and policy, as well as basic user-friendly Web features. The questions for this section included the following:

1. Does it feature or provide links to the items that follow?
    a. Sources of archived information (e.g., laws, policy documents, etc.)
    b. Sources of current information (e.g., reports, newsletters, press)
    c. Databases (e.g., Web access to downloadable statistics)
    d. A "what is new" section (can be titled differently)
    e. Public services (true services and/or substantive service information)
2. Is a downloading feature available?
3. Is a search feature available?
4. Is a site map available?
5. Is a help feature available?
6. Is the date the site was last updated (mm/dd/yyyy) available?
7. Is there an e-government policy or statement clearly available?
8. Are there one-stop shops or "single windows" available?
    a. If yes, is it universal (i.e., central or connected to all services)?
    b. Are there other modalities available (specify focus and services, e.g., contracts, employment)?
9. Is there a separate e-government portal or section?
10. Is there any homeland-security or terrorism-related information on the home page, either as an alert or a link to such information?

Stage II was also evaluated for each ministry Web site. Question 10 on homeland security was added to the 2004 UN report due to researchers' identification of this feature as a common trend on national home pages, especially in North America and Europe.

Stage III: Interactive Presence

Stage III involves interactive presence ranging from downloadable forms to specific contact information for public officials. The questions included are as follows:

1. Can one download or print forms for any specific service?
   a. If yes, how many different types of forms are there (up to 6 or more)?
2. Can one submit online forms for any specific service?
   a. If yes, how many different types of forms can be submitted (up to 6 or more)?
3. Is the "contact us" feature available?
   a. Is the contact person's or office's name given?
   b. Is the telephone number given?
   c. Is the e-mail address given?
   d. Is the postal address given?
   e. Is the fax number given?
4. Is there audio and/or video capability?
5. Is a security (secure link) feature clearly available or indicated?
6. Is an electronic-signature feature clearly available or indicated?

Stage III questions were also answered for each ministry site, though all questions were dummy-variable prompts and not quantitative in nature.

Stage IV: Transactional Presence

Stage IV evaluates whether the country provides for opportunities for online transactions. Few Latin American countries had advanced to this level of e-government development. The following questions were put forth:

1. How many types of online transaction services exist?
2. Can the user pay online for the following?

    a. Fees for any public service

    b. Fees for penalties (e.g., motor-vehicle violations)

    c. Taxes

    d. Fees for postal services

3. Is an online payment facility available for payment by the following?

    a. Credit card

    b. Bank or debit card

    c. Bill to the user's home

4. Can providers of goods and services bid online for public contracts (e-procurement)?

Stage IV questions were also answered for each ministry site, though all questions were dummy-variable prompts, not quantitative.

Stage V: Networked Presence

Stage V represents the highest e-government development with features that facilitate two-way communication—ranging from discussion groups and online surveys to Web comments and online consultation. The questions included are as follows:

1. Is there a Web comment form?

    a. Is a response time frame indicated for submitted forms or e-mails?

2. Is there a calendar or directory of upcoming government events?

3. Is there an online poll or survey?

4. Is there a formal online consultation facility?

5. Is there an open-ended discussion forum?

6. Does the online consultation allow feedback on policies and activities?

7. Is there a direct or clear statement or policy encouraging citizen participation?

8. Does the site offer any e-mail sign-up option, either as a formal Listserv or simply for news items?

Like Stages III and IV, Stage V was included in each ministry-site survey, but the quantitative questions were converted into dummy-variable prompts. Question 8 regarding e-mail or Listserv sign-up options was added to the 2004 UN report due to the increasing presence of this important communications feature in leading e-government systems, including systems in many Latin American nations.

Qualitative Evaluation: E-Participation Measure

In addition to the analysis of the five stages based on the Web measure assessment model, an evaluation of e-participation features was also undertaken. This survey posed several questions in three general categories: e-information (providing information resources to citizens), e-consultation (engaging in consultation with citizens), and e-decision-making (offering consideration of citizen input). Unlike the previous evaluations, this survey was qualitative in nature with researchers ranking each question from 1 to 5 (*never* to *always*). These responses were not calculated into the E-Government Readiness Index, but used for other analyses. Conversely, the quantitative scores for each of the five stages were incorporated into an overall country composite score and indexed out of the highest score of 1.0. The intra- and interregional findings for Latin America will be presented in the following part.

Findings and Discussion

Since the same E-Government Readiness Index was used in both 2003 and 2004, time-series comparisons, as well as intra- and interregional comparisons, can be drawn from the data set. For the purposes of this chapter, the findings of the 2003 and 2004 UN reports will be divided into four main subparts: (a) interregional comparisons of Latin American countries vs. the rest of the world regions, (b) intraregional comparisons of Latin American countries in 2003 and 2004, (c) common features and best practices of high-performing Latin American countries, and (d) a brief discussion on e-participation in Latin America.

Interregional Analysis: Latin America Lags Behind North America and Europe

Latin America, as a region, fares relatively well in comparison to the rest of the world, but does not host any of the top e-government performers. In the global e-government rankings for 2003, Latin America did not place among the top 20, with Chile scoring the highest in 22nd place (*UN Global E-Government Survey 2003*, 2003). Mexico (30th), Argentina (31st), Brazil (41st), and Uruguay (47th) were also identified within the top 50 countries surveyed. Overall, with an e-government readiness score of 0.442, Latin America ranked third among world regions, behind North America (0.867; for UN purposes, North America comprised only the United States and Canada) and Europe (0.558), but ahead of South and Eastern Asia (0.437), Western Asia (0.410), the Caribbean (0.401), Oceania (0.351), South Central Asia (0.292), and Africa (0.246).

Similarly, the 2004 e-government readiness rankings reinforce the finding that the Latin America region as a whole compares well with the rest of the world, but that no individual country places among the top 20 in e-government readiness. Once again, Chile is the Latin American front-runner at 22nd place in the world (*UN Global E-Government Readiness Report 2004*, 2004), with the four other regional leaders also among the top 50 countries: Mexico (30th), Argentina (32nd), Brazil (35th), and Uruguay (40th). Additionally, Colombia drastically improved to enter into the top 50 at 44th place. As a region, however, Latin America in 2004 (0.4558) slipped from third to fourth, behind North America (0.8751), Europe (0.5866), and South and Eastern Asia (0.4603).

While the regional ranking dropped, the overall regional score increased by 3.80% (0.0138), from 0.4420 to 0.4558. Clearly, this regional score is also above the world average (0.4127). Furthermore, of the 20 Latin American countries surveyed, only 8 countries ranked below the world average: El Salvador (0.4034), Ecuador (0.3924), Bolivia (0.3863), Suriname (0.3474), Paraguay (0.3408), Guatemala (0.3391), Honduras (0.3301), and Nicaragua (0.3216). (Note that Paraguay's E-Government Readiness Index score dropped dramatically from the 2003 level because much of the e-government infrastructure was off line for reconstruction during the 3-month evaluation period in 2004. If its Web site would have been fully functional as in 2003, Paraguay would have ranked far above the world average.) While Latin America has much to learn from the rest of the world with respect to e-government, it

Table 1. E-government vs. Web measure indices (2004)

Country	Readiness Index Score (World Ranking)	Web Measure Index Score (World Ranking)	Ranking Difference (Web:Readiness)
Chile	0.6835 (22)	0.884 (6)	16
Mexico	0.5957 (30)	0.784 (11)	19
Argentina	0.5871 (32)	0.643 (22)	10
Brazil	0.5675 (35)	0.637 (14)	21
Uruguay	0.5481 (40)	0.483 (48)	-8
Colombia	0.5335 (44)	0.641 (23)	21
Peru	0.5015 (53)	0.517 (41)	12
Panama	0.4907 (54)	0.523 (40)	14
Venezuela	0.4898 (56)	0.517 (42)	14
Guyana	0.4243 (71)	0.208 (103)	-32
Costa Rica	0.4188 (73)	0.174 (113)	-40
Belize	0.415 (76)	0.216 (98)	-22
El Salvador	0.4034 (79)	0.394 (57)	22
Ecuador	0.3924 (82)	0.243 (87)	-5
Bolivia	0.3863 (88)	0.255 (84)	4
Suriname	0.3474 (105)	0.05 (161)	-56
Paraguay	0.3408 (109)	0.108 (138)	-29
Guatemala	0.3391 (111)	0.317 (72)	39
Honduras	0.3301 (113)	0.243 (88)	25
Nicaragua	0.3216 (121)	0.274 (80)	41
Average:	*0.4558 (69.7)*	*0.4055 (66.4)*	*3.30*

is not far behind the world leaders as a whole. As will be discussed in the subsequent subparts, Latin America has many high-performing countries that demonstrate best practices, and the region as a whole appears to be advancing in both e-government capacity and willingness.

Before making interregional comparisons, it should be noted that the E-Government Readiness Index incorporates the scores from the Web Measure Index—the bulk of our research and analysis—with the Telecommunications Index and the Human-Capital Index. When the Web Measure Index is considered separately, the Latin American rankings are even more impressive. Table 1 outlines the differences between these rankings for 2004.

On average, Latin American countries rank roughly three places (3.30) higher in the world rankings under the Web Measure Index than the E-Government Readiness Index. This disparity in rankings reflects a general theme in the region: That Latin American countries have the Web-site research and development in place, but they often do not have the capacity and resources to ensure broad Internet access for their populations. The 2004 UN report summarizes these ranking differences with respect to Latin America.

However, the fact that some of these South and Central American countries do not qualify for the overall E-Government Readiness Index shows that despite considerable improvements in expanding and consolidating their e-government portals, the effective outreach and access eludes the majority of the populations. With limited human and technological infrastructure support, many countries that invest in e-government tend to lose out in the set of world comparative rankings when assessed for overall e-readiness.

This points to an important lesson in e-government and ICT for development planning. Whereas it is important to focus on improving access to service delivery, e-government programs must be placed in, and run concurrently with, an integrated framework aimed at improving infrastructure and educational skills. Countries may lose out on overall e-government readiness and their development goal of achieving access to all if the progress is not evenly balanced. For example, Mexico, which ranked 11th among the top 25 in assessment of its e-government program alone, was ranked 30th when ranked by the composite E-Government Readiness Index (*UN Global E-Government Readiness Report 2004*, 2004)

Table 1 illustrates similar trends for other regional countries. While Latin America is advancing on pace with respect to Web measures, the region has significant ground to make up in terms of providing more comprehensive Internet access to its citizens.

Intraregional Analysis: First- and Second-Tier Divide in Latin America

In addition to the disparity between the E-Government Readiness and Web Measure Indices in Latin America, there also exists a great chasm between the top 9 countries and the bottom 11. As Table 2 illustrates, the first-tier Latin American countries all rank within the top 60 globally, while the second-tier countries rank outside the top 70. The difference between the lowest ranking first-tier country, Venezuela (0.4898, 56th), and the highest ranking second-tier country, Guyana (0.4243, 71st), is .0655. In other words, Venezuela scores 15.4% higher than Guyana and ranks 15 places higher than any second-tier country. Furthermore, all six countries that lost ground in the index scores are found among the second-tier countries. Table 2 outlines this disparity in greater detail. Countries that lost ground in index scores are in bold.

Table 2. E-Government Readiness index scores (2003-2004)

	Country	2004 Index Score (World Ranking)	2003 Index Score (World Ranking)	Index Change (Ranking Change)
1 S T	Chile	0.6835 (22)	0.671 (22)	0.0123 (0)
	Mexico	0.5957 (30)	0.593 (30)	0.003 (0)
	Argentina	0.5871 (32)	0.577 (31)	0.01 (-1)
	Brazil	0.5675 (35)	0.527 (41)	0.041 (+6)
T I E R	Uruguay	0.5481 (40)	0.507 (47)	0.041 (+7)
	Colombia	0.5335 (44)	0.443 (57)	0.091 (+13)
	Peru	0.5015 (53)	0.463 (53)	0.038 (0)
	Panama	0.4907 (54)	0.434 (62)	0.057 (+8)
	Venezuela	0.4898 (56)	0.364 (93)	0.126 (+37)
2 N D	Guyana	0.4243 (71)	0.422 (72)	0.002 (1)
	Costa Rica	**0.4188 (73)**	**0.427 (66)**	**-0.008 (-7)**
	Belize	**0.415 (76)**	**0.422 (71)**	**-0.007 (-5)**
	El Salvador	**0.4034 (79)**	**0.409 (80)**	**-0.006 (1)**
	Ecuador	0.3924 (82)	0.378 (85)	0.014 (3)
	Bolivia	**0.3863 (88)**	**0.411 (78)**	**-0.025 (-10)**
T I E R	Suriname	0.3474 (105)	n/a	n/a
	Paraguay	**0.3408 (109)**	**0.413 (75)**	**-0.072 (-34)**
	Guatemala	0.3391 (111)	0.329 (109)	0.010 (-2)
	Honduras	0.3301 (113)	0.28 (124)	0.050 (11)
	Nicaragua	**0.3216 (121)**	**0.324 (112)**	**-0.002 (-9)**
	Average:	*0.4558 (70)*	*0.442 (69)*	*0.0138 (+1)*

As Table 2 indicates, the top nine or first-tier countries were actually only eight in 2003. The 2004 UN report indicates why Venezuela made the leap from the second- to first-tier status:

In South and Central America, the greatest improvement was made by Venezuela (0.489) in the past year, which was reflected in the jump from 93rd position in 2003 to 56th in 2004. A new national Web portal was established in 2004 (http://www.gobiernoenlinea.ve). A strong commitment to education is reflected in vast improvements in its educational online services (http://www.me.gov.ve), which now rival those in the top 20 in the world. In addition to basic information, the government offers interactive features such as user registration capability, a poll and open discussion forum, and a clear statement and policy encouraging public participation in education policy and development (*UN Global E-Government Readiness Report 2004*, 2004; errors in original).

The Venezuelan success story presents hope to other second-tier countries in Latin America such as Guyana (0.4243, 71st), Costa Rica (0.4188, 73rd),

Belize (0.415, 76th), El Salvador (0.4034, 79th), Ecuador (0.3924, 82nd), and Bolivia (0.3863, 88th) who all rank higher than Venezuela did in 2003 (0.364, 93rd). These countries are all within striking distance of first-tier status, and only minor adjustments appear to be needed in order to break the top-70 rankings.

In addition to Venezuela's improvement, Colombia experienced dramatic improvement, rising 13 ranks from 57th in 2003 (0.5335) to 44th (0.443) in 2004. Conversely, Paraguay's 2004 performance (0.3408, 109th) dropped dramatically from the 2003 level (0.413, 75th). However, much of Paraguay's e-government infrastructure was offline for reconstruction during the 3-month evaluation period in 2004. If the national home page would have been fully functional as it was in 2003, Paraguay would have remained within the top 80 in the world rankings.

The Latin American Front-Runners: Common Features and Best Practices

While vast differences exist between the first- and second-tier e-government countries in Latin America, an interesting phenomenon is developing among the first-tier countries: Their e-government development reveals many common features and trends. In fact, by analyzing the advancement in these countries from 2003 to 2004, it becomes clear that these first-tier countries have borrowed each other's best practices and have built upon proven methods in Latin America. They may also be borrowing from outside the region, observing long-standing leaders (long standing at least within the context of e-government, which is still just in its infancy) such as the United Kingdom, the United States, Canada, and others. Following the lead of nations outside the region without planning for the cultural, political, and institutional nuances of the various Latin American countries can result in a successful technical implementation that nevertheless is a failure or less than successful in its applied practice.

These e-government trends, a number of which will be outlined below, are noteworthy for a variety of reasons, not the least of which is that they highlight some of the very changes that governments may or may not go through in the face of the current information revolution. As Nye (2002, p. 11) points out, "the effects on central governments of the third information revolution are still in their early stages." For Latin America and its history of strong central governments, these impacts may be profound. It remains to be seen how this historical institutional model in Latin America will affect the strategic development and implementation of e-government in the region. The top-down, strong national government model can, for instance, lead to both positive and potentially negative outcomes regarding e-government. In a general sense, the e-government leaders in Latin America have gotten where they are today partially because of strong national government support and planning for e-government. This is clearly a positive, and to the extent that this type of top-down planning and implementation leads to the rapid spread and take-up of valuable e-government services at the local level, it will prove to be highly effective (note that the UN report does not cover local e-government activities other than as sidebars to the main study).

Four of the more important and telling e-government trends—citizen portals, online services and transactions, e-mail sign-up and user registration, and user-friendly, citizen-centered information—will be explored in greater detail below. Several case studies of best practices in particular countries are also presented.

Citizen Portals and One-Stop Shopping

One of the most predominant common practices among first-tier countries in Latin America involves the implementation of various one-stop-shopping features. This emerging trend aims at making e-government resources more easily accessible with all important citizen-focused information and services centralized at one site. These citizen portals collect services from various government sites and consolidate them on one page. It is clear that the development of these citizen portals is extremely important for making e-government more accessible and user friendly to citizens. The following four case studies, each exemplifying a different approach to citizen portals, stand out as particularly noteworthy.

Determining What the Citizen Wants: Chile's *Gobiernochile* (http://www. gobiernodechile.cl)

In 2003, Chile was identified as having one of the most advanced citizen portals in the world. Chile's national home page is specifically directed to its citizens—as opposed to some countries that focus on foreign visitors—and, as such, the government has placed easy access links on the front page. For instance, the Web site provides up-to-the-minute information on the president's schedule, as well as current news on what the government is doing. In addition to easy-to-access information, the front page provides a link to all online transactions and services, regional-government Web sites, and laws relevant to marriage, consumer safety, and civil and criminal defense. Perhaps the most effective feature of the Chilean Web site is that the government has made decisions about which information and services are most important and has included that information on the front page. Instead of overwhelming the user with countless options, it focuses on those that are most important to the citizen (*Gobiernodechile.cl*, 2004).

Comprehensive Services and Information for the Citizen: Argentina's *Gobiernoelectronico* (http://www.gobiernoelectronico.ar)

In contrast to Chile's national home page, Argentina offers a more comprehensive one-stop-shopping approach with numerous links to various information sources and online services. The Argentine government does not appear to tailor the information to that which is of greatest priority to the citizen, but instead, it groups the information into several clear categories. For instance, the services and information provided by the three branches of government are listed by icons at the top of the Web page, while the local-government divisions are listed on the left column of the Web page. General transactions and services options are listed by category in the center of the Web page, and additional links to national newspapers, weather outlets, tourism centers, and so forth are listed in the right column. Current news, legislation, and policy options are also listed in a separate box at the bottom of the page. The Argentine approach to one-stop shopping is in stark contrast to the Chilean model in that Argentina attempts to list all resources. Chile prioritizes and tailors its one-stop shopping to the most pertinent information and services. Both are effective because they are clearly organized and user friendly (*Gobiernoelectrónico.ar*, 2004).

Providing All but Focusing on a Few Key Citizen Services—A Hybrid Approach: Brazil's *E.Gov* (http://www.e.gov.br)

Brazil's one-stop shopping is perhaps the most effective in Latin America because it combines the Argentine and Chilean approaches. Similar to the Chilean model, the Brazilian Web site provides the most pertinent information and services, situated in the center of the Web page as well as the right-hand column. However, like the Argentine approach, the Brazilian Web site includes all information and services in the left-hand column, categorized by ministry and/or department. The most effective best practice is found at the top of the Web page: The Brazilian Web site includes 13 images with subtitles that represent the most desired citizen services, ranging from tax payment and health services to legislation information and utilities. The image logos make the site particularly user friendly (*Portal de Serviços e Informações de Governo*, 2004).

Transactions Only: Mexico's *Tramitanet* (http://www.tramitanet.gob.mx)

Mexico's approach to one-stop shopping is very different from the other three case studies since it is limited to transactions and services, not information. The front page divides services and transactions by two distinctions: electronic vs. nonelectronic transactions, and services for citizens vs. those for businesses. By clicking on one of the four boxes, the citizen is directed to all of the services within the category. For instance, the electronic-services option lists all services that the government provides online, while the business-services box lists all electronic and nonelectronic services for businesses. These divisions help the citizen narrow down the information and interact with the government in an efficient manner (*Tramitanet*, 2004).

Online Services and Transaction Options

Related to the trend toward providing integrated citizen portals, another noteworthy trend in Latin America is the move to providing true online services and transactions. The number and variety of online services and transaction options increased exponentially in Latin America from 2003 to 2004, with the first-tier countries leading the way. One of the distinguishing features between first- and second-tier countries concerns whether extensive services and online transaction options are available. Second-tier Web sites are primarily information centers with limited, if any, online services and transaction opportunities, while first-tier countries all seem to be moving government services online. The following four case studies illustrate the depth and breadth of services provided online in Latin America.

E-Procurement at Its Best: Brazil's *Comprasnet* (http://www.comprasnet. gov.br)

The Brazilian government provides an e-procurement Web site for government contracts for goods and services. *Comprasnet* provides information on relevant legislation and current news on the economic development of the country. More importantly, it provides an online bidding site for government contracts, as well as links to services for new and emerging businesses in Brazil. To use the online services, the Web site installs specific software for the user's computer and allows for online registration of potential government contractors (*Comprasnet*, 2004).

National Online Employment Database: Chile's *InfoEmpleo* (http://www. infoempleo.cl)

With *InfoEmpleo*, Chile facilitates an online national employment database to help citizen employees find jobs and private employers fill employment slots—the only such government-sponsored online employment network found in Latin America. The front page divides services into two main categories: (a) those for employers to post job openings, and (b) those for workers to find jobs for which they qualify. Employers can also scan the postings of potential employees. The government service is free and easy to use, and registration is required. Additionally, the front page lists those jobs that are most sought after, as well as provides links to private employment Web sites and other useful resources (*InfoEmpleo*, 2004).

Education Online: Venezuela's Education Ministry Web Site (http://www. me.gov.ve)

The top nine Latin American countries have all developed extensive education-ministry Web sites. Venezuela, for example, offers an education-ministry Web site that includes over 30 online education-related transactions and services, as well as citizen surveys and user registration capability for additional services. Services include payment for continuing-education courses, teacher licensing and credentialing, and information for other legal documents related to education. The Web site also allows users to customize the Web site through online registration that entitles users to access additional services and information. The front page is extremely user friendly and includes up-to-date news, a searchable events calendar, and an easy-to-use directory of services and information in the left-hand column (*Website of Ministerio de Educación y Deportes*, 2004).

Mexico's Multi-Pronged Approach: *Tramitanet, eMexico, and Foros*

Mexico provides a multifaceted approach to online services and transactions. First, as explained in a previous case study, *Tramitanet* (http://www.tramitanet.gob.mx) is a one-stop-shopping citizen portal with services for both citizens and businesses. Second, *eMexico* (http://www.e-mexico.gob.mx) is an extensive e-government site with online information and services categorized into 10 "communities." Users are asked to click on the image that corresponds to their community, for example, women, immigrants, senior citizens, business owners, and students, and the relevant online services and information are presented. The Web site also lists the most commonly requested services for each community. Last, *Foros* (http://www.foros.gob.mx) provides a networking presence for citizen discussion groups on national law and policy. Discussions and postings are divided by topics, as well as by specific legislation, and all registered citizens can post messages to be read by other citizens and the government. The Web site appears to be used extensively as over 100,000 messages have been posted this year. In summary, Mexico's triple combination of online services and transactions provide citizens with easy-to-use methods to interact with government to address needs, comment on policy, and find pertinent information (*eMexico*, 2004; *Tramitanet*, 2004; *Website of Presidencia de la República: Foros*, 2004).

These case studies constitute just a few examples of the extensive online services and transaction opportunities being developed by first-tier Latin American countries. The 2003 and 2004 snapshot views indicate that these first-tier countries are constantly and rapidly developing additional online services to meet citizen needs. Conversely, the second-tier countries are lagging behind and focus on providing information.

E-Mail Listserv and User Registration Options

Two related personalization features are being developed among the first-tier Latin American e-government pioneers: e-mail Listserv options for up-to-date news and information, and user registration options for additional services, including e-mail accounts, discussion-group access, and so forth. The Chilean government's Web site, for example, provides citizens with the option to subscribe to daily, weekly, and/or monthly e-mail updates (*Gobiernodechile.cl*, 2004). Similarly, at the *eMexico* Web site, the Mexican government provides citizens a range of online user registration features to obtain a national e-mail account and access citizen discussion groups (*eMexico*, 2004).

Importantly, these services allow citizens to participate more fully in the democratic decision-making process by having current information on government practices and by allowing users to express their views to government with other citizens. In 2003, UN researchers did not find these options among most national home pages; however, 1 year later, they were prevalent in most, if not all, first-tier countries in Latin America. The emergence of these services merits further research and discussion to more fully understand their effect on e-government and e-participation.

Overall Citizen-Oriented, User-Friendly Services and Information

Finally, one of the most significant advancements in Latin American e-government concerns the first-tier countries' emphasis on simple and effective information displays and online services. While this trend is much more nuanced then the other trends involving tangible online features, services, and information, overall ease of use and access to information are the ideal for all online services and information.

As the 2004 UN report notes with Chile, first-tier national home pages in Latin America provide citizens with important information and direct access to online services (*Gobiernodechile.cl*, 2004; *UN Global E-Government Readiness Report 2004*, 2004). They also typically provide an up-to-date calendar of important events and direct links to the Web sites of national ministries and regional governments. First-tier performers all seem to have keyed in on this common feature of providing user-friendly, citizen-oriented Web sites that allow citizens to easily access critical information and online services. Simplicity and readability appear to be key objectives in Latin American e-government development.

These four key e-government features, shared in various ways by the leading e-government Web sites, illustrate the growing trend among Latin American e-government entrepreneurs: Top-performing countries are imitating, and perhaps learning from, the best practices of their neighbors, as well as the best practices of other world leaders in e-government. As the 2003 and 2004 UN reports indicate, these countries are not developing in a bubble, but instead, are observing the advancement made by other countries and adapting other countries' unique developments into their own e-government infrastructures. The significance of this practice of sharing and borrowing ideas, apparently done at this stage by primarily informal channels, merits further research and discussion.

E-Participation: The Qualitative Assessment

While the e-government readiness analysis was purely a quantitative study,
the 2004 UN report also included a qualitative study on e-participation. Outside of the UN nomenclature, e-participation is often called e-democracy and
attempts to determine the extent to which e-government tools and features
"are conducive to an online deliberative and participatory process between
the government and citizen" (*UN Global E-Government Readiness Report
2004*, 2004, p. 65). E-participation, at its core, is about breaking down barriers to the public sphere, an important governance, community, and political concept being tackled by numerous thinkers and researchers (Jenkins &
Thorburn, 2003). Initial research on Latin America left the impression that
e-participation is extremely underdeveloped in the region. However, this may
be a relative strength in comparison to the rest of the world. Table 3 reports
the e-participation scores and world rankings.

The average world e-participation ranking for Latin American countries
is almost 60 (58.75), which is over 10 rank places better than the average
world e-government readiness ranking for Latin American countries in 2004
(69.7). This also bests the region's average Web Measure Index score in 2004

Table 3. E-participation rankings (2004)

Country	Index Score	World Ranking
Mexico	0.7705	6
Colombia	0.623	12
Chile	0.6066	14
Panama	0.2787	28
Venezuela	0.2787	28
Honduras	0.2623	32
Argentina	0.2459	35
Brazil	0.2459	35
El Salvador	0.2459	35
Peru	0.2131	41
Bolivia	0.1475	53
Nicaragua	0.0984	66
Costa Rica	0.0656	75
Guatemala	0.0656	75
Uruguay	0.0656	75
Ecuador	0.0492	84
Guyana	0.0492	84
Belize	0.0164	123
Paraguay	0.0164	123
Suriname	0	151
Average:	*0.22*	*58.75*

(66.4). These findings raise additional questions for research and discussion. Can these quantitative e-government studies be effectively compared to the qualitative e-participation survey? Are the e-participation world rankings skewed due to global inadequacy in e-participation development? What is the correlation between e-government and e-participation development? How can surveys be better developed to more precisely measure e-participation in both quantitative and qualitative means? Further research and discussion are required to produce satisfactory answers to these questions.

Conclusion

This chapter on the United Nations global e-government readiness reports of 2003 and 2004 indicates where Latin America is in relation to the rest of the world; namely, as a whole, Latin America is among the strongest regions in the world and shows significant year-over-year progress. Chile, Mexico, Argentina, Brazil, Uruguay, and Colombia all rank among the top 50 countries with respect to e-government readiness. However, no individual Latin American country ranks among the top 20 in the E-Government Readiness Index, though several do appear in the top tiers of the Web Measure Index and E-Participation Index. These findings reflect the disparity between a well-developed e-government infrastructure and the lack of access for opportunity for these countries' general populations. In other words, while Latin American countries might have created effective Web systems and strategies, citizens cannot easily use them because the population lacks broad access to the Internet.

Furthermore, there exists a great dichotomy between the region's first-tier e-government countries (Chile, Mexico, Argentina, Brazil, Uruguay, Colombia, Peru, Panama, and Venezuela) and the second-tier group (Guyana, Costa Rica, Belize, El Salvador, Ecuador, Bolivia, Suriname, Paraguay, Guatemala, Honduras, and Nicaragua). The first-tier countries share several common features, including one-stop-shopping citizen portals, citizen-friendly online services and information, ample online services and transaction options, and e-mail, Listserv, and user registration options. Based on the results from 2003 and 2004, it appears that these first-tier countries share and borrow best practices. Additionally, the Venezuelan case study demonstrates that many of the second-tier countries could jump into the first tier by making minor adjustments and refinements to their e-government infrastructure.

Now that the UN report has established where Latin America currently stands in its development of e-government services, the question becomes, what lies ahead? Additionally, what should the region earmark as top priorities for further development? The findings of the 2004 UN report outline three specific priorities for future development of e-government on a global scale:

- **Governments Need to Adopt Access for Opportunity as a Policy Goal:** This objective is extremely important in Latin America, where there is a large gap between Web development and citizen access to the Internet. Until the general population has broader access to e-government resources, Latin American countries will struggle to develop and effectively utilize online government resources.

- **Governments Need to Focus on Knowledge Societies:** This UN objective focuses on governments sharing ideas so as not to have to reinvent the wheel. As discovered by comparing the 2003 and 2004 UN reports, Latin American countries appear to often share and/or borrow best practices; however, this collaborative process could be further formalized and developed in order to create a more fluid exchange of ideas, technology, and proven methods.

- **Governments Need to Include ICTs in All Planning Initiatives:** This UN objective is also being realized in Latin America, at least within the first-tier countries, in that these countries are constantly and rapidly increasing the variety and quantity of services and information provided online. Nevertheless, Latin American countries should make a deliberate effort to integrate all government ministries and functions online. The creation of information-technology departments and an official e-government policy would greatly assist this effort (*UN Global E-Government Readiness Report 2004*, 2004).

The 2004 UN report also emphasizes the need to develop a legal framework to deal with e-government, as well as education programming to train new public servants on how to use the applicable e-government infrastructure.

In addition to the 2004 UN report conclusions, the findings of this chapter suggest three additional priorities with specific applicability to Latin America. These recommendations are of primary importance to the advancement of the region as a whole:

- **Latin America Needs to Bridge the Gap Between First- and Second-Tier Countries:** As discussed earlier, there exists a great divide in development between the top 9 countries and the bottom 11. Since 2003, Venezuela crossed this divide into the top-tier group, and a half dozen other second-tier countries could also make that leap in 2005 by refining and revamping their e-government infrastructure. To achieve this end, these second-tier countries need to borrow best practices from the first-tier performers, and perhaps a formal collaborative effort would be the best approach to sharing ideas and building the region as a whole.

- **Latin America Needs to Embark on Stage V by Creating a Networked Presence:** The top-tier e-government countries in Latin America have all entered to some extent into Stage IV of the Web measure assessment model in that they have begun to not only offer basic online services, but also to facilitate online transactions, whether that be tax payments, e-procurement, or other citizen-to-government contracting or transacting. However, few countries have entered Stage V, which involves creating a networked presence with two-way communication between citizens and government. Latin American countries should look to establish these networks through formal online consultation facilities, Web comment forms, and direct e-access to government officials. This is the region's new frontier.

- **Latin American Nations Should Institutionalize Regional E-Government Best-Practices Sharing and Implementation:** It is clear that the top-tier e-government countries in Latin America have spent significant time and resources on implementing useful e-government systems and features. It is also apparent that at some level, the leaders are learning from each other, either by sharing information and practices, or simply by emulating and refining the successful practices of their neighbors. This kind of regional best-practices sharing and implementation can and should be institutionalized in Latin America.

By bridging the gap between the top and bottom countries in Latin America, by pioneering into Stage V of online presence, and by institutionalizing regional e-government best-practices sharing and implementation, Latin America could emerge as a leading region in e-government worldwide. More importantly, citizens will have better access to critical information and government services, and governments will cut costs by moving transactions and services online, thus helping to shape the very face of Latin American culture in the digital era, notwithstanding the cultural assumptions and trends that shape the way Latin Americans will ultimately use e-government technology (Galston, 2002). In any case, these priorities as outlined above seem paramount for future development in the region.

A postscript to this chapter must be included. Besides analyzing the current state of Latin American e-government through the UN report and outlining key priorities for future development in the region, this chapter also underscores the importance of quantitative comparative studies. In this young field of e-government, anecdotal case studies and qualitative analyses alone are insufficient to capture the meaning and substance of e-government development; quantitative studies are needed to place the case studies in context and to offer a broader vision of the current state of e-government development. This contextual background engenders a more accurate perspective of how individual success stories and failures correspond with the growing trends of development.

References

The 2002 e-readiness rankings: A white paper from the Economist Intelligence Unit. (2002). New York: The Economist Intelligence Unit.

Accenture. (2002). *Egovernment leadership: Engaging the customer.* New York: Author.

Accenture. (2003). *Egovernment leadership: Realizing the vision.* New York: Author.

Annan, K. (2001). *UN press release.* United Nations. Retrieved December 24, 2004, from http://www.unicttaskforce.org/welcome/

Comprasnet. (2004). Retrieved November 15, 2004, from http://www.com-prasnet.gov.br

Curtin, G. G., Sommer, M. H., & Vis-Sommer, V. (Eds.). (2003). *The world of e-government.* New York: Haworth.

eMexico. (2004). Retrieved November 15, 2004, from http://www.e-mexico.gob.mx

Galston, W. A. (2002). The impact of the Internet on civic life: An early assessment. In E. C. Kamarck & J. S. J. Nye (Eds.), *Governance.com: Democracy in the information age.* Washington, DC: Brookings Institution Press.

Gobiernodechile.cl. (2004). Retrieved December 12, 2004, from http://www.gobiernodechile.cl

Gobiernoelectrónico.ar. (2004). Retrieved December 15, 2004, from http://www.gobiernoelectronico.ar

Graafland-Essers, I., & Ettedgui, E. (2003). *Benchmarking e-government in Europe and the U.S.* Santa Monica, CA: RAND.

InfoEmpleo. (2004). Retrieved from November 15, 2004, from http://www.infoempleo.cl

International City-County Management Association (ICMA). (2002). *Electronic government 2002.* Washington, DC: Author. Retrieved May 15, 2005, from http://www.icma.org

Jenkins, H., & Thorburn, D. (2003). Introduction: The digital revolution, the informed citizen, and the culture of democracy. In H. Jenkins & D. Thorburn (Eds.), *Democracy and new media.* Cambridge, MA: MIT Press.

Jupp, V. (2003). Realizing the vision of e-government. In G. Curtin, M. Sommer, & V. Vis-Sommer (Eds.), *The world of e-government.* New York: Haworth.

Nye, J. S. J. (2002). Information technology and democratic governance. In E. C. Kamarck & J. S. J. Nye (Eds.), *Governance.com: Democracy in the information age.* Washington, DC: Brookings Institution Press.

Portal de serviços e informações de governo. (2004). Retrieved December 27, 2004, from http://www.e.gov.br

Siew, L., & Leng, L. Y. (2003). E-government in action: Singapore case study. In G. Curtin, M. Sommer, & V. Vis-Sommer (Eds.), *The world of e-government.* New York: Haworth.

Tramitanet. (2004). Retrieved December 27, 2004, from http://www.tramitanet.gob.mx

UN benchmarking e-government: A global perspective. (2002). New York: United Nations. Retrieved December 27, 2004, from http://egovaspac.apdip.net/resources/readiness/undpepa-aspa2001.pdf

UN global e-government readiness report 2004: Toward access for opportunity. (2004). New York: United Nations. Retrieved December 27, 2004, from http://www.unpan.org/egovernment4.asp

UN global e-government survey 2003. (2003). New York: United Nations. Retrieved December 27, 2004, from http://www.unpan.org/egovernment3. asp

UNICT. (2004). Information & Communications Technologies (ICT) Task Force. Retrieved December 22, 2004, from http://www.unicttaskforce.org/index. html

Website of Ministerio de Educación y Deportes. (2004). Venezuelan Education Ministry. Retrieved November 15, 2004, from http://www.me.gov.ve

Website of Presidencia de la República: Foros. (2004). Retrieved November 15, 2004, from http://www.foros.gob.mx

West, D. M. (2002). *Urban e-government 2002.* Providence, RI: Taubman Center for Public Policy.

West, D. M. (2003). *Urban e-government 2003.* Providence, RI: Taubman Center for Public Policy.

Endnotes

[1] The United Nations published these reports in print and online format, which can be accessed and downloaded free of charge from the United Nations Online Network in Public Administration and Finance. *UN Global E-Government Survey 2003* is available at http://www.unpan.org/egovernment3. asp, and *UN Global E-Government Readiness Report 2004: Toward Access for Opportunity* is available at http://www.unpan.org/egovernment4.asp.

[2] One of the authors (Christopher J. Walker) was responsible for surveying all countries in Latin America for both the 2003 and 2004 UN reports and possesses advanced fluency in Spanish and Portuguese. The other author (Gregory C. Curtin), in addition to serving as the principal investigator for the project, served as the supervising researcher over Latin America to ensure regional and global consistency.

Chapter VII

Tracking E-Government in South America:
Origin and Impact of E-Government Strategies in Argentina, Chile, and Uruguay[1]

María Frick, Argentina

Abstract

The existing disparity regarding the achievements of electronic-government development in the Southern Cone area is owed to implementation processes characterized by the coexistence of organizational isomorphism patterns along with each country's own institutional framework. Insofar as electronic government was developed within the public administration's modernization processes, and that said processes were financed almost entirely by international credit institutions, there is a similarity among the different strategies implemented; the same responds to a middle-level policy transfer process. However, institutional environments have exerted a decisive influence on the effective implementation of the original schemes, thus determining significant differences regarding the impacts of each policy. This chapter develops this perspective, understanding that acknowledgement of this path covered may contribute to adapting strategies to the frameworks in which they have been introduced, thus fostering amortization of resources invested, survival of initiatives, and use of electronic-government benefits in the construction of an efficient and transparent public administration open to citizens.

Introduction

Initially, a technological aura surrounded electronic government and seemed to isolate it from the characteristics and influences of every state policy. However, despite the initial enthusiasm, its development has eroded the mere technological expectations, thus revealing its similarities with all public policies. Electronic government is a complex and multidisciplinary phenomenon whose benefits depend on major political, technical, and administrative efforts and understandings.

In Latin America, national e-government policies have already been implemented, and it is possible to observe the results of these features.

Upon an initial analysis, we observe the existence of projects within the region with significant results in administration transparency and efficiency. These initiatives reveal the innovation capacity of certain public organizations as well as the real benefits of the use of new technologies in state administration.[2] However, a thorough analysis reveals that at the domestic policy level, these cases are organized within the region in a pattern of similarities and differences that form an unequal development map regarding results attained.

Despite the existing multiplicity as regards each country's own features, the region accounts for homogeneous characteristics regarding the strategies implemented at the domestic level. In the Southern Cone especially, electronic-government strategies exhibit technical-formal similarities in relation to administration goals, contents, and management methods. There are similarities that coexist with each country's institutional framework, thus determining that, beyond the existence of isolated successful projects, we may observe that the capacities and impacts of each policy are significantly different.

In this sense, there are clear traces of complex political, technical, and administrative processes as regards the adaptation of the new technological proposal of a virtual government. Therefore, this chapter aims at analysing this network of electronic-government implementation projects at the national level in Argentina, Chile, and Uruguay. Specifically, it shall explore the origins of their implementation features and the possible paths leading to adaptation among original administrative patterns and those effectively under implementation along with the results obtained according to each macropolitical environment.

Thus, we shall divide the presentation into two parts, pursuant to two hypotheses. The first one states that there is a homogeneity pattern regarding e-government strategies within the Southern Cone, resulting from an original matrix and conditioning aspects shared by the countries of the region within the framework of state reform and modernization processes. The second hypothesis establishes that the effective implementation of these strategies as well as of the results obtained by them is determined, eventually, by the institutional characteristics of each environment.

Following a brief introduction of neo-institutionalism possibilities as a theoretical context for this analysis, we shall thus describe e-government emergence and spreading within the South American agenda and the similarities of policies implemented regarding their formal-structural outline. This analysis is conducted from the perspective of institutional isomorphism and policy transfer. The same states that the existence of similarities is owed to shared framework conditions and forces. Then we shall analyse the possible incidence of institutional frameworks and governability structures in the performance of these outlines. This exploration is developed through the notions of state capacity and embedded autonomy. The same, as from their characteristics at the intermediation level—corporate agreements, policy networks, and party structures—explain the existing differences among the various countries vis-à-vis common challenges.

Insofar as the inexistence of specific indicators prevents the conduction of a more in-depth analysis, this chapter's nature is confined to exploratory research. Theoretically speaking, the aim of this chapter is limited specifically to the description of phenomena that are common to political science and that repeat themselves over again within the new public-administration arena. From a practical perspective, this chapter aims at contributing to the consolidation of ongoing policies and to the exploitation of resources invested in such a complex and potential area as electronic government. Overall, the ultimate goal is to join efforts for the consolidation of a new action sphere that slowly wakes up from its virtual nature and claims real and specific efforts within the region.

Neo-Institutionalism as an Analytic Framework

The configuration of electronic-government development strategies and experiences in South America should be analysed from a perspective that discloses the relationships between the emergence and adoption of organizational formats and the game forces and factors that have led to their implementation that nowadays determine their development. A perspective that both enables and enriches this connection is that of neo-institutionalism.

Neo-institutionalism is a line of thought that understands individuals' actions and their collective expressions as coming from the mediation of social structures and individual behaviours. These mediations, known as institutions, refer to a society's formal and informal rules, which, through conventions, codes of conduct, behaviour rules, and laws and agreements, regulate human interaction.

Initially, institutions arise as a strategy to overcome the collective action dilemma: They represent agreements and strategies created at the social level that limit opportunistic actions and favour collective well-being. However, at the same time as institutions regulate conflicts, they also establish power structures that outline and determine exchange possibilities among agents. Therefore, each institutional framework with its own features is responsible for explaining the distribution of power structures and the exchange and coordination possibilities among social, political, and economic actors.

Different fields of knowledge have made several contributions to institutions' analysis, which have established different disciplinary perspectives. However, all new institutionalisms share the statement that, insofar as institutions condition individual preferences, the same are considered relevant in order to understand and explain interaction among individuals.

For the purpose of this chapter, two neo-institutionalist lines of thought are of special significance: the politological line of thought and that resulting from the organization theory and sociology.

From the political-science perspective in particular, neo-institutionalism arose during the '80s as an attempt to overcome the methodological individualism supported by the behaviourist approach.

Behaviourism expanded within the academic agenda as a reaction against ancient classical institutionalism, which in turn was accused of being formalist, normative, and poor as regards the generation of comparative results. Influenced by political philosophy and law, this tradition was based on the study of political regimes and the state stemming from the law and the constitution, thus adopting an exclusively descriptive approach, strongly normative and that often generated juxtaposed results. Alternatively, behaviourism proposed an explanation of politics and its results based on the adding up of individual interests. During the '70s and '80s, behaviourism successfully built a science in which individuals are the centre of politics and the latter is the result of the addition of individual interests (Rivas Leone, 2003).

By incorporating critics made by this science to classical institutionalism, politological neo-institutionalism resumes the study of government structures in an attempt to revaluate the importance of institutions in human events. However, on this occasion, this approach adopts an intermediate scope perspective, oriented toward intermediation interests. The same arises as a functional-descriptive approach, which, although it does not deny the role and importance of individual actors, it confers institutions a more autonomous role.

New institutionalism claims that institutions compose the group of rules and traditions originated from organizational routines. These routines become key elements for political dynamics insofar as they limit individual preferences, provide information on the costs and benefits of the various alternatives, and legitimise actions. Decision-making processes and processes involving institutional change become thus complex networks formed by actors, transaction costs, routines, and game rules, wherein institutions establish the adding up and negotiation of interests as well as their integration to the establishment of collective values and aspirations (Rivas Leone, 2003).

Specifically, politological neo-institutionalism has conferred special relevance to the role of the state, its relationship forms with civil society, and the characteristics of its decision-making processes. From this perspective, institutions become a central factor in the capacity of the state to perform its duties. Public-policy decisions are determined by the governance structure in the sense that political institutions fix transaction costs among actors and determine the adoption of and expectations on policies (Repetto, 2003).

From this perspective, the state and its organizations fail to be subordinated to social groups' interests (state elites, capitals, or interest groups) as they possess their own interests, which differ from those of other agents (Evans, 1996). Furthermore, they are immersed in social networks. Actors involved in the elaboration of public policies (members of the political class, capitalists, and civil servants) interact according to the political dynamics resulting from interaction within institutional environments. These environments configure the structure of the strategic game generated around the various public problems and establish the characteristics of this process, that is, what issues should be discussed and what issues should be accepted as immutable, who the allies and who the opponents are, how coalitions are articulated and how these should be amended or sustained in time, and to what extent agreements reached are reliable and bound to be fulfilled (Repetto, 2003).

In the case of the disciplinary branch stemming from organization theory and sociology, neo-institutionalism arises out of the rejection of rational actor models and the consideration of institutions as independent variables, as held by constructivism, rational-action literature, and the contingence school. From these perspectives, collective decisions may be understood as the mere addition of individual interests and institutional change arises as a result of intentional schemes. Thus, the institutional outlining results from the minimisation of transaction costs among actors or as a rationality function that harmonises contextual conditions, the nature of duties, and operating factors and their consequences on the values aimed at (Martínez Nogueira, 2002).

Contrary to the above, the organization institutionalist school stems from the verification that schemes do not respond only to individual qualities or reasons, nor to context duties and conditionings. Instead, these result from the features of the framework wherein they are immersed. In this sense, organizations are immersed and determined not only by their internal specific aspects, but also by the social, cultural, and historic frameworks where they belong.

Therefore, contrary to the views of institutional economists and public-election theoreticians, this branch of institutionalism states that opportunism and imperfect information are neither the only factors nor the most significant ones. Upon considering organizations as the result of a special historic and cultural development, institutionalisation is viewed as a process whereby some social relationships and actions are given for granted as a state of affairs wherein common knowledge defines what is significant and what actions are deemed feasible (March & Olsen, 1989). Neo-institutional sociology states that most forms and procedures may be understood as specific practices of cultural origin. In this sense, it highlights the non-reflexive, routine, and presupposed nature of the most part of human behaviour and states that institutional agreements are reproduced because quite often, individuals fail to come up with adequate alternatives (Romero, 1991).

Thus, from this perspective, organizations are open institutions in which internal structures and performance routines reflect the cultural and social rules and structures of the environments in which they are immersed. These environments operate as rational myths insofar as they provide sense to and legitimise organizations, supporting in this way their survival. Furthermore, they structure their action and limit their optimisation capacity, thus favouring some groups in which interests are secured by prevailing sanctions and compensations (DiMaggio & Powell, 1991).

Within a common line of thought, the complementary nature of politological and organizational views is of special value when analysing the features and the implementation stages of e-government within our region. Their combination enables the analysis of the operating factors behind organizational schemes along with the adaptation of these schemes to specific macropolitical frameworks. Insofar as this analysis allows for identification and understanding of political dynamics and their results in terms of public decisions' formulation and application, neo-institutionalism thus becomes, from the perspective of this chapter, a rich framework for the analysis of electronic-government strategies in the Southern Cone area.

Therefore, the study of these South American strategies is proposed herein as a first instance, stemming from the dissemination patterns of organizational models developed by DiMaggio and Powell (1991) and the contributions made by Dolowitz and Marsh (1996) on policy transfer. Second, the analysis shall focus on the possible incidence of the institutional framework in implemented schemes through the concepts of state capacity (Repetto, 2003) and embedded autonomy (Evans, 1996), both from the politological line of thought of the neo-institutionalist school.

E-Government in the South American Agenda

Generally speaking, e-government emergence and development within the South American agenda is determined by coincidences. In the first instance, beyond the features and results of some specific projects, it can be stated that, at the domestic level, its implementation accounts for a common background and reference models. A framework involving the transformation of the development model, reformulation of the state's role, and modernization of public administration is the arena that accompanies and determines its evolution.

As in the '70s, not only in Latin America but also worldwide, the poor performance of the state slowed down economic growth, thus generating high inflation and unemployment rates. In the Southern Cone in particular, the consequences of economic globalisation and the increase of international interests influenced the import substitution regimes, thus originating a fiscal crisis that paralysed states and questioned their role in the economy, their financial and administrative capacity, and their legitimate nature regarding the articulation of civil society's interests. In search of initiatives that would enable the recovery of certain stability and before the urge for financial aid, political elites adopted, in the early '80s, the neo-liberal paradigm principles. Hand in hand with the international agenda, a liberal market under a neutral macroeconomic policy and a minimal state became the successful growth strategy.

This radical change resulted in a series of structural reforms. With the purposes of achieving basic macroeconomic balance, resuming growth, and effectively allotting resources, financial and commercial policies were liberated, and public-expenditure priorities were established along with new fiscal and tax criteria; also, privatisation and economy deregulation measures were taken along with a state modernization process that aimed at increasing efficiency, effectiveness, and transparency of financial operations. Therefore, the techniques suggested by the new public administration were incorporated to the agenda; moreover, decentralization and decongesting actions were implemented along with the creation of new surveillance mechanisms, the expansion of officers' management skills, and the incorporation of new state-budget criteria.

The expansion of new information and communication technologies converged within the region with these series of reforms, thus originating the first versions of an electronic government. In search of the benefits thereof, the new tools were incorporated to the administrative modernization agenda, especially regarding the efficiency increase of budget execution, financial administration, and customs and tax management. In general, these projects were implemented inside the central administration through the state modernization bodies. Some specific examples are the financial information integrated systems in Argentina (Intragrated System of Financial Information (SIDIF)), Chile (Information System for the Financial Administration of the State (SIGFE)), and Uruguay (SIIF), and customs administration systems MARIA (Argentina), LUCIA (Uruguay), and ISIDORA (Chile).

Despite the efforts made, these measures proved to be insufficient to rescue countries from the economic emergency. Although they were able to reduce inflation rates and to gradually resume the economic growth process, the same failed to achieve macroeconomic stabilization. On the other hand, the state's pulling away from the economy bore direct consequences such as the rise of unemployment, labour-market precariousness, impairing public services, and an increase in inequality.

In view of this scenario and upon the doctrinal revision of international credit institutions and creditors, the region commenced, in the late '80s, a second series of reforms. Without having closed the first cycle in many cases, a new goal was added to the public agenda to wit: a process aimed at equal, democratic, and transparent growth wherein the state resumes its role as progress articulator. This vision implied a more moderate approach regarding the state-market relationship and a more participative strategy regarding public administration; with reference to electronic government, this vision was translated into the acknowledgement of the need for state coordination in technology incorporation (previously derived to the market) and renewed attention to the consolidation and creation of new participation mechanisms between the government and civil society.

Therefore, between 1995 and 2000, a series of strategies were implemented in the Southern Cone to promote the information society and that incorporated the existing electronic-government initiatives; the same implied universal access to new technologies and their implementation in areas such as trade, health, and education. Within the specific e-government sphere, the transparency of public organizations and service rendering to citizens became the main goals. Projects were promoted for the use of the Internet for public services' rendering and to foster contact with civil society; further, hand in hand, with an increasing expansion of new technologies, government agendas acquired higher publicity and public presence.

As from this common path covered, a marked trend may be observed within the Southern Cone in terms of institutional structures engaged in the implementation of electronic-government initiatives: There is a government agenda entrusted to an institution directly under the supervision of the presidency, or another institution related thereto, associated with the modernization of the state that takes the e-government implementation responsibility as part of the national agenda (Reilly & Echeverría, 2003). Simultaneously, these organizations are linked to the information-society strategic development plans, toward which coordinating institutions also exhibit similar characteristics: They tend to be established under commissions in the executive government area that are a part of ministerial institutions and public bodies on the one hand and decentralized entities and private-sector companies on the other.

Although the general secretariat remains always within the executive area, its duties relate mostly to the coordination of the different actors involved in each project area.

According to the above, these techno-formal similarities coincide with public administration's modernization process. The first reforms implied institutional change processes that required high-level leadership and galvanized techno-political organizations loyal to the executive power and strong enough to execute transformation projects (Camou, 2001). Insofar as e-government formed part of these strategies, its implementation was developed within modernization institutions isolated from the social and corporate pressures that may be generated by changes in the development model.

On the other hand, the second series of reforms required structures to co-ordinate the action of scattered actors, and that could be able to overcome, through local embedded leaderships, resistance to institutional change (Camou, 2001). Therefore, strategies were associated with participative management structures that conferred protagonism to the different social actors under the state's coordinating role. In turn, vertical structures isolated under executive-power protection did not lose their powers, but became a part of national projects integrated toward the information society.

Thus, these features may be recognised in the three countries under study.

In Argentina, the electronic-government strategy development has been entrusted to the National Bureau for Information Technologies' Innovation Management (ONTI), which is under the supervision of the Strategic Coordination Unit of the ministerial cabinet head office. This cabinet was established in 1994 as a direct presidential advisory entity with the aim of implementing the institutional reform.[3] Moreover, in 2000, the National Program for Information Society Development (PSI) was created; the same operates within the communications' secretariat of the Ministry of Infrastructure and Housing and is engaged in the articulation of the sector's entities and resources pursuant to the national goals and policies regarding information-society development, the promotion of universal Internet access, electronic-government development, and the training of specialized human resources, along with investment promotion and the development of new technologies in general.

In Chile, the Interministerial Committee for Public Administration Modernization is in charge of electronic-government implementation. This institution was established in 1990 within the framework of the Presidential General Secretariat Ministry as advisor to the executive power and is also responsible for the implementation of the state reform and modernization project.

Figure 1. E-government implementation structure in the first and second reforms introduced

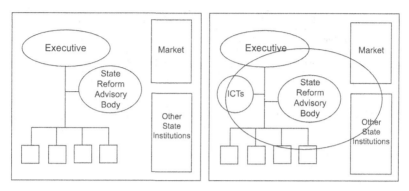

Moreover, in 1999 the New Communication and Information Technologies' Committee was established as presidential advisor with the responsibility of coordinating the action of the various ministries and public institutions within the ICTs' sphere. Its goal is to put forward policies and to encourage initiatives in five different working areas: access promotion, electronic government, incorporation of new technologies at the corporate level, human-resources training programs, along with citizens' information and participation.[4]

In Uruguay, the first electronic-government projects were implemented within the working sphere of the Executive Committee for State Reform (CEPRE), an entity under the supervision of the Budget and Planning National Bureau (OPP), supervised, in turn, by the presidency, and in charge of providing assessment on the formulation of development schemes and programs.[5] Moreover, actions aimed at information-society promotion have been, since 2000, within the scope of the National Committee for Information Society (CNSI). This entity is operated directly by an executive-power management unit and is formed by the president, national universities' representatives, and representatives of the telecommunications and software sector.

In general, it is observed that the features associated with the incorporation of electronic government to the South American agenda exhibit marked temporal coincidences. In this sense, it may be stated that the incorporation of electronic government to the South American agenda bears a common original matrix and shared conditionings.

Just as in the case of other policy arenas, the public-administration modernization process has originated, regarding the electronic-government develop-

Table 1. Organizational strategies for electronic-government implementation within the Southern Cone area

	First generation	Second generation
Argentina	National Bureau for Information Technologies Management Innovation, Ministerial Cabinet Head Office (1994)	National Program for Information Society Development, Ministry of Infrastructure and Housing (2000)
Chile	Presidential General Secretariat Ministry (1990)	New Communication and Information Technologies' Committee (1999)
Uruguay	Executive Committee for State Reform, Budget and Planning National Bureau, Presidency (1996)	National Committee for Information Society, Presidency of the Republic (2000)

ment, the dissemination of implementation patterns that reflect the prevailing conditions and ideas of each period on the state administration responsibilities, structure, and forms. Furthermore, insofar as the reform movement entailed direction shifts, several generations of organizations may be identified that bear significant similarities among each other (Martínez Nogueira, 2002).

Organizational Strategies and Policy Transfer

Stemming from the assumption of a shared original matrix and common determining aspects, the features relative to electronic-government implementation in the Southern Cone area may be analysed under the policy-transfer hypothesis, that is, as the result of a process wherein acquaintance with ideas, institutions, policies, and programs of a given period or place are introduced within the development of policies and programs of another period or place (Dolowitz & Marsh, 1996).

Within the framework of organizational neo-institutionalism, this conception poses the existence of three ideal types of policy transfers that vary according to the conditions that lead policy selectors to take into consideration certain models or nations in particular. There is a voluntary transfer when the emulation responds to a free government decision, either due to the unsatisfactory results achieved by policies applied to date or due to uncertainty regarding the future. There is a coercive transfer when emulation is based on the unilateral nature of an issuer to dictate recommendations to a receptor. Finally, there is a type of transfer called indirect coercive or middle-level transfer. This does not depend on the direct intervention of agents that motivate a change, but rather on the "global economy's structural power." Four structural factors determine this transfer: external factors, technological changes, economic interdependence, and competitiveness (Dolowitz & Marsh, 1996).

Specifically, the indirect coercive transfer coincides with the institutional isomorphism notion (Dimaggio & Powell, 1991), also developed within organizational neo-institutionalism. This conception refers to the process that forces a population's organizational units to resemble the rest of the units that bear the same environmental conditions. Just as in the case of the policy-transfer notion, institutional isomorphism may exhibit different features according to the mechanisms that generate it: Coercive isomorphism results from formal and informal pressures exerted by society's cultural expectations; mimetic isomorphism results from uncertainty in terms of a poor understanding of organizational technologies, the ambiguity of working objectives, and symbolic uncertainty; and, normative isomorphism results from behaviour models and rules created and legitimised through experts' and professionals' networks.

Regarding the development of electronic-government strategies within the Southern Cone, it is possible to detect the variables that promote both the notion of policy transfer and that of institutional isomorphism. In this sense, through these variables, we may achieve an explanation on how Latin American governments and public administrations have chosen to pursue their e-government initiatives and how initiatives are taking place in the region.

In the first place, as described herein, Southern Cone countries have been, since the late '70s, immersed in an unsatisfactory environment and suffering from exhaustion due to their development models, which led them to search for stability solutions. Simultaneously, the search for credit access immersed them in a coercive transfer relationship regarding international financing institutions' recommendations.

In general, state structural reform and modernization projects have been implemented within Southern Cone countries with the financing aid of institutions such as the International Monetary Fund (IMF), the World Bank (WB), the United Nations (UN), the Organization for Economic Cooperation and Development (OECD), and the Inter-American Development Bank (IADB). These institutions have exercised certain coercion over the national agendas through the negotiation of action strategies in the implementation of loans (Peres & Stallings, 2000). This is evidenced also in technological-innovation policies. When European countries provide assistance in designing biosafety legislation, for example, they may model the legislation on the precautionary standards set in Europe even though that might not be the preferred stance of the country receiving the assistance (Programa de Naciones Unidas para el Desarrollo [PNUD], 2001).

Based on the above, as long as electronic-government strategies in Argentina, Chile, and Uruguay have been financed mainly by the Inter-American Development Bank under larger credits for the public administration's reform and modernization,[6] it could be stated that the IADB's role has definitely influenced the organizational isomorphism process.

As in other modernization process aspects, it could be stated that its preferences played an outstanding role to the extent that the availability of operational models implemented in other frameworks for the execution of similar projects could have fulfilled the desire for the reduction of risks associated with innovation, thus ensuring a predictable execution of disbursements.[7]

Within the conceptual framework of policy transfer and within the general context, another variable that must be taken into account in electronic-government incorporation within the Southern Cone area is the possible uncertainty that countries may have suffered vis-à-vis the expansion of new technologies, as well as the loss of positions regarding appropriation.

In 1999, while in the United States and Europe Internet users numbered 48 million and 24.6 million respectively, and the Net was becoming a part of social and economic life, 65% of the Latin American population had never accessed the Internet. Already it was evident that this digital breach of information society, built on the existing socioeconomic distribution, could reinforce and reestablish inequality structures both at the domestic and international level. New technologies were creating a completely new sector wherein most developed countries were at the forefront of progress and which appropriation consolidated both as complex and indispensable for economic diversification and integration into the global economy of developing countries.

By the late '90s, information and communication technologies along with the related industries were among the most dynamic sectors of the world economy. In 1999, a growth of between $2.2 and $3 billion was estimated for this sector for the year 2005. Also, while Web pages increased at a rate of 7.3 million daily, it was estimated that the worldwide electronic-commerce volume directly to consumers would increase from $25,000 to $233,000 billion by the year 2004 (PNUD, 2001). New technologies offered at that time possibilities for export increase, the creation of new jobs, and economy diversification. In general, the ICT sector required less initial capital and infrastructure investments than traditional sectors, thus providing, on the other hand, a high labour demand (PNUD).

However, although the information society seemed to be able to offer the potential for development, no Latin American country held a position of importance within the new digital arena. In 1999, only 0.5% of Latin Americans possessed Internet access. There were 23 hosts for every 10,000 inhabitants and 44 computers for every 1,000 inhabitants; in developed countries, these values accounted for 30% regarding Internet access, 811 hosts, and 353 computers. In the Latin American region, there were no technological nodes, and universities and research centres lacked the capacity to implement new technologies. Furthermore, there were no companies specialized in providing expertise on the matter, nor were there economic stability and entrepreneurial dynamism to set up new companies or to make these new ideas available to the market (PNUD, 2001).

In general, Latin America joined the information-technology revolution at a late stage. In 1999, users slightly numbered 1.6 million and knowledge on new technologies was confined to specific segments of scientific, technological, and professional elites (Equipos/Plus, 1999). Within this framework of loss of competitiveness, Latin American governments encountered also marked social expectations on this new and almost unknown action sphere. Forty-one percent of the Latin American population estimated that the government was responsible for ensuring and regulating computer and Internet access (Equipos/Plus, 1999).

Therefore, it may be assumed that, within this scenery, the increasing urgency and the need to find effective solutions may have led to the adoption of already tested models without considering the aspects that would enable their successful adaptation to the local field, thus supporting in this way a transfer process similar to those observed in other technological-innovation areas.

Finally, within the analysis referred to as policy transfer and institutional isomorphism, it is worth highlighting the influence of the generation of an international consensus on the conceptualisation and solution of public-administration problems, also regarding the use of information technology as a potential tool. This normative rule is the result of common sense in professionalism created gradually through interinstitutional networks and policy communities (Martínez Nogueira, 2002).

Although Latin American government leaders have often expressed their political desire to use new technologies to achieve development,[8] this common sense was developed mainly along with international intergovernment institutions, thus highlighting the poor contribution of local institutions. Apart from a demand induced by programs supported by international financial institutions, the region accounted for a significant cooperation from specialized international sectorial bodies that supplied a real demand by governments, thus contributing to the initial development and maintenance of the e-government agenda.

Among them, the Latin American Centre for Administration and Development (CLAD) played a vital role in the research, assessment, and promotion of administrative knowledge. It is worth highlighting also the efforts made by United Nations Education Science and Culture Organization (UNESCO), the Organization of American States (OAS), and the Institute for Connectivity of the Americas (ICA-IDRC)(International Development Research Centre). The prompt activity of these bodies regarding the financing and dissemination of innovation projects, and the generation of analysis and case studies, along with the creation of professional networks and training schemes have played a vital role in the development of new technologies within the Latin American agenda.[9]

Despite the fact that variables proposed by policy-transfer models and institutional isomorphism may not be exhaustive and, although there are no specialized studies or specific indicators that allow for a more in-depth analysis of these factors, it is possible to outline from them the determinations that shaped the emergence of electronic-government strategies within the Southern Cone. Also, we may take the risk of explaining the existing similarity among implementation models. Within a revision and reformulation framework of the states, uncertainty about the information society and technological innovation, the coercion of financing institutions, social expectations on the role of the state, and the legitimating of models and concepts through professionals' networks may have determined the design pattern of national strategies in the Southern Cone.

Specifically, regarding the first hypothesis stated herein, it may seem plausible to state that the similarity of strategies implemented in Argentina, Chile, and Uruguay respond to a middle-level transfer process that occurred simultaneously. This statement coincides with an institutional isomorphism process of a normative and coercive basis. Finally, at the first stage of these policies, the influence of a mimetic process based on uncertainty and lack of local knowledge of the development and potential of new technologies for state administration should not be ruled out.

Because Institutions Matter

Electronic-Government strategies in the Southern Cone area respond to an original matrix that determined similar incorporation and implementation forms among the countries of this region. From the organizational point of view, this homogeneity is reflected in a coincidence regarding the goals and methods of the various national agendas. However, upon observing these strategies from the perspective of their impacts, it may be evidenced that they exhibit significant differences. Despite the fact of sharing a common original strategic model, policies have yielded unequal results.

In general, electronic-government development may be considered a three-stage process. The first stage relates to the emergence of projects that arise spontaneously and in an isolated manner within the different organizations. At the second stage, upon acknowledgement of the need for a coordinated agenda at the national level, a specialized e-government office is set up and a working agenda is outlined. Finally, during the third stage, upon institutionalisation of the project, the e-government office undertakes more specific initiatives in integration, coordination, and standardization areas, and government bodies begin to take over the agenda (Reilly & Echeverría, 2003).

From this perspective, despite the original similarities of the strategies implemented, we may observe significant differences within the region in the development level achieved. While Chile has moved on to the third stage, Uruguay, despite having acknowledged the need for an e-government-coordinated agenda, has failed to institutionalise it at a national level. Leadership efforts have been unsuccessful and the National Committee for Information Society has left the project in the hands of CEPRE, which has implemented specific projects according to its own working agenda (Reilly & Echeverría, 2003). Finally, Argentina is situated at an unequal development stage. Neither ONTI nor PSI have been able to consolidate themselves as national agendas, and electronic-government projects still emerge in an organic manner at a lower level.

These disparities are further enhanced if we take as an indicator of the results obtained the online government presence. In the Southern Cone, the interpretation of this index reinforces disparity among the policies implemented: While Chile accounts for a 0.83 development score and is ranked among the governments with higher presence worldwide, Argentina scores 0.62, a value considerably higher than the 0.35 score of Uruguay (UN, 2003). Therefore, it is clear that, although similar models inspired the strategies, their implementation yielded dissimilar results. Thus, the feasibility and the degree of acceptance of each policy were owed both to its generic qualities and to the specific framework wherein it was applied.

Therefore, the analysis of strategies must go beyond the formalities of schemes and contents so as to visualize their correspondence with the features and requirements of each institutional framework. To track electronic government in South America, it is thus necessary to expand our views and to adopt an approach that allows us to compare implementation processes within the different environments.

In view of this need, the state-capacity notion becomes a potential analysis tool. Within the framework of politological neo-institutionalism, this concept refers to the ability of government instances to materialize into public policies, the maximum possible levels of social value, given certain context restrictions and according to certain collective definitions aimed at defining the fundamental public problems and the specific social value to be provided by the state response in each case (Repetto, 2003).

Moreover, the state capacity may be analysed from two dimensions. The first one refers to the administrative efficiency to implement official goals, and it depends on the type of recruitment, bureaucratic training, hierarchy levels, services, and degree of specialisation that characterize the bureaucratic administration. Thus, the higher the knowledge, expertise, and professional nature of the bureaucratic organization, the higher the state's capacity to defend the positions associated with its functions.

The second dimension refers to the state's political capacity to make decisions that represent and express the interests of actors involved in a given public action arena. Understanding that the implementation of policies is performed within a specific set of social bonds that tie the state to society, and that said implementation faces uncertainty and requires constant renegotiation of goals and commitments, the political capacity takes into account the level of conflict among actors; furthermore, it refers to the efficiency of civil servants in defining and defending the government agenda.

The state capacity, considered under these two dimensions, is conditioned by a country's institutional framework, that is, the legislative, executive, and judicial institutions by formal and informal customs and norms, and by the nature of the conflict among the different contending interest groups within society. In this sense, the same is linked to the conception of embedded autonomy that states that problem-identification processes, public policies' outlining, and implementation processes depend both on state endogenous processes and also on the relationship between state administrative bodies and private agents (Evans, 1996).

According to this conception, the existing network between internal consistency (autonomy) and external connectivity (embedding) explains the specific experiences regarding state-capacity degrees evidenced in certain public-policy areas: Each subsystem of policies operates associated with institutional networks that bring together social and state actors with the most varied interests and ideas. In this way, the state capacity depends not only on coherent administrative organizations and expert and well-motivated bureaucratic institutions, but also on the type of political interaction, regulated by certain rules, norms, and customs established by state actors and by the political system (Repetto, 1998). From this perspective, differences among South American electronic-government policies may be thus explored, not from the formal-structural vision of the organizational dimension, but as the type of political interaction within each specific case.

Therefore, it is worth highlighting the special value of the indicators developed by Kaufmann, Kraay, and Zoido-Lovatón (1999; see Table 3). These authors created a quantitative approach to the governance notion composed of three groups of analytic categories that refer to the key elements of a country's institutional framework. The first group relates to government selection, supervision, and reelection processes. Indicators such as voice, accountability, and political stability refer to the political process, civil liberties, political rights, and the perceptions on the possibility of government destabilization.

The second group refers to the respect of citizens and the state for the institutions that regulate their interaction. In turn, this group is divided into the rule of law that groups various indicators on the incidence of crime, efficacy, and predictability of the judicial system and agreement reinforcement, and also control of corruption understood as the exercising of public power for private benefit.

Finally, the third group refers to the state's capacity to formulate and implement policies. The variables within this group include government effectiveness, which combines perceptions on the quality of public-services rendering and of bureaucracy, the competence and independence of public employees regarding political pressures, and the quality of public commitments. The second variable is the regulatory quality, which includes perceptions on policies, especially those that result in market performance, or those that as an excessive regulatory burden impose restrictions on the development of entrepreneurial and commercial freedom.

Although this methodology still accounts for a strong margin of inaccuracy, all the same it allows us to make approximate calculations within the region of the state capacity level regarding electronic-government implementation and to explain the differences in the results obtained despite the original similarities.

Specifically, the possibility of comparing governance values with the only indicators available in terms of electronic government is of special interest, that is, the e-Gov Index and the e-Gov Readiness Index, both developed by the United Nations (2003).

Generally speaking, the e-Gov Index measures governments' development regarding e-government according to the number and features of the national government Web sites in terms of information dissemination, service delivery, and interactive participation. The E-Government Readiness Index, also developed by the United Nations, complements these measurements with the telecommunication access dissemination index and the human-development index in order to visualize the generic capacity or the attitude of the public sector to use information and communication technologies for encapsulating in public services and deploying to the public quality information and effective communication.

From the correlation of these indicators with governance values, we may thus observe the incidence, in general terms, of institutional variables in Latin American development of electronic government. The correlation coefficients of these variables exhibit the determination of the norms, habits, and government institutions regarding the capacity of the public administration to take possession and make use of the potential of new information and communication technologies (see Table 2).

First of all, regarding online government presence, we observe the specific determination of government effectiveness and rule-of-law variables. In this sense, it may be assumed that those governments with higher administrative capacity and bureaucratic quality tend to exhibit higher Web development. Also, insofar as the features of legal frameworks affect information and services delivery on the Internet, this presence depends also on the quality and predictability of regulatory agreements and frameworks.

On the other hand, regarding e-Gov readiness, we observe the influence of all institutional variables with the sole exception of political stability. The political-process features, the predictability of agreements, the administration's transparency levels, the bureaucratic effectiveness, and the regulatory frameworks possess, as in other public-action dimensions, a direct incidence

Table 2. Variables of incidence in electronic-government implementation in Latin America

Governance indicators (1)	Web presence (1)		e-Gov readiness (2)	
	R	*Sig. level*	R	*Sig. level*
Government effectiveness	0.63	0.01	0.73	0.01
Regulatory quality	0.45	Not significant	0.49	0.05
Rule of law	0.49	0.05	0.63	0.01
Control of corruption	0.46	Not significant	0.58	0.05
Political stability	0.30	Not significant	0.37	Not significant
Voice and accountability	0.30	Not significant	0.47	0.05

Note: (1) Kaufmann, Kraay, & Mastruzzi (2003). (2) UN (2003). N=18

in the state capacity to incorporate new communication and information technologies.

However, two observations should be made.

In the first place, despite statistical values, the political-stability variable cannot be excluded from the analysis. Although perceptions on the possibility of government destabilization may not exert a direct influence on electronic-government policies implementation, political stability may account for an indirect incidence regarding power leaders' fragmentation. Generally speaking, it is quite unlikely that the connection of a given state administration, even a consistent one, to a fragmented group of power leaders increases their ability to implement their decisions. On the contrary, it seems likely under this scenery is the increase of transaction costs. Consequently, the performance of effective intertemporal exchanges that allow for the generation of long-term and high-quality policies is thus hindered (Spiller & Tommasi, 1999). Insofar as it is not possible for Latin America to consider its victory regarding stability achievement from this perspective, for the region, political stability is not a variable that should be ruled out completely from the analysis.

Second, it is worth highlighting the difference between regional values and the same correlations performed with developed countries. If governance indicators among the 20 most populated countries according to the OECD are correlated, it is observed that these indexes do not bear significant incidence in the impacts generated regarding electronic government. Although this chapter does not aim at conducting an in-depth analysis on the possible causes of these differences, it is worth highlighting them in view of future research tasks or in terms of a thorough analysis of local development.

Beyond these appreciations, from the interpretation of these data it may be held that, in general, despite the fact that strategies are originated under an organizational isomorphism pattern, the effective electronic-government development in Latin America is determined by the institutional conditions wherein it has been immersed. The state capacity within an innovation and coordination area such as electronic government is closely linked to the institutional dynamic features in terms of the relations among government powers, political conflict characteristics, and power distribution, along with the formal and informal rules and customs that regulate interaction among actors. Despite its initial bureaucratic aura, in electronic government, just as in other government spheres, political institutions still matter.

This verification does not confer any particular feature to e-government and it does not entail any contribution whatsoever to public policies' analysis. However, it still enables us to move forward on safer grounds regarding the analysis of the factors that yielded the above-mentioned diverse results in the Southern Cone. The founding bases and the institutional features of each country thus explain the conditions that determined the variety of state capacity levels in each country and the different results obtained in the e-government arena.

Argentina

In Argentina, the online presence of government organizations accounts for a 0.62 score, and government capacity to incorporate new technologies scores 0.58. This capacity is determined both by online development attained and by telecommunication dissemination levels and the country's human-capital level, with scores of 0.19 and 0.92 respectively (see Table 3). All these indicators are well above the Latin American average, thus showing that Argentina is not in a bad position comparatively speaking as regards e-government development. However, this country is still at the initial stage of electronic-government development. The reasons for this inconsistency can be found within the features of its institutional framework.

Argentina exhibits (except for the voice and accountability variable) governance indicators remarkably lower than the Latin American average (see Table
3). The most critical values are observed specifically in the regulatory quality,
political stability, and control of corruption, with scores of 19.06, 23.80, and
27.8 in relation to average scores of 52.83, 43.34, and 42.44 respectively.

Generally speaking, it can be stated that Argentina's institutional performance
hinders the generation of effective long-term policies. Institutional features
such as political fragmentation, electoral laws, and congress organization
along with political practices such as the acceptance of the necessity and
urgency decrees and the executive power's discretion in budget allotting
hinder the generation of intertemporal agreements deemed necessary (Spiller
& Tommasi, 2000).

In first place, the peculiar combination of electoral laws, political fragmentation,
and executive practices erodes congress' capacity to control the administrative
performance and to put pressure on the effectiveness and professionalism
of bureaucratic frameworks. On the other hand, the executive power's high
rotation prevents the development of cooperation and coordination norms
deemed essential for an organized, coherent, and consistent performance of
government activities. The bureaucratic organization's feasibility depends
rather on the quality of the officer in charge and on capturing administrative
institutions as a strategy for e-government's effective implementation than
on the administration as a policy-generating machine (Spiller & Tommasi,
2000).

This scenery is accompanied also, in the case of Argentina, by an administrative reform process characterized by the voracious logic of public expenditure
reduction and by the absence of any vision whatsoever on the modernization
or reformulation of procedures. This reform has resulted in an irreversible
authority and political-power decentralizing process that, although it decen-
tralizes decision-making processes and favours federalization, also hinders
the implementation of policies at the national level.

Just as in other public-policy spheres, this governability structure generates
strong weaknesses regarding e-government development. The initiatives
currently in force show an uncoordinated and erratic increase of new technologies' implementation within the administrative performance. First of
all, the ONTI has not been effective as the government's designated leading
agency to drive the move to e-government. The overload from the combination of both planning and implementing responsibilities, and the placement
as an office at the lower end of the administrative hierarchy overtaxed its

capacity and its ability to deliver on its demanding mandate (World Bank, 2002). This is thus reflected in the absence of a specific electronic-government project that goes beyond the mere statement of the intention to develop future working plans.

On the other hand, although placement of PSI within the Ministry of Infra-structure and Housing may be considered as a strategy to ensure direct access to operational responsibility on the matter, within an institutionally weak framework as described before, this decision bears negative consequences. Within a framework of high political rotation, the close association to a ministry generates vulnerability and uncertainty regarding the continuance of a task, as well as isolation from the rest of the decision-making and ad-ministrative structures.

Hence, the effectiveness and impact of the various programs in place has been poor so far. A good number of public entities (projects, programs, commis-sions, etc.) have their own sites and define their dissemination of information strategies and modalities of service delivery in almost autonomous ways. As a consequence, there has been a proliferation of different architectures, systems, and applications; high–cost, disparate, and low-volume purchasing practices; the absence of standards for service quality and content; and little if any follow-up to ensure effective results (World Bank, 2002).

Moreover, Argentina lacks the adequate political leadership to enable defini-tion and implementation of an electronic-government strategy. There is no real commitment at the political apex of the cabinet, possibly for lack of a concrete understanding of the benefits and requirements of electronic govern-ment. Also, because of economic and institutional decentralization pressures, there is a lack of willingness from government agencies to cooperate in the formulation of common policies and discipline in implementing them instead of fighting for turf and resources. Within a framework of high rotation and the erosion of control mechanisms, individual agency programs appear more a grab for resources and turf than a commitment to results. While program objectives invariably are desirable and meaningful, they rarely are unbundled operationally into effective action programs (World Bank, 2002).

Chile

In Chile, online government presence accounts for a 0.84 score and govern-ment capacity to incorporate new technologies scores 0.67. These values are well above regional average values of 0.44 and 0.40, with the same relationship regarding telecommunication-dissemination and human-capital indexes (0.28 and 0.90 respectively). With reference to governability indicators, Chile stands out at the regional level due to its institutional consolidation. This country, with an average 87.4 score, almost doubles the regional average and is closer to developed countries (see Table 3).

From the political point of view, Chile accounts for deep-rooted centralization and institutions that, with a high degree of autonomy, reinforce the central state's ample authority. This centralism may be further verified in political parties' ideas and practices, which have played a vital role in structuring a system of clientelist relations between the state and society. The same is characterized by vertical networks of groups that stem from every community toward the nation's centre (Marcel, 1996).

Historically, the Chilean state's institutional origin fulfilled all the basic requirements to build a solid, stable, and functional public apparatus. Also, reform and modernization processes resulted in a significant reduction of productive functions and a redefinition of private-sector roles regarding social-services delivery along with a fiscal cutback process that implied a tough learning process in terms of public expenditure control. However, these changes failed to be accompanied by similar changes in the forms of directing, administering, and handling the state apparatus (Marcel, 1996).

On the other hand, Chile stands out for having undertaken the state reform and development model under an authoritarian regime. Since 1982, owing mainly to this factor, Chile has held a sustained development without the need for critical interventions or the implementation of drastic measures. Furthermore, this country has not faced the problems arising in general during state reform processes, such as fiscal crisis, extended corruption, and evident inefficiencies, or serious arguments on the state's adequate scope or goals.

Hence, the post-adjustment state is more an institution builder than a direct economic agent. In fact, most part of the Chilean administrative reform during the early '90s was centred on bureaucracy's moral and expertise reconstruction, thus expanding expenditure significantly, in part through a sustained real increase in public-sector salaries.

The civil government was able to support these measures on the basis of tax increase and because the economy adopted a unique growing pace until the late '90s. Fiscal resources from different sources were added to administrative resources, whose availability is associated with ample temporal perspectives,

Table 3. Variables of incidence in electronic-government implementation in the Southern Cone: National values

	Argentina	Chile	Uruguay	Latin American average
Government effectiveness*	37.60	86.06	68.60	40.64
Regulatory quality*	19.06	90.20	67.00	52.83
Rule of law*	27.08	87.10	69.10	40.67
Control of corruption*	27.80	90.70	75.80	42.44
Political stability*	23.80	85.90	79.50	43.34
Voice and accountability*	52.50	84.30	77.80	51.73
Country average*	31.31	87.38	72.97	45.28
e-Gov readiness**	0.58	0.67	0.51	0.44
Web presence**	0.62	0.84	0.36	0.40
Telecommunication Index**	0.19	0.28	0.24	0.12
Human-Capital Index**	0.92	0.90	0.92	0.82

Note: * Kaufmann, Kraay, & Mastruzzi (2003) ** UN (2003)

a professional ethos among the highest bureaucracy levels, and an accumulated administration tradition (Torre, 1997).

Furthermore, this process resulted in a balanced relationship among the executive and legislative powers aimed at preserving political stability and at democratising government strategies. Regarding the Pacto de la Concertación (Conciliatory Alliance), the executive power confined its powers to the system's centralization and leveled itself by encouraging the voicing and accountability of achievements.

Therefore, within this solid institutional framework, the Chilean electronic government has been able to stand out as one of the most developed governments worldwide. Moreover, it can be stated that Chile bears a twice-reinforced state capacity. First of all, it accounts for a highly efficient bureaucracy that operates within a predictable regulatory framework. Second, this apparatus operates within a context of political stability and predictability of agreements, with little margin for the exercising of public power in private benefit. Additionally, there is an explicit commitment of the president of the republic toward information-society development that has played a vital role in e-government development and the success of new technologies' dissemination in terms of connectivity.

Uruguay

In Uruguay, the online presence of government institutions accounts for a mere 0.36 score, despite its 0.51 score in the e-Gov Readiness Index. Paradoxically, Uruguay possesses human-capital values as high as Argentina (0.92) and a telecommunication-dissemination level even higher than this neighbouring country (0.24; see Table 3). Furthermore, Uruguay accounts for a similar institutional consolidation to that of Chile, which in turn is well above the regional average. Thus, how can we explain such a poor development level? Uruguay is, in this sense, a paradox and exhibits, just like its peers, its own peculiarities.

In the Uruguayan case, the demographic volume could be considered as a possible incidence factor. As in other information-society spheres, the population is a determining factor of online government presence levels. Insofar as new technologies facilitate communication with citizens, the territorial extension and demographic density constitute dynamic aspects for state innovation. Undoubtedly, in the case of Uruguay, this factor may not be left out. However, this aspect does not seem to explain the poor performance regarding electronic government. Explanations should be searched instead in the features and performance of the country's institutions.

The Uruguayan political system is characterized as having originated within the political parties' framework, which endowed it with a peculiar imbrication of politicians, technicians, and bureaucrats. Historically, the Uruguayan state stood out due to the role of political parties as personnel selection and promotion actors and, at the same time, as central actors in the state governing process. This double nature determined the state's colonization by party structures. The Uruguayan state ranges between autonomy and captivity and depends on a political network characterized by the arrangements and commitments culture, and by a multiple balance and vetoes logic (Caetano, 1995).

Contrary to Argentina, bureaucratic schemes resulting from this political network are quite functional to the system. Proportional representation at the House of Representatives establishes the control of the legislative power over the executive power, which allows for mutual party control and maintains bureaucracy's politicization under functional levels. However, this functionality bears negative consequences regarding the country's innovation capacity (Ramos, Narbondo, & Filgueira, 2002).

Although the government structure is characterized by a moderate to strong presidency, the institutionalisation and competence degree of the party system, with sectors that account for considerable organizational autonomy, adds negotiation instances to the political process and increases the number of actors with a vetoing power within the policy-formulation process. This complex political network regarding bureaucracy is characterized by a strongly structured and stable nature that limits all innovative drastic interventions or those that may lead to an innovative breakup. Uruguay bears the rigidity and the entrenchment of a senior clerk, that is, the effective capacity to resist any transformation attempt that may affect its interests and convictions regarding the adequate formats for public administration (Ramos et al., 2002).

This immobilisation is reinforced by political patronage and network structures associated with political authorities. In general, with the aim of leveling costs and benefits, the elites pass the laws and decrees that enable the implementation of innovative policies; however, they do not determine the corresponding controls and punishments. In this way, they allow for the agenda's discursive execution, facilitating at the same time implementation processes that respect the interests of both parties and state power structures. Therefore, mid-level authorities and party leaders (often in charge of state performance units, the state's last step of direct political appointment) administer the selection of winners and losers in policy implementation; furthermore, although in some cases they adhere to the policy in force at the moment, they render it heterogeneous regarding its achievements (Ramos et al., 2002).

In the last years, in addition to this performance pattern, we find the repercussion of the modalities and the results of the state reform implementation. In Uruguay, salaries have served as a variable for public expenditure cutbacks, thus enhancing the diversity among salaries and devaluating the administrative profession. Consequently, the tension between the political sector, responsible for the decision making, and the qualified technical-professional group is solved in favour of a political leadership. In general, this leadership fails to take into account the specialized assessment of its institutional apparatus; in turn, it accounts for its own reliable staff and professional experts hired from outside the public administration. As a result, there are marked deficiencies at the policy-planning level as well as in the regulation and quality-control capacities and administration transparency (Ramos et al., 2002).

Undoubtedly, within the framework of a deeply static and politicized administration, political commitment with policies is vital. The effective performance of projects, especially within the context of articulated strategies, calls for constant dialogue and promotion activities that generate support and establish alliances. Also, if the strategic relevance assigned and the understanding of goals is only shared in part, e-government implementation becomes a conflict arena regarding guidelines and activities. As a matter of fact, electronic government in Uruguay seems to have been encouraged within this framework.

The CNSI was created by President Batlle upon having taken office. Although initially it seemed to possess the necessary strength for its institutionalisation, it was never able to define its information-society strategy; currently, the project is quite unarticulated, lacking clear goals and cohesion (IADB, 2003). Given the institutional characteristics, the particular situation regarding the existing economic crisis, and a government hindered by the weakening of political support, the CNSI's agenda has failed to account for, during its development, any possibilities of appropriation by politicians and public employees. Currently, although this country is implementing a public administration modernization program, modernization components through electronic-government solutions and capacities are extremely weak and hardly taken into account (Inter-American Development Bank (BID), 2003). Despite the fact that this country possesses the necessary resources for full electronic-government development, political dynamics generated by their institutional frameworks seem to stop any real innovation.

Therefore, stemming from each country's institutional features, it seems possible to find an explanation regarding the different conditions that in each country determined different state capacity levels and diverse results in the e-government arena. In this sense, it may be stated that while in Argentina, the bureaucratic apparatus is immersed in social networks and political fluctuations, and lacks tools that enable the necessary autonomy to comply with its agenda, Uruguay and Chile possess the administrative capacity required for the generation of agreements deemed necessary for the development of long-term policies. However, while the Chilean public administration has achieved strong state autonomy, Uruguay is still entirely tied to party politics and depends on the constant conciliation and renegotiation of goals, thus drowning itself in an immobility status that hinders institutional change.

As a conclusion to the second hypothesis, we may state that, just as in other public-policy spheres, in electronic government, institutions do matter. Although this confirmation does not entail any new ideas, it brings to us the e-government vision as a real public-policy sphere. By detaching virtual fantasies of technological promises from e-government implementation, and by asserting the significance of the institutional framework for the region, we may then draw our attention toward the need for reinforcing efforts and to adapt the features of ongoing projects so as to amortize the work carried out up to date and strengthen its success and survival possibilities.

In developing countries, this sincere acknowledgement is as necessary as it is promising. Only by recognising weaknesses and features of the path covered shall we be able to benefit from each society's strong features and thus enhance the use of tools that favour the search for new effectiveness, transparency, and citizen participation levels.

Conclusion

Upon the exploration of electronic-government implementation strategies in the Southern Cone area, the diagnosis that applies is that of a network characterized by the coexistence of organizational isomorphism with institutional frameworks typical of each country. Consequently, the region exhibits significant differences in the goals achieved. Chile is the regional leader while Argentina accounts for an erratic policy, which has still yielded positive results. Uruguay is immersed within a framework of relative immobility and poor exploitation of available resources.

Therefore, two conclusions apply for the region.

The first conclusion states that, insofar as electronic-government development was held within the framework of state reform and public-administration modernization processes, and that these processes were financed, almost in their entirety, by international credit institutions, the origin of strategies implemented responds to a middle-level transfer process; additionally, we find a mimetic process based on uncertainty and ignorance at the local level regarding the new development and potential relative to the use of technology in state administration.

The second conclusion suggests that institutional frameworks exert a decisive influence on the effective implementation of electronic-government strategies. Online government presence and electronic-government development capacity indexes are correlated with state capacity levels; furthermore, differences in the impacts produced at the national level only seem to be explained through the particular features of each country's institutional context.

In this sense, it may be concluded that readiness for e- government is not only a technology issue, requiring an examination of government itself. As in any other public-action arenas, the problem with institutional change relies on the fact that it is easier to commence it than to sustain it and, in general, management capacities are the most difficult obstacles for its survival.

The implementation of e-government is thus a management task that must be assessed in the overall context of the organizations and their environments. In terms of a vision for the future, this implies the consideration of strategies to be implemented not according to the need for different actions, resources, or regulatory regimes, but from the nature of the activity to be undertaken. This aspect entails a revision of the proposed goals and strategies and their adaptation to the institutional context wherein they are immersed in order to enhance resources and efforts to achieve maximum results. It is only through this acknowledgement that resources invested shall be fully exploited, and that results obtained shall be both tangible and effective.

In terms of state action, the above statement implies new efforts in order to generate the awareness of technical, political, and administrative sectors on the potential of new technologies for state administration, the creation of specialized leaderships, duly committed with initiatives, and the generation of a responsible attitude toward ongoing projects. On the other hand, at the academic level, this implies the need for urgent involvement in this subject and the generation of studies and indicators aimed at technical cooperation and assessment.

Presently, these projects are under implementation though resources used are, almost in their entirety, owned by third parties. Hopefully, the fact of being aware of the origins and the impacts generated by these strategies up to date shall enable us to start taking real steps in the new digital government world.

Note

María Frick is a Uruguayan political scientist engaged in electronic government studies and new technologies for the strengthing of democracy.

References

Benedetti, P. (1999). *Aspectos institucionales de la administración pública: Implicancias para la Argentina* [Public administration institutional aspects: Implications for Argentina]. Retrieved October 30, 2004, from *http*://www.fgys.org/pdf/DT%2022%20PDF.pdf

Bonifacio, J. A. (1996). *Redes de cooperación inter-administrativa en América Latina* [Inter-administrative cooperation networks in Latin America]. Retrieved October 13, 2004, from http://www.cefir.org.uy/docs/dt16/10bonifa.htm

Caetano, G. (1995). Las representaciones sociales y políticas en el Uruguay moderno (1900-1933) [Social and political representations in modern Uruguay (1900-1933)]. *PRISMA, 1*. Retrieved October 31, 2004, from http://www.argiropolis.com.ar/documentos/investigacion/publicaciones/prismas/1/representaciones.htm

Camou, A. (2001, September). *La segunda generación de reformas del estado en sus laberintos* [Second generation state reforms in their labyrinths]. Paper presented at the 23rd International Congress of the Latin American Studies Association, Washington, DC.

DiMaggio, P. J., & Powell, W. W. (1991). The iron cage revisited: Institutional isomorphism and collective rationality in organizational fields. In P. J. DiMaggio & W. W. Powell (Eds.), *The new institutionalism in organizational analysis* (pp. 267-292). Chicago: University of Chicago Press.

Dolowitz, D., & Marsh, D. (1996). Who learns what from whom: A review of the policy transfer literature. *Political Studies, 64*, 343-357.

Equipos/Plus. (1999). *Oportunidades de cooperación para la investigación de políticas públicas de acceso a Internet* [Cooperation opportunities for Internet access public policies]. Montevideo, Uruguay: Author.

Evans, P. (1996). El estado como problema y como solución [The state as a problem and as a solution]. *Desarrollo Económico, 35*, 140.

Inter-American Development Bank. (2003). *Manual.gob. Estrategias de gobierno electrónico en los países de la región 1: La definición de un modelo de análisis y estudio de casos* [Manual.gob. Electronic government strategies in countries within the region 1: Defining an analysis model and case studies]. Retrieved September 14, 2004, from http://www.iadb.org/sds/itdev/doc/manual_gobes.pdf

Kaufmann, D., Kraay, A., & Zoido-Lovaton, P. (1999). *Aggregating governance indicators.* Policy research working papers. N. 2195. World Bank. Available at: http://www.worldbank.org/wbi/gac

Kaufmann, D., Kraay, A., & Mastruzzi, M. (2003). *Governance matters II: Governance indicators for 1996-2002.* World Development Bank. Retrieved September 14, 2004, from http://econ.worldbank.org/view. php?id=919

Marcel, M. (1996). Modernización de la gestión pública: La experiencia Chilena [Public administration modernization: The Chilean experience]. Retrieved October 13, 2004, from http://www.cefir.org.uy/docs/ dt16/06marcel.htm

March, J. G., & Olsen, J. P. (1989). *Rediscovering institutions.* New York: The Free Press.

Martínez Nogueira, R. (2002). Las administraciones públicas paralelas y la construcción de capacidades institucionales: La gestión por proyectos y las unidades ejecutoras [Parallel public administrations and institutional capacity construction: Administration by projects and executing units]. *Reforma y Democracia, 24.* Retrieved October 13, 2004, from http://www.clad.org.ve/rev24/marnog.pdf

Peres, W., & Stallings, B. (2000). *Crecimiento, empleo y equidad.* Santiago de Chile, Chile: Economic Commission for Latin America and the Caribbean (ECLAC).

Programa de Naciones Unidas para el Desarrollo (PNUD). (2001). *Informe sobre desarrollo humano 2001: Poner el adelanto tecnológico al servicio del desarrollo humano* [Report on human development 2001: Placing technological development at the service of human development]. United Nations. Retrieved July 13, 2004, from http://www.undp. org/hdr2001/spanish/spidhtod.pdf

Ramos, C., Narbondo, P., & Filgueira, F. (2002). *La economía política de la reforma de la administración pública y los servicios civiles de carrera: La experiencia de Uruguay en los años 90* [Political economics of public administration reform and qualified civil services: Uruguay's experience in the 90s]. Proceedings of the Latin American Centre for Development Administration (CLAD). Retrieved May 22, 2003, from http://unpan1. un.org/intradoc/groups/public/documents/CLAD/clad0043202.pdf

Reilly, K., & Echeverría, R. (2003). *El papel del ciudadano y de las OSC en el e-gobierno: Un estudio de gobierno electrónico en ocho países de América Latina y el Caribe* [Citizens and CSOs' role in e-government: An electronic government study in eight countries of Latin America and the Caribbean]. Communications' Progress Associations (APC). Retrieved July 25, 2004, from http://www.katherine.reilly.net/docs/EGOV&OSCenALC.pdf

Repetto, F. (1998). *Notas para el análisis de las politicas sociales: una propuesta desde el institucionalismo.* en Perfiles Latinoamericanos, N°12, Mexico.

Repetto, F. (2003). *Capacidad estatal: Requisito necesario para una mejor política social en América Latina* [State capacity: A necessary requirement for a better social policy in Latin America]. Retrieved May 22, 2003, from http://www.clad.org.ve/fulltext/0047522.pdf

Rivas Leone, J. A. (2003). El neoinstitucionalismo y la revalorización de las instituciones [Neo-institutionalism and reappraisal of institutions]. *Reflexión Política, 9.* Retrieved July 25, 2004, from http://editorial.unab.edu.co/revistas/reflexion/pdfs/pan_49_3_c.pdf

Rodal, E. (2003). *Programa para el establecimiento del gobierno electrónico en América Latina y el Caribe (PEGE-LAC): Conceptos, estrategias y aplicaciones que el Banco Interamericano de Desarrollo viene desarrollando en la region* [Program for electronic government establishment in Latin America and the Caribbean (PEGE-LAC): Concepts, strategies and applications developed by the Interamerican Development Bank within the region]. Retrieved May 22, 2003, from http://unpan1.un.org/intradoc/groups/public/documents/CLAD/clad0047346.pdf

Romero, J. (1991). El nuevo institucionalismo en el análisis organizacional [The new institutionalism within the organizational analysis]. In P. J. DiMaggio & W. W. Powell (Eds.), *The new institutionalism in organizational analysis.* Chicago: University of Chicago Press.

Romero, J. (1999). Estudio introductorio. Los nuevos institucionalismos: sus diferencias, sus cercanias. In P.J. DiMaggio and W.W. Powell, (1999) (Eds.) El nuevo institucionalismo en análisis organizacional. México: Fundación de Cultura Económica.

Scott, W. R., & Meyer, J. W. (Eds.) (1994). *Institutional environments and organizations.* London: Sage.

Spiller, P. T., & Tommasi, M. (1999). *Los determinantes institucionales del desarrollo Argentino: Una aproximación desde la nueva economía institucional* [Institutional determiners of Argentine development: An approach from the new institutional economics]. Retrieved October 30, 2004, from http://www.fgys.org/pdf/DT%2033.pdf

Spiller, P., & Tommasi, M. (1999). *Las fuentes institucionales del desarrollo argentino.* Hacia una agenda institucional. United Nations Development ment Porgramme (UNDP)/ Fundacíon Gobierno y Sociedad. Editorial Universidad de Buenos Aires. Buenos Aires, Argentina.

Torre, J. C. (1997). *Las dimensiones políticas e institucionales de las reformas estructurales en América Latina* [Political and institutional dimensions of structural reforms in Latin America]. Santiago de Chile, Chile: Economic Commission for Latin America and the Caribbean (ECLAC).

United Nations (UN). (2003). *UN global e-government report: Survey 2003.* Retrieved September 3, 2004, from http://www.unpan.org/egovernment3.asp

World Bank. (2002). *Electronic government and governance: Lessons for Argentina.* Retrieved September 3, 2004, from http://topics.developmentgateway.org/egovernment/rc/filedownload.do~itemId=294205

Endnotes

[1]   Translation by Alejandra Sobadjian (mast@fibertel.com.ar)

[2]   In general, these cases have been analysed and disseminated as good practices and form part of e-government history at the local level. For a survey of best practices within the region, see http://www.icamericas.net/Cases_Reports/E-Gov_Best_Practices.

[3]   In Argentina, although the ministerial cabinet head office has been in charge of institutional reform and democracy-strengthening strategies, including the incorporation of new technologies since 1994, it was not until 2002 that ONTI was created as a specific area for technological innovation regarding administrative modernization.

[4]   It is worth highlighting the development of a participation strategy within the state reform project in Chile as from 1997 through the creation of the Interministerial Committee for Public Administration Modernization.

5   The CEPRE's background relates directly to the State Reform Sectorial Commission, dated 1995, and to the OPP's performance (reestablished in 1995 following the dictatorship period).

6   Inter-American Development Bank (http://www.iadb.org) and Reilly and Echeverría (2003)

7   A document that consolidates this transfer trend is Manual.Gob (BID, 2003).

8   Declaration of Florianopolis, Declaration of South American Presidents, Summit of the Americas, European Union Latin America and the Caribbean Summit (Rodal, 2003)

9   It is worth highlighting the implementation of projects such as the Observatory for Information Society (http://www.unesco.org.uy/informatica/observatorio), Inventory on Projects on Information and Communication Technologies in Latin America and the Caribbean, Prizes of Latin American Digital Cities, Latin American Network of Education Portals, Regional Fund on Digital Innovation of the Americas, Virtual Parliament of the Americas (http://www.icamericas.net), Electronic Government Leaders' Network of Latin America and the Caribbean (Red GeALC) (http://www.redgealc.net), and a distance learning course titled "Introduction to Formulation of Electronic Government Strategies" (http://www.educoea.org), among others.

Section III

Local Studies

This section approaches several e-government issues at the local level. In particular, the final part of the book presents to chapters that compare the state of e-government and e-democracy in Latin American municipalities, one particular case study in one of Latin America's biggest cities, and one project conducted at the local level that shows a cooperation strategy between Europe and Latin America

Chapter VIII

E-Government in Latin American Cities:
An Assessment of Selected City Web Sites

Marc Holzer,
Rutgers, The State University of New Jersey at Newark, USA

Tony Carrizales, Marist College, USA

Richard Schwester, John Jay College of Criminal Justice, USA

Abstract

*This chapter examines e-government practices in Latin American cities. Empha-
sis is placed on five areas: privacy and security, usability, content, services, and
citizen participation. In* Digital Governance in Municipalities Worldwide, *Holzer
and Kim (2004) evaluated e-government in the largest municipality in each of
100 countries. Included in this study were the largest cities in 15 Latin American
countries. This chapter focuses on these 15 cities, highlighting those that received
the highest overall index score. In addition, five cities with above-average scores
in the five e-government component areas are assessed. Although this chapter
does not take into consideration all e-government practices in Latin America, it
does provide benchmark cases for cities in the Latin American region.*

Introduction

The purpose of this chapter is to examine e-government practices in Latin American cities. In *Digital Governance in Municipalities Worldwide*, Holzer and Kim (2004) evaluated e-government in the largest municipality in each of 100 countries. That study was based on research conducted by the E-Governance Institute of the National Center for Public Productivity at Rutgers University-Newark and the Global e-Policy e-Government Institute at Sungkyunkwan University (South Korea). Cities were selected using statistics from the International Telecommunication Union (ITU). From the ITU data, 98 United Nations member countries were identified based on an online population greater than 100,000. Of the 100 city Web sites assessed, 15 were from Latin American countries: Tegucigalpa, Honduras; Ciudad de Mexico, Mexico; Panama City, Panama; San Jose, Costa Rica; San Salvador, El Salvador; Sao Paulo, Brazil; Buenos Aires, Argentina; Santa Fe De Bogotá, Colombia; Montevideo, Uruguay; Santiago, Chile; Guayaquil, Ecuador; Caracas, Venezuela; Asuncion, Paraguay; La Paz, Bolivia; and Lima, Peru. The official city Web sites were not available for Havana, Cuba, and Santo Domingo, Dominican Republic. Guatemala City, Guatemala, could be evaluated by only one of the required two evaluators, and therefore was not included.

Literature Review

E-Government and Latin America

Chile is regarded as having one of the most advanced telecommunications infrastructures throughout Latin America. In terms of mobile-phone service, Chile has the highest level of integration. As of 2003, there were 48.8 mobile phone subscribers for every 100 individuals. This compares favorably to countries such as Mexico (28.3 subscribers per 100) and Brazil (26 subscribers per 100). Chile is a leader in Internet integration as well. Based on 2003 data, there were 20.3 individuals online for every 100. This compares to only 10.8 in Argentina, 9.5 in Brazil, and 6.2 in Mexico (Economist Intelligence Unit, 2005b).

The Chilean government is rapidly integrating new technologies in an effort to construct a sound e-government infrastructure. Specifically, the Chilean tax authority (the Servicio de Impuestos Internos) is at the forefront of the country's e-government movement with the implementation of its Internet-based invoicing system. By 2006, it is estimated that more than 50% of all invoices will be Internet based, with this percentage rising to over 80% by 2009. The government is moving forward with what has been dubbed "Ruta 5 Digital," which is a high-capacity digital cable network designed to connect central, regional, and local governments. Chile is also working to bridge the digital divide through an emphasis on computer literacy and increased Internet access (Economist Intelligence Unit, 2005a). In terms of citizen participation, Chile's national congress is developing an Internet-based consultative medium called *Virtual Senator*, which should afford citizens opportunities to contribute to the policy-making process (Padget, 2005).

Mexico was one of the first Latin American countries to implement e-government services with the development of Comprasnet. Launched in 1996, Comprasnet is an Internet-based procurement system that was envisioned as a means by which the procurement process could be made more efficient, more transparent, and less costly. In fact, uncovered purchase inconsistencies regarding furnishings for President Vicente Fox's palace. CompraNet has paved the way for DeclaraNet and TransmitaNet. DeclaraNet is an electronic-based tax-return system, while TransmitaNet provides electronic access to more than 2,000 federal and state forms (Padget; 2005).

Brazil's Government Net (RedeGoverno) is a federal-government portal site that offers numerous services, which include income-tax declarations and payments, school enrollment forms, and distance learning, as well as information regarding retirement and social-security benefits. At the municipal level, Porto Alegre established its Participatory Budget Process in 1989, which allows the citizenry to consult on proposed budgetary decisions regarding public services and administration. Since 2001, the Porto Alegre government has enhanced its Participatory Budget Process through the use of the Internet. Specifically, four telecenters were created throughout Porto Alegre, which allow individuals to communicate electronically with officials in the Participatory Budget Process. These telecenters also offer access to numerous government services, and they serve to bridge the digital divide and promote active citizenship (Improvement & Development Agency [IDeA] & the Society of Information Technology Management [Socitm], 2002).

Governments throughout the world are increasingly using the Internet as a means of engaging citizens (Holzer & Kim, 2004). Internet applications have the potential to reconnect citizens and decision makers, publicizing views presented by consultative parties, and providing greater opportunities for citizens to influence public policy. According to Kakabadse, Kakabadse, and Kouzmin (2003), the Internet may alter the dynamic of representative democracy, giving citizens a direct means of influencing the public policy-making process. This may include virtual town-hall meetings, online consultation portals, and other Internet-based applications where citizens can debate policy and convey their views. Through advanced Internet applications, citizens are able to participate more freely and consult on public policies (Holzer, Melitski, Rho, & Schwester, 2004; Holzer & Schwester, 2005).

Previous literature on e-government has highlighted best-practice cases throughout the world; however, these cases have been primarily at the national level. Research at the local level provides an opportunity for municipalities to use benchmarks for which the practice and use of e-government are more appropriate. In the case of Latin America, Holzer and Kim (2004) indicate that the region lags in digital governance performance when compared to cities in Oceania, Asia, Europe, and North America. Before Latin American cities can fully utilize the highest ranked cities (Seoul, Hong Kong, Singapore, New York, and Shanghai) as benchmarks, they must first build on best-practice cases in their region.

Moon (2002) has developed a framework for e-government development adapted from Hiller and Belanger (2001), which consists of five stages:

1.   Information dissemination
2.   Two-way communication
3.   Service and financial transactions
4.   Vertical and horizontal integration
5.   Political participation

The final stage reflects the ability of the Internet to utilize interactive modes of communications such as bulletin boards, real-time chats, and live broadcasts. These functions, Moon (2002, p. 426) suggests, "enable government to promote public participation in policy-making processes by posting public notices and exchanging ideas with the public." A similar approach toward

e-government development includes phases beginning with information dissemination and concluding with transforming government (Balutis, 2001).
These models of e-government hierarchies are ideal for studying e-government practices; however, an important issue to be taken into consideration
by Latin American municipalities is that each of the different phases of
e-government implementation relies on the completion of a previous phase
(Melitski, 2004).

When attempting to move too rapidly through the stages of e-government, the
initial stages begin to erode. Melitski (2004, p. 653) points out that "instead
of maintaining accurate and timely information online, the focus of many
managers has been to move to the next 'stage' of implementation, and the
result is a plethora of outdated and inconsistent information on many government Web sites." The following municipal e-government cases, in addition
to serving as best-practice examples in Latin America, also provide a basis
for effective Web sites, and questions are posed in the areas of privacy and
security policy, usability, content, services, and citizen participation.

Methodology

This research examines e-government practices throughout select Latin
America cities, which have been chosen in accordance with their population
size, the total number of individuals using the Internet, and the percentage
of individuals using the Internet. The rationale for selecting the largest cities
stems from previous research, which suggests that there is a positive relationship between population and e-government capacity at the local level
(Moon, 2002; Moon & deLeon, 2001; Musso, Weare, & Hale 2000; Weare,
Musso, & Hale, 1999).

The instrument for evaluating these municipal Web sites consisted of five
components: (a) privacy and security, (b) usability, (c) content, (d) services,
and (e) citizen participation. The research instrument is one of the most extensive in e-government research today, utilizing 92 measures (see Table 1
and Appendix). In developing the overall score of a municipality, each of the
five categories was equally weighted, with a highest possible score of 100.

Table 1. E-government measures (Source: Holzer & Kim, 2004)

E-Government Category	Number of Key Concepts	Raw Score	Weighted Score	Keywords
Security/ Privacy	19	28	20	Privacy policies, authentication, encryption, data management, and use of cookies
Usability	20	32	20	User-friendly design, branding, length of home page, targeted-audience links or channels, and site search capabilities
Content	19	47	20	Access to current and accurate information, public documents, reports, publications, and multimedia materials
Service	20	57	20	Transactional services involving purchase or register, and interaction between citizens, businesses, and government
Citizen Participation	14	39	20	Online civic engagement, Internet-based policy deliberation, and citizen-based performance measurement
Total	92	203	100	

Findings

Among the 15 city Web sites evaluated, Sao Paulo, Brazil (36.11), and Buenos Aires, Argentina (32.79), had the highest overall index scores. These two cities ranked 21st and 28th respectively among the cities evaluated worldwide. In the area of privacy and security policy, Santiago, Chile, ranked highest among the Latin American cities with a score of 3.21. In the area of usability, Ciudad de Mexico ranked third highest among the Latin American cities with a score of 10.63, behind Sao Paulo and Buenos Aires. In the area of content, Montevideo, Uruguay, ranked third highest among the Latin American cities with a score of 5.74, behind Sao Paulo and Buenos Aires. In the content area, the highest ranking cities in the category are singled out, excluding the two best-practice cities of Latin America, in order to provide a range of cities as benchmarks for regional study. In the area of service, Santa Fe de Bogotá, Colombia, ranked third highest among the Latin American cities with a score of 5.96, behind Sao Paulo and Buenos Aires. Finally, in the area of citizen participation, Tegucigalpa, Honduras, ranked highest among the Latin American cities with a score of 9.74 and was third overall among the 100-city study of municipalities worldwide.

Latin American Best Practices: Sao Paulo, Brazil

The highest overall score of those municipalities studied in Latin America was achieved by Sao Paulo, Brazil (36.11). Sao Paulo was also ranked 21st overall among the 100 municipalities studied, and received its highest score in the area of usability. The city's score of 14.38 was 15th overall in this area, and in the area of service, its score of 9.12 led to a 9th-place ranking. The remaining areas of content, citizen participation, and privacy resulted in rankings of 22nd, 25th, and 45th respectively. Sao Paulo received a score of 0 in the area of privacy, along with nearly half of the countries in Latin America.

As well as Sao Paulo did in Latin America, its overall score of 36.11 was roughly half that of Seoul, Korea's (73.48), which was the highest ranked municipality in the study. In addition, although Sao Paulo has one of the highest online populations in the world, the ratio of those online to the overall city population is disappointingly low. This is a trend throughout the Latin American municipalities studied and for the region as a whole. The gap between those who have access to the Internet and those who do not is often referred to as the digital divide. The digital divide has historically impacted lower socioeconomic individuals. The Internet as a communication medium also tends to favor individuals with strong writing skills. The other digital divide, or the "gap between those who not only know how to contact government but understand enough about it to be it able to sift and sort their way through a perhaps poorly designed computer website," (Stowers, 2003, p. 22) adds to the problems of access in e-government. Kuttan and Peters (2003) set forth four types of divides as defined in the literature:

1. Information-technology usability
2. Computer access
3. Broadband speed
4. Internet access

Table 2. Findings

Ranking	City	Country	Score	Privacy	Usability	Content	Service	Participation
21	Sao Paulo	Brazil	36.11	0.00	14.38	8.51	9.12	4.10
28	Buenos Aires	Argentina	32.78	0.00	12.18	7.66	8.07	4.87
32	Tegucigalpa	Honduras	31.20	2.14	10.00	5.11	4.21	9.74
41	Santa Fe de Bogotá	Colombia	25.69	2.14	10.00	5.53	5.96	2.05
43	Montevideo	Uruguay	24.44	2.86	10.63	5.74	3.16	2.05
48	Ciudad de Mexico	Mexico	22.40	0.36	10.63	4.68	5.96	0.77
53	Panama City	Panama	19.90	0.00	10.00	3.83	3.51	2.56
59	San Jose	Costa Rica	18.16	0.36	9.06	2.98	4.74	1.03
60	Santiago	Chile	17.84	3.21	5.94	3.83	2.81	2.05
61	Guayaquil	Ecuador	17.73	1.07	9.38	2.77	2.98	1.54
64	Caracas	Venezuela	15.96	0.00	7.81	2.77	3.33	2.05
65	Asuncion	Paraguay	15.15	0.00	6.25	3.19	2.63	3.08
67	San Salvador	El Salvador	14.29	1.07	8.44	2.34	1.93	0.51
77	La Paz	Bolivia	8.55	1.07	4.06	2.55	0.35	0.51
78	Lima	Peru	6.24	0.00	4.69	0.85	0.70	0.00

The significance of the digital divide becomes increasingly apparent when policy makers in government give additional weight to feedback and communications with the citizens via the Internet. The problems of the digital divide plague even the best cases in Latin America, such as Sao Paulo (Figure 1).

Latin American Best Practices: Buenos Aires, Argentina

The second highest overall score of those municipalities studied in Latin America was that of Buenos Aires, Argentina (32.79), and the city was ranked 28th overall among the 100 municipalities studied. Buenos Aires received its highest score in the area of usability. The city's score of 12.188 was 34th overall in the category. In the area of service, its score of 8.07 led to a 12th-place ranking. The remaining areas of citizen participation, content,

Figure 1. Web site of Sao Paulo (Available at http://www.prefeitura.sp.gov. br. Accessed December15, 2004)

and privacy resulted in rankings of 19th, 28th, and 45th respectively. Buenos Aires also received a score of 0 in the area of privacy.

One of the most overlooked functions of e-government is privacy and security. Abramson and Morin (2003) outline three major challenges that confront the public sector in terms of implementing e-government. These challenges include financing and pricing e-services, adopting new technologies, and security and privacy. Similarly, Reddick (2004) identifies privacy and security as 2 of 12 hurdles that have had a negative impact on the growth of e-government. Heiman (2003) proposes 10 recommendations for public-sector information security. His primary recommendation is to implement an IT governance structure that is all inclusive. He states that the structure should be inclusive of all stakeholders, with all branches of state government and local units of government represented so as to develop policies, standards,

Figure 2. Web site of Buenos Aires (Available at http://www.buenosaires.gov. ar. Accessed December15, 2004)

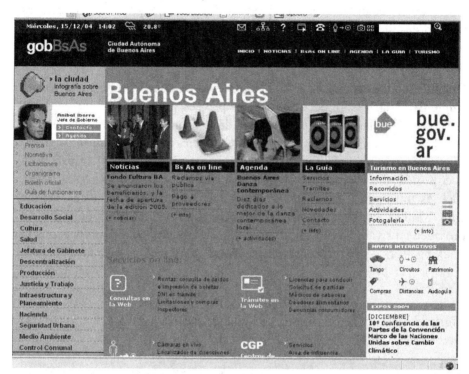

and security plans. Hiller and Belanger (2001, pp. 28-29) recommend that government "must meet the legal requirements to install confidence and trust in government," and "government must gain individual confidence and trust by addressing privacy perceptions." These are just a few of the recommendations based on privacy and security upon which many of the Latin American municipalities can build. Buenos Aires was one of the overall best practices in Latin America, but in the area of privacy and security, it received a score of 0. Additional opportunities for a more private and secure Web site are discussed below in the case of Santiago, Chile.

Privacy and Security Policy: Santiago, Chile

In the area of privacy and security policy, Santiago, Chile, ranked highest among the Latin American cities with a score of 3.21. Santiago was also ranked 23rd overall among the 100 municipalities studied. An essential question to take into consideration for municipal Web sites is, "Does the site have a privacy or security statement or policy?" Over 68% of all municipalities studied did not provide a privacy or security statement at all. One of the reasons that Santiago had an above-average score was that it was able to provide such a statement.

One method for expanding a privacy policy is to make it available beyond a single page. That is, direct access to the privacy policy should be available on every page that requires or accepts data. Moreover, privacy statements should make available information about agencies collecting data through the Internet and the type of information that is being collected. If any information is collected, the manner in which it will be used should also be disclosed, such as third-party disclosure, mailing lists, or managerial access to the data. Neither Santiago nor any of the other Latin American municipalities provided a privacy policy addressing the use of cookies or Web beacons in tracking users. With respect to security, some areas of consideration include

Figure 3. Web site of Santiago. Available at http://www.ciudad.cl. Accessed December15, 2004.

password-restricted pages, digital signatures, and functions that check for viruses during downloads. One last consideration for municipal Web sites is the identification of a contact person for inquires into security and privacy issues.

Although Santiago may be viewed as a benchmark for municipalities in Latin America, any municipalities that aspire to above-average scores in privacy and security should emulate worldwide best practices. The top-ranked municipalities worldwide are Hong Kong, Singapore, and New York, with scores of 15.36, 11.79, and 11.07 respectively.

Usability: Ciudad de Mexico, Mexico

In the area of usability, Ciudad de Mexico, Mexico, ranked third highest among the Latin American cities with a score of 10.63, behind Sao Paulo and Buenos Aires. Ciudad de Mexico also ranked 48th overall among the 100 municipalities studied.

As a whole, the municipalities in Latin America averaged the lowest scores in usability when compared to other regions throughout the world. The Web site of Ciudad de Mexico, however, reflects some basic user-friendly Web characteristics. These include having a search function, navigation bar, and consistent color and formatting.

There are other areas of potential improvement for the home page of Ciudad de Mexico and most Latin American municipalities. For instance, a home page that does not require numerous screens to view is considered a positive function of usability. In cases where long documents or pages require more than three to four screens, there should be alternate methods for viewing, such as a .doc or .pdf file. Web sites that allow citizens to submit information via online forms are user friendly if they incorporate explicit notation, information for fixing errors, and fields that do not require resubmitting all information when errors are found. Most Web sites have search functions, but additional means for enhancing usability include the ability to limit the scope of a search. Search functions that provide advanced search options and the ability to narrow a returned search by performing a sub-search also benefit users. Additional areas of Web site usability include having a site map, the date information was added for recent updates, and links for targeted audiences (e.g., youth, family, businesses, public employees, etc.).

Figure 4. Web site of Ciudad de Mexico (Available at http://www.df.gob.mx/. Accessed December15, 2004)

Sao Paulo, Buenos Aires, and Ciudad de Mexico can be viewed as benchmarks of usability for municipalities in Latin America. Worldwide best practices in the area include the top-ranked municipalities of Hong Kong, Jerusalem, and Seoul, with scores of 19.38, 18.75, and 17.50 respectively.

Content: Montevideo, Uruguay

In the area of content, Montevideo, Uruguay, ranked third highest among the Latin American cities with a score of 5.74, behind Sao Paulo and Buenos Aires. Montevideo was also ranked 40th overall among the 100 municipalities studied. Although Montevideo, with a below-average score, is not necessarily a best practice in the region, its inclusion adds a useful case to the study of e-government municipalities in Latin America.

Figure 5. Web site of Montevideo (Available at http://www.imm.gub.uy/. Accessed December15, 2004)

Montevideo did include many of the basic characteristics of e-government content, such as information about the location of offices, listings of external links, and contact information for agencies and departments or employees and public officials. Moving beyond basic Web site content, many municipal Web sites worldwide also provide information such as minutes of public meetings, city regulations, agency mission statements, calendars of events, and budget information. An additional level of Web site content includes the ability to purchase or order documents online, geographic information systems (GIS) capabilities, and an emergency or alert mechanism.

Montevideo, Sao Paulo, and Buenos Aires can be viewed as benchmarks for municipalities in Latin America. Worldwide best practices in the content dimension include the top-ranked municipalities of New York, Stockholm, and Singapore, with scores of 14.68, 14.68, and 14.04 respectively.

Figure 6. Web site of Santa Fe de Bogotá (Available at http://www.alcal-diabogota.gov.co. Accessed December15, 2004)

Service: Santa Fe de Bogotá, Colombia

In the area of service, Santa Fe de Bogotá, Colombia, ranked third highest among the Latin American cities with a score of 5.96, behind Sao Paulo and Buenos Aires. Montevideo was also ranked 23rd overall among the 100 municipalities studied. The early 1990s witnessed the use of the Internet by city governments primarily for service and information delivery and was a reflection of what Ho (2002) identifies as the bureaucratic paradigm. Ho suggests that the late 1990s marked the emergence of e-governance as a paradigm shift toward public-service delivery. "One-stop service centers" via the Internet have not required vast reorganizations of personnel, and a government Web site can serve as a "convenient and cost-effective platform for centralized service provision" (Ho, p. 436).

Santa Fe de Bogotá has begun to increase services online as suggested above. However, most Latin American municipalities have not reflected any paradigm shift. Some services that Web sites provide include paying for utilities such as water, electricity, and gas, filing or paying taxes, paying fines or tickets, and applying for permits. Some additional services that are reflected in best-practice Web sites worldwide include searchable databases, allowing users to file complaints, access private information such as educational and medical records, customize the main city home page depending on individual needs, and receive timely responses to requests for information.

Santa Fe de Bogotá, Sao Paulo, and Buenos Aires can be viewed as benchmarks for municipalities in Latin America. Worldwide, the top-ranked municipalities in this area are Seoul, Hong Kong, and Singapore, with scores of 15.44, 14.04, and 13.33 respectively.

Citizen Participation: Tegucigalpa, Honduras

In the area of citizen participation, Tegucigalpa, Honduras, ranked highest among the Latin American cities with a score of 9.74. Tegucigalpa also ranked third overall among all of the worldwide municipalities studied. Of the five categories, citizen participation is the only one where a Latin American municipality scored in the top five worldwide. Although the Latin American municipalities as a whole still scored below average, Tegucigalpa was a clear exception.

The basic questions asked when considering online citizen participation include the following. Does the Web site allow users to provide comments or feedback to individual departments and agencies through online forms? Does the Web site allow users to provide comments or feedback to elected officials (e.g., the mayor or city council)? Tegucigalpa takes online communication to the next level. The high score in citizen participation comes in part from the Web site's "Chat with the Mayor" section. The ability to log in and chat with a mayor is not a common practice among municipalities. This practice can be attributed to the initiative of Tegucigalpa's mayor. Additional possibilities of government-citizen communication via the Internet are exemplified by Seoul's OPEN (Online Procedures Enhancement for Civil Applications) system. Holzer and Kang (2002) highlight the significant government reforms that Seoul underwent beginning in 1998, specifically the OPEN system's ability to "enhance transparency in bureaucracy through the posting of many specific descriptions and administrative criteria for public service" (p. 44).

Figure 7. Web site of Tegucigalpa (Available at http://www.alcaldiadetegu-cigalpa.com. Accessed December15, 2004)

In addition to communication with city officials, other forms of citizen participation include Listservs, newsletters, and bulletin boards. Best practices include functions such as discussion forums on policy issues, e-meetings in real time, synchronous video of public events, an online citizen satisfaction survey, and a citywide performance-measurement system published online.

In terms of citizen participation, Tegucigalpa is a benchmark for municipalities in Latin America and can also serve as a best-practice case for municipalities worldwide. Additional best practices in citizen participation include the top-ranked municipalities of Seoul, Rome, and Singapore, with scores of 15.64, 10.51, and 9.74 respectively.

Conclusion

The cases cited above highlight e-government best practices in Latin American municipalities, as reported in the 2004 study *Digital Governance in Municipalities Worldwide* (Holzer & Kim, 2004). Although this study did not take into consideration all e-government practices in Latin America, this chapter has provided benchmark cases for cities in the Latin America region. Overall, Sao Paulo, Brazil, and Buenos Aires, Argentina, ranked in the top third of all 100 municipalities studied worldwide. A focus on the five categories (privacy and security policy, usability, content, service, and citizen participation) is important for developing e-government practices in Latin America.

The municipalities discussed reflect similar types of governments and capacities, thereby serving as models or benchmarks. It should be noted that political and cultural externalities impact the adoption of e-government best practices throughout the region. Underscoring this, Holzer and Kim wrote the following:

Even though some cities have improved their own applications, and are now known as "best practices," they may not be easily adopted by other cities which have different cultures and institutions. Innovative applications regarded as best practices must be revised and adapted, depending on specific cultures and institutions. (p. 87)

It is important for e-government practices to not attempt to function beyond a city's capacities and capabilities. A strong foundation for e-government is the best approach for Latin American municipalities, and this foundation can be developed around the questions we have set out and by surveying the benchmark cases we have identified. Although the Latin American region as a whole is in the early stages of e-government, building upon established practices will determine the region's success in the long run.

References

Abramson, M. A., & Morin, T. L. (2003). The e-government challenge. In M. A. Abramson & T. L. Morin (Eds.), *E-government 2003* (pp. 1-14). Lanham, MD: Rowan and Littlefield Publishers.

Balutis, A. (2001). E-government 2001, Part I: Understanding the challenge and evolving strategies. *The Public Manager, 30*(1) 33-37.

Economist Intelligence Unit. (2005a, March 9). *Chile telecoms: Growth focused on Internet and data.* Retrieved August 30, 2005, http:www. eb.eiu.com/index.asp?layout=show_article&article_id=1598104759

Economist Intelligence Unit. (2005b, February 11). *Chile: Telecoms and technology background.* Retrieved August 30, 2005, http:www.eb.eiu. com/index.asp?layout=show_article&article_id=1018084901

Heiman, D. (2003). Public-sector information security. In M. A. Abramson & T. L. Morin (Eds.), *E-government 2003* (pp. 297-328). Lanham, MD: Rowan and Littlefield Publishers.

Hiller, J., & Belanger, F. (2001). *Privacy strategies for electronic government* (E-government series). Arlington, VA: PricewaterhouseCoopers Endowment for the Business of Government.

Ho, A. T.-K. (2002). Reinventing local governments and the e-government initiative. *Public Administration Review, 62*(4), 434-444.

Holzer, M., & Kang, H.-S. (2002). Building transparent bureaucracy in the city of Seoul: A holistic view of Seoul metropolitan government. In M. Holzer & K. Byong-Joon (Eds.), *Building good governance: Reforms in Seoul* (pp. 29-50). Newark, NJ: National Center for Public Productivity and Korea: Seoul Development Institute.

Holzer, M., & Kim, S.-T. (2004). *Digital governance in municipalities worldwide: An assessment of municipal Web sites throughout the world.* Newark, NJ: National Center for Public Productivity.

Holzer, M., Melitski, J., Rho, S.-Y., & Schwester, R. (2004). *Restoring trust in government: The potential of digital citizen participation.* Washington, DC: IBM Endowment for the Business of Government.

Holzer, M., & Schwester, R. (2005). ICTs as participatory vehicles. In M. Khosrow-Pour (Ed.), *Encyclopedia of information science and technology* (pp. 1372-1378). Hershey, PA: Idea Group Incorporated.

Improvement & Development Agency (IDeA) & the Society of Information Technology Management (Socitm). (2002). *Local e-government now: A worldwide view.* Retrieved May 1, 2005, from http://www.locregis. net/aaa/LEGNUK.PDF

Kakabade, A., Kakabade, N.K., & Kouzmin, A. (2003). Reinventing the democratic governance project through information technology? A growing agenda for debate. *Public Administration Review, 63(1)*, 44-60.

Kuttan, A., & Peters, L. (2003). *From digital divide to digital opportunity.* Lanham, MD: The Scarecrow Press, Inc.

Melitski, J. (2004). E-government and information technology in the public sector. In M. Holzer & S. Hwan Lee (Eds.), *Public productivity handbook* (2nd ed., pp. 649-672). New York: Marcel Dekker.

Moon, M., & deLeon, P. (2001). Municipal Reinvention: Municipal values and diffusion among municipalities. *Journal of Public Adminstration Research and Theory 11*(3), 327-352.

Moon, M. J. (2002). The evolution of e-government among municipalities: Rhetoric or reality? *Public Administration Review, 62*(4), 424-433.

Musso, J., Weare, C., & Hale, M. (2000). Designing Web technologies for local governance reform: Good management or good democracy. *Political Communication, 17*(1), 1-19.

Padget, J. (2005). E-government and e-democracy in Latin America. *IEEE Intelligent Systems, 20*(1), 94-96.

Reddick, C. G. (2004, March). *A two-stage model of e-government growth.* Paper presented at the 2004 National American Society for Public Administration Conference, Portland, Oregon.

Stowers, G. N. L. (2003). The state of federal Websites: The pursuit of excellence. In M. A. Abramson & T. L. Morin (Eds.), *E-government 2003* (pp. 17-52). Lanham, MD: Rowan and Littlefield Publishers.

Weare, C., Musso, J., & Hale, M. (1999). Electronic Democracy and the diffusion of municipal Web pages in California. *Administration and Society, 31*(1), 3-27.

Appendix: Criteria for Web Site Evaluation

Privacy/Security	Usability	Content	Service	Citizen Participation
1-2. A privacy or security statement/policy	20-21. Home-page length, page length	40. Information about the location of offices	59-61. Pay utilities, taxes, fines	79-80. Comments or feedback
3-6. Data collection	22. Targeted audience	41. Listing of external links	62. Apply for permits	81-82. Newsletter
7. Option to have personal information used	23-24. Navigation bar	42. Contact information	63. Online tracking system	83. Online bulletin board or chat capabilities
8. Third-party disclosures	25. Site map	43. Minutes of public meetings	64. Apply for licenses	84. Online discussion forum on policy issues
9. Ability to review personal data records	26-28. Font color	44. City code and regulations	65. E-procurement	85. Scheduled e-meetings for discussion
10. Managerial measures	29-32. Forms	45. City charter and policy priority	66. Property assessments	86. Online surveys/polls
11. Use of encryption	33-38. Search tool	46. Mission statements	67. Searchable databases	87. Synchronous video
12. Secure server	39. Update of Web site	47. Budget information	68. Complaints	88-89. Citizen satisfaction survey
13. Use of cookies or Web beacons		48-49. Documents, reports, or books (publications)	69-70. Bulletin board about civil applications	90-92. Performance measures, standards, or benchmarks
14. Notification of privacy policy		50. GIS capabilities	71. FAQ (frequently asked questions)	
15. Contact or e-mail address for inquiries		51. Emergency management or alert mechanism	72. Request information	
16. Public information through a restricted area		52-53. Disability access	73. Customize the main city home page	
17. Access to nonpublic information for employees		54. Wireless technology	74. Access private information online	
18. Use of digital signatures		55. Access in more than one language	75. Purchase tickets	
19. Function of checking virus		56-57. Human-resources information	76-77. Webmaster response	
		58. Calendar of events	78. Report violations of administrative laws and regulations	

Chapter IX

Defining and Measuring E-Democracy:
A Case Study on Latin American Local Governments[1]

Marc Navarro, Universidad Pompeu Fabra, Spain

Abstract

The aim of this chapter is to define and to measure electronic democracy. In order to achieve this purpose, first, different conceptual perspectives about the interconnection between new information and communication technologies and democratic institutions are described. Second, a definition of electronic democracy and its relationship with classical theories on representative democracy is provided. Third, with this description, an index to measure the stage of development of electronic democracy in a given political system is developed. Fourth, the index is tested in some Latin American municipalities. Finally, with the obtained results, some conclusions about the level and nature of electronic-democracy implementation in the region are described. The chapter adopts an institutional approach to understand the impact of ICTs on institutions that illustrates how difficult defining and measuring this reality can get.

Introduction

The study about the relationship between technological change and institutions has been a controversial topic in the social-sciences context. There are several researchers that try to illustrate, both from a positive and negative perspective, the impact of technological advances along history. This literature refers to several issues: economic development (Jorgenson & Stiroh, 1999), democracy promotion (Ott, 1998), public administration (Fountain, 2001), or business performance (Brynjolfsson & Hitt, 2000).

Recently, along with the rise of the Internet, the World Wide Web, and computer-mediated communications, there has been a growing concern about how to analyze the impact of ICT on political institutions. In this sense, there is a lot of research intended to show how ICTs have been adopted by some institutions, such as public administration (Criado, 2003; Fountain, 2001; Ho, 2002), political parties (Nixon & Johansson, 1999; Norris, 2001), or parliaments (Kingham, 2003; Louvin & Alderdice, 2001; Norris, 2001; Zittel, 2001). The results and conclusions of this kind of research have led to an increasing interest about the influence of ICTs on the whole political process (Hacker & van Dijk, 2000a; Hague & Loader, 1999; Tsagarousianou, Tambini, & Bryan, 1998; Wilhelm, 2000).

Despite the efforts to determine and to explicitly state the result of the relationship between ICTs and political institutions, it seems that bidirectional analysis has not been as important for researchers. In fact, apparently, scholars have paid less attention to research on the institutional characteristics that promote technological change. Nevertheless, this is starting to become a recurring issue and some authors, such as Parto (2003) or Taylor (2002), have already focused on it. In particular, based on an empirical study on how political institutions affect technological progress in the long run, Taylor maintains that a country's type of governmental structure plays an important role in technological innovation. He argues that centralized governments tend to ignore innovation at the first stages and that they are slower on technological diffusion in comparison to decentralized governments.

In the same context, Pippa Norris (2001) focuses on the political process and states that there is slight empirical evidence to support that differences in the political system can explain the development of an electronic government policy. In spite of it, she observes that the federal countries, and therefore more decentralized ones, have a greater tendency to introduce digital-government strategies. Other studies, like the one carried out by Trechsel, Kies,

Mendez, and Schmitter (2003), develop a comparative analysis among the parliaments of the European Union, and conclude that no institutional variable can explain the use of ICTs by parliaments or by political parties.

The same argument can be found in comparative studies related to parliaments although empirical evidence are not very solid. These analyses support that presidential regimes that promote a closer relationship between the politicians and their electorate have greater incentives to introduce technological innovations. On the contrary, parliamentary systems show less interest in technology (Zittel, 2001).

The study about the implications that ICTs have on political institutions is more and more important as a result of the irruption of the Internet in society and, specifically, in the political scenario. The analysis of the relationship between ICTs and democracy has given rise to new terms that define the new situation. Terms like teledemocracy, digital democracy, cyberdemocracy, or virtual democracy have become popular in the academic context. For the purpose of this chapter, the word *electronic democracy* will be used since it has become the most commonly accepted term.

When we refer to electronic democracy, a few questions should be answered. First, a definition of electronic democracy as well as a description of the way it relates to the classical theories of democracy is required. Second, there is a need to understand how electronic democracy takes place or, in other words, which indicators can be used in order to measure the level of implementation of electronic democracy in a political system.

Regarding the studies on electronic democracy, it should be noted that most of them have been carried out on developed countries. The ICT impact on developing countries seems to have been paid less attention to by scholars due to the technological gap between both of them. Nonetheless, some efforts have been undertaken by these countries, especially in Latin America, that should be considered. Because of it, we judge it necessary to attend to the technological development in this region, and to evaluate in which stage of electronic democracy it is. In order to do so, we will develop our case study on the main Latin American capitals since we suppose that they will be the most technological developed cities in the region.

This chapter intends to give an answer to these inquiries. In order to do so, it will be structured as follows. To begin with, some of the theoretical perspectives in the field will be described. In the second place, taking into account the previous findings, the meaning of electronic democracy will be approached. Finally, a battery of indicators will be suggested as a way to measure electronic democracy. This set of indicators will be the basis to develop an index that quantifies the level of implementation of electronic democracy in the following 17 Latin American local governments: Asuncion, Bogotá, Brasilia, Buenos Aires, Caracas, Guatemala, La Paz, Lima, Managua, Mexico DF, Montevideo, Panama, Quito, San José, San Salvador, Santiago, and Tegucigalpa.

ICT and Institutions: A Brief Literature Review

The study of the impact that ICTs might have on the political process has given rise to a broad debate among scholars. This is due to the fact that the political process is related to a complex institutional structure of information flows to which ICTs can contribute in several ways. Because of it, to take an institutional approach can contribute to understanding better this embeddedness between both realities.

Institutions, as the rules by which actors interact with each other, organize the society. That means that an institution is any socially imposed constraint upon human behavior. As North (1990) notes, institutions are the rules of the games for human interaction. By limiting the actions of humans, it is then possible to give actors some expectations about the actions of others. They thus facilitate human interaction. That is important for us in that institutions build complex and huge information flows between them.

Institutions do not remain unchangeable over time. On the contrary, institutional development is what encourages the evolution of a society. An institutional change occurs when a change in actors' relative power takes place. The acquisition of new knowledge or abilities for a given actor causes changes in its relative power. This new situation results in a restructuring of actors' negotiation guidelines (North). The actor with new knowledge or capability will want to modify the interchange rules in order to obtain better benefits. Therefore, it will want to change the existing institutions. To sum up, a change in the relative power, with the perception of this change for the other actors, is the great impulse for an institutional change.

Thus, regarding ICTs, when institutional change occurs, it is not because the ICTs promote a reorganization in the institution. The new technologies' impact on the institutional change may take place as a result of the opportunities that ICTs make available to the actors. Actors in a given institutional situation use the new opportunities offered by ICTs, organizing their force inside the institution. So, ICTs can accelerate the taking place of activities that set up networks of the institutional framework. Following this approach, new technologies impact the institutions, amplifying the ready existing forces, not creating news (Agre, 2002).

This fact leads to the obvious question about the potential of ICTs to change anything in the current model. Depending on the answer to this question, a classification can be set up with two different models, according to Agre (2002): the amplification model and the reinforcement model.

The amplification model, the one that we will adopt along this chapter, maintains that ICTs alone do not change anything. Nonetheless, they can expand the existing actors' skills who, in fact, are the ones that can promote institutional change. Consequently, and because ICTs introduction is still at its early stages, it is too soon to witness any changes in the contemporary institutions.

Modern institutions developed through the interaction of multiple forces. In this context, the amplification model wonders about the transformation of the interaction among these forces. Therefore, this perspective is more interested in the results than in the causes and, in this sense, it supports that the changes brought about by the use of ICTs will not take place within the whole institutional framework. To predict the consequences of widespread ICTs, it will be necessary to examine the forces at work in the current institutions.

In other words, according to the amplification model, ICTs are introduced within the existing institutional structure and contribute to the forces that these institutions have determined. Thus, they expand the forces already organized within the institutional framework. These forces increase their relative power and, therefore, are the ones that promote institutional change. In this sense, the amplification model is not based on a normative theory of democracy; it does not adopt a normative position. Instead, it recognizes that different normative theories will probably lead to different empirical investigations (Agre, 2002).

For a better understanding of the amplification model, let us contrast it with the reinforcement model, which is prevalent in the literature. This one identifies a structural challenging feature of the political system and wonders about the potential of ICTs to solve the problem. This trend usually adopts a participatory vision of democracy and asks whether ICTs can contribute to enable a broader number of citizens involved in the political process. The conclusions of its supporters are generally negative because they commonly presume that all the new information and communication technologies do is to reinforce the existing structures instead of contributing to solve the perceived problem (Agre, 2002).

The reinforcement-model followers assume that ICTs only can strengthen democracy if they expand opportunities for political participation, such as direct participation of citizens in decision-making or deliberation in the policy process. In doing so, most of them conclude that ICTs are not capable to achieve this. Consequently, new technologies have no impact on democracy. But, as Norris (2001) notes, this is an excessively limited normative yardstick.

Indeed, the reinforcement model suggests that, in practice, ICTs fail when it comes to transforming the existing models of democratic participation, giving rise to a more pessimistic vision about ICTs' ability to bridge the gap between the representatives and the represented. For the followers of this model, ICTs have not provoked an substantial change that have alter the institutional framework.

Since the model expects that ICTs' introduction will resolve all the problems that threaten current democracies, the empirical studies carried out under this premise have come up with negative conclusions that remark that ICTs give rise to the same existing political process and do not contribute to a more participatory democracy (Chadwick & May, 2003; Hagen, 2000; Halle, Musso, & Weare, 1999; Karakaya, 2003; Margolis & Resnick, 2000; Thornton, 2002).

One of the most important differences between both models is that the amplification model is not based on a normative theory of politics. In fact, it defends that different normative theories have to drive different empirical inquires. Several authors have based their work on the amplification model and have adopted different normative patterns of democracy that have resulted in different results in relation to ICTs' potential. In this sense, this perspective supports that there is no theoretical basis for electronic democracy. Instead, there is just theoretical basis for democracy (Requejo, 2002). This stated, how do these theories deal with the electronic-democracy concept?

Van Dijk (2000) is one of the authors that adopt this approach. He carried out an eminently theoretical work about the relationship between different views of democracy and ICTs' repercussion on them. He identified six models of democracy (pluralistic, participatory, libertarian, legalistic, competitive, and plebiscitary) and observed the direction that the information and communication flows took among the actors of the different political systems.

For him, this was a decisive element to interpret the potential relationship between politics and ICTs.

Norris (2003) carried out a similar work. She took into account the thesis of the pluralistic democracy, the direct democracy, and the representative democracy and analyzed how these normative patterns could be used to evaluate the role of ICTs in the government. In her research, contrary to the opinion of the reinforcement-model followers, she supported that there are several ways in which ICTs can strengthen democracy, especially in relation to issues such as transparency or public services delivery. Therefore, on one hand, she backed that ICTs expand the existing forces. But, on the other, she denied that ICTs alone are able to stimulate new forms of participation.

The amplification model worries about how people are interrelated within the institutional framework. Within this system, ICTs are ubiquitous because they can affect almost every arrangement (Agre, 2002). Therefore, the amplification of existing forces can result in a status quo transformation by means of the alteration of the existing information channels. This statement leads to the conclusion that the impact of ICTs on politics cannot be foreseen. As a result, if change takes place, it will be political, not technological. In other words, if democracy does not benefit from technology, institutions, not technology, are to be blamed. But, if ICTs are able to reinforce democracy, then technology should be planned and such programming will have to be sensitive to the different political theories and paradigms of democracy (Barber, 2001).

The amplification model is focused on the broadening of the current forces. However, the introduction of ICTs does not necessarily impact all the actors. Therefore, the embedding of ICTs can lead to different results depending on the actors affected. What is more, it may lead to no institutional change at all. This situation has been analyzed by Barber (1999) who sets up three possible scenarios as a result of the interaction between democracy and technology. He maintains that such a combination can give rise to three settings. The first one is based on complacency and it simply is a mimetic reproduction of the current attitudes and tendencies. It is called the Pangloss Scenario, it is based on the market, which benefits the most.

The second option is a scenario dominated by technological determinism as a result of the expansion of the government capacities related to indirect surveillance and citizenship control (Pandora Scenario). Finally, in the third scenario, technologies foster democratic life. This third alternative is focused on the amplification of citizen capacities (Jeffersonian Scenario).

Barber's (1999) underlying idea is that technology alone cannot give rise to a specific democratic model. Thus, the results produced by the different models will be determined by the quality of the political institutions and the character of its citizens.

In conclusion, technology can transform the existing institutions or give rise to no institutional change. The interconnection between ICTs and democracy can aggravate the problematic features of democracy or can help alleviate them; it can leave everything as it was or can bring about new problems that did not previously exist (Subirats, 2002). Once described the approach that we will use along the chapter, we are ready to develop the next part our work: what electronic democracy is and how to measure it.

Defining Electronic Democracy

Once some of the main research issues about the impact of ICTs on political institutions have been explained, there is a need to clarify the meaning of electronic democracy for the rest of the chapter. The delimitation of this concept will lead to the second of our purposes: to split the concept into several elements in order to carry out an empirical analysis.

Electronic democracy is a concept that has been normally used in relation to the implementation of ICTs to the democratic process. Some examples include online communities, online discussions, or online lobbying (Moore, 1999). In this sense, it can be said that there are as many notions about electronic democracy as ideas about democracy. Also, due to the early stage of the concept, there exists great confusion about its meaning (Riley, 2003). Regarding the genesis of the concept, three main roots can be identified (Grönlund, 2002):

- The Internet culture found within what has been called "virtual communitarians," that is, people who use ICT within the framework of social organizations
- Government rationalization efforts that have become apparent as a result of programs such as eEurope
- The critical mass of Internet users in many countries

It is not only interesting to learn about the origins of the concept but also about its scope. As the enlargement model supports, for the purpose of this chapter, ICTs are not an independent force that either strengthens or weakens democracy, but they are a tool that amplifies the trends and forces that are already present in the political system. This belief does not imply that ICTs are not able to contribute to a change in the current institutional balance. On the contrary, the main idea to be emphasized is that ICTs are not immune to the institutional architecture within which they are implemented. Therefore, their impact depends on the institutional framework within which they are put into action.

Depending on the effect of ICTs on the institutional design and on the actors, the balance will be specifically changed. This transformation does not necessarily lead to an institutional development. However, this result cannot be predicted in advance nor can it give rise to theoretical guidelines about the future performance of political systems, as we stated above.

Nonetheless, our interest is electronic democracy. That means that our focus of attention embraces the ICTs' implementation on institutions of representative democracy, not in the whole institutions included in a given political system. As a result, we need to make up a definition of the term. In doing so, we will be able to establish the different elements included in the definition and, after that, develop our index to measure electronic democracy.

The concept of electronic democracy to be used throughout this chapter will consider the employment of ICTs (such as the Internet, interactive broadcasts, or digital phone systems) in the policy-making process, always under every pattern of representative democracy (Hacker & van Dijk, 2000b). More exactly, the focus of interest is the policy-making process, from the design of the political agenda to the implementation of the policy. Therefore, electronic democracy is defined as the use of different mechanisms offered by ICTs that can be embedded on policy-making process. In other words, the use of ICTs to reinforce representative democracy (Macintosh, 2004).

This is a very comprehensive definition, since we believe that specialized literature has been too often excessively demanding with the concept of electronic democracy. Many times, it has been assumed that ICTs would only reinforce democracy if they are able to expand the opportunities for political participation, such as in the case of direct participation in the policy-making process, deliberation in the political process, or electronic voting (Norris, 2001).

The role of ICTs in a representative democracy should take into consideration all the institutions and organizations within which the function of representation is used. It should bear in mind what kind of new opportunities

Figure 1. The policy making process

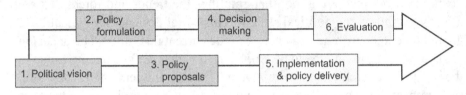

are created after the implementation of new information and communication channels in terms of strengthening the link between the representatives and the represented. It should wonder about the enlargement of information channels, the search for transparency and accountability, and the promotion of participation. Otherwise, similar conclusions to those of some studies could be reached.

In order to define the concept, it is necessary to exactly specify what policy making is. Just as Dahl (1992) supported, the policy-making process has two discernible parts: (a) the agenda setting, and (b) the decision about the solution to be adopted. The agenda setting refers to the pronouncement of a topic. During this phase, politicians select (or reject) the issues to be tackled in the next stage. During the second phase, politicians try to reach a solution and make a final decision about the definitive approval or refusal of the policy.

The decision-making process is provisional until the end of the second stage. During this period, several debates, votes, amendments, and agreements take place, but still they are preliminary actions that can be object to changes during the last phase of the decision-making process. In fact, it is not until the end of this last phase that decisions do become compulsory. Decisions are only obligatory at the end of the decision-making process (Dahl).

As Figure 1 suggests, the policy-making process comprises the gray boxes, while the white ones refer to the policy delivery and implementation process. The first phase of the policy-making process, when the agenda is set, considers the two first gray boxes, while the second phase, related to the decision about a solution, takes shape in the two following boxes.

During the different stages of the policy-making process, one can observe that there are several openings for the implementation of ICTs. In the first place, between the initial political vision and the policy formulation, there are opportunities for the represented to make requests to the representatives.

Also, there are chances for the citizens to set online discussions. These debates can help develop the political agenda.

Second, once the policy has been formulated and the phase of proposals is opened, ICTs can highly contribute to enlarge the channels of diffusion of the formulated policy. Also, the government can arrange debates and deliberations. It can also develop surveys in order to have important information about the public opinion with regard to the policy proposal.

Third, previous to the end of the final policy, ICTs offer valuable opportunities to the citizens since they allow them to write and send the last proposals and consultations about the policy. Also, thanks to ICTs, political institutions can offer a large amount of information about the state of the art, about the representatives' views and opinions, and about the different policy rough drafts and versions along the whole process.

To sum up, ICTs have a lot of potential to reinforce the policy-making process. Depending on the objective to be pursued, ICTs can contribute to the democratic process in three different ways, which, in turn, means that three subconcepts can be obtained from the electronic-democracy term (Kubicek, Westholm, & Winker, 2003; Organization for Economic Cooperation and Development [OECD], 2001; Tsagarousianou, 1999):

- **Information:** Electronic democracy offers a high potential for the improvement of political information and transparency. For the purpose of this chapter, it is especially important to consider the new channels that citizens can use to collect information. This kind of information is related to the politicians' opinions and to the task of their governments and parliaments as well.

- **Communication and consultation:** Electronic democracy can enrich communication and consultation between citizens and politicians in the design of public policies. In fact, dialogue may increase as a result of a greater interaction between the represented and the representatives, of the improvement of communication channels, and of the enlargement of citizens' capacities to question politicians. Moreover, electronic democracy can significantly support discussions in the public sphere.

- **Participation:** This sort of channel offers a better relationship with the government, in which citizens are involved in the policy in a direct way. This happens when the participation is oriented to the policy making and the result of it is compulsory for elected authorities.

What is more, these three elements can give rise to three different levels of civic involvement in the policy-making process. The predominance of one model or another will depend on the focus of attention or reinforcement of the different initiatives. As a result, and taking into account the three electronic democracy subconcepts mentioned above, three situations related to public participation may occur (Macintosh, 2004):

- **Electronic enabling:** It refers to how ICTs can be used to expand the relevant information in a more understandable and accessible way for the citizenship.
- **Electronic engaging:** It refers to politicians' concern about consulting with a wider audience with the objective of obtaining deeper contributions as well as supporting the deliberative discussion on public policies.
- **Electronic empowerment:** It refers to how information and communication channels are released to support participation and to facilitate bottom-up communication with the aim to influence the political agenda.

Measuring Electronic Democracy

This section is aimed at itemizing each of the three electronic-democracy components that have been previously developed. In order to do so, for each of the listed elements (information, communication and consultation, and deliberation), several ICT-enabled procedures have been selected. When determining the set of variables that describe each group, a technological limitation has been considered. Thus, this section deals with an ideal electronic-democracy concept, taking into account what technology is able to pursue nowadays. Nevertheless, the different features listed have not been selected from an ideal model. Instead, they have been adopted from many different international experiences.[2]

This chapter gathers the most important.

Information

Information distribution is one of the basic principles of democracy, that is, a one-way relation in which government produces and delivers information for use by citizens. It can cover both passive access to information upon demand by citizens and active measures by government to disseminate information to citizens (Coleman & Gotze, 2001).

The first issue to be tackled will have to do with the provision of understandable and accessible information to the citizens. It has been usually a matter of top-down communication that does not allow for an interaction between the issuer and the government, with no interaction between the source and the recipient. Depending on the objective to be pursued, three types of information can be identified (Lenk, 1999): (a) basic information about the government, (b) information on public-services eligibility and on legal rights and doubts, and (c) information on planning and on the policy-making process.

Although the concept of electronic democracy was earlier defined as the introduction of ICTs in the policy-making process, it is interesting to also take into account the provision of basic information about the government, about the politicians, and about other legal issues. This is so because this sort of information is very useful to make the most about the other dimensions of electronic democracy. In short, information allows the citizens to be aware about the basic structure and components of their government and to be more qualified to participate in the policy-making process.

Thirteen variables have been selected to depict the three information categories. They are listed below:

a. Basic information about the government. For this first type of information, the following variables have been considered: (a) structure, history, and functions of the city council, (b) members of the council, and (c) members of the government.

b. Information on legal data. The identified variables are as follows: (a) access to regulations, whether all of them or merely to those related to economic issues, (b) access to the municipal law, (c) access to the last electoral results, and (d) access to the municipal budget.

c. Information on planning and on the state of policies. This category's variables are the following: (a) access to the state of the regulations (both general and economic), (b) access to the full calendar of the council's meetings, (c) access to the government program, (d) access to the council-meeting documents, and (e) access to the government-meeting documents.

Communication and Consultation

Representative democracies need a good communication between citizens and their representatives in order to reduce the principal-agent problem. Political engagement becomes absolutely relevant in this respect, opening channels to connecting them, especially for hearing voices in policy debates that often do not have this chance to do it. Communication and consultation channels are needed in order to build a relation based on partnership with the government, in which citizens engage in the policy-making process. It recognizes the role for citizens in proposing policy options and shaping the agenda and the policy outputs. For this proposal, we consider a set of channels in which ICTs can improve the communication and consultation of our democracies.

Communication and consultation channels seek to support an active participation and facilitate the bottom-up ideas to influence both the political agenda and policy-making process. The citizens are emerging as producers rather than just consumers of policy. It is a recognition that there is a need to allow citizens to influence policy formulation.

This group of channels considers new channels offered by ICTs to improve the bidirectional information in the policy-making process. Two types of procedures are taken into account. On one hand, there are the communication channels. These are channels launched by the government with the objective of welcoming opinions about a specific or a general item.

On the other hand, there are consultation channels. They are those procedures that allow the citizens to present their opinions and ideas and to discuss with politicians in order to make a difference on the agenda or to make clear their reactions to the government initiatives or to any member of the council actions.

The main difference between both systems is that consultation channels are led by the government and they are used during a restricted period of time. On the contrary, communication channels are up for an unlimited period of time.

The means ICTs offer to enhance communication schemes are as follows:

- **Requests mailbox:** This is the simplest form of communication between the politicians and the citizens. It consists of supplying a way to send opinions, complaints, or questions. The advantages that this system presents are related to letting people reveal their ideas in a direct way. It is a complement to the classical requests mailboxes that are found on site.

- **E-mail:** It is commonly said that this is the queen of ICTs applications to democracy (Coleman & Gotze, 2002). It has to do with giving the citizens the chance to send their opinions via electronic mail from a public access point. Messages can be sent to the mayor, to all the government members, or to the whole council.

The consultation channels that this group gathers, and which electronic-democracy analysts have paid more attention to, is the one related to the potential of ICTs for discussion and for the enlargement of the public space (Barabas, 2002; Coleman & Gotze, 2002; Trénel, 2004; Wilhelm, 2000; Witschge, 2003). In fact, the Internet has been usually perceived as a channel that allows debates among a lot of people.

Scholars maintain that the Internet offers a solution to the problems of effective participation because it allows the management of discussion and deliberation on a large scale (Witschge, 2004). Authors also support that online debates and the end of space and time limits could give rise to a democracy improvement beyond compare throughout history (Wilhelm). These channels are the following:

- **Surveys:** This practice consists of opening a communication channel where citizens can be consulted about a specific theme in order to give their opinions (Richard, 1999).

- **Online fora:** These systems allow citizens to discuss an issue or facilitate debates between the citizens and some politicians. The topics approached are usually suggested by some members of the government or by a particular politician (Rosén, 2001).

- **E-petition:** This option is related to the citizens' right to propose issues that they think should be taken into consideration by the legislative or executive body, depending on who the recipient is (Rosén, 2001).

- **Electronic opinion polls:** This option is related to a discussion on a specific service. The participants have the opportunity to learn about an issue and to discuss it, questioning experts and stating their opinions.

- **Chats:** They are based on a direct dialogue between one or several citizens and a politician who are using the computer at the same time.

Anyone connected to the Web page can have access to the discussion in process (Rosén, 2001).

- **Dialogue pages:** A dialogue page is a special electronic page set up around an issue that interests many people. It usually contains a lot of information about the topic under discussion such as background papers, assistance documents, maps, and all that the citizens need in order to develop an opinion and express it (Rosén, 2001).

- **Online focus groups:** This is a tool that allows for in-depth exploration of an issue by the means of an open discussion among a group of eight people who represent a particular sector. The discussion is led by a trained facilitator (Coleman & Gotze, 2002).

- **Electronic panels:** It has to do with citizens' involvement in a discussion with certain representatives. The debate can be focused on a particular service or on public services in general. It can be an open debate or a closed discussion that only allows for specific guests (Coleman & Gotze, 2002).

Participation

Participation refers to the activity oriented to decision making with a compulsory result for authorities. Even in a representative democracy, the ability of citizens to express their political views along the mandate is a fundamental principal. The channels offered by ICTs to enhance participation to elevate opinions directed to representatives can take place in multiple ways.

The growing literature on electronic democracy has focused on the ability of ICTS to enhance participation. New information and communication technologies are commonly perceived as being of great value in allowing new participation channels. ICT allows registering the political attitudes and inclinations of the citizens regarding a given policy. In this sense, instead of physically going to polls, people could vote from home. That is perceived by some scholars as an opportunity to vote more frequently and on more issues. So, referenda and polls could spread since the vote is less expensive. ICTs reduce the time and space problem. The channels offered by ICT on participation are the following:

- **Referenda:** They consist of asking a question of the whole population related to a decision that has to be made. It may help the politicians to adopt or refuse that decision (Coleman & Gotze, 2002).

- **Electronic vote:** It is related to the use of ICTs in any type of elections, be it a representatives election or another type of election under regulation control.

Methodology

In this section, the research method used in order to carry out the empirical analysis will be described. After this explanation, the Electronic Democracy Index (EDI) will be developed from the data obtained from the empirical test.

The technique to be used will be the content-analysis one. This is a qualitative technique based on the study of the social reality through the observation and the study of the documents written in the context of one or several societies. The content analysis will be implemented by examining the municipal Web pages of our sample. The purpose of this observation will be to determine the existence or nonexistence of each of the variables that describe the EDI.

Table 1. Electronic-democracy tools

1. Information	2. Communication and Consultation	3. Participation
1a. Functions of the city council	2a. General mailbox	3a. Referenda
1b. Members of the council	2b. General e mail	3b. Electronic vote
1c. Members of the government	2c. E-mail of members of the government	
1d. Council-meeting documents	2d. E-mail of members of the council	
1e. Government-meeting documents	2e. Requests mailbox by type of policy	
1f. Council-meeting calendar	2f. Survey	
1g. Access to economic regulations	2g. Online forum	
1h. Access to general regulations	2h. E-petition	
1i. State of new regulation	2i. Opinion polls	
1j. Municipal law	2j. Chats	
1k. Electoral results	2k. Dialogue pages	
1l. Government program	2l. Online focus groups	
1m. Municipal budget	2m. Panel meetings	

After obtaining the data, the EDI will be elaborated. For the index development, an equal value (1) will be assigned to each one of the variables that make up the information and participation clusters. In the case of the communication and consultation category, a value of 0.5 for the variables 2a, 2b, 2c, 2d, and 2e will be assigned due to the fact that this set of variables has a smaller impact on electronic democracy. This sort of channel makes it difficult to measure the impact on policy-making processes since nobody knows who is receiving the request. And, in case that message goes to the right person, evaluating the impact of it will continue being tough. The remainder of the variables of this group will be valued with 1.

Next, the results obtained from each of the three groups of variables will be weighed up with a value between 0 and 1. Finally, each of the categories that make up the EDI will be grouped in only one result, that is, a final value of the EDI. This figure will be a number between 0 and 1. This way of proceeding implies that there will be two types of results: one related to the index as a whole and one related to the values of each of its components. Therefore, it will be possible to know which component has been developed with more emphasis and, consequently, has greater influence on the index as a whole.

Empirical Results

Just as was mentioned beforehand, this study focuses on the analysis of the Web pages of 17 municipalities in Latin America that correspond to the capitals of 17 countries in the region. The 17 cities that make up the sample are Asuncion (Paraguay), Bogotá (Colombia), Brasilia (Brazil), Buenos Aires (Argentina), Caracas (Venezuela), Guatemala (Guatemala), La Paz (Bolivia), Lima (Peru), Managua (Nicaragua), Mexico DF (Mexico), Montevideo (Uruguay), Panama (Panama), Quito (Ecuador), San José (Costa Rica), San Salvador (El Salvador), Santiago (Chile), and Tegucigalpa (Honduras).

One of the first observations that the obtained results give rise to regards the most used ICT mechanisms in Latin American municipalities. As Figure 2 shows, the preferred local government channels are focused on information. Communication and consultation, and especially participation, do not seem to have been paid the same attention to by governments.

These results, which show that communication and consultation channels have been more developed than participation, coincide with the results of

Figure 2. EDI's variables in Latin American municipalities

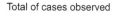

Total of cases observed

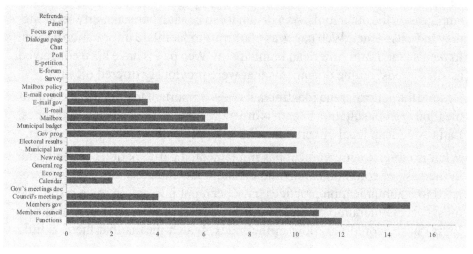

other empirical studies that have been carried out (Beierle & Cahill, 2000; Chadwick, 2003; Kakabadse, Kakabadse, & Kouzmin, 2003; Moon, 2002; Norris, 2003; Thornton, 2002; Trechsel et al., 2003).

With regard to the communication and consultation channels, there are important differences between the two types of systems previously identified. Communication channels (that concern variables 2a, 2b, 2c, 2d, and 2e) have been set in more municipalities than consultation ones (related to variables 2f to 2m). Actually, consultation channels have not been implemented in the municipalities of the set.

At this point, it is important to note that the existence of electronic-democracy devices does not guarantee that they will be used. Some researches have tried to investigate the real use of electronic-democracy tools by public officials. For instance, Salvador, Cortéz, Sánchez, and Ferrer (2004) and Navarro (2004) show that, in Catalonian municipalities, messages sent to the e-mail addresses displayed on the Web pages were not frequently replied to. These studies demonstrate that the percentage of unanswered e-mails was 30.9% and 47.4%, respectively. This test has not been conducted for the purpose of this chapter because it is out of our scope. Nevertheless, it would be interesting to test the variables in future research to check their use.

Once the data for each category has been obtained, it is possible to develop the EDI. As Table 2 shows, the municipalities of the sample have widely developed the information channels offered by ICTs while they have placed less emphasis on the other tools. As a result, it can be said that, generally speaking, they have used their Web pages as platforms to facilitate information access. In fact, so far, Latin American municipality Web pages have been conceived as sites to post online documents that were previously offered off line.

Despite the general trend identified, it is also important to notice that communication and consultation channels are more popular than participation ones. Latin American local governments have hardly paid attention to the latter.

What is more, no government has implemented participation channels and, in the case of communication and consultation channels, only the ones related to communication practices have been put into action. As a result, the most successful municipalities under the model (Brasilia, Buenos Aires, and Lima) have scored very low in the index, which means that there is little

Table 2. The IDE and its components in Latin American municipalities

	Information	Communication & Consultation	Participation	EDI
Brasilia	0.846	0.238	0	0.361
Buenos Aires	0.615	0.238	0	0.284
Lima	0.538	0.238	0	0.259
Quito	0.538	0.190	0	0.243
Santiago	0.538	0.190	0	0.243
Ciudad de México	0.538	0.095	0	0.211
Asunción	0.385	0.238	0	0.208
Bogotá	0.538	0.048	0	0.195
Montevideo	0.385	0.190	0	0.192
Tegucigalpa	0.462	0.095	0	0.186
Caracas	0.308	0.143	0	0.150
Panamá	0.385	0.048	0	0.144
San Salvador	0.385	0.048	0	0.144
La Paz	0.308	0.048	0	0.118
San José	0.308	0.048	0	0.118
Guatemala	0.231	0.048	0	0.093
Managua	0.154	0.095	0	0.083
Average	0.439	0.132	0	0.190

concern about implementing an ICT-related system that has a real impact on the policy-making process. This output may lead to the conclusion that what local governments really want is to introduce a cosmetic reform instead of showing a real interest in electronic democracy. Therefore, it can be concluded that opening the policy-making process to the citizens is not a priority for Latin American municipalities.

Although participation channels have not been implemented, some other conclusions can be drawn from the other electronic-democracy mechanisms. In fact, those municipalities more concerned about the introduction of different models (and not only interested in one of them) have scored better in the EDI. Another trend can also be identified: All of the local governments of the set have scored higher in relation to the information than in relation to communication and consultation. Latin American municipalities are an example of the causal relationship between information and participation. Therefore, when a city is interested in widely informing its citizens, it is also interested in implementing also communication and consultation tools, and vice versa. The main exception to this rule is Bogotá. This city has a middle-high score on information and a very low score on communication and consultation.

Some Tentative Conclusions

This chapter has dealt with one of the most controversial issues in social science nowadays: the relationship between democracy and ICTs. It has aimed at defining and measuring what electronic democracy is in order to move research forward. The approach adopted has allowed for an empirical analysis about the level and the nature of electronic-democracy implementation in Latin American municipalities. Furthermore, it has been the intention of this chapter to illustrate how difficult measuring the new reality can get.

In order to achieve the purpose of the chapter, first, different conceptual perspectives about the interconnection between ICTs and political institutions, in general, and ICTs and democracy, in particular, have been approached. Second, a definition of electronic democracy as well as a description of its relationships with representative democracy has been provided. This explanation has facilitated the measurement of the stage of development of electronic democracy in a political system that has been possible thanks to the EDI.

Third, the index has been tested in some Latin American municipalities. The obtained results have led to some conclusions about the trends of electronic-democracy implementation in the region.

The outputs of this work are similar to those reached by other studies. The EDI shows what local governments' priorities are in relation to electronic democracy. It has been shown that local governments focus on information. As previously stated, the municipal Web pages have been basically used as a platform to post online information that was offered off line before the introduction of ICTs in governments and public administrations. Also, it has been illustrated that the introduced methods of the second subgroup have just taken the form of communication systems. The consultation mechanisms have not been considered at all by the public officials, and neither have the participation tools offered by ICTs.

The low average score of EDI shows that electronic democracy in Latin American municipalities is in its first stage of implementation. Thus, it is a process in development. As a result, it is difficult to recognize any changes in the actors' capabilities within the institutional framework, as the enlargement model supports. For the time being, no institutional change can be observed as the consequence of implementing ICTs in the policy-making process. Nonetheless, this change may happen in the following years once electronic democracy is more developed and these transformations and new tools are better assimilated.

In fact, it can also be argued that the introduction of ICTs in the Latin American municipalities' policy-making process can be described as a cosmetic reform instead of a real transformation toward a full electronic democracy. Although information channels have been practically the only channels that have been implemented, their importance has also to be remarked on. In this sense, it is true that when a citizen is well informed and has wide access to data related to the government and to politicians, she or he can contribute to foster a more accountable local polity. Therefore, information is essential for a proper democracy. Furthermore, information tools could give rise to a critical mass that demands the implementation of the other electronic-democracy instruments.

The opportunities provided by new channels of information and communication are, indeed, very important for strong democracy. Those channels are the core of representative democracy. We should not depreciate the opportunities for civic engagement generated via ICTs providing transparency, openness, and the accountability of government, as well as the importance of the strength

of the channels of interactive communication between citizens and institutions. An increase in public information will produce a stronger and more
accountable mandate from the people to their chosen representatives.

An informed citizenry is a prerequisite to maintaining the social contract
between government and those governed by it. Government must accept the
responsibility to provide to its citizens as much as possible access to public
information on government activities. In this sense, Latin American cities
have started to publicize important information on the Web regarding their
activities. So, access to information is now easier to get than a few years ago
thanks to the use of new technologies by officials. That is the first step.

As we stated before when we explained the amplification model, it is too
early to evaluate the impact these mechanisms have had on actors' capabilities. That is particularly important for societies in Latin America since the
implementation channels of electronic democracy have been developed in
recent years. So, the opportunities that ICTs can make to the actors are still
undiscovered, maybe because the actors are unconscious about their new
capabilities or because the potential impact has not been developed yet on
the actors' strategies.

It would be interesting for future research to test the different variables that
integrate the EDI. As many analyses reveal, the implementation of electronic-democracy tools is not a guarantee of its use. This is why it would be
interesting to check the instruments and to develop a system of punishment
for not using them. Also, reviewing the evolution of every municipality in the
long term would bring light to find out what the motivations and the behavior
of different types of government are in relation to digital democracy. This
analysis could represent an important contribution to the field.

This first study has tried to assess the level of electronic-democracy implementation in Latin American municipalities. The results show that, so far, cities
are at a preliminary stage. A full description of the developments of electronic
democracy—and the effective use of its tools—in the municipalities of the
sample as well as of the possible relationships between ICTs and the municipal
institutional framework should be approached in future research.

References

Agre, P. (2002). Real-time politics: The Internet and the political process. *The Information Society, 18*(5), 311-331.

Barabas, J. (2002, September). *Virtual deliberation: Knowledge from online interaction versus ordinary discussion.* Paper presented at the Prospects for Electronic Democracy Conference, Pittsburgh, PA.

Barber, B. (1999). Three scenarios for the future of technology and strong democracy. *Political Science Quarterly, 113*(4), 573-589.

Barber, B. (2001). The uncertainty of digital politics: Democracy's uneasy relationship with information technology. *Harvard International Review, 13*(1), 42-47.

Beierle, T., & Cahill, S. (2000). *Electronic democracy and environmental governance: A survey of the states* (Discussion Paper 00-42). Washington: Resources for the Future.

Brynjolfsson, E., & Hitt, L. (2000). Beyond computation: Information technology, organizational transformation and business performance. *Journal of Economic Perspectives, 14*(4), 23-48.

Chadwick, A. (2003). Bringing e-democracy back in: Why it matters for future research on e-governance. *Social Science Computer Review, 23*(4), 443-455.

Chadwick, A., & May, C. (2003). Interaction between states and citizens in the age of Internet: "E-government" in the United States, Britain and the European Union. *Governance, 16*(2), 271-300.

Coleman, S., & Gotze, J. (2002). *Bowling together: Online public engagement in policy deliberation.* London: Hansard Society.

Criado, I. (2003, September). *El desarrollo de innovaciones tecnológicas en las administraciones públicas: Lecciones sobre las páginas Web.* Paper presented at the Sixth Congress of the Spanish Political and Administration Science Association, Barcelona, Spain.

Dahl, R. (1992). *La democracia y sus críticos.* Barcelona, Spain: Paidós.

Fountain, J. E. (2001). *Building the virtual state: Information technology and institutional change.* Washington, DC: The Brookings Institution Press.

Grönlund, A. (2002, August). *E-democracy and e-government: State of the art*. Paper presented at the 68th IFLA Council and General Conference, Glasgow, Scotland.

Hacker, K., & van Dijk, J. (Eds.). (2000a). *Digital democracy: Issues of theory and practice*. London: Sage Publications.

Hacker, K., & van Dijk, J. (2000b). What is digital democracy? In K. Hacker & J. van Dijk (Eds.), *Digital democracy: Issues of theory and practice*. London: Sage Publications.

Hagen, M. (2000). Digital democracy and political systems. In K. Hacker & J. van Dijk (Eds.), *Digital democracy: Issues of theory and practice*. London: Sage Publications.

Hague, B., & Loader, B. (Eds.). (1999). *Digital democracy: Discourse and decision making in the information age*. New York: Routledge.

Halle, M., Musso, J., & Weare, C. (1999). Developing digital democracy: Evidence from Californian municipal Web pages. In B. Hague & B. Loader (Eds.), *Digital democracy: Discourse and decision making in the information age*. London: Routledge.

Ho, A. (2002). Reinventing local governments and the e-government initiative. *Public Administration Review, 62*(4), 434-444.

Jorgenson, D., & Stiroh, K. (1999). Information technology and growth. *American Economic Review, 89*(2), 109-115.

Kakabadse, A., Kakabadse, N., & Kouzmin, A. (2003). Reinventing the democratic governance project through information technology? A growing agenda for debate. *Public Administration Review, 63*(1), 44-60.

Karakaya, R. (2003, April). *The use of the Internet for citizen participation: Enhancing democratic local governance?* Paper presented at the Political Studies Association Annual Conference, Leicester, United Kingdom.

Kingham, T. (2003). *E-parliaments: The use of information and communication technologies to improve parliamentary processes*. Washington, DC: The World Bank Institute.

Kubicek, H., Westholm, H., & Winker, R. (2003). *Prisma strategic guideline 9: eDemocracy*. Prisma Project. Retrieved May 13, 2005, from http://www.prisma-eu.net/deliverables/sg9democracy.pdf

Lenk, K. (1999). Electronic support of citizen participation in planning process. In B. Hague & B. Loader (Eds.), *Digital democracy: Discourse and decision making in the information age*. London: Routledge.

Louvin, R., & Alderdice, J. (2001). *Regional parliaments in the Internet era* (General Report to the General Assembly of Presidents of the European Regional Legislative Assemblies, CALRE).

Macintosh, A. (2004, January). *Characterizing e-participation in policy making.* Paper presented at 37th Hawaii International Conference on System Sciences, HI.

Margolis, M., & Resnick, D. (2000). *Politics as usual: The cyberspace revolution.* Thousand Oaks, CA: Sage.

Moon, J. (2002). The evolution of e-government among municipalities: Rhetoric or reality? *Public Administration Review, 62*(4), 424-433.

Moore, R. (1999). Democracy and cyberspace. In B. Hague & B. Loader (Eds.), *Digital democracy: Discourse and decision making in the international age.* London: Routledge.

Navarro, M. (2004). *Coaliciones de gobierno y desarrollo tecnológico: Un análisis comparado de la democracia electrónica en los municipios de Catalunya.* Unpublished master's thesis, Open University of Catalonia, Catalonia, Spain.

Nixon, P., & Johansson, H. (1999). Transparency through technology: The Internet and political parties. In B. Hague & B. Loader (Eds.), *Digital democracy: Discourse and decision making in the information age.* New York: Routledge.

Norris, P. (2001). *Digital Divide: Civic Engagement, Information Poverty, and the Internet Worldwide.* Cambridge: Cambridge University Press.

Norris, P. (2003). *Deepening democracy via e-governance* (Draft chapter for the UN World Public Sector Report). Retrieved May 13, 2005, from http://ksghome.harvard.edu/~pnorris/ACROBAT/e-governance.pdf

North, D. (1990). *Institutions, institutional change and economic performance.* Cambridge: Cambridge University Press.

Organization for Economic Cooperation and Development (OECD). (2001). *Citizens as partners: Information, consultation and public information in policy making.* Paris: Author.

Ott, D. (1998). Power to the people: The role of electronic media in promoting democracy in Africa. *First Monday, 3*(4). Retrieved May 13, 2005, from http://www.firstmonday.dk/issues/issue3_4/ott

Parto, S. (2003). *Technological change and institutions: A case study* (Research Memoranda No. 036). Maastricht, The Netherlands: Maastricht Economic Research Institute on Innovation and Technology.

Requejo, F. (2002). Bases teòriques de la democràcia electrònica. In C. Amorós (Ed.), *Democràcia electrònica i portals de l'Administració*. Barcelona, Spain: Ministry of Universities, Research and Information Society, & Public Administration School of Catalonia.

Richard, E. (1999). Tools of governance. In B. Hague & B. Loader (Eds.), *Digital democracy: Discourse and decision making in the information age*. London: Routledge.

Riley, C. (2003). *The changing role of the citizen in the e-governance & e-democracy equation*. Ottawa, Canada: Commonwealth Center for Electronic Governance.

Rosén, T. (2001). *E-democracy in practice: Swedish experiences of a new political tool*. Retrieved May 13, 2005, from http://www.e-democracy. gov.uk/documents/retrieve.asp?pk_document=67&pagepath=http:// www.e-democracy.gov.uk/knowledgepool/

Salvador, M., Cortés, R., Sánchez, R., & Ferrer, L. (2004). *Els ajuntaments de Catalunya a Internet: Un estudi comparat de les pàgines Web (2000-2003)*. Barcelona, Spain: Pompeu Fabra University.

Subirats, J. (2002). Los dilemas de una relación inevitable: Innovación democrática y tecnologías de la información y de la comunicación. In H. Cairo (Ed.), *Democracia digital: Límites y oportunidades*. Madrid, Spain: Trotta.

Taylor, M. Z. (2002, August-September). *A study of the comparative political economy of innovation: How political institutions affect long-run technological progress*. Paper presented at the American Political Science Association Annual Conference, Boston.

Thornton, A. (2002). Does Internet create democracy? *Ecquid Novi, 22*(2), 126-147.

Trechsel, A., Kies, R., Mendez, F., & Schmitter, P. (2003). *Evaluation of the use of new technologies in order to facilitate democracy in Europe: E-democratizing the parliaments and parties of Europe*. Geneva, Switzerland: C2D-Research and Documentation Centre on Direct Democracy, University of Geneva.

Trénel, M. (2004). *Measuring the quality of online deliberation: Coding scheme 1.1.* Social Science Research Center Berlin. Retrieved May 13, 2005, from http://www.wz-berlin.de/~trenel/tools/quod_2_4.pdf

Tsagarousianou, R., Tambini, D., & Bryan, C. (1998). *Cyberdemocracy: Technology, cities and civic networks.* London: Routledge.

Van Dijk, J. (2000). Models of democracy and concepts of communication. In K. Hacker & J. van Dijk (Eds.), *Digital democracy: Issues of theory and practice.* London: Sage.

Wilhelm, A. (2000). *Democracy in the digital age: Challenges to political life in cyberspace.* New York: Routledge.

Witschge, T. (2003). *Online deliberation: Possibilities of the Internet for deliberative democracy.* Amsterdam: Amsterdam School of Communications Research.

Zittel, T. (2001, April). *Electronic democracy and electronic parliaments: A comparison between the US House, the Swedish Riksdagen, and the German Bundestag.* Paper presented at the joint sessions of the Workshops of the European Consortium for Political Research, Grenoble, France.

Endnotes

[1]   Many debts have been incurred in writing this chapter. Above all, I would like to thank Mikel Barreda, Rosa Borge, Ana-Sofía Cardenal, Andrea Costafreda, and Mila Gascó. All remaining errors are my own.

[2]   For specific international examples of almost every electronic democracy tool, see Kubicek et al. (2003).

Appendix

Table 3. The components of EDI in Latin American municipalities

	Information													Communication and Consultation													Participation	
	1a	1b	1c	1d	1e	1f	1g	1h	1i	1j	1k	1l	1m	2a	2b	2c	2d	2e	2f	2g	2h	2i	2j	2k	2l	2m	3a	3b
Asunción	1	0	1	0	0	0	1	1	0	0	0	1	0	0.5	0.5	0.5	0.5	0.5	0	0	0	0	0	0	0	0	0	0
Bogotá	1	1	0	0	0	0	1	1	0	1	0	1	1	0.5	0	0	0	0	0	0	0	0	0	0	0	0	0	0
Brasilia	1	1	1	1	0	1	1	1	1	1	0	1	1	0.5	0.5	0.5	0.5	0.5	0	0	0	0	0	0	0	0	0	0
Buenos Aires	1	1	1	0	0	1	1	1	0	1	0	0	1	0.5	0.5	0.5	0.5	0.5	0	0	0	0	0	0	0	0	0	0
Caracas	0	0	1	0	0	0	1	1	0	1	0	0	0	0.5	0.5	0	0	0.5	0	0	0	0	0	0	0	0	0	0
Ciudad de México	0	0	1	1	0	0	0	1	0	1	0	1	1	0.5	0.5	0	0	0	0	0	0	0	0	0	0	0	0	0
Guatemala	1	1	1	0	0	0	1	0	0	0	0	0	0	0	0.5	0	0	0	0	0	0	0	0	0	0	0	0	0
La Paz	0	0	1	0	0	0	1	0	0	1	0	1	1	0	0.5	0	0	0	0	0	0	0	0	0	0	0	0	0
Lima	0	1	1	0	0	0	1	1	0	1	0	1	1	0.5	0.5	0.5	0.5	0.5	0	0	0	0	0	0	0	0	0	0
Managua	1	0	1	0	0	0	0	0	0	0	0	0	0	0.5	0.5	0	0	0	0	0	0	0	0	0	0	0	0	0
Montevideo	1	1	1	0	0	0	1	1	0	0	0	0	0	0.5	0.5	0.5	0	0.5	0	0	0	0	0	0	0	0	0	0
Panamá	1	1	1	1	0	0	0	0	0	0	0	1	0	0.5	0	0	0	0	0	0	0	0	0	0	0	0	0	0
Quito	1	1	1	1	0	0	1	1	0	1	0	1	0	0.5	0	0.5	0.5	0.5	0	0	0	0	0	0	0	0	0	0
San José	1	0	0	1	0	0	1	1	0	1	0	1	0	0	0.5	0	0	0	0	0	0	0	0	0	0	0	0	0
San Salvador	0	1	1	0	0	0	1	1	0	1	0	0	0	0	0.5	0	0	0	0	0	0	0	0	0	0	0	0	0
Santiago	1	1	1	0	0	0	1	1	0	1	0	0	1	0	0.5	0.5	0.5	0.5	0	0	0	0	0	0	0	0	0	0
Tegucigalpa	1	1	1	0	0	0	1	1	0	0	0	1	0	0.5	0.5	0	0	0	0	0	0	0	0	0	0	0	0	0

Table 4. Web pages analyzed

Asuncion	http://www.mca.gov.py/inicio.html
Bogotá	http://www.bogota.gov.co/bogota/home1.php
Brasilia	http://www.distritofederal.df.gov.br/
Buenos Aires	http://www.buenosaires.gov.ar/
Caracas	http://www.alcaldiamayor.gov.ve/2004/
Ciudad de Mexico	http://www.df.gob.mx/
Guatemala	http://www.municipalidaddeguatemala.gob.gt/
La Paz	http://www.ci-lapaz.gov.bo/
Lima	http://www.munlima.gob.pe/
Managua	http://www.managua.gob.ni/
Montevideo	http://www.montevideo.gub.uy/
Panama	http://www.municipio.gob.pa/
Quito	http://www.quito.gov.ec/
San José	http://www.msj.co.cr/
San Salvador	http://www.amss.gob.sv/pages/index.html
Santiago	http://www.ciudad.cl/
Tegucigalpa	http://www.alcaldiadetegucigalpa.com/index2.html

Chapter X

Contributing to Socially Relevant Public Policies on E-Governance:
The Case of the Genesis of the Communes in Buenos Aires City

Roxana Goldstein, Centro de Estudios sobre Ciencia,
Desarrollo y Educación Superior [Centro REDES], Argentina

Abstract

This chapter aims to introduce a conceptual framework and a case study that can contribute to deepen the understanding of the relation among the information and knowledge society, democracy, and development. In this chapter, it is argued that this relation has as its core issue the reinforcement of the governability and the governance oriented to development through the use of ICTs. Special focus is made on the contribution that ICTs can make in the consolidation of a public space where multi-actor, open, well-informed, equitable and transparent participatory processes allow all social actors to deliberate on the proposal elaboration and decision-making processes related to the public policies that shape their life conditions. It is expected that the preliminary contributions presented in this chapter will contribute to enrich the proposal elaboration and the decision-making processes of the public policies on e-governance through a new approach that takes into account the complexity, multidimensionality, and qualitative aspects that characterized the social impact of ICTs in LAC societies.

Introduction

We can identify a first stage of public policies on ICTs and the information and knowledge society (IKS) in the Latin American and Caribbean region, which was mainly oriented to the development of the technological infrastructure needed to provide access to ICTs and advanced services based on them. This infrastructure development supports the expansion of these technologies from the generalization of the Internet.

Several research projects have been carried out in order to analyze the scope, success, and restraints that these policies have presented in terms of their performance about the objective of inserting the Latin American societies into the IKS.

A first and basic observation has already been largely analyzed and corresponds to the restraints that these policies have had in terms of the universalization of access to ICT and to the Internet for the whole society. It is known that the unequal social and geographical distribution of access to ICTs, known as the digital divide, represents a threat to social cohesion as it reinforces the preexisting social gaps.

Moreover, we know that a merely quantitative analysis, one that allows us to know the amount of computers, telephones, and Internet connections per inhabitant, does not offer a full comprehension about the shape that the IKS is taking in the region, about how its development impacts society, and about how the diffusion of ICTs is contributing to overcome development barriers in the region.

Now, if we consider that a merely quantitative analysis about how the IKS advances is not sufficient to understand its complex implications on development, we must conclude that neither will those public policies supported on the mentioned analysis be efficient.

In the Latin American and Caribbean region, there exists a growing stream of thinking that is oriented to research and action in favor of the development of an IKS that impacts positively on social, political, economic, and human development for the societies.

The pursued objective in this chapter is to bring about new focuses and to open new analysis lines that can contribute to enrich that stream of thinking, which is based on the need for understanding the complexity, multidimensionality, and qualitative aspects that characterized the social impact of ICTs through the development and advance of the IKS.

In this chapter, then, are joined some conceptual tools for the analysis and some preliminary conclusions that we have reached up to now through the fulfillment of two activities that allow us to advance in the understanding of the two faces in the relation among IKS, democracy, and development.

On the one hand, there are introduced the basic elements of the conceptual framework and the preliminary conclusions reached within the research project "Evaluation of the Social Impact of ICTs in Local Participatory Processes: ICTs and Democratic Governability Reinforcement" that was carried out at the Center for Studies on Science, Development and Higher Education (Centro REDES)[1] of Argentina.

On the other hand, there are introduced the basic elements of an incipient initiative that constitutes the germ of a participatory public policy on e-governance within the context of the beginning of the administrative and political decentralization process in Buenos Aires, which is considered a strategic opportunity for social, political, economic, and human development for the city.

At the moment this chapter was written, it was considered that the elements herein joined, that emerge from these two experiences, are not yet consolidated concepts, but processes still being elaborated on and in permanent revision.

The need to overcome development barriers that our society faces leads us to search for new ways to try to open new paths that lead us to more rich and complex conceptualizations, those that can at the same time become decisions, actions, and results capable to contribute to enlarge the opportunities for all to live a worthy life.

The IKS is then a threat and an opportunity, and presents a field of research and action related to its implications that is pursued to enlighten through this chapter.

Conceptual Framework. Part I:
Socially Relevant Public Policies on ICTs and the IKS in the Frame of a New Relationship Between State and Society

Our Perspective About Governability, Governance, and Public Policies for Human Development

The International Labor Organization (ILO), as Romel Jurado (2005) says, defines public policies as:

the result of a set of processes through which social demands are transformed into political options and into public authorities decision issues, being this the reason why they cannot be considered as simply administrative acts of the central politic power but as social products emerging from a cultural and economic context, and inserted in a power structure and in an specific political project. (p. 4)

Then, how must the scenario where the public policies are generated be in order to orient them effectively and efficiently to social-needs satisfaction in an equitable, transparent, opportune, and legitimate manner?

As Nuria Cunil Grau (1997) describes, during the 20th century, liberal democracy suffered the shift of the decision-making orbit of public-interest issues from the political sphere to the administrative and government spheres through the adoption of logics of action supported on a technocratic vision of the problems to be solved jointly, particularly in Latin America, with lobbyist, clientelistic, and prebendary logics of incidence. This action and incidence logics contribute to "depublicization," in the sense of making it not visible and not accessible for all social actors, and to "depoliticization," in the sense of taking it off the political arena—the central problems that our society faces in terms of development—generating a public space where neither these problems appear in the agenda, nor are there debate and deliberation instances for consensus construction, and where there is a lack of pertinent information to nourish the processes in which opinion that supports decisions is built.

In front of this model that led to a development failure in the region, particularly to a dual model of IKS, Cunil Grau (1997) opposes another option supported upon Habermas' public-space notion and other authors' further theories. The sense of this option is to allow for a rearticulation of the relationship between state and society through the construction of "sensitive spaces" and "bridges" where the communicative power of an autonomous public space could convert into political will. Sensitive spaces or bridges must be directly inscribed into an institutional reform of politics and administration from which the state makes access to its decision and action mechanisms public and democratic. This is supposed to disarticulate clientelism, elitism, prebendaries, and privileges, but also excessive bureaucracy, among other negative aspects. Such a reform that allows the formation of a public space where collective problems can recover their public condition, in both senses of being visible and accessible by every social actor, to be dealt with in a political process where a diversity of autonomous actors (from political and economic power) could intervene freely and openly, with equal opportunities, and where communicative power formed through public, open, and informed deliberation is susceptible to convert into concrete action.

In such a public space, civil society, now conceived as a heterogeneous and diverse set of social identities, can enlarge its influential possibilities, passing from only being a control and incidence agent to actively participate in proposal elaboration and decision-making processes on public government administration within the framework of a new state and society cooperation scheme, not anymore sustained by a partnership approach where civil society plays the role of the performer of decisions made in other spheres and without its direct participation (generally between state and market). As Mayntz (2003) says, this new mode of governing or "governance" is "different from the old hierarchical model in which state authorities exert sovereign control over the people and groups...[it] refers to a basically non-hierarchical mode of governing" (p. 1) characterized by "a larger degree of cooperation and by the interaction between state and non-state actors within mixed—state and private—decision networks" (Mayntz, 2000, p. 1), including, from our perspective, not only corporate actors but social actors as well.

But, what are we talking about when we talk about governance? Following Joan Prats' (2001) definition, it is considered that governance is "institutions and rules that set the limits and the incentives for the construction and functioning of interdependent networks of actors (government, private sector and civil society)" (p. 114). As Prats continues, "the concept of governance has two dimensions: a) a structural dimension, referring to the institutional arrangements already existing in a given society, b) a dynamic or process dimension, referring to the actions of the actors that may affect the structural dimension" (p. 115).

Which conditions must this governance fulfill to produce a governability oriented to human development? Prats (2001) states, as an initial characterization of governability, that:

A social system is governable when it is sociopolitically structured so as to allow all strategic actors to interrelate in order to take collective decisions and solve their conflicts according to a system of rules and formal or informal proceedings—that may register different levels of institutionalization—within which they may formulate their expectancies and strategies. (pp. 103-104)

The author continues:

the conflict can be solved—positively—in new rules of games that incentivize development through the necessary institutional changes or—negatively— through the widening of the distributive coalition to the new actors, without altering institutionality—patrimonialist, populist, clientelistic, chieftaincy, mercantilist, corporative...that block development (p. 130)

As can be seen through this summary, not only the results—peaceful conflict resolution—but the processes through which those results are reached—a diversity of autonomous actors interacting and building consensus through formal and informal institutions in an open and free public space—are important to orient governability and governance to human development.

ICTs and Their Impact on Society

As we have analyzed in a previous work, we consider that "[r]eal world and virtual world are mutually inscribed entities. One of them cannot be understood without considering the other. The processes that occur at both sides of virtuality are mutually imbricated" (Goldstein, 2005, p. 74).

Following this premise, we are interested in studying some aspects that are part of this imbrication, particularly, the way in which the diffusion and appropriation of ICTs can influence life conditions of the whole society.

As it is well known, communication, information, and knowledge are crucial strategic resources in the informational society in which we are immersed, and the possibilities to generate, use, and take advantage of them will determine the opportunity to live a worthy life for all of us and for future generations; therefore, active public policies defined in a large, open, and well-prepared public space are needed in order to protect the right to access to these resources for all.

In other words, both the need to invest in ICT diffusion paths and the fact that the right for all to communication, information, and knowledge must be protected justify the need of active public policies on ICTs and IKS.

Which criteria must be taken into consideration when defining ICTs and IKS public policies in order to make them significant for our societies' development?

ICTs and IKS Public Policies Oriented to Social, Political, Economic, and Human Development

Until now, as before mentioned, IKS evolution in our region has responded to a development pattern in which ICTs contribute to deepen the problems that our society is facing, especially inequality, reflected in a social divide constantly enlarged since the '70s.

How do we revert this situation? How do we relate ICTs and development in a positive way?

Kemly Camacho (2003), in her research about ICTs' social impact on nongovernment organizations (NGOs) in Central America, defines the dimensions of equitable access, the using with sense and the social appropriation of ICTs, put together in the concept of the social impact of ICTs.

This definition of the social impact of ICTs emerges from the need for being able to establish evaluation parameters for policies, programs, and actions on ICTs oriented to CSOs (social organizations) that allow us to differentiate policies only centered on providing access from other policies that incorporate actions oriented to generate skills, to a strategic use of ICTs, and to appropriate them in order to produce new useful knowledge to achieve the strategic objectives and missions of the CSOs that implement them.

How do we extrapolate this concept to society and its development?

Social Impact of ICTs and Development: Enlarging the Framework of Reference

Daniel Pimienta (2003), a prestigious ICT-for-development (ICT4D) actor in the Caribbean region, clearly exemplifies this in his document *La Brecha Digital: ¡A Ver A Ver!*, where he shows the difference between an ICT user devoted to entertainment in a cybercafé and another one in a community technology center creating social capital and knowledge to surpass development barriers.

It is clear that if we are interested in using ICT tools to surpass regional development barriers, we need something more than access, even more than digital training; moreover, we need to produce new knowledge with them (what we call appropriation). In this context, knowledge is considered the solution for society's problems. A society appropriates technology as it uses all its potential for its own benefit: Following this reasoning, the social appropriation of ICTs occurs when a society uses these technologies to produce knowledge to solve its own problems that restrain development, in other words, to surpass its development barriers.

Having reached this point, there emerges three dimensions to be analyzed:

1.   Up to which point is this social appropriation of ICTs translated into a life-quality improvement for our societies in our development? This means, up to which point are ICTs being development enablers? This is what we would try to measure as social impact (relating it to results, effects, and impacts in the long term).

2.   Up to which point is this social-appropriation process translated into an ICT local design that matches our needs? In other words, how much are we adjusting the design of local solutions based upon ICTs to our own needs? Or, are we consuming ICTs designed in other contexts trying to profit from them, but only adapting to them? Expressing it in another way, how much are we contributing to create a virtue circle that reinforces ICTs' local industries and local knowledge economies, turning them into dynamic forces that push economic and social development?

3.   How much are ICTs, their associated public policies and actions, and the way in which they are being defined participating in the improvement of life conditions for our societies and installing new practices? In Michele Leclerc-Olive's (2004) words, are they creating positive impacts

in the normative framework in which these "situated political actions" are inscribed? Are ICTs acting as enablers of a cultural change?

In any case, these dimensions are convergent as more positive impact is to be obtained as social actors strongly participate in the design of ICT-based solutions (be they policies, programs, or actions), when ICTs are integrated both as development enablers (first dimension) and as economy dynamic forces (second dimension), a virtue circle that can only be activated as society surpasses cultural limitations that its practices present and that act as development barriers. This is where ICT policies and actions can contribute in the generation of new surpassing practices (third dimension).

How do we redefine ICTs' social-impact dimensions in terms of development through public policies?

In order to identify the relation between ICTs and development through the impact concept and through the three dimensions above mentioned, new questions must be asked:

- **Equitable access:** Are ICTs enlarging the public-policy scope? Are ICTs contributing to equate the development levels of the different social groups, reducing social gaps? Are ICTs reinforcing the equity of the public policy? Or are ICTs' benefits reaching only the more advantaged social sectors?

- **Using with sense:** Are ICTs being used to reach the public policy's strategic objectives? Are ICTs being used through strategies that are adequate to reinforce the positive effects of this policy or to reduce its negative effects? Do ICTs in this policy reinforce its opportunity, quality, and transparency?

- **Social appropriation:** Are ICTs facilitating collective knowledge-production processes within the frame of this policy? Are ICTs enlarging these processes to reach new actors?

We can add two dimensions to this analysis:

- **The impact on IKS-related industries:** Is the use of ICTs in this policy contributing to reinforce local ICT industries?

- **The impact on the normative framework:** Is the use of ICTs in this policy contributing to install new practices and a new know-how that contributes to the society's development?

Conceptual Framework. Part II: The Relation Among IKS, Democracy, and Development Toward E-Governance Public Policies Oriented to Development

Based on the conceptual framework detailed before, the objective pursued in this section is to present the main ideas that guide our work, supported with the intention to establish an integral conceptual framework that helps us to understand the crucial role of e-governance as the intersection among IKS, democracy, and development.

As Robert Dahl (1998) affirms, it is considered that a plain democracy must have the following elements so as to guarantee political equality and the equal capacity of every citizen to influence state policies: effective participation; vote equality; the possibility of informed understanding; effective final control upon the public agenda; an institutional system in charge of elective representatives that guarantees free, fair, and frequent elections; the support of freedom of expression; the provision of alternative information; free and autonomous associations; and the inclusion within the citizenry of the whole adult population.

Enlarging this model on the base of the premises drawn by David Held (1996) in the democratic autonomy model, and making use of Cunil Grau's (1997) arguments, we can add the following:

- An institutional framework receptive to experiments with new organizational forms
- Mixed spaces for effective participation in the proposal elaboration and in decision making on public-interest issues
- Horizontal, heterogeneous, multi-actor networks where there is free and democratic interaction for consensus construction about socially relevant public issues

- A participative culture widely extended through the diversity of social actors and to the diversity of social organization spheres
- A diversified civil society, deeply organized and active around its interests and cultural and social identities
- Information and communication systems that guarantee the equitable access and the free consumption and production of relevant information to nourish the public space

We consider that ICTs have many elements to contribute to the consolidation of a democratic system like the one described above, following Criado Grande, Ramilo Araujo, and Serna's (2002) definition of electronic government:

The new government model that is proposed (Electronic Government) will be able to better solve social problems (guaranteeing governability) as far as it is capable of establishing rules, principles and values that enable the necessary institutional change (neo-institutionalism) so that governments and Public Administration are be able to generate consensus among those social critical actors capable to articulate joint answers to the social problems (policy networks) improving in a continuous way the quality of the policies and public services (NPA). (p. 31)

The following are examples:

- In transparency through the diffusion of public information, e-vote, e-procurement, the enabling of social control on public administration, and political parties' system reform
- In efficiency through e-administration within the frame of the state reform
- In services through e-services and unique entry point implementations
- In state and society relationships, opening new communication channels between public servants and citizens, or facilitating citizen participation
- In the building of social capital through e-society policies, reinforcing citizen networks, and facilitating the free production and circulation of information

In this chapter, the last two points are especially focused on and are considered as integrating what is known as e-governance, being that they are core issues when considering the use of ICTs to reinforce a governance oriented to development.

The Two Faces of the Relation Between ICTs and Citizen Participation

Two paths should be followed in order to build a positive relation in terms of social impact between ICTs and citizen participation:

1. The use of ICTs in participatory processes, what we call e-governance, means ICTs helping to build a heterogeneous and large public space, democratizing access both to the consumption and production of information and knowledge, enlarging access to proposal elaboration and decision-making processes, consolidating deliberation processes where opinion is built, and strengthening mixed spaces between state and society for deliberation and decision making within the frame of a new relationship between them.
2. Citizen participation in public policies on ICT and IKS means civil society's involvement in participatory processes for the design, implementation, and execution of ICT and IKS public policies.

In the crossroads of both paths is citizen participation in public policies on e-governance.

Besides this, we also must consider that there are several factors that condition the effectiveness and efficiency of a public policy on e-governance. What preparation is necessary for a society to facilitate successful policies on e-governance oriented to development?

E-Readiness Concept: The Preparation to Take Advantage of E-Governance

What infrastructure and culture are necessary to be developed in order to be ready—as a society looking for integral and equitable development—to take advantage of ICTs, especially the Internet, when they are applied to governance reinforcement?

We consider the list Heeks (2001) exposes as a set of conditioning factors for e-governance in development countries, that we resume as follows: to count on adequate ICT infrastructures, legal frameworks, institutional frameworks, leadership and strategic thinking, integrated ICT policies defined as part of integral governance programs, and adequate ICT initiatives set to real context needs.

The main idea here, what Richard Heeks (2001) tries to show in his work and we share with him, is that these conditioning factors for e-governance must be attended to and planned through adequate policies in order to have an "e-prepared" society in a way that shall lead to a positive impact in society as a whole, dearticulating the vicious circle built between digital divide and social gaps.

ICTs in Citizen Participation: Studying the Social Impact of ICTs in Governability and Governance

In this section, the most significant issues identified in the conceptual framework and some preliminary conclusions are presented, both arising from the research project "Evaluation of the Social Impact of ICTs in Local Participatory Processes: ICTs and Democratic Governability Reinforcement" that is carried out at Centro REDES of Argentina.[2]

This research has as its main objective the production of recommendations for public policies on electronic governability based upon the obtaining of outstanding information on the impact of ICTs in local participatory processes in Argentina, particularly in Buenos Aires.

Our inquiries start from the assumption that the consolidation of these processes is a fundamental stage in democracy reinforcement and in the enlargement of democratic governability for human development in our society. From this point of view, one way of using with sense and socially appropriating ICTs is revealed through the contribution that these technologies have and can have in the consolidation of those political instruments that enable citizen participation in the elaboration of public-policies proposals and in decision-making processes concerning government.

This research focuses on the analysis of the generation and diffusion of information and knowledge (GDIK) processes that are generated in the framework of the application of citizen participation political instruments. Why? Because information and knowledge are the crucial strategic resources in the IKS, and considering this, the way in which these resources are generated and diffused in the context of local participatory processes with the help of ICTs is the key to promote the social impact of the ICTs in the strengthening of democratic governability oriented to human development.

Which are the political instruments of citizen participation that contribute more to democratic reinforcement? Which barriers face these instruments for their implementation? How can ICTs contribute to their beating? What processes of the generation and diffusion of information and knowledge characterize these political instruments? How can ICTs reinforce and promote the impact of these political instruments in democratic governability? How can ICTs contribute to enrich deliberative processes in which citizens have the opportunity to be involved to influence government decisions that condition their lives? Do we have a methodological framework to study ICTs' impact?

These are some of the questions that the mentioned research tries to respond to.

The Specific Conceptual Framework of the Research

Starting from a socio-centric and integral perspective of the problem, we take into consideration those premises introduced above about socially relevant public policies, about the social impact of ICTs and development, and about the new public space within which the frame of a new relationship between state and society exists. Articulating these conceptual frameworks developed by Cunil Grau (1997) with those developed by Michele Leclerc Olive (2004), Héctor Poggiese (1994),[3] and the PPGA/FLACSO Argentina Group (Redín & Morroni, 2002)—all of them prestigious researchers and practitioners of participatory processes—the following have been identified:

- The most significant characteristics that can convert a participatory process into a successful instrument that can help to overcome the development barriers that our delegative democracy model imposes

- The generation and diffusion of information and knowledge[4] processes within these participatory processes

- The opportunities for a positive social impact of ICTs for development within these GDIK processes

In order to briefly summarize,[5] the next five axes of analysis of a participatory process and its more relevant identified aspects are presented:

- **The context:** The most significant characteristics of the context in which the participatory process takes place, and that can be considered as external and internal factors, including the social and political context, the preceding normative framework (political culture or decision-taking attitudes and styles), motives, circumstances in which the participatory process is decided to be developed, and strategic actors involved in this decision

- **The general characteristics:** The type of participatory instrument,6 leadership, political involvement, coordination style within the team in charge, social issues and central themes, the kind of focus (social or techno centered), and scope (local, national, regional, global)

- **The preparation:** The preparation of relevant social actors to be active players in the participatory process, amount of social organizations within the central topic of the participatory process, previous participatory experiences in the field, social perception of citizen participation, and normative-legal-institutional framework

- **The participatory device:** A characterization of the participatory device implemented at each stage of—elaboration, execution, follow-up—of the participatory process. This characterization includes the following:

  - Type of participatory device (legitimating device, communicating device, or hybrid forum)[7] based on its scope of openness (the solution is known before the process takes place or is elaborated within the participatory process), completion (Does the participatory process include both the proposal elaboration process and the decision-making process about those proposals? Or are final decisions taken outside the participatory process? Are proposals elaborated within the participatory process only considered as inputs of decision-making processes that take place outside the participatory scenario where the participatory process occurs?), reflexiveness (Is the opinion of the participants being formed during the participatory process through free and open deliberation and debate? Or is it formed individually without any exchange or direct interaction?), publicness (scope of the diffusion of the participatory process itself, and of the consensus and results reached), plurality (scope of the diversity of social actors involved in the participatory process), and transparency (public diffusion of the participatory process mechanisms, rules, and procedures)

- The methodology and stages are as follows:[8]
  - Is it associative between state and society?
  - Does it articulate the roles of each social actor and organization involved?
  - Does it allow circular planning, execution, and control phases?
  - Does it introduce an integral focus on the social issue, capturing its complexity and multidimensionality?
  - Is it equitable? Does it include consensus construction mechanisms that allow equal opportunities to be heard, to introduce own views, and to incise opinion formation?
  - Is the participatory process conceived as an open process, allowing permanent aggregation of new actors?
  - Does the participatory process include registration processes that guarantee public access to the information and knowledge managed within the process, to the evolution and advances reached in each stage, and to the contributions made by every actor involved?
  - Does the participatory process include procedures for the future preservation and public access to all records once the participatory process is concluded?

- Results, effects, and impacts, both of the results reached at the participatory process and of the participatory process itself includes the following.
  - **Impact on the normative framework:** New participatory practices, new know-how, new political culture, and the consolidation of a permanent public space related to the central social issue of the participatory process
  - **Impact on development goals** (both millennium goals and development goals at the local and national level)

Once we have identified the relevant characteristics of a participatory process—those aspects that are significant in helping a participatory process to contribute in the creation of a new public space and a more successful relationship between state and society—the next stage consists on the identification of the GDIK processes, especially those in which ICTs can have a significant impact. Those GDIK processes include the following:

- Coordination of the team in charge. Communication, information production, collaborative work and proposal elaboration, document elaboration and circulation, and decision making
- Identification of the relevant, necessary, existing, and available information about the central issue of the participatory process and its search, recovery, compilation, source identification, digitalization, format standardization, and in general all information management tasks that guarantee adequate and opportune relevant information availability
- Strategic social actors' identification. The identification of specialists, decision makers and takers, relevant social actors, relevant social organizations and their CEOs, and governmental agencies involved
- Setting a unique entry point for public access to all the relevant information related to the participatory process. Built of a public library, repositories, portal, or Web pages, or any other information infrastructure that allows free and open public access to the relevant information
- Inter-institutional coordination. Agreements, procedure settlements for information supplying and access, and the settlement of standards
- Best-practices identification and recording. Coding, recording, online and public access setting
- Recording of the different stages of the participatory process. Recording of reports, proceedings, meetings, debates, and all the activities developed, and the recording of agreements and consensus reached at each stage: decisions, conclusions, and results reached within the participatory process.
- Publicity of the participatory process. The preparation of different materials for raising awareness and publicity, specially adapted to the different social sectors and social actors involved, the dissemination of these materials, and the preparation, publicity, and diffusion of the participatory process agenda

- Collaborative knowledge creation and knowledge sharing. Debates; discussion forums; knowledge sharing within communities of practice; collaborative production of documents and proposals; collaborative work coordination; synthesizing, filtering, and management of information; synthesizing of contents created within the debate processes.

- Publicity of results and products of the participatory process. The preparation of different materials about contents, agreements, resolutions, proposals, decisions reached at the participatory process; and their diffusion to all social actors

At this point, we want to understand the relationship between GDIK processes in the participatory process and the concept of the social impact of ICT in development described above. For that purpose, we must identify the following:

- **Equitable access:** Adequate preparatory ICT planning, including inter- and intra-institutional coordination, infrastructure availability, capacity building, mixed strategies combining traditional and new ICTs, and ICTs application development

- **Using with sense:** Strategic planning on the use of ICT applications that enable all social actors involved to produce and to consume information; uni-, bi-, and multidirectional communication; free and open information and knowledge exchange; debates and deliberation; consensus construction; collaborative working; individual and collective decision taking; and recording, preserving, and protecting information

- **Social appropriation:** To evaluate how ICTs are contributing to capacity building, to social capital building, to strengthen trust, to achieve development goals, to improve coordination, to permanent networks, to reduce time and costs, and to equate opportunities for all actors

- **Knowledge-economy-related industries:** The use and consumption of hardware, software, Internet connections, telephone services, ICT application developments, technological exchanges, SMEs (small and medium-sized enterprises), and corporative and academy providers, and new jobs creation

- **Normative framework:** A new perception of ICTs, know-how about ICTs that can be applied in everyday activities, raising awareness on information and communication rights, new legal-institutional rules, a new social organization, and best practices

Citizen Participation in E-Governance Policies

Both UN-DESA's (2003) and Reilly and Echeverría's (2003) research show that e-governance is an incipient field of action, and many preparation actions must be taken in order to create the favorable scenarios where public polices on e-governance could be oriented to development.

In this chapter, an experience of citizen participation in e-governance is introduced that can be the beginning of a positive process of a social understanding of the social impact of ICTs and of the strategic relations among IKS, democracy, and development.

The Case of the Decentralization Transition Process and the Socially Relevant Public Policies on E-Governance in Buenos Aires City

At this point, the above case will be introduced as an example that even when initiatives are at their initial stage, we still can learn more about e-governance, citizen participation, and their relationship with socially relevant ICTs and IKS public policies in a Latin American context.

Describing the Argentinean Context

The new millennium came along with a series of social, political, and economic phenomena that converged into the failure of a model that, extended to all the mentioned dimensions, has generated the biggest social gap in Argentine history.

This scenario was characterized by the constant widening of this social gap together with the autonomization of the leading establishment (the detachment of political, economic, and union leaders from those who they represent), the constant pressure of external debt, the flight of capital, the increase of unsatisfied basic needs, and the fast withdrawal of the state from public-problems assistance.

This explosive "cocktail" led to the social, political, economic, and institutional crisis that exploded in December 2001.

At that moment, a general questioning about the ruling model burst into the public space, and a demanding citizenry demanded new actors and new ways to solve public-interest issues. The scenario becomes full of effervescence, protest, and a claim for recovering a more active role in public affairs. The need to re-create a public space with new actors and to recover collective issues to public matters in politics.

Soon protest became proposal, and proposal became incidence and demand for a more active participation in the elaboration and decision-making processes in government and administration action.

Particularly in Buenos Aires, parallel with the context described, public administration reform started within which new participatory democracy instruments and administrative and political decentralization started to be formulated, both being consecrated in the Buenos Aires Constitution in 1996.

Following this mandate, a first stage of decentralization started, which included a process of de-concentration through administration and participation centers[9] (CGPs), the creation of new institutions with a de-concentrated or decentralized strategy including CSOs in their policies and interventions, the implementation of the Urban Strategic Plan, and the starting of the participatory budgeting process. At the same time, a hard debate began about future administrative and political decentralization through communes[10] that should have been set and ruled by 2001 as the constitution established.

The Participatory Elaboration Process for Communes Law

After several failures to approve a law for the future communes, in 2004 a participatory elaboration process (PEP)[11] started in order to facilitate citizen participation in the elaboration process of a proposal for the mentioned law. This proposal was to be ready for approval by the end of 2004.

The PEP for the communes law was first conducted by the government, the legislature, and a group of active neighbors. When it had just started, the government abandoned the process, but it continued with the coordination of the legislature commission and the help of a few neighbors.

The procedure was the following. Forty six neighborhood meetings were organized (one of them for each neighborhood in the city) in which legislators of each party represented at the legislature presented his party's position about the subject of communes. After that, neighbors could make their questions and comments, and all this was registered in order to process the 46 meetings altogether in a synthesis process. In the middle of the whole process, as many neighbors could not attend their neighborhood meeting, another option was implemented to collect citizens' ideas: Social organizations would be able to open their own debate spaces (named debate autonomous spaces;[12] finally there were about 200) in order to collaboratively elaborate with their members, affiliates, or citizens their own contributions. Finally, a commission for the purpose of synthesizing all the contributions was integrated by legislator assistants, members of the CD&PC[13] and LCABA,[14] and neighbors. The result of the process was collected in a final synthesis document, and was incorporated into the law project that the CD&PC then submitted for its approval process following the necessary steps established by the regular procedure. The Participative Project of the Communes Law was treated in debate in the legislature session on November 30, 2004. A political arrangement between legislators postponed its final approval and an ad hoc commission was created in order to negotiate the conflictive topics.

Finally, the communes law was approved on September 1, 2005. As its main aspects, we must mention that it guarantees participatory democracy, establishes exclusive and concurrent competences for communes and for the central government, establishes the boundaries for future communes in accordance to the citizens' wishes and with a population average of 200,000 inhabitants each, and establishes an election date for 2007.

The Participatory Program for Transition Toward Communes

The results obtained through the consultation process, and the communes law itself, are not sufficient in order to organize such a complex process that the transition to communes would demand. Having noticed this, some social organizations advocated citizen participation and closely following the whole process, decided to promote a new participatory process in order to elaborate a proposal that takes into consideration all the aspects that were still not covered, especially those related to the effective implementation of the participatory mechanisms consecrated in the constitution.

That is why FLACSO Argentina and a group of social organizations decided to start the meeting called Buenos Aires VIVA V: Towards a Participatory Program for Transition to Communes.

A Buenos Aires VIVA V process (*V* stands for *the fifth*) is a participatory process where citizens, NGOs, social organizations, and academic and government actors meet to deliberate and debate openly and freely about strategic topics related to the city. They have been organized since 1996, and they count on the methodological assistance of PPGA-FLACSO Argentina Group.

The Buenos Aires VIVA V, which is related here, took place from May to July 2005. Its main objective was to create an associative space between state and society in order to strategically plan the future transition to city decentralization, guaranteeing the implementation of the participatory instruments pre-established in the city constitution.

The Buenos Aires VIVA V was organized by a group of citizens and social, academic, and government organizations, joined freely and openly.

The Buenos Aires VIVA V Methodology

During May to July 2005, a cycle of meetings took place— an initial seminar, then three regional meetings—in order to present the relevant topics related to the transition to communes. Workshops in different quarters allowed the participatory elaboration of proposals under an umbrella of four strategic axes that were set up by the promoter group, and finally there was a closing final meeting where the results reached through the whole process were presented.

At this final meeting, it was decided that those valuable results would be considered the starting points for a participatory transition program that would be coordinated by the SD&PC[15] of the Buenos Aires government, with the same organization of Buenos Aires VIVA V as its foundational basis and the same spirit of aggregation and associative administration of the permanent new actors.

The referred program was launched during July 2005, and it is in its starting phase, strongly concentrated in the addition of new actors and the definition of a complete proposal for the transition process, which will start as soon as the Law for Communes is approved, what is considered imminent today.

Which are the strategic axes that were defined to work on at this Buenos Aires VIVA V? The promoter group, based on previous experiences related to the communes problem, and considering all the contributions made during the initial seminar, decided to create four working groups for the regional meetings, which were organized as itinerary workshops; each group oriented to debate and to gain consensus on the following:

- Mapping the urban social tissue through the recognition of best practices about citizen participation, citizen networking collaboration, and associative administration between state and society
- Building capacities and skills, and the definition of the necessary skills for every social actor involved and the definition of a plan of activities and organizations that would allow the whole city to be prepared to participate in the future decentralized administration
- The networked information and communication system that would allow the free and open access and creation of relevant information, deliberation in order to create consensus about the strategic issues, and the collaborative elaboration of proposals and the decision taking about the transition
- The administration and organization of the participatory transition program, which was oriented to define the institutional issues, government sectors' responsibilities, civil society's role, and how the different strategic actors were going to be involved

Buenos Aires VIVA V Results

Final results are being joined in a final document (in elaboration), but a preliminary document[16] already available let us know that important consensus has been reached by a group of organization and citizens that were involved in the Buenos Aires VIVA V. Especially related to the networked information and communication system, it was agreed that:

The Networked information and communication system is a set of procedures, resources and infrastructure through which participants would be both consumers and producers of information, guaranteeing: a) the free, open and democratic flow of strategic public information about the Transition Program, b) the democratic participation in proposals and projects elaboration, c) the permanent access to the public communication space. The system will com-

bine a variety of communication and information channels: interpersonal, telephone, massive and local media, electronic media, others. The system will guarantee a multidirectional communication within a wide community of citizens, social organizations, government and other strategic social actors allowing the consolidation of a network of social organizations and social actors involved in the process. (FLACSO/PPGA, 2005, p. 9)

The Research Results

In this section we are presenting a brief summary of the most significant findings we have come through the already mentioned research. It is important to notice that it is not a political analysis of the PEP, which is out of the boundaries of this work, but an attempt to put together some data and information that would lead us to have a better understanding of the institutional and emerging GDIK processes that are taking place in the city related to e-governance and citizenry building.

In accordance to the Communes Law for Buenos Aires City No. 1777, the city will be divided into 15 communes, with an average of 200,000 inhabitants each, their boundaries being established in accordance to the neighborhoods' identities expressed along the PEP and in its final synthesis document, as follows.

For a better analysis of the available data, a regrouping by zones has been made.

The Buenos Aires City in Context Before the PEP for Communes Law

Buenos Aires has had its political and administrative autonomy since the Argentine Constitution reform in 1994 and the Buenos Aires Constitution promulgation in 1996. This constitution establishes the institutional mechanisms for the implementation of a participatory democracy.

The city has 2.7 million inhabitants, being the most populated city of Argentina, and together with its surrounding metropolitan region (the Great Buenos Aires), it has 11 million inhabitants. The Great Buenos Aires consists of almost 30% of the total country population, forming the biggest urban

Figure 1. Buenos Aires' commune neighborhood map based on Communes Law No. 1777 (http://www.barriada.com.ar/mapabaires.htm)

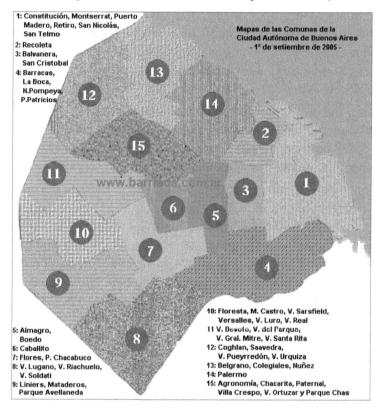

Table 1. Zones and future communes at Buenos Aires (Decentralization and Citizen Participation Commission, http://www.legislatura.gov.ar)

Zone	Future Commune
1 - North	2 - 13 – 14
2 - Historic Center	1 – 3
3 - South	4 - 8
4 - Center	5 - 6 - 7
5 - West	9 - 10
6 – Northwest	12 - 11 – 15

conglomeration in the country and one of the most important of the Latin American region.

The Civil Society Development Index Report (UNDP-BID-GADIS, 2004) reveals that Buenos Aires presents an active flow of people from and to the Great Buenos Aires, with 1.6 million entering and 0.6 million exiting. At the same time, 45% of the city's working force is composed of commuters from the Great Buenos Aires (UNDP-BID-GADIS).

Besides this, the city is the seat of the national authorities and is the most important commercial and cultural center of the country, with 73% of its geographical GDP (gross domestic product) related to services (32% financial, 22% commercial, and 18.7% communal and personal services).

At the same time, the city presents an HDI level of 0.867[17] (UNDP, 2002), the highest level in Argentina, with an income gap of 15, which has increased 30.4% compared to 1995 (UNDP). It is important to notice that this income gap is not equally distributed among the city neighborhoods. Buenos Aires has suffered its own fragmentation process during the '90s, resulting in some neighborhoods with a high quality of life, like those in future communes 13, 14, and 2 in the north, and some neighborhoods with a low quality of life, such us those in future communes 4 and 8, the south. Middle quality of life conditions can be found in future communes within the historic center, center, west, and northwest zones.

The Civil Society in Buenos Aires

The Civil Society Development Index report (UNDP-BID-GADIS, 2004) shows that there are more than 9,000 social organizations in the city, many of them oriented to topics related to education and health, with a high proportion of affinity organizations (62%), and a higher proportion than in the rest of the country of supporting organizations (24.2%). The proportion of grassroots organizations is 9.8%, lower than in the rest of the country, and the proportion of networks is significant at 3.4%.

We must especially mention the organizations devoted to rights defense, with a strong presence of those advocating human rights, civic rights, women and consumers rights, and ecology and environment preservation (UNDP-BID-GADIS, 2004).

On the other hand, as mentioned in the IDSC report (UNDP-BID-GADIS, 2004), there is a scarce significance of international and philanthropological funds, a high tendency to network in interrelationships and agreements, and scarce communicational visibility and incidence of legislative power.

How Much was Known in Buenos Aires About Decentralization and Communes Before the PEP?

In spite of being a subject that started to be treated in the city at the moment the city was declared autonomous and its constitution promulgated in 1996, the subject is still scarcely known by the citizens. As stated by the Creer y Crecer Foundation (2004), only 9.8% of citizens know the scope of the decentralization into communes, while only 27.6% have had any reference on the subject; 12.7% among those surveyed were in the range of 40 to 49 years old, 7.5% were in the range of 18 to 29 years of age.

The Citizen Participation in Buenos Aires

There exists a very important antecedent on citizen participation in the City, which is the experience of the participatory budgeting. This process has already 3 years of existence, and according to results given by recent research (Creer y Crecer Foundation, 2004), it has yielded very low levels of knowledge among the citizens: Only 19% of them declare to have heard about the subject, while 81% state never to have heard about this participatory process; only a 2% declare having participated at least in one of the meetings that are part of the participatory budgeting process.

Among the reasons given for not having participated in the participatory budgeting process, 44% of the surveyed citizens state the lack of time, while 20% state not having been informed about the meetings (Creer y Crecer Foundation, 2004).

On the other side, many participants seem to feel defrauded by the results obtained, and think that their ideas and proposals have not been taken into consideration. They perceive discretion of some degree in the selection of the proposals since the methodology of the participatory budgeting process does not foresee it being enforceable, while the decision taking and the correspondent execution of the decisions taken are subject to the further city executive-power approval.

The Access to Internet in Buenos Aires

There is scarce information about the access, availability, use, and appropriation of ICTs, and specifically about the Internet in the city, and even more scarce information yet related to the neighborhoods in which the city is made up.

Nevertheless, a survey carried out by the Creer y Crecer Foundation in April 2004 reveals that 49% of the population of the city above 18 years old uses the Internet; 47% are women and 51% are men. These figures constantly decrease as age grows.

Furthermore, if we deepen the analysis by communes and zones within the city, we can realize that the north and historic center zones achieve the highest level of access to the Internet, with it being distributed as follows.

The GDIK Processes

In this subsection we will describe the GDIK processes identified at the institutional level, those that were planned and carried out by the city authorities, and both the government and the legislature authorities as well.

Those processes were planned on a general, global basis, and then problems were solved as they appeared. Mixed strategies were implemented for the calls for the meetings; these included brochures, pamphlets, small posters, e-mails, and personal communication.

Notices of the meetings and advances of the process were widespread through e-bulletins periodically prepared and distributed. Results of every neighborhood meeting were tape recorded. Results of the debate autonomous spaces were sent through paper folders specially prepared for that purpose, and, in a few cases, with diskettes.

Table 2. Access to Internet by age in Buenos Aires (Source: Creer y Crecer Foundation, 2004)

Age	18-29	30-39	40-49	50-59	60 or more
Access (%)	80.7	66.5	58.5	43.2	10.8

Figure 2. Access to Internet in Buenos Aires (Source: Creer y Crecer Foundation, 2004)

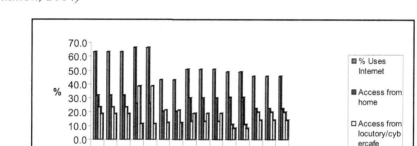

During the neighborhood meetings, legislators and their teams presented their position and the attending citizens were to ask their questions and present their suggestions. Introductive material was given to the public.

All this registered material is preserved at the LCABA, and can be requested by any citizen.

The synthesis process was carried out by a group of legislators, their teams, and their citizens, who deliberated and gained consensus on the fundamental and most mentioned ideas within the presented proposals.

The final synthesis document, the previous pre-projects, the Participatory Project of Communes Law, the bulletins, and other complementary documents can be accessed online through the legislature's Web page.

No special budget was assigned for ICT access, implementations, or use related to this project.

No strategic planning was made about e-readiness topics, including both CD&PC personnel and citizenry.

These GDIK processes were in charge of the CD&PC, and financial resources were absorbed by the commission and the legislature budget.

Technological resources were provided by the Commission from its permanent equipment, and occasionally by the Commission personnel.

ICTs strategies were in charge of permanent personnel of the commission, with advance technical knowledge. There was no special or additional training, nor were additional personnel hired. No external consultants were required.

PEP Results Analysis

References:

- PEP Publicity Effectiveness = % Attendant CSOs by Commune/CSOs Invited by Commune

- Total Outreach = (% Attendant Citizens by Commune/Total Attendant Citizens) + (% Attendant CSOs by Commune/Total Attendant CSOs) + (% Debate Autonomous Spaces Presented by Commune/Total Debate Autonomous Spaces presented)

- Previous Knowledge Commune Average: Average of Previous Knowledge by Neighborhood within Commune

- Uses Internet (%) = Men and Women Above 18 Years Old by Zone (Creer y Crecer Foundation, 2004)

Figure 3. PEP publicity effectiveness, total outreach, previous knowledge about communes, and use of the Internet

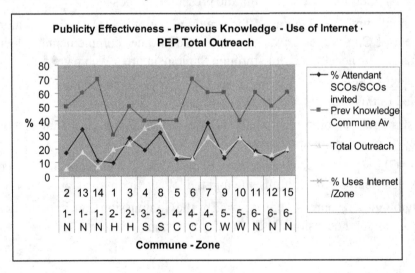

The above analyzed data does not allow us to conclude that a correlation between access to the Internet and the PEP publicity effectiveness exists; neither do they reveal a correlation between access to the Internet and the outreach of the PEP (attendant citizens and attendant CSOs and debate autonomous spaces presented) as shown in Figure 3.

In this sense, it seems that other aspects have influenced more directly, such as the strong presence of the various political parties of the city in each neighborhood (this is the case of Communes 4 and 8 in the south), or the strong involvement of citizens and CSOs in previous participatory processes such as the participatory budgeting (for example, Commune 7 in the center).

The already mentioned data in Figure 3 reveal a likely direct correlation between the previous knowledge about communes and the outreach of the PEP in each commune.

A Brief Analysis of the Participatory Device

The PEP was conceived as a process oriented to introduce the citizenry all along the city. Based on the typology defined by Michele Leclerc Olive (2004), we can identify that the 46 meetings responded to a methodology more oriented to being legitimating and communicating devices than to be a hybrid forum, considering that legislators were invited to present their proposals, and the citizens then were able to ask some questions, but no debate or collaborative working sessions were implemented. This top-down implementation, and the lack of knowledge about the topic that the citizenry had suffered during their neighborhood meetings, was the germ of an unsatisfactory feeling that was perceived by the PEP coordinators, and generates the creation of the debate autonomous spaces, through which CSOs were free to debate and prepare their own proposals, that then would be included in the synthesis process.

The synthesis process itself has had some weaknesses; not all the information about the 46 meetings and the debate autonomous spaces was ready and available on time, reducing the transparency and clearness of the process.

What happened in parallel beyond the institutional boundaries? A rich and active social tissue, even when it was a small proportion of citizens, started to create their own emerging system of GDIK processes, giving the shape to a public space where debate and collaborative work allowed them to elaborate and communicate information and knowledge about the future communes. Many CSOs performed as information and communication nodes for their networks, through personal contact, neighborhood media, or electronic bulletins.

The CD&PC commission made its own publicity of the process through brochures, small posters, and pamphlets that were disseminated in each neighborhood, but the most important role that the commission was asked to play was to be the source of reliable data and information about the process and its history. This role was fulfilled in a high but relative degree because the lack of resources and previous planning conspired against the full availability of information on the legislature's Web page. Anyway, the e-bulletin sent periodically by the commission was mentioned by the attendants who received it as one of the most effective information tools within this process.

What Do Attendants Think of the PEP?

As part of this research, a survey was carried out addressed to the attendants of the PEP, and also personal interviews with key actors were made.

Through these interviews and survey, we can learn that there exists a polarization among participants.

The opposing positions differ in the perception of the process itself, with it being highly positive for those who participate more actively and with a higher incidence in the coordination and organization of the PEP.

The above-mentioned surveyed citizens with a positive perception of the PEP, who represent the larger group, also declare having achieved high degrees of incidence and declare that the resulting law reflects to a great extent their expectancies.

The other group, a minority one that reflects a negative perception of the PEP, is made up of a heterogeneous group of citizens, social actors, and political actors that could not have a strong incidence at the beginning of the process due to political or ideological rivalries with the CD&PC commission authorities, because they perceive a certain degree of discretion in the selection of the topics to be debated during the process, or because they feel frustrated because their proposals were not included in the final result.

What Do PEP Attendant Citizens Think of ICTs' Impacts on the PEP?

The surveyed citizens, who count with access to the Internet, consider as positive the role of ICTs, and especially of the Internet, in the consolidation of an active neighborhood network dealing with communes and decentralization in the city. Many of them have made an explicit reference to their belonging to the *"Vecinos del Encuentro"* network, which they consider has significantly increased its membership and communicational capabilities owing to the Internet.

At the same time, advantages and disadvantages have been pointed out about the use of the Internet in the different instances of the PEP: speedier processes, easy access to information from abroad about similar processes, fast and easy distance communication (subject to having enough skills), relatively low costs, and a useful tool for continuous contact if on-site meetings are difficult to arrange due to lack of time or long distances.

These advantages are counterbalanced by some disadvantages that citizens perceive, among those mostly mentioned are that the Internet can become a discriminatory tool as many citizens are not familiar with its use, it increases communication but not acquaintance among people, there is a lack of official and governmental information available, there is no organized information, there are a lack of skills to operate with this tool, and there is a lack of adequate and easy access in less developed zones of the city.

The PEP Impacts on the Normative Framework and the Consolidation of New Political Practices in Buenos Aires

As Poggiese (2005) says (whom we agree with after the analysis made through this research), different rationalities can be identified in the public space about the PEP and the present transition-to-communes program:

- Neighborhood movements and independent neighbors that bring along with them a tradition of citizen exertion transpired by a strong mistrust over politicians and government. This mistrust vision conspires in part with the possibility of building associative public administration scenarios, as the transition-to-communes program, since these actors are less disposed to build consensus with the government.

- Traditional CSOs and neighborhood associations, which have had a strong commitment with the PEP and the communes law. These social actors feel their autonomy and empowerment to be at risk, both the autonomy and the empowerment they earned through their active involvement in the PEP for the communes law. Besides this, some of those social movements bring along with them traditions of political incidence nearer to the old practices of lobbies, pressure, expert consultancies, and partnership with state than to the associative public-administration modality, which implies trust, openness, and a collaborative attitude, elements that are as from now being built between many of those social actors and the government. This associative modality represents something new, new practices that would be necessary to learn.

- Neighborhood networks already developing associative public-administration practices and projects with the government. Differing from the two other groups mentioned before, those social actors have an integral vision of the problems that the city is facing and are strongly oriented to consensus construction.

Preliminary Contributions to Socially Relevant Public Policies on E-Governance

Which are the most significant problems and opportunities that decision makers on public policies on ICTs and IKS must take into consideration in order to design equitable policies?

The case related in this chapter, analyzed through both the research about the social impact of ICTs in participatory processes and the participatory public policies on e-governance in the transition program to communes in Buenos Aires, allow us to reach some preliminary conclusions that are presented at this point.

First, it is necessary to identify some initial problems that are faced when defining public policies on ICTs, particularly in our region:

1. **The conceptualization of the digital divide:** We consider that it is important to think about this divide not only in terms of access to tech-

nological infrastructure, but in terms of access both to the infrastructure and to the culture necessary for everybody to profit from this available structure. A typical aspect of ICTs is that in order to use them and to profit from them and take advantage of all their potential, some special capacities, abilities, and skills are needed: cognitive skills, special training, and a variety of advanced skills and capacities known as "digital alphabetization." To successfully manage oneself in a digital world, this kind of alphabetization is necessary, and this means that the digital infrastructure without the complementary human capital needed for their appropriation is not sufficient to generate social benefits for the society as a whole.

2.   **The conceptualization of the IKS:** It is important to enlarge this concept from Castells' (1999) vision to David and Foray's (2001) perspective, who affirm that IKS will become true depending on:

> *the proliferation of knowledge-intensive communities. These communities...are characterized by their strong knowledge production and reproduction capabilities, a public or semi-public space for learning and exchange and, the intensive use of information technologies. ...Only when increasing number of communities displaying those very characteristics are formed across a wide array of cognitive fields, when professional experts, ordinary users of information, and uninitiated students are brought together by their shared interest in a given subject.* (p. 23)

3.   **The definition of a strategic vision about ICTs:** From the point of view expressed in this chapter, we feel that it is necessary to consider, in the Latin American context, which are the strategic aspects about these technologies when we think of their impact on our societies' development.

There are basically two strategies when thinking about the impact of ICTs in less developed societies.

a.   The new economy industries' development. ICTs as resource developers through the development of their related local industries

b.   ICTs as social, political, economic, and human development enablers

We consider that the first perspective constitutes a partial focus on this subject, while the second perspective represents an integral vision facing development issues within IKS framework. This second perspective, considered as the vision that must lead ICT public-policies definition processes, must be shaped within the framework of the social impact of ICTs in development, including in their analysis and design processes the concepts of equitable access, using with sense, social appropriation, their impact on the knowledge economy, and their impact on the normative framework in the context in which those policies are being applied.

4.   **The definition of an adequate process for the design, implementation, and evaluation for ICT public policies:** We consider that ICT public policies must rely on the necessary legitimacy that an open, multiactor, and agreed-upon process must give, where the mentioned consensus is gained through a deliberative process in which all social sectors were equitably represented, equally informed, and equitably enabled for participation

5.   Especially related to e-governance public policies, through the analysis of the Buenos Aires case presented above, we can reaffirm that some critical aspects must be taken into consideration, having been already mentioned in previous works.[18]

   a.   The need for strategic planning on ICT actions integrated into governance strategies (ICTs integrated, neither isolated, idolized, nor ignored; Heeks, 2001)

   b.   The importance of e-preparation (for social, political, and government actors)

   c.   The necessary previous awareness about the social impact of ICTs to all strategic actors

   d.   The need of participatory planning

   e.   The importance of political will

   f.   The need of intra- and inter-coordination between actors

   g.   The relevance of trust and social capital

   h.   The need for complementary traditional and innovative strategies

How can all these problems be faced with an integral approach? Both the research and the process presented in this chapter, and the findings we have come through their analysis, has encouraged us to consider that the conceptual framework presented here in this chapter could be a useful tool to help understand the still underexplored imbrications between the virtual and physical worlds, specifically those revealed in participatory processes, and in governability and governance reinforcement through the use of ICTs. The qualitative analysis performed to study the case of the PEP for the communes law of Buenos Aires has as its main purpose the situating of the analysis of e-governance in the historic context in which it is being developed. As Tesoro, Arambarri, and González Cao affirm (2002), we also consider that the sociopolitical and institutional contexts are conditioning factors for the success of the e-governance projects. The case of the PEP for the communes law and the conceptual framework introduce new elements that can help to understand how these cultural and institutional factors interact with the e-governance initiatives.

Conclusion

The building of a new government model, and its effective implementation in the real world, based on the synthesis of the best practices that can be rescued from neo-institutionalism, the policy networks, and the new public administration experiences in Latin America, within the transition to the IKS, is at the same time the opportunity to build a new public space with its own new complexity. ICTs and IKS public policies, especially those related to e-governance, will be crucial to shape a new public space where all citizens will have the opportunity to get involved in the decision-making processes related to those public affairs that impact on their human development.

The role of the state, as a key actor in this context, will be to guarantee equal opportunities to all citizens to actively participate in this new public space, ensuring equal capabilities for all to be able to appropriate those participatory processes (virtual and on-site access, skills and habits to be able to appropriate all available mechanisms), reinforcing the weakest actors, creating synergies between institutional processes and emerging processes within society, establishing a permanent flow of reliable and full public information, and strengthening its own capacities to coordinate and articulate associative public administration spaces between state and society.

Many significant uses of ICTs have been identified along this chapter, which allow us to be optimistic about the potentially positive social impact of ICTs on democracy and development. But we must not forget about ICTs' risks and constraints, at least the still existing digital divide, the unequal distribution of capacities that allow social appropriation of ICTs, the existing mistrust about ICT use and application, the still high ICT costs, the bureaucracy and concentration of information as traditions that are difficult to change, and a delegative democracy model that conspires against development.

On the other hand, specially focusing on e-governance public policies, both UN-DESA (2003) and Reilly and Echeverría's (2003) research agree and affirm that there are really few public policies in e-government that are oriented to citizen participation in proposal elaboration and decision-making processes. And this is more evident about citizen participation on e-governance policies.

But the present moment can be an inflection point, an opportunity to turn this tendency around. There are many e-government initiatives at their initial phase in the region, and an international consensus is being built about its strategic relevance to improve social, political, and human development.

In order to lead these e-government and e-governance policies to development, it is necessary to overcome technocentric visions through the full comprehension of the potential social impact of ICTs.

To spread this full understanding to all social sectors, awareness raising is needed, which must cover a wide scope of social, political, and governmental actors and decision makers.

At the same time, participatory processes should be carried out in order to facilitate all strategic actors' involvement. Within the frame of a new relation between the state and society, these participatory processes would allow the enlargement of those policies' scope, passing from a vision of citizens as clients to a vision of citizens as proactive actors in the shaping of their own society.

A participatory scenario like this will lead to a new model of government that, as Criado Grande et al. (2002) say, "improves the quality of its public policies, that gives better responses to social problems, that enlarges the opportunities to consensus construction among all social actors, that allows an institutional and cultural change needed to enlarge its actions legitimacy," in other words, an e-government oriented to social, political, economic, and human development for Latin American and Caribbean societies.

References

Camacho, K. (2003). *Internet, ¿cómo vamos cambiando?* San José, Costa Rica: Fundación Acceso & IDRC.

Castells, M. (1999). *La era de la información: Economía, sociedad y cultura: Vol. 1. La sociedad Red.* Mexico DF, Mexico: Siglo XXI Editores.

Creer y Crecer Foundation. (2004). *Encuesta sobre comunas: La ciudad real.* Buenos Aires, Argentina: Creer y Crecer Foundation.

Criado Grande, J. I., Ramilo Araujo, C., & Serna, Miguel S. (2002). *La necesidad de teoría(s) sobre gobierno electrónico: Una propuesta integradora.* Retrieved March 3, 2004, from http://www.clad.org.ve/fulltext/0043103.pdf

Cunil Grau, N. (1997). *Repensando lo público a través de la sociedad.* Caracas, Venezuela: CLAD & Editorial Nueva Sociedad.

Dahl, R. (1998). *On democracy.* New Haven, CT: Yale University Press.

David, P., & Foray, D. (2001). *An introduction to the economy of the knowledge society.* Retrieved May 25, 2005, from http://www.merit.unimaas.nl/publications/rmpdf/2001/rm2001-041.pdf

Facultad Latinoamericana de Ciencias Sociales/Planificación Participativa y Gestión Asociada (FLACSO/PPGA). (2005). *Buenos Aires viva V. Documento final: Preliminar, 311*(39). Buenos Aires, Argentina.

Goldstein, R. L. (2005). Sociedad de la información, democracia y desarrollo local: Las TIC como herramientas para el fortalecimiento de procesos decisorios participativos participativos en la gestión local. In S. Finquelievich (Ed.), *E-gobierno y e-política en América Latina* (pp. 73-103). Buenos Aires, Argentina: LINKS.

Heeks, R. (2001). *Understanding e-governance for development.* Retrieved April 2, 2003, from http://www.man.ac.uk/idpm/idpm_dp.htm#ig

Held, D. (1996). *Modelos de democracia.* Madrid, Spain: Alianza Editorial.

Jurado, R. (2005). *Material del curso "políticas públicas para TIC y equidad social": Diplomatura en políticas públicas para Internet 2005.* FLACSO, Quito, Ecuador.

Leclerc Olive, M. (2004). *Les villes: Laboratoires de démocraties?* Retrieved June 3, 2005, from http://www.isted.com/programmes/prud/syntheses/Atelier_A/Leclerc-Olive.pdf

Mayntz, R. (2000). Nuevos desafíos de la teoría de governance. *Instituciones y Desarrollo, 7*. Retrieved November 12, 2005, from http://www.iigov. org/id/attachment.drt?art=187660

Mayntz, R. (2003). *From government to governance: Political steering in modern societies.* Paper presented at the Summer Academy on IPP, September 7th-11th, Wuerzburg, Germany. Retrieved November 20, 2005, from http://www.ioew.de/governance/english/veranstaltungen/Summer_Academies/SuA2Mayntz.pdf

Pimienta, D. (2003). *La brecha digital: ¡A ver a ver!* Retrieved May 15, 2006, from http://funredes.org/mistica/castellano/ciberoteca/tematica/esp_doc_wsis1.html

Poggiese, H. (1994). Metodología FLACSO de planificación gestión. *Serie de Documentos e Informes de Investigación, Nro. 163.*

Poggiese, H. (2005). *Racionalidades alternativas sobre desarrollo urbano para la configuración de las comunas descentralizadas, en la ciudad autónoma de Buenos Aires.* Buenos Aires, Argentina: FLACSO Argentina Redes PPGA (Planificación Participativa y Gestión Asociada).

Prats, J. (2001). Gobernabilidad democrática para el desarrollo humano: Marco conceptual y analítico. *Instituciones y Desarrollo, 10*, 103-148. Retrieved December 12, 2005, from http://www.iigov.org/id/article.drt?edi=187384&art=187477

Redín, M. E., & Morroni, W. (2002). *Aportes metodológicos para la ampliación democrática de la toma de decisiones y la participación social en la gestión sociourbana.* Paper presented at the seminar Gestao Democratica das Cidades, Metodologías de Participación, Redes y Movimientos Sociales, Porto Alegre, Brazil.

Reilly, K., & Echeverría, R. (2003). *El Papel del ciudadano y de las OSC en el e-gobierno: Un estudio de gobierno electrónico en ocho países de América Latina y el Caribe.* Retrieved July 22, 2005, from http://katherine.reilly.net/docs/EGOV&OSCenALC.pdf

Tesoro, J. L., Arambarri, A. J., & González Cao, R. (2002). *Factores endógenos y exógenos asociados al desempeño del gobierno electrónico: Hallazgos emergentes de un análisis exploratorio de experiencias nacionales.* Retrieved April 29, 2004, from http://www.clad.org.ve/fulltext/0043105.pdf

UNDP. (2002). *Aportes para el desarrollo humano de la Argentina/2002.* United Nations Development Program, Banco Interamericano de Desarrollo, Gadis. Buenos Aires, Argentina: United Nations Development Program.

UNDP-BID-GADIS. (2004). *Índice de desarrollo sociedad civil de Argentina: Total país.* Buenos Aires, Argentina: Edilab Editora.

UN-DESA. (2003). *World public sector report 2003: E-government at the crossroads.* United Nations Department of Economic and Social Affairs. New York: United Nations Publications.

Endnotes

[1]   Its name in Spanish: "Centro de Estudios sobre Ciencia, Desarrollo y Educación Superior" ("Centro Redes") (http://www.centroredes.org.ar). Director: Dr. Mario Albornoz. Area: "Política y Gestión del Conocimiento —Políticas para la Sociedad de la Información". Area Coordinator: Lic. Rubén Ibáñez. Research Team: Lic. Roxana L. Goldstein.

[2]   Research Project:"Evaluation of the Social Impact of ICTs in local participatory processes: ICTs and democratic governability reinforcement". Director: Lic. Rubén Darío Ibañez. Research Team: Lic. Roxana L. Goldstein.

[3]   "PPGA FLACSO Argentina": Stands for "Planificación Participativa y Gestión Asociada—FLACSO Argentina", the name in Spanish for the Group of Participatory Planning and Associative Administration at FLACSO Argentina. Director: Dr. Héctor Poggiese.

[4]   "GDIK" Processes: Generation and Diffusion of Information and Knowledge Processes.

[5]   They are summarized here the main aspects. For further analysis see Document "Evaluación del Impacto Social de las TIC en los procesos participativos locales: Las TIC en el fortalecimiento de la gobernabilidad democrática en Buenos Aires - Argentina", at http://www.centroredes. org.ar/template/template.asp?nivel=documentos&cod=00.

[6]   Following Michele Leclerc Olive´s (2004) perspective, we differentiate "participatory instrument" from "participatory device". A participatory instrument could be referendum, popular consultation, participatory

budget. A participatory device is the way a participatory instrument is implemented in a given context, for example the Participatory Budgeting at Buenos Aires, The Participatory Budgeting at Porto Alegre, etc.

[7]   From Michele Leclerc Olive's (2004, pp. 4-5) Typology.

[8]   Based on Redín and Morroni's (2002) perspective.

[9]   "CGPs" stands for "Centros de Gestión y Participación", the name in Spanish of the Administration and Participation Centers.

[10] A "Commune" is an administrative and political subdivision of a district.

[11] "PEP": Participatory Elaboration Process for Communes Law.

[12] "DAS": Debate Autonomous Space.

[13] "CD&PC" stands for "Comisión de Descentralización y Participación Ciudadana", the name in Spanish of the Decentralization and Citizen Participation Commission of the LCABA.

[14] "LCABA" stands for "Legislatura de la Ciudad Autónoma de Buenos Aires", the name in Spanish of the Buenos Aires Autonomous City Legislature.

[15] "SD&PC" stands for "Secretaría de Descentralización y Participación Ciudadana", the name in Spanish of the Decentralization and Citizen Participation Secretary of Buenos Aires Government.

[16] Buenos Aires VIVA V—Final Document—Preliminary Version. 2005.

[17] Human Development Index. Last measurement available. Corresponds to year 2000.

[18] Heeks (2001); Reilly and Echeverria (2003); Tesoro, Arambarri and González Cao (2002), among others.

Chapter XI

Electronic Delivery of Public Services to Citizens:
The eGOIA Project

Petra Hoepner, Fraunhofer Institute FOKUS, Germany

Linda Strick, Fraunhofer Institute FOKUS, Germany

Manuel Mendes, Universidade Católica de Santos [Unisantos], Brazil

Romildo Monte, Centro de Pesquisas Renato Archer [CenPRA], Brazil

Roberto Agune, Governo do Estado de São Paulo, Casa Civil, Brazil

Sergio Bolliger, Governo do Estado de São Paulo, Casa Civil, Brazil

Alejandra Ciurlizza, CONCYTEC, Peru

Abstract

The main goal of the EU @LIS demonstration project Electronic Government Innovation and Access (eGOIA) is the provisioning of demonstrators that show future-oriented public-administration services to a broad public in Latin America. The vision of the eGOIA project is the provision of a single virtual space supporting the interaction of citizens (independent of social status, gender, race, abilities, and age) and the public administration in a simple, future-oriented, and cost-effective way. A software infrastructure is developed in order to allow the access of citizens through the Internet to integrated public services at several levels: local government (municipalities), regional government (state), and federal government. The trial of the demonstrator will be performed in São Paulo state and in municipalities in Peru.

Introduction

E-government is being implemented in most countries in the world, not only the most developed, but also in countries under development like those from Latin America. E-government is the use of information and communication technologies in public administrations combined with organizational change and the development of new skills in order to improve public services and democratic processes.

To serve citizens and enterprises with a variety of services in the social, educational, and security sectors is a main goal of public administrations. One important category considered in this chapter deals with the delivery of life-event services (birth, employment, etc.) to citizens (Vintar, Kunstelj, & Leben, 2002), as are already in place for Austrian citizens (HELP, n.d.). These services include the delivery of personal documents and the payment of taxes, constituting a large class of situations in Latin America.

The development of ICT and very specifically of the Internet gives new opportunities to enhance the delivery of such services to the citizens. Other channels are not excluded, but in eGOIA (Electronic Government Innovation and Access), the main access channel will be the Internet, as a complementation (not replacement) of already existing physical delivery options.

The growing availability of public services introduced by public agencies on the Internet requires that the government take initiative to convert the present, physical-presence relationship with citizens into a future-oriented electronic community. The interaction of citizens with the public administration has to be encouraged to choose new ways of access for the benefit of all participating parties.

E-government services hide the level of complexity lying behind the services offered to the citizen and enterprises. Each life event is associated with the relevant actions and interactions with and between the public administrations. The services may imply either a single business process or several business processes to be performed in a given sequence between different administrations and sectors.

As happens in other countries, increasingly in Latin America, services are already being delivered in front offices (Prisma, 2003) with citizens' physical attendance and the intervention of public servants. "One-stop" places (e.g., Poupatempos or Save Time in Sao Paulo, Brazil) are created enabling citizens to access several public services in the same location rather than visiting different agencies and locations where the services are performed.

These front offices are normally located in cities and include expensive ICT infrastructures, connecting them online with the equipment and people—the back offices—already existent in traditional departments of the public administration, where the services are really executed.

eGOIA intends to complement these front offices with the creation of an electronic virtual front office where different kinds of actions and information with respect to the services can be displayed. One of the goals is to alleviate the number of citizens going to the physical front offices (these systems had great success and tend to overcrowd), thus avoiding new high investments and operational costs. In cities like Sao Paulo, as well as in the majority of big cities in the rest of Brazil, this is not a question of being modern and simply adopting the new ICT technologies trend, but, much more, it is a question of giving to all people the possibility to get the service quality of already existing installations.

On the other hand, as computer networking becomes increasingly important to economic and social success, many people in inner cities (e.g., less favored citizens living in the slums) and isolated rural areas are failing to acquire the new technology. This is especially true for low-income and underserved people who do not have the possibility to access the new technology and to benefit from its usefulness. In underserved communities, proper tools for making use of these technologies are required to profit from the benefits of these new developments, and eGOIA addresses this user group specifically.

To accelerate the development of the information society in Latin America and to reinforce the partnership between the European Union (EU) and Latin America, the European Commission launched a cooperation program called Alliance for the Information Society (@LIS; European Commission, n.d.-a). Within this program, "demonstrators" are developed to show the opportunities of ICT to a broad public.

The EU @LIS project eGOIA (http://www.egoia.sp.gov.br) intends to improve existing Latin American approaches and physical-presence attendance systems, like Poupatempo, toward a future-oriented e-attendance system in order to achieve the following:

- **Support less skilled people by Internet access points:** This includes the improvement of the user interfaces and services to fit people's needs based on a life-situation-focused approach.

- **Integrate public-administration services to provide a one-stop shop for citizens:** Integration comprises adaptation of front-office processes for easy usability and access to back-office processes in an open and standardized fashion that features the reusability of components.

- **To study the process of multiplying the experiences and solutions into other Brazilian states, and other Latin American countries, in particular to Peru**

One of the main goals in the eGOIA project is the transfer of experiences and the reuse of proven e-government solutions in Germany and across Europe. Although it seems that architectural guidelines and interoperability frameworks together with service solutions are easy to transfer, the sociocultural context is different, and these architectural guidelines and interoperability frameworks need to be adapted for Latin America.

The next section provides an overview of current needs in Brazil and Peru with respect to e-government, and more specifically to the virtual delivery of services, resulting in the choice of services implemented in eGOIA. The following sections describe in more detail the architectural and technological aspects of the demonstrators built in eGOIA. The chapter closes with some comments about future work and conclusions.

Current Needs in Brazil and Peru

Brazil and Peru are the target Latin American countries for demonstrating e-government services within the eGOIA project. In addition to this, the pre-conditions and requirements of different e-government levels are tackled: the state level, municipal level, and federal level. The requirements within the project are strongly related to the main user group of eGOIA: the citizens.

São Paulo and Brazilian States

The creation of citizens' services centers (physical front offices) in almost all the Brazilian states (nowadays 23 out of 27 existing states), which gather several agencies carrying out services from any area of the government in a unique space, has created a great advance in improving significantly the image of the public administration in Brazil (http://www.centraisdeatendi-mento.sp.gov.br/).

Before these initiatives, the public agencies were considered as archaic places dominated by the image of bureaucracy with a lack of information and ex-planation. Today, the citizens' services centers have been transformed into paradigms of efficiency, effectiveness, and respect to the citizens' rights, not only for the public administration but also for the private sector.

The facilities introduced by these centers support the performance of hundreds of services in a single space. However, even though carried out in one single space, the citizens are required to present several times the same personal data and documents for each administrative service. It is important to note that 90% of the public services offered in Brazil still require the presence of the citizen. The challenge here is to construct virtual citizen services centers, where it will be possible to access public services and information without the obligatory repeated proof of certificates. This will lead to a new quality of relationship between state and citizen.

Technically, each of the services currently provided uses its own database. These databases, usually built more than three decades ago, cannot respond to the new demands of electronic service provisioning. That means that there is a need for the integration, adaptation, and restructuring of the legacy databases.

The technical challenges eGOIA faces are therefore twofold: provide inte-grated electronic services to the citizens with an easily usable front end (access channel and user interface) and provide the integration of existing legacy systems into a newly organized back-office environment. These challenges are common to all e-government approaches, in Latin America as well as in Europe or on other continents. Naturally, various other factors influence the success of e-government systems; for example, so-called good-practice examples are awarded in the Stockholm Challenge ("Awarded Public Gov-ernment Projects," n.d.).

eGOIA has chosen the region of São Paulo for its initial local-community demonstrations. The São Paulo state population is now over 37 million inhabit-ants. It is bigger than the Canadian population, the same size as Argentina's, and almost half of Germany's.

The citizens of the São Paulo region already have the possibility of access-ing public-administration services in single physical places, namely, the Poupatempos (Poupatempo, n.d.). Poupatempos are increasingly demanded and require expansion, which is associated with high expenditures due to the extensive infrastructure needed for high-quality services. A shortcoming is that in this physical-presence environment, people will always have to appear and queue up in person for each service required. This led to the requirement of the São Paulo state government to enhance this administration system into a future Internet-based e-government system available to all citizens in São Paulo and in rural areas, which are currently lacking the possibility of access to new technologies and services.

Besides the requirements of state governments such as São Paulo state, also municipalities and their needs have to be considered.

Municipalities in Brazil and their Needs

Brazil is a highly decentralized federation. Its 27 states (including the federal district) have 5,560 municipalities, each of them having its own direct elected legislative and executive branches. According to their population, Brazilian cities can be classified as very small (less than 5,000 inhabitants; 1,371 cities), small (between 5,000 and 20,000 inhabitants; 2,688 cities), medium (between 20,000 and 100,000 inhabitants; 1,275 cities), large (between 100,000 and 500,000 inhabitants; 194 cities), and very large (more than 500,000 inhabitants; 32 cities).

Since 1998, due to a legal decree, all the municipalities are being obliged to publish their accounts through the Internet. Although they were not prepared to do that, they started working on their internal processes and on the automation of their information systems in order to not only comply with the law, but also to improve the quality and availability of the municipal public services.

These efforts have been supported in the last years by some programs of the Brazilian government that were created in order to help municipalities to improve their administrative and fiscal management. The most important supporting programs are PMAT (Program for the Modernization of the Tax Administration and Management of the Basic Social Sectors, http://www.bndes.gov.br/programas/sociais/municip.asp) and PNAFM (National Program to Support the Administrative and Fiscal Management of Brazilian Municipalities, http://www.fazenda.gov.br/ucp/pnafm/).

As a result of the efforts being made by the municipalities and with the support of PMAT and PNAFM, several Brazilian cities have developed and implemented information systems aiming for municipal management needs related to the automation of their administrative procedures. A recently published survey conducted by the Brazilian Institute for Geography and Statistics (IBGE) shows that the great majority of the municipalities computerized internal activities, but only 24% of the municipalities have their own Web site on the Internet.

Analyzing this situation, the conclusion is that the municipalities have concentrated their work so far on in-house activities, implementing information systems that organize and computerize their internal processes. Now, they will have to focus their investments on the production of Internet applications for online services directly for the users (citizens, businesses, organizations, etc.). The new municipal information systems will have to deal with the same problems as state-government systems, such as the integration of systems, services, and data (back-office procedures), and the support of appropriate access channels (front-office procedures). These are exactly the problems that the eGOIA project is tackling.

Municipalities in Peru

Peru is a country with a population of almost 28 million inhabitants. The Office of the Prime Minister is the state institution that governs, through the Commission for the Development of the Information Society (CODESI), national policy on ICT (http://www.codesi.gob.pe/). Furthermore, it leads, through the portal of the Peruvian state and the respective laws, the application and expansion of electronic government in public administrations.

Other state institutions that have experienced interesting progress on the subject are the Superintendence of Tax Administration (SUNAT), the National Superintendence of the Public Records Offices (SUNARP), and district councils such as Miraflores that offer exemplary electronic portals.

However, most public institutions and district councils, which are the demonstration environment of eGOIA, just started to adopt this process and merely resorted to preparing simple electronic portals to meet the legal requirements and to avoid administrative sanctions due to omission.

In this regard and in order to implement the eGOIA demonstration project, three districts were selected that represent the country's diversity. First is San Borja, a middle-class residential district of the capital, followed by Villa El Salvador as a reflection of a vast popular and emerging sector of the city of Lima, and finally Cajamarca, a historical city of the northern Sierra that represents the rural areas of the country.

To provide Internet access to a broad public, a new and popular private business emerged at the end of the '90s and beginning of the year 2000 to the install public Internet booths. Such services are offered at a very low price to the users and are therefore expanding rapidly.

While Peru emerges as a leading country in the use of the Internet through public booths, the large majority of them are used by young students. It is clear then that the Peruvian population lacks training in ICT, which threatens to become a critical bottleneck regarding the benefits of the expansion of information and communication technologies.

It is necessary that, from the macro point of view, a comprehensive plan be defined and executed, including economic, administrative, political, and legal aspects. From a specific point of view, actions are required to allow an increased connectivity in provinces, to design user-friendly and useful electronic portals, and to provide funds for technological equipment in the public agencies. The permanent training of the actors involved and the constant dissemination of the benefits of e-government among the population is a fact that has been considered in eGOIA through a plan for the dissemination of results and presentation of advantages to the districts established in the interior of the country.

The starting point of eGOIA was a diagnosis of the situation of each one of the districts chosen for the project. Thus, inquiries were made in each locality participating in this project. The samples were designed and applied to determine the level of knowledge of ICT and to identify the municipal services that could be offered in the future through the Internet.

The relevant information obtained from these studies reflects a scarce level of knowledge of ICT among the population of Villa El Salvador and Cajamarca. Furthermore, the insufficient level of preparation of the municipal employees in terms of electronic government and the poor level of equipment and infrastructure of the Villa El Salvador district council were recognized. Local initiatives are required on a broad spectrum to teach the basics of ICT and the Internet.

Figure 1. Business aspects of the eGOIA Demonstrator

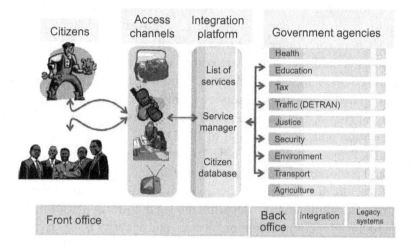

The eGOIA Demonstrator

The general aspects, architecture, design principles, and system development as applied in eGOIA are described below.

General Aspects

The eGOIA Demonstrator is an e-government demonstration system (see Figure 1) that will support the interaction of citizens with different types of e-government services through the Internet, either through home personal computers or through different types of public citizen points of access (CPAs), which can be located in a variety of places such as Poupatempos, libraries, Internet cafés, public kiosks, and so forth.

The eGOIA Demonstrator comprises the following:

- **Back-office integration:** Concentrates on a unified approach to access already existing and newly emerging government services. Requirements for faster development cycles, decreased effort, and greater software reuse motivate the creation and use of middleware and middleware-based solutions. The envisaged solution creates a virtual boundary around application components (e.g., e-government services) that interact with each other only through well-defined interfaces and define the standard mechanisms to compose and execute components in generic component servers. Valuable experiences on how to proceed to an integrated e-government service architecture were provided by the senate of Berlin, Germany, through its e-government project VeZuDa (Unification and Consolidation of the Data of the County of Berlin; VeZuDa Project, 2004). The objective of this project was the conception and prototypical realization of a distributed and secure back-office infrastructure for the city of Berlin, providing access to various data of different administrative departments via a uniform platform. Based on middleware, communication, access, and security issues have been solved to connect governmental departments and to develop services to request data from different database systems.

- **Front-office integration:** Besides the integration of back-office processes, the main factor for the acceptance of e-government services is an intuitive user interface integrating the access to the diverse e-government services available. This will be achieved by concentrating on certain life situations that are non-technical and easy to follow by the target user group. eGOIA will provide access to the e-government services in the CPAs.

The implementation of the eGOIA Demonstrator has been planned in two phases. During eGOIA Phase 1, started in October 2003 and finished in May 2005, the main activities were as follows:

- Definition of criteria and requirements to select the services to be demonstrated in the context of citizen attendance systems in the state of São Paulo and in Peru
- Analysis of different European best-practices examples
- Definition of the architecture for the Demonstrator and usage of well-proven technologies
- Development of a first prototype of the Demonstrator with the corresponding training of developers

The second phase starts in May 2005 and ends in September 2006 with the following goals:

- Development of enhanced demonstrators based on the experiences obtained in Phase 1 while considering applications with increased needs with respect to the interoperability of horizontal and vertical levels of governmental services
- Expanding the experiences made in São Paulo to other Brazilian states
- Dissemination and exploitation of demonstrators to other governmental levels, such as the local (municipalities) and the federal level

Architectural Framework

The architectural framework remains a work-in-progress framework for the project time and will be improved and further developed along with the realization of services in response to the challenges of the evolving new technologies. It will lead at the end of the project to a general architectural framework that reflects the experiences and provides recommendations for ICT strategies as part of an e-government master plan. For building the eGOIA Demonstrator, the integration procedures demand the coordination of different government departments and cooperation with the public-administrative staff. The distribution of the data used by the eGOIA Demonstrator and the autonomy of the government departments responsible for the data result in a complex structure, which is expressed in a customer-supplier relationship and demands negotiation among the several public administrations in terms of service-level agreements. The architectural framework addresses the issue of the interoperability of e-government services at several levels. This will cover the interoperability issues regarding the different government departments and the interoperability of existing applications or pilots as well as the development of new e-government services.

To achieve a future-proof and interoperable solution, eGOIA assessed relevant standardization efforts and best-practice experiences in the field of e-government. This included, for example, the European Commission (n.d.-b) IDABC program, the German Standards and Architectures for E-Government Applications (SAGA; Federal Ministry of the Interior of Germany, KBSt Unit, 2003), the UK E-Government Interoperability Framework (e-GIF; "Policies

Figure 2. Reference model for open distributed processing in eGOIA

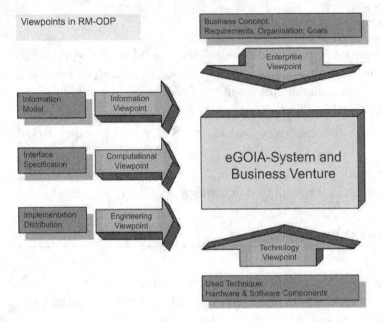

and Specifications," 2004), and the U.S. Federal Enterprise Architecture (FEA, n.d.). Out of these standards, eGOIA has defined some basic guidelines for the definition of the overall architecture that are briefly described in the following sections.

Use of ODP as a Reference Model

SAGA suggests the use of the Reference Model of Open Distributed Processing (RM-ODP) (see Figure 2) to describe e-government applications. RM-ODP provides a basis for an architectural separation of concerns in distributed systems (RM-ODP, 1996). The analysis of the application is broken down into different viewpoints in order to reduce the complexity of the overall architecture. This makes the demanding system easier to understand and hence better to handle. The object-oriented paradigm is the basis of RM-ODP, which promotes clear-cut structures, reusability, and the updating capability of the models, components, and systems created.

Figure 3. Usage of RM-ODP in eGOIA

It has to be kept in mind that RM-ODP is a highly sophisticated set of concepts and its applicability to a broad community seems quite difficult, especially without the provision of tools. The project has decided to use the new concepts of software engineering, which is known as MDA (model-driven architecture). The usage of RM-ODP in eGOIA is shown in Figure 3.

Adoption of MDA for System Development

In early 2001, the Object Management Group (OMG) described the general principles for MDA.

The MDA facilitates a model-centric software development process, which substantially reduces the time to market for complex e-government services and applications. The relationship between ODP viewpoints and MDA languages can be found in David Frankel Consulting (2003).

MDA defines three kinds of models for development:

- Computation-independent model (CIM)
- Platform-independent model (PIM)
- Platform-specific model (PSM)

The eGOIA project is using the Medini toolset for model-based software development (IKV++ Technologies, n.d.-b). Medini assists the software-development process by using the unified modeling language (UML; *Introduction to OMG's Unified Modeling Language*, n.d.), enterprise distributed object computing (EDOC; *UML Profile for Enterprise Distributed Object Computing*, n.d.), and the meta-object facility (MOF). In addition, Medini supports different middleware platforms, such as enagoOSP (IKV++ Technologies, n.d.-a), which is also used in the project.

Figure 4. MDA-driven development process

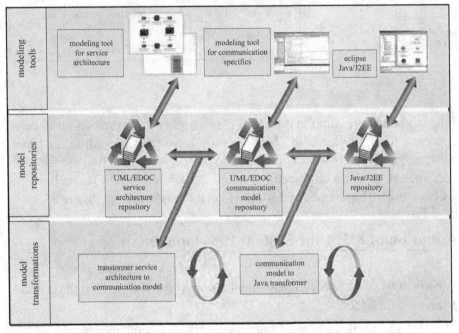

The Medini toolset can be used for the different phases in the development process for a software system as shown in Figure 4:

- The modeling tool for service architecture based on UML and EDOC directly support the abstract PIM and refined PIM modeling steps.

- The modeling tool for communication specifics (PSM) based on UML and a UML profile for enagoOSP support the enagoOSP platform-specific modeling (in the future, other platforms or technologies, such as Web services, will be considered).

- Code can be derived from models that are directly integrated into the Integrated Development Environment (IDE) of eclipse (http://www.eclipse.org/).

Use of a Service-Oriented Middleware

A middleware supporting a service-oriented architecture (SOA) provides for reorganization of software applications and infrastructure into a set of interacting services. SOA benefits include reduced interdependency between software assets, allowing individual software assets (components) to become building blocks that can be reused in developing other applications (application assembly and composition). The enagoOSP is a distributed middleware platform providing a uniform service access, execution, and management environment, particularly across different administrative and technological domains. It enables the integration, composition, and management of existing and emerging application services based on different programming languages, different access technologies, and different service technologies. Beyond this, it provides a controlled (secure) and uniform access to these services by means of one-stop shopping and single-sign-on capabilities including customization by means of profiles to the customers and end users. It is based on Common Object Request Broker Architecture (CORBA) and Java 2 technologies.

Some details of the first-phase developments are presented in the next section. Prospects of eGOIA Phase 2 are discussed in the last section of the chapter.

eGOIA Demonstrator Phase 1

To realize the eGOIA Demonstrator, relevant public services had to be selected and implemented. All services will be executed in a real environment and infrastructure.

Service Selection

Service selection for the eGOIA Demonstrator is based on a combination of pragmatic and ideal criteria. Since it will be hardly possible to assess in depth every existing service, the eGOIA project has applied a combination of criteria that ensures as much as possible the highest payoff with the minimal risk, while taking into account the characteristics of the technology available in the project.

The selection of eGOIA governmental services to be demonstrated at first has been narrowed down to a small number of candidates, which have the main focus on the service-integration vision and which are important public services for citizens based on the needs in Latin America.

In summary, the practical steps taken were the following:

1. Select a small number of candidate e-services on the bases of the combination of the following criteria: high payoff, minimum risk, and constraints of technology available to the project.

2. Conduct deep scrutiny of candidate services in terms of comparative gains with existing systems, technical and legal difficulties, users, management of change, and so forth.

3. Apply relevant leading-edge experiences of e-government services in Europe and Brazil and Latin America today, and see which ones add complementary richness.

4. In the light of all inputs, select the e-services that will become the base of the eGOIA Demonstrator.

In the following, a summary of the services selected is given.

Brazil, São Paulo State

For the first demonstration of the eGOIA system, a service collection has been chosen that relates to the civil identification and the specific life event of a citizen that had his or her identification card lost or stolen. The services selected are provided by the Public Safety Secretary of São Paulo state, the institution responsible for all the procedures related to citizen identification, such as the issuance and cancellation of the citizen's identification card (ID card), fingerprint-reliable authentication, the control of stolen ID cards, and so forth.

The ID card is the Brazilian national citizen identification document, which has national validity and is issued at the state level. It is a very important document as it must be presented to apply for all official documents.

Some examples of life situations show the importance of ID cards in Brazilian everyday life. It is required, for instance, from employers for any labor agreement, from third parties for any contractual relationship, from financial agents and those in commerce for buying on credit, and, above all, from the governmental agencies for public services, such as education, medial care, and so on, as well as for rights petitions and document issuance.

The ID-card issuing is the most demanded citizen identification service. In the São Paulo Poupatempos, an average of over 85,000 ID cards are issued per month. This requires a complex resources infrastructure, not only due to the high demand, but also because it is a very complex document. It is printed on special paper, contains citizen personal data as well as a photograph, fingerprints, and signature. Every issuance requires a lot of data handling, including fingerprints collections and validation.

The three ID-card services selected for the first phase of the eGOIA Demonstrator are the following:

- **ID-card replacement service:** Most frequently, ID-card replacement is asked for if the current document has been lost or stolen. Today, the ID-card replacement request is done only personally in the police stations or in the Poupatempo agencies. When a citizen desires to get an ID-card replacement, he or she has to present some documents, and fingerprints and a new photo have to be taken. The main goal of ID-card replacement service in the eGOIA demonstration is to provide an integrated service that supports citizens with lost or stolen ID cards to request a replacement of this document via the Web. As fingerprints are not yet transferred electronically, this service allows the premodification of personal data (to be validated in Poupatempo), schedules a date in Poupatempo, and informs about the documents to be provided regarding the personal situation of the citizen (e.g., social situation, age).

- **ID-card cancellation service:** The ID-card cancellation is accomplished to avoid the improper use of an ID card that was stolen or lost. The goal of ID-card cancellation service in the eGOIA demonstration is to automate this activity by updating the civil identification database. The integration of the legacy systems that this service requires will provide promptness in the ID-card cancellation process.

- **ID validity consult:** ID validity consult is a new service that the state of São Paulo will provide to institutions such as banks, businesses, commerce, and others that have registered themselves to access the service. The objective is to prevent the improper use of a cancelled ID card. A business user will log into the eGOIA Demonstrator, enter the ID card number and issuance date, and then gets the information about the ID-card cancellation status. The business user will be charged for this service.

Peru

In the Peruvian case, a municipal set of services was identified as important for the citizens: tax information and in the future tax payment.

In Peru, the usage of a taxpayer code is widespread. The taxpayer's code is a number allocated by a district council to an individual who owns a plot of land or a real-estate property, either finished or in construction within the jurisdiction of the district.

The purpose of the service for the payment of taxes through the Internet is to offer the citizens a quick and efficient method to pay their taxes using credit or debit cards. This type of payment can be made from the Internet booths authorized by the district councils.

To do so, the first thing that the citizen would have to do is to identify himself or herself with a taxpayer's code through the district council's portal. The referred taxpayer's code shall be validated in the revenues system of each district council.

Once the personal information of the citizen has been validated, he or she will be able to view all the kinds of municipal taxes that have to be paid, selecting those to pay and the amount to pay.

Finally, once the citizen selects the tax and the amount to be paid, he or she will carry out the electronic operation with a credit card through the eGOIA demonstrational system, which will interact as a payment corridor.

Initially, only the tax information service is implemented.

Aspects of Implementation

The functional multilayer software architecture of the eGOIA Demonstrator is shown in Figure 5.

Figure 5. eGOIA Demonstrator software architecture

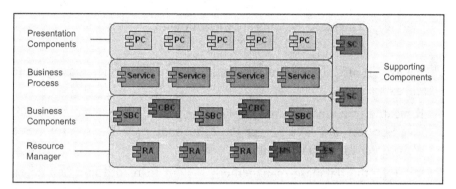

The main components of the eGOIA Demonstrator architecture are the following:

- Presentation components (PCs) handle the interaction with the user.

- Service components implement a business process through the composition of single business components (SBCs) and composite business components (CBCs).

- SBCs implement an atomic functionality that can be reused by CBCs and services.

- CBCs are composed of SBCs.

- Supporting components (SCs) are for generic usage. Examples are logging, notification, authentication, and media converters (HTML [hypertext markup language], wireless application protocol(WAP), voiceXML [extensible markup language]).

- Resource components manage resources such as resource adapters (RAs) that provide the bridge between the business layer and the different legacy systems and databases; a component to access an e-mail system (ES); and a metadata system (MS) to manage data objects, that is, a representation of a concept (citizen, ID Card, tax, etc.) in the government domain. It is a document model representation used by components to exchange data.

The choice of software to be used in the first version considered good practices from project partners, as well as a degree of stability to support the execution of the services. The main systems are the following:

- enagoOSP, already introduced as middleware for service management and execution

- Tomcat, a free, open-source implementation of a servlet container for Java Servlets and Java Server Pages technologies. It also provides a Web server for Web accessibility.

- MySQL, the database-management system to record and handle all eGOIA Demonstrator system information, but not the legacy application data.

The Demonstrator Infrastructure and Environment

The first prototype of eGOIA will demonstrate the selected integrated services in real use and toward three stakeholders: the citizens, accessing government-to-citizen (G2C) services at a CPA; business actors accessing government-to-business (G2B) services by their own computers; and government actors, accessing government-to-government (G2G) services and providing the G2C and G2B services.

For these purposes, the prototype will be launched in a government-controlled environment that, because it is offering real services, allows complete step-by-step access, supervision, and evaluation.

In order to guarantee such conditions, Poupatempo Guarulhos (http://www.poupatempo.sp.gov.br/pguarulhos/ptg.htm) has been chosen as the demonstration environment. It is located in the Guarulhos municipality, which is 17 km away from the São Paulo state capital, yet integrated into its metropolitan area. It has a large and very poor population: about 1 million people with an annual per capita income of $5,700. In fact, it is the 13th largest city in Brazil (It is the largest one that is not a capital of a state).

The Poupatempo Guarulhos is a citizens' services center of São Paulo state, where a large variety of public services in a single physical place are offered to the people. Their attendance is about 143,000 per month. The Poupatempo Guarulhos users' profile assures us that the demonstration will be carried out according to the defined target population.

Inside the Poupatempo Guarulhos, among the various public agencies, there is also one of the state's free citizens' points of access to public services on the Internet, called e-Poupatempo (http://www.poupatempo.sp.gov.br/e-poupatempo/). Its attendance is, on average, 70,000 people per month. In e-Poupatempo, people are assisted by trained personnel in their activities.

In the eGOIA trial, several institutions are involved besides São Paulo casa civil and its related companies.

The Instituto de Identificação Ricardo Gumbleton Daunt (IIRGD) is the institution responsible for ID cards and the owner of the respective database the ID-card services work on. The e-Poupatempo will support people in the access and usage of the eGOIA services. One of the reasons the Poupatempo Guarulhos was chosen is that it hosts also in its e-Poupatempo the Poupatempo Usability Lab (Filgueiras, Aquino, Tokairim, Torres, & Barbarian, 2004). In-depth assessment and evaluation of people's ability and satisfaction are performed in the usability lab, which will comprise also the eGOIA services. With its resources, people using the set of services may be filmed, and all their actions will be recorded to be analyzed. People's behavior, doubts, and questions will also be recorded by the lab's employees. Social profile research, requirements verification, and satisfaction-level polls can easily be done based on the available data. For the demonstration regarding the G2B service ID Validity Consult, the Banco do Povo Paulista agency will be involved, which is also located in the Poupatempo Guarulhos. Banco do Povo Paulista is a state-government agency responsible for loans for low-income people.

An additional advantage of Poupatempo Guarulhos is given by the fact that very closely located is the Blind People Association, whose partnership will help in testing the accessibility for disabled people.

The organizational agreements between all those agencies required an extensive preparation phase. The official trial will start in August 2005. The infrastructure of the eGOIA trials is shown in Figure 6.

The e-Poupatempo in Guarulhos is attended on average by 350 people per day. From their statistics, we know that about 15 people per day access the electronic police report, which is the first one to be executed in the chain of integrated services offered to the citizens in eGOIA. So, we estimate that there will be up to 15 well-controlled demonstrations per day, restricting the Internet access of the demonstration to those machines available in the e-Poupatempo.

If an ID card was stolen or lost, the electronic police report triggers the automatic cancellation of the ID card in the system. Integrated to the execu-

Figure 6. eGOIA prototype trial environment

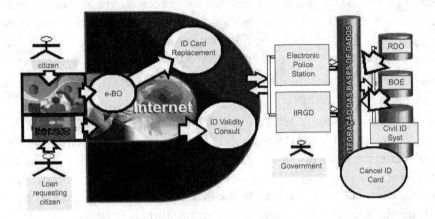

tion of this life event, the citizens may ask for an ID-card replacement, with the respective service thereby scheduling an appointment in a Poupatempo agency in order to collect fingerprints and to get the new ID card.

For the demonstration regarding the G2B service that queries if an ID card is valid or cancelled (ID Validity Consult), the Banco do Povo Paulista agency was chosen as the business trial user. To apply for a loan, one of the conditions is the presentation of a valid identity card. The identity document of the loan applier is verified by the agency manager, but currently there are no means to check if the ID card is perhaps cancelled. The demonstration prototype is going to provide this new kind of service. From Poupatempo statistics, we know that there are about 20 loan requests per day, so this is the expected amount of daily ID validity consulting during the demonstration period, restricting the prototype to the consultation from this agency.

eGOIA Demonstrator Phase 2

Assessment and Dissemination Activities

Together with the first Demonstrator, it is necessary to create a plan (strategic, tactic, operational) that mediates the interactions between the eGOIA project and the governments, facilitates the identification of Demonstrator opportunities, defines governmental segments, and enlarges the identification of customer and governmental needs.

To prepare the regional dissemination and multiplication of results, meetings took place with the representatives of public-service agencies in Cuiabá (Mato Grosso state, Brazil). The Brazilian state participants were Ganha Tempo (Mato Grosso do Sul), SACI (Pará), SAC (Bahia), DETRAN (Pernambuco), Central do Cidadão (Rio Grande do Norte), and Serviço de Atendimento Imediato ao Cidadão, Na Hora, Brasília (federal district). The initial aim was to gather information on existing e-government processes, technology used, requirements, legal aspects, and so forth of the services potentially selected for the demonstration project. Out of this experience, a recommendation for a master plan will be drawn up comprising strategic guidelines for e-government implementations in the future. In addition to that, technological and organizational change-management issues will be addressed.

In Peru, initial contacts with the municipalities have been established, and information was gathered about the actual situation in Peru. There is a big impact on the commonly used CPAs (Internet cabinas) in Peru to the Demonstrator.

Cooperative Government

The first phase of eGOIA was focused on the Poupatempo pilot, which has its own restrictions and needs. In the second phase, the Demonstrator should be extended to support other Brazilian states as well as municipalities and potentially the federal level. With the diversity of administrations involved, constraints and differences between authorities appear.

First of all, each federal, state, and local administration is organized differently in order to provide services for citizens through a variety of regional, local, or municipal offices. Although there is no standard structure of administrations, it is hoped that it might be possible to define a common eGOIA architecture onto which the particular implementations could be mapped.

Another issue for eGOIA deployment is that not only are administrations differently organized, but there exist different technological preconditions. Different infrastructures popped up in all areas because no standardized platforms were available. Therefore, it is critical that eGOIA runs on multiple platforms without imposing the requirement to replace the systems.

Another important issue is the access to already existing systems. These legacy systems are by definition existing systems that have to stay and cannot be changed. eGOIA will have to adapt to and interact with these systems rather than replace them. Last but not least, the technological costs have to be considered. There are a significant number of municipalities that do not even have Web portals or Web pages.

Finally, as it is well known from other best practices, eGOIA Phase 2 e-government systems should facilitate horizontal (agencies of the same level, that is, either federal, state, or local) and vertical (agencies belonging to different levels, which can include the federal, state, and local) information sharing and application interaction. eGOIA Phase 2 should provide a basis for this kind of problems: the so-called cooperative government.

An interoperability framework for e-government services must be defined such that public administration, enterprises, and citizens can interact across borders (e.g., the EIF; *European Interoperability Framework*, 2004). Interoperability is the keyword to enable cooperative government for efficient information exchange over heterogeneous technology and organizational domain boundaries.

Conclusion

Traditional and often still paper-supported administrative procedures cannot be transferred to the digital world just as they are without modification. Instead, the introduction of e-government processes and structures will often necessitate some reorganization (German Federal Office for Information Security (BSI), 2004). If the change process is actively pushed forward, then there is a unique opportunity to improve efficiency and to achieve permanent quality.

This chapter described the eGOIA approach to achieve a sustainable and future-proof e-government service environment that fits the needs of different user group segments.

In the first phase of eGOIA, as described in this chapter, the main goals were to develop the core components of the Demonstrator, based on a well-defined set of services. This implementation is being tested in a real environment (e-Poupatempo Laboratory) where the satisfaction of users will be measured.

Table 1. Access level on ICT (http://www.teleco.com.br/uitdai.asp)

Access	High	Superior	Medium	Low
Number of Countries	25	40	62	59
First Country	Sweden (0,85)	Ireland (0,69)	Belarus (0,49)	Zimbabwe (0,29)
Last Country	Israel (0,70)	**Brazil (0,50)**	Armenia (0,30)	Niger (0,04)

The eGOIA Demonstrator of this phase technically already comprises the integration of back-office procedures (integration of services and access to existing distributed databases for the benefit of the citizen) and front-office procedures (supporting appropriated access channels and the functionalities of the services). These integration tasks are not at all simple techniques. Therefore, technological tendencies in the IT area were considered and an architecture concept was introduced.

eGOIA started already the second and last phase where several demonstrators will be deployed also at state, municipal, and federal levels. Different scenarios of cooperative government are under analysis. For this phase, new platform concepts will be considered, with a strong emphasis on interoperability aspects.

eGOIA has chosen in Brazil the region of São Paulo state for its initial local-community demonstrations. In the case of Peru, another complementary way has been decided, aiming at the support of municipalities (San Borja, Villa El Salvador, and Cajamarca).

Internet connectivity problems are not explicitly handled by eGOIA, and, actually, the project is mainly based on the fact, in the case of Brazil, that Brazilian telecommunication infrastructure is able to support all the e-government solutions to be demonstrated. According to an index of the International Telecommunication Unit (ITU, http://www.itu.int/home/, November 2003), among 186 countries, Brazil presents a "superior" access level on ICT, slightly over the medium level (see Table 1). In order to verify the specific regional situation in Brazil, the ITU index methodology has been applied to the Brazilian states. São Paulo state, the one where the eGOIA demonstration will be running, presents a better situation than the Brazilian average index. But even the worst connectivity level, in Maranhão state, may be classified in the medium category.

Infrastructure is the most important starting point for the eGOIA project proposals toward citizenship e-inclusion. Of course, this depends on the initiatives concerning digital-divide fighting. Even in states like São Paulo, where you may find a fairly good infrastructure, one must count on other initiatives running parallel to the eGOIA project to improve access to the usual infrastructure in very poor regions. One example of this is the new program to be launched in the Ribeira Valley, the poorest region of the state. It aims at forming a regional virtual community, based on a public free wireless connection to Internet, provided by the government to the municipality's territory. Programs like this have been already launched in other municipal areas of the São Paulo state. Recognizing the connectivity problem in Latin American countries, the EU @LIS program also funds the project ALICE (*America Latina Interconectada Con Europa*, n.d.) to improve the connectivity. The RedCLARA high-speed research and education network came into service on September 1, 2004 (*Latin American Cooperation of Advanced Networks*, n.d.).

But beyond the Internet connections, one may still count on the access to equipment and knowledge. That is why the eGOIA Demonstrator does not stress citizen access to the services from home. This access will be provided anyhow through the general government portal already in use (http://www. cidadao.sp.gov.br). eGOIA considers Internet access to e-services to be provided in e-Poupatempos and other public e-including programs, like Acessa São Paulo (http://www.acessasaopaulo.sp.gov.br), which educates people to use the Internet. These e-inclusion solutions may be developed according to regional particularities. In Peru, for instance, although the ICT penetration level is still low, there is a phenomenon called Internet booths, public booths, or cabins, which are located nationwide. It means that this for-profit business provides access to computing, communications, and the Internet to the public for a low fee, which reduces the problem regarding the lack of connectivity.

eGOIA is now defining a new e-government model for Latin America and is concerned with the adoption of best practices and their adaptation to the local needs in a subset of activities (e-services for citizens) that are part of other ambitious initiatives toward e-government in Brazil and Peru.

Due to the nature of the partners, from the beginning, the project was inserted in local programs, with a total commitment to local needs and considering the local socioeconomic and cultural context.

Besides that, eGOIA represents an excellent opportunity to analyze already existent best or worst practices and evaluates, with reduced risks, the use of new technologies through the partnership with relevant European institutions.

eGOIA is not simply transposing models and technologies already existent in Europe, but selects the best of them for the solution of real Peruvian and Brazilian situations.

Acknowledgments

This chapter described the work undertaken and in progress in the context of eGOIA (ALA/2002/47-446/1087), a 3-year project (2003-2006) that is partially funded by the Commission of the European Union's @LIS program. The authors would like to acknowledge all eGOIA partners.

Disclaimer

This publication has been produced with the assistance of the European Union. The content of this publication is the sole responsibility of the eGOIA Consortium and can in no way be taken to reflect the views of the European Union.

References

America Latina Interconectada Con Europa (ALICE) project. (n.d.). Retrieved July 5, 2005, from http://alice.dante.net/

Awarded public government projects. (n.d.). *Stockholm Challenge.* Retrieved July 5, 2005, from http://www.stockholmchallenge.se/index.html

German Federal Office for Information Security (BSI). (2004). Top priority e-government: Guidelines for heads of public agencies. *E-government manual.* Retrieved July 5, 2005, from http://www.bsi.bund.de/english/themes/egov/download/1_Chef_en.pdf

David Frankel Consulting. (2003). *Applying EDOC and MDA to the RM-ODP engineering and technology viewpoints* (Version 01-00). Retrieved July 5, 2005, from http://www.net.intap.or.jp/e/odp/odp-techguide.pdf

European Commission (n.d.-a). *Alliance for the Information Society.* Retrieved July 5, 2005, from http://europa.eu.int/comm/europeaid/projects/alis/overview_en.htm

European Commission. (n.d.-b). *IDABC program.* European eGovernment Services. Retrieved July 5, 2005, from http://europa.eu.int/idabc/

European interoperability framework for pan-European e-government services v 1.0. (2004). Retrieved July 5, 2005, from http://europa.eu.int/idabc/servlets/Doc?id=19529

Federal enterprise architecture. (n.d.). Retrieved July 5, 2005, from http://www.whitehouse.gov/omb/egov/a-1-fea.html

Federal Ministry of the Interior of Germany, KBSt Unit. (2003). *SAGA: Standards and architectures for e-government applications* (Version 2.0, English version). Retrieved July 5, 2005, from http://kbst.bund.de/Anlage304417/Saga_2_0_en_final.pdf

Filgueiras, L., Aquino, P., Tokairim, V., Torres, C., & Barbarian, A. (2004, August). *Usability evaluation as quality assurance of e-government services: The e-Poupatempo case.* Paper presented at the Fourth International Conference on E-Commerce, E-Business, E-Government (I3E 2004), Toulouse, France.

HELP. (n.d.). *Citizen portal of the Federal Chancellery in Austria.* Retrieved July 5, 2005, from http://www.help.gv.at/

IKV++ Technologies. (n.d.-a). *enagoOSP (open service platform).* Retrieved January 5, 2005, from http://www.ikv.de/content/Produkte/osp_e.htm

IKV++ Technologies. (n.d.-b). *Medini toolset.* Retrieved July 5, 2005, from http://www.ikv.de/content/ENGLISH/Products_Services/Technology.htm

Introduction to OMG's unified modeling language. (n.d.). Retrieved July 5, 2005, from http://www.omg.org/gettingstarted/what_is_uml.htm

Latin American Cooperation of Advanced Networks (CLARA). (n.d.). Retrieved July 5, 2005, from http://www.redclara.net/en/index.htm

Policies and specifications. (2004). *United Kingdom e-government interoperability framework.* Retrieved July 5, 2005, from http://www.govtalk.gov.uk/schemasstandards/egif.asp

Poupatempo. (n.d.). *O que é o Poupatempo?* Retrieved July 5, 2005, from http://www.poupatempo.sp.gov.br

Prisma. (2003). *Prisma strategic guidelines: eAdministration.* Retrieved July 5, 2005, from http://www.prisma-eu.net/deliverables/SG1administration.pdf

Reference Model of Open Distributed Processing (RM-ODP). (1996). *ISO/IEC 10746-3: Information technology–Open distributed processing–Reference model: Architecture.* Geneva, Switzerland.

UML profile for enterprise distributed object computing (EDOC). (n.d.). Retrieved July 5, 2005, from http://www.omg.org/technology/documents/formal/edoc.htm

VeZuDa Project. (2004). VeZuDA als grundlage für eine e-government-dienste-plattform. *Splitter, 1.* Retrieved July 5, 2005, from http://www.lit.berlin.de/BVC/splitter/sp1-2004/vezuda.htm

Vintar, M., Kunstelj, M., & Leben, A. (2002, April). Paper presented at the 10th NISPAcce Annual Conference, Cracow, Poland. Retrieved July 5, 2005, from http://www.nispa.sk/news/papers/wg2/Vintar.doc

About the Authors

Mila Gascó holds an MBA and a PhD in public-policy evaluation and received the Award Enric Prat de la Riba, granted to the best PhD thesis on public management and administration, given by the Escola d'Administració Pública de Catalunya in Barcelona, Spain. She is a senior analyst at the International Institute on Governance of Catalonia and an associate professor at the Universitat Oberta de Catalunya (Open University of Catalonia). She has a wide teaching experience (she worked as a full professor in the Rovira i Virgili University in Tarragona, Spain) as well as a broad researching experience. She has taken part in numerous national and international seminars, has published both in Spanish and English, and has supervised some PhD theses. Dr. Gascó has also collaborated with several institutions such as the provincial government of Barcelona (Diputació de Barcelona), the World Bank Development Gateway, the United Nations Program for Development, the University of Hull in the United Kingdom, the mayor's office in Valencia (Venezuela), and the governments of Brazil and the Dominican Republic. Her main interests are related to public policies that allow the transition of a society to the so-called knowledge era (in particular, she is interested in e-government and e-governance), to the use of ICTs for human development, and to public-policy evaluation.

* * *

Roberto Agune is the coordinator of the São Paulo State's Strategic Information System and of the São Paulo State's Public Administration Quality Committee Core Support Group, as well as the executive secretary substitute of the Public Administration Quality Committee. Mr. Agune was the president of the São Paulo State's Information Science Council (CONEI). His undergraduate degree is in architecture from the University of São Paulo and he has postgraduate degrees in educational planning, and urban planning and administration.

Sergio Bolliger holds a BA in architecture and a master's degree in philosophy. In the eGOIA project (Electronic Government Innovation and Access), he is the leader of Subproject 3 (Improving Accessibility and Acceptance of E-Government Services). Since 2002, he has been the project manager of Fundação do Desenvolvimento Administrativo (FUNDAP), a public foundation for administrative development. As such, he coordinates a public-services-quality core group for the chief of staff of the government of the state of São Paulo, which gathers specialists from FUNDAP, Companhia de Processamento de Dados do Estãdo de Sao Paulo (Prodesp) (the government ICT company), and Poupatempo (a governmental program for high-quality public-services provision). From 1997 to 2002, he worked directly in the Poupatempo Program's implementation and management, being responsible for the coordination of the operational units since 2000. Before 1997, he worked for 18 years in the São Paulo City Hall in several areas.

Tony Carrizales received his BA from Cornell University and his MPA from the Cornell Institute of Public Affairs. He is a senior associate for the National Center for Public Productivity in the Graduate Department of Public Administration. Mr. Carrizales serves as an assistant editor for *Public Voices* and *Chinese Public Administration Review*. His research interests include e-government and citizen-driven government performance.

Alejandra Ciurlizza holds an MA in sociology from the University of Sheffield (England) and a BA, also in sociology, from the University of Louvain (Belgium). She is an external adviser to the president of the Peruvian National Science and Technology Council (CONCYTEC) in matters concerning the information society. She participates in the meetings for the establishment of the National System in Science, Technology and Technology Innovation

(SINACYT) and represents CONCYTEC in the Directory of the National Institution of Research and Training in Telecommunications (INICTEL). Furthermore, she plays a major role in developing the information society in Peru, Comisión Multisectorial para el Desarrollo de la Sociedad de la Información (CODESI) and participates in the National Committee for the Edition of Scientific Publications. She has participated in various information projects such as the Network of Networks of Latin America and the Caribbean, the Network of Commercial Opportunities in the Andean Region, and the Information Network of the Latin American Association of Development Financing Institutions. She is a founder of the Documentation Center of the Catholic University of Peru. She has published several articles in the field of information policies.

Gregory Curtin holds a PhD in political science and JD (Juris Doctor) in law. He is a research professor and director of the E-Governance Lab at the School of Policy, Planning and Development at the University of Southern California (USC). He is also the founder and editor-in-chief of the *Journal of E-Government* and lead editor of the recently published *World of E-Government*. In addition to these publications on e-government, he serves as the principal investigator for the ongoing United Nations Global E-Government Readiness Survey and Report.

Alberto Etchegaray holds a master's degree in public policy from Georgetown University (USA), a bachelor's degree in legal and social sciences from Universidad Diego Portales (Chile), and a certificate in management and business from Universidad de Barcelona (Spain). Mr. Etchegaray was a governance and civil-division consultant for the Inter-American Development Bank (IADB) from 2002 to 2003, a modernization-of-state senior advisor for the ministry of the presidency cabinet, and a chief of staff in the deputy ministry of the presidency cabinet. He has written several papers and reports on the relationship between the market and the civil society as well as on the initiatives toward the modernization of the Chilean public sector. He has led a national educational program that has financially supported more than 35,000 economically poor students.

María Frick is a Uruguayan political scientist engaged in electronic-government studies and new technologies for the strengthening of democracy. She has obtained her degree at the Universidad de la República, Uruguay. Currently, she is finishing a postgraduate course on communication theory at the Universidad de Buenos Aires (UBA), Argentina. Regarding her specialization area, she has worked for the Political Science Institute of the Universidad de la República, the Institute for Connectivity in the Americas/IDRC (International Development Research Center), and the Organization of American States (OAS).

J. Ramón Gil-Garcia is a postdoctoral fellow at the Center for Technology in Government, and an adjunct professor at the Rockefeller College of Public Affairs and Policy and at the Department of Management Science and Information Systems in the business school of the University at Albany, State University of New York (SUNY). His research interests include e-government success, interorganizational information systems, information-technology implementation, government reform and new public management, and government information strategy and management. Gil-García has published in various journals including *Government Information Quarterly*, *European Journal of Information Systems*, *Public Finance and Management*, and *The International Public Management Journal*.

Roxana Goldstein holds a postgraduate degree in public policies for the Internet (FLACSO, Facultad Latinoamericana de Ciencias Sociales, Latin American School of Social Sciences, Ecuador), and a postgraduate specialist diploma in electronic government (Universitat Oberta de Catalunya, International Institute on Governance of Catalonia, Spain). She also holds both a BA in information systems (School of Engineering, Buenos Aires University, Argentina) and a BA in humanities and social sciences (University of Palermo, Argentina). She is a consultant and a researcher at the Centro de Estudios sobre Ciencia, Desarrollo y Educación Superior-Centro Redes in Buenos Aires (Argentina), and a member of the PPGA (Socio-Urban Participatory Planning and Associative Management) Project at FLACSO Argentina.

Patricio Gutiérrez holds both an industrial-engineering degree from Universidad de Chile and a master's in public management from Universidad Adolfo Ibañez. Mr. Gutiérrez has relevant e-government experience, working for the general secretariat of the presidency ministry at the Public Modernization and Reform Project. He has been the e-government coordinator since

2002. In this assignment, Mr. Gutierrez has the main role as supervisor of the e-government agenda implementation of the Digital Agenda of Chile. In addition to this, he also updates periodically the activities of the government of Chile in e-government matters. He has been a presenter in several conferences about topics such as electronic government, digital signature, and the use of ICTs in government.

Petra Hoepner is a senior scientist and project leader at Fraunhofer Institute FOKUS (Fraunhofer Institut für Offene). In this function, she is concerned with project management, coordination, and technological development in various projects with a focus on e-government. She led several European and national projects at FOKUS, is the project manager for the European Union @LIS project eGOIA, and is member of the body of experts for Standards and Architectures for eGovernment Applications (SAGA) of the German Federal Government Coordination and Advisory Agency for IT. Petra Hoepner has worked for FOKUS since 1990. Prior to this, she worked as a system specialist at Nixdorf Microprocessor Engineering GmbH. She received her diploma in computer science from Technical University (TU) of Berlin in 1980.

Marc Holzer holds a PhD in political science and a master's of public administration, both from the University of Michigan. He is chair and professor of the Graduate Department of Public Administration, Rutgers University-Newark, and executive director of the National Center for Public Productivity. Dr. Holzer is a past president of the American Society for Public Administration (2000-2001) and a fellow of the National Academy of Public Administration.

Ester Kaufman is an attorney at law from UBA. She also holds a master's in social sciences (FLACSO, Argentina) and a postgraduate degree in the international cooperation of project developments (Organización de Estados Iberoamericanos Universidad Nacional de Educación a Distancia (OEI-UNED), Spain). She coordinates the FLACSO Project on e-government. She has written book chapters, journalistic articles, and CDs. She teaches and directs research projects within the management program of Instituto Nacional de Adminstración Pública (INAP) and the Digital Government Postgraduate Program at UNTREF (University of Tres de Febrero, Argentina). She has given seminars in several Latin American countries targeted at mayors and government officials. She advises local government on associative e-government models. She has given several lectures at international events.

Luis Felipe Luna-Reyes holds a PhD in information science from the University of New York at Albany. He is currently a professor of business at the Universidad de las Américas in México, where he leads the Research Group on Strategy Analysis in Institutions and Organizations. Luna-Reyes is also a member of the Mexican National Research System. His current research focuses on electronic government and on information-systems development, use, and implementation across functional and organizational boundaries. He has published book chapters and articles in various journals including *System Dynamics Review* and *European Journal of Information Systems*.

Manuel Mendes graduated with a degree in electrical engineering in 1965 at the Technical University of Berlin, and received his PhD in engineering at the same university in 1968. Dr. Mendes works for Centro de Pesquisas Renato Archer (CenPRA) in the technical management of the eGOIA Project and other projects in electronic government. He was a research assistant at the Heinrich Hertz Institute from 1968 to 1969 and a postgraduate lecturer in the same period at the TU. He also was a senior researcher at the Max von Laue-Paul Langevin in Grenoble (France). Since 1969, he has been a full professor in computer engineering at UNICAMP, Universidade Estadual de Campinas; from 1983 to 1985, he was director of Centro Technológico papa Informática (CTI) (former CenPRA); and at several occasions he was an invited professor and researcher at the University of Darmstadt and the FOKUS Institute in Germany. He has taught at different universities such as TU Berlin, TU Darmstadt, UNICAMP Campinas, (USP-POLE) in São Paulo, PUCCAMP in Campinas, UNIMEP Piracicaba, and Unisantos in Santos. His research interests are Web service systems, metadata management systems, and model-driven software development.

Romildo Monte graduated in physics and has a master's degree in computer science. He works for CenPRA, being mainly concerned with project management and multiproject coordination. He is CenPRA's representative in the eGOIA Project Management Committee. As director of CTI's Computer Institute of the Ministry of Science and Technology, he coordinated from 1994 to 2000 the Brazilian Software Quality and Productivity Program, aiming at the generation and dissemination of technology for software quality evaluation and improvement. He was a member of the Installation Committee of the Brazilian Information Society Program. From 1988 to1993, he was one of the coordinators of the Brazilian Software Plant Project. In this project, he worked at International Software Systems Inc. in Austin, Texas. During the '70s and '80s, he executed technical activities in software development and computer technical support, and managed teams and projects for the data-processing centers of the Universities of Sao Paulo and Minas Gerais.

Marc Navarro is a PhD candidate in political science and a member of the research team State Transformation in Latin America: New Institutional Designs, Civil Service and Regulatory Policy at Pompeu Fabra University (Spain). He earned a diploma in advanced studies in political and administration sciences and a master's degree in information and knowledge society from the Open University of Catalonia. His research interests are related to subnational institutions and their impact on development. Regarding that topic, he has written several articles and conference proceedings on decentralization, multilevel governance, federalism, electronic democracy, new technologies, and party systems.

Marcos Ozorio de Almeida works at the Ministry of Planning, Budget and Management of Brazil. Besides his duties in the area of public procurement policy design and implementation for the executive branch, he advises on e-government issues and elaborates and executes reform projects and programs financed by multilateral organizations in the public sector. Mr. Ozorio advises some foreign governments on procurement reform and coordinates e-government cooperation initiatives with other countries. He has coordinated the government's participation in the Country Procurement Assessment, done by the World Bank, and the implementation of e-procurement, supported by the Inter-American Development Bank. He has worked on the establishment of a Latin American network of e-government and e-procurement specialists with the Organization of American States and has been a speaker on ICT for transparency on procurement with the World Trade Organization. Also, he has helped the United Nations Commission on International Trade Liberalization, with the present initiative to incorporate e-procurement into the framework of the Model Law on Government Procurement. Mr. Ozorio has also written papers on e-procurement for Centro Lationamericano de Administración para el Desarrollo (CLAD), Consumer Unity and Trust Society (CUTS) of India, and OAS.

Jennifer S. Rojas-Bandera holds a BS in industrial engineering from the Universidad de las Américas in México. She is currently working toward her master's in industrial engineering. She is a research assistant at the business school and a member of the Center for Research on Physics and Applied Mathematics.

Marco Aurélio Ruediger holds a PhD in sociology from the University Research Institute of Rio de Janeiro (IUPERJ) and a master's in management and urban policy from the New School for Social Research in New York. He is currently working as a professor and researcher in the Brazilian School of Public and Business Administration in the Getúlio Vargas Foundation, for which he is also the coordinator of the master's course in public administration. As a consultant, he has coordinated modernization and institutional development projects for FGV/EBAPE with agencies of the Brazilian federal government. Dr. Ruediger has held a number of public positions including that of state subsecretary for public administration in Rio de Janeiro. He is currently affiliated with the National Center of Digital Government of the John F. Kennedy School of Government (Harvard University), and has participated actively in international and national congresses, such as the American Society for Public Administration (ASPA), International Politicial Science Association (IPSA), ANPOCS, and ENANPAD. His research interests are connected to the modernization of state structures, issues of local development, and the extensive use of technologies to support a digital government as a central element in a strategic interrelation between the state and civil society.

Richard Schwester received his BA from the Johns Hopkins University and his MA from Rutgers University-Newark, both in political science. He is a senior research associate for the National Center for Public Productivity in the Graduate Department of Public Administration, Rutgers University-Newark. Mr. Schwester serves as assistant editor of *Public Performance & Management Review*.

Linda Strick has been working with Fraunhofer FOKUS since 1988 as a senior researcher. She was responsible for several projects of the European Commission in the area of architecture, design, and implementation for distributed systems. She has also worked for several international industry partners in projects that address ubiquitous computing for personalized access to distributed information. She was involved in international standardization activities with respect to architect- and model-distributed systems and several projects in the area of developing modeling tools. She is also doing consultancy for system integration projects and has published a number of papers for conferences and journals.

Christopher Walker is a joint-degree candidate (June 2006) in law and public policy from Stanford Law School and Harvard University's Kennedy School of Government. He is a Foreign Languages and Area Studies (FLAS) fellow at the David Rockefeller Center for Latin American Studies at Harvard University and has published several articles on various issues of law and policy in Latin America. He is also the principal research associate over Latin America for the ongoing United Nations Global E-Government Survey and Report. In addition to his research interests in Latin America, he served as editor in chief of the *Stanford Law and Policy Review* in 2004 and 2005, and currently serves as managing editor of the *Stanford Law Review*.

Index